The Freelance Photographer's Market Handbook 2005

The Freelance Photographer's Market Handbook 2005

Edited by John Tracy
& Stewart Gibson

BFP BOOKS London

All information was believed correct at the time of going to press. However, market information is subject to change, and readers are advised to check with the publication concerned before preparing a contribution. Members of the Bureau of Freelance Photographers are kept in touch with changes in the marketplace through *Market Newsletter*. Every care has been taken in the compilation of this book, but the publisher can assume no responsibility for any errors or omissions, or any effects arising therefrom.

A catalogue record for this book is available from the British Library

ISBN 0-907297-55-2

21st Edition

Published for the Bureau of Freelance Photographers by BFP Books, Focus House, 497 Green Lanes, London N13 4BP. Typesetting and page layout by BFP Books. Text set in New Century Schoolbook. Printed in Great Britain by Biddles Ltd.

CONTENTS

PREFACE

Our 21st anniversary edition coincides with the final coming of age of the digital revolution – at least as far as freelancing is concerned.

As predicted last year, the phrase "digital media accepted" is no longer to be found in this book. We have rapidly reached the stage where virtually all picture buyers will accept digital files without raising an eyebrow.

Thus, where no specific preference is stated, it can now be assumed that all markets listed here are happy to accept pictures in both film and digital formats.

What is notable is that a considerable number of markets are now expressing a definite preference for digital submissions. Most have made that leap from acceptance to preference in just the past 12 months.

This was inevitable once the digital revolution really took hold. Once the quality was there, editors and publishers soon recognised the substantial savings in time and expense that handling digital images can mean. Not to mention the freedom from worries about lost or damaged original transparencies!

Those digital files do need to be of high-quality though, whether they be digital capture or scanned from film. As far as digital capture is concerned, this means that a well-specified digital SLR is required for any serious level of freelancing.

As for trends in magazine publishing itself, there has been little of note over the past 12 months. The only major event in the market has been the arrival of weekly magazines for men.

The almost simultaneous launch of IPC's *Nuts* and EMAP's *Zoo Weekly* early in 2004 has certainly shaken up the men's market, generating a circulation of some 1.5 million copies a month between them. And as we go to press, two further entrants into this field are expected. But whether these weeklies seriously damage the market for the established monthlies remains to be seen.

The ongoing move to digital by picture buyers continues to be reflected in the agency world, where the past year has again seen numerous closures, mergers and takeovers as older agencies struggle to change their methods and digitise their stocks.

At the same time there have been plenty of new entrants to the agency scene. Almost without exception these newcomers are solely on-line operations, holding and selling images only in digital form. Naturally most expect photographers to supply them in digital form as well, although some are still prepared to scan submissions in-house.

Despite the almost universal acceptance of digital there remain markets where film is required. For the high-end glossy magazine, or the large-format calendar publisher, a medium format transparency is still the standard to hold to. One day soon digital will catch up with this standard too, but perhaps not for a while yet.

ABOUT THE BFP

Founded in 1965, the Bureau of Freelance Photographers is today the major body for the freelance photographer. It has a worldwide membership, comprising not only full-time freelances, but also serious amateur and semi-professional photographers. Being primarily a service organisation, membership of the Bureau is open to anyone with an interest in freelance photography.

The most important service offered to members is the *Market Newsletter,* a confidential monthly report on the state of the freelance market. A well-researched and highly authoritative publication, the *Newsletter* keeps freelances in touch with the market for freelance work, mainly by giving information on the type of photography currently being sought by a wide range of publications and other outlets. It gives full details of new magazines and their editorial requirements, and generally reports on what is happening in the publishing world and how this is likely to affect the freelance photographer.

The *Newsletter* also includes in-depth interviews with editors, profiles of successful freelances, examples of successful pictures, and other general features to help freelances in understanding and approaching the marketplace.

The *Newsletter* is considered essential reading for the freelance and aspiring freelance photographer, and because it pinpoints launches and changes in the marketplace as they occur, it also acts as a useful supplement to the *Handbook*. The *Handbook* itself is an integral part of BFP membership services; members paying the full annual fee automatically receive a copy every year as it is published.

Other services provided to members for the modest annual subscription include:

● Advisory Service. Individual advice on all aspects of freelancing is available to members.

● Mediation Service. The Bureau tries to protect its members' interests in every way it can. In particular, it is often able to assist individual members in recovering unpaid fees and in settling copyright or other disputes.
● Exclusive items and special offers. The Bureau regularly offers books and other useful items to members, usually at discount prices.
● In the Services section of this *Handbook* can be found a number of companies providing special discounts to BFP members on production of a current membership card. Amongst various services members can obtain comprehensive photographic insurance cover at competitive rates.

For further details and an application form, write to Bureau of Freelance Photographers, Focus House, 497 Green Lanes, London N13 4BP, telephone 020 8882 3315, e-mail mail@thebfp.com, or visit the BFP website at www.thebfp.com. Or if you wish to join right away, you'll find an application form at the back of this book, after the main index, on page 259.

HOW TO USE THIS BOOK

Anyone with the ability to use a camera correctly has the potential to make money from their pictures. Taking saleable photographs isn't difficult; the difficulty lies in finding the market. It isn't enough for you, the photographer in search of a sale, to find what you think *might* be a suitable market; rather you must find *exactly* the right magazine, publisher, agency or whatever for your particular type of work. Many a sale is lost when work which is, in itself, technically perfect fails to fulfil the total requirements of the buyer.

The Freelance Photographer's Market Handbook has been designed to help resolve these difficulties. It puts you in touch with major markets for your work, telling you exactly what each is looking for, together with hints and tips on how to sell to them and, wherever possible, an idea of the rates they pay.

The *Handbook* covers five big markets for your pictures: magazines (by far the largest), newspapers, book publishers, picture agencies, and card and calendar companies. There are three ways of using the book, depending on the way you need or wish to work:

1. If you are out to sell to magazines and you can offer coverage on a theme particularly applicable to a certain type of publication (eg gardening, angling, sport) turn to the magazine section and look for the subject. The magazines are listed under 36 categories, each of which has a broad heading covering specific magazines. The categories are in alphabetical order, as are the magazines within those categories. You need only read through them to discover which is best for your type of work.

2. If you have a set of pictures that fall into a specific photographic category (landscapes, children, celebrities etc), turn to the subject index on page 21. Look up your chosen subject and there you will find a list of all the mag-

azines with a strong interest in that particular type of picture. You then have only to look up each one mentioned in the appropriate section for precise details of their requirements. (If in doubt as to where to find a particular magazine consult the general index at the back of the book.) There are separate subject indexes for book publishers and agencies on pages 170 and 197 respectively.

3. If you are looking for the requirements of a specific magazine, book publisher, agency, card or calendar publisher, whose name is already known to you, simply refer to the general index at the back of the book.

Some points to remember

With this wealth of information open to you, and with those three options for finding the right market, there is no reason why you shouldn't immediately start earning good cash from your camera. But before you rush off to submit your images, here are some points worth bearing in mind and which will help you to more successful sales:

1. The golden rule of freelancing: don't send people pictures they don't want. Read the requirements listed in the various parts of this directory and obey them. When, for instance, a Scottish magazine says they want pictures of all things Scottish with the exception of kilts and haggis, you can be sure they are over-stocked with these subjects. They are not going to make an exception just for you, however good you think your pictures might be.

2. When working with colour film, and unless the listing states otherwise, always supply transparencies rather than prints. Unless otherwise stated, it can be assumed that any size of transparency, from 35mm up, can be accepted. Digital images supplied on CD are usually acceptable, but always check this point with your chosen market in advance.

3. When submitting pictures, make sure they are accompanied by detailed captions. And don't forget to put your own name and address on each photograph/CD.

4. If you have an idea for a picture or feature for a particular publication, don't be afraid to telephone first to discuss what you have in mind. Nearly every editor or picture buyer approached when the *Handbook* was being compiled said they would be delighted to hear from potential freelances in advance,

rather than have inappropriate pictures or words landing on their desks.

5. If seeking commissions, always begin by making an appointment with the appropriate person in order to show your portfolio and/or cuttings. Do not turn up at a busy editor's office unannounced and expect to be met with open arms.

6. Enclose a stamped addressed envelope if you want a posted submission returned if unsuccessful.

APPROACHING THE MARKET

You've chosen your market, taken the pictures and written the captions. Full of hope and expectation, you put your work in the post. A week later, it comes back with a formal rejection slip. Why? Where did you go wrong?

You have only to look through the pages of this book to see that there are a lot of markets open to the freelance photographer, yet the sad fact remains that a great many of those who try their hand at editorial freelancing fail the first few times, and many never succeed at all. That isn't meant to be as discouraging as it might sound. On the contrary, because so many freelances fail, *you*, with the inside knowledge gleaned from these pages, stand a better chance of success than most. What's more you can gain from the experience of others.

So let's take a look at some of the areas where the inexperienced freelance goes wrong. Knowing the common mistakes, you can avoid them and consequently stand the best chance of success with your own work.

The first big mistake made by the novice is in the actual format of pictures supplied. The easiest types of photograph to take and produce today are colour print and digital. Unfortunately, both can be difficult to sell.

The smaller enprints produced by commercial processors never sell – except in the most exceptional of circumstances. While many markets do accept larger, high-quality prints, most buyers in the publishing world much prefer colour slides (transparencies), or digital files scanned from slides. The only exception here is newspapers, which do prefer to work from prints or digital files.

Images taken with digital cameras are now acceptable to most markets, but ideally need to be produced on a well-specified digital SLR in order to provide the quality parameters necessary for high-quality reproduction. Lesser-quality digital images are even less saleable than colour prints.

Most magazines are all-colour, but a number of smaller publications do still use black and white, while many up-market publications like to use a proportion of high-quality monochrome imagery. In this case, high-quality black and white prints will be required.

The quality of your work must be first class. Images should be pin-sharp and perfectly exposed to give strong, saturated colours. Slight under-exposure of around one-third to half a stop may be acceptable, but over-exposure never. *Never* send over-exposed, washed-out pictures.

A few markets – such as calendars and greetings cards, or certain specialist picture libraries – continue to prefer larger format transparencies for ultimate reproduction quality. If your chosen market stipulates a larger format, don't send 35mm.

While most markets now accept images in digital form, each will have specific technical requirements or preferences that should be ascertained before submission. Some will consider digital files as samples only, but require slides or prints for reproduction. Always check with your chosen market for their precise requirements in this area.

Unless otherwise stated in an individual entry, it can be assumed that all the markets listed here accept digital submissions as well as traditional film.

So much for picture format, but what of the actual subject of your pictures? Here again, a lot of fundamental mistakes are made. The oldest rule in the freelancing book is this: don't take pictures, then look for markets; find a market first and then shoot your pictures specifically with that market in mind.

Every would-be freelance knows that rule; yet the many who ignore it is frankly staggering. Remember that rule and act accordingly. First find your market, analyse it to see the sort of pictures it uses, then go all out to take *exactly* the right type of picture.

Editors see a lot of pictures every day, and the vast majority are totally unsuited to their market. Of those that are suited, many are still rejected because, despite being the right *type* of pictures, the subjects are still uninspiring. They are subjects the editor has seen over and over again; and the type that the magazine will already have on file. So once again, the work gets rejected.

Remember this and learn from it. Most of the pictures that fall on an editor's desk are pretty ordinary. If you want to make yours sell, you have to show them something different. It might be a fairly straightforward view of an unusual subject, or it might be a more common subject, seen and photographed from a new angle. Either way, it will be different.

So when you set out to take your pictures, really look at your subject and, even before you press the shutter, ask yourself, why am I taking this picture? Why will an editor want to buy it? What's so different or unusual about it? How can I make a few changes here and now to give it a better chance of success?

Good, traditional picture composition also plays a part in a picture's chances. Many would-be freelances submit pictures of people in which the principal subject is far too small and surrounded by a wealth of unwanted, distracting detail. So make a point, whenever you shoot, of moving in close and really filling the viewfinder with your subject.

Many potentially saleable landscapes are ruined by a flat perspective. So watch out for, and try to include, foreground interest in such pictures.

People at work on a craft or a hobby can be good sellers, but a good many pictures depicting such subjects are shot candidly without the necessary thought needed to really show the subject to its best. Always pose pictures like these before you take them.

Finally, a word about presentation. It's true that a good picture can often find a sale, no matter how badly it is presented; but it is equally true that bad presentation can have a negative influence on an editor or picture buyer and so ruin your chances of success. So why make things difficult for yourself?

When you send prints or CDs, make sure they are stiffly packed between thick cardboard or in cardboard envelopes. Present slides in plastic filing wallets and make them easy to view with the minimum of fuss.

With digital submissions, an editor will appreciate a print-out of thumbnail images for quick reference.

If you are sending words – either captions to pictures or a full-blown article – always type them, rather than writing them by hand. Text for articles should be printed on one side of the paper only with double spacing between lines and with good margins on each side. If submitting text on disk, always include a "hard copy" print-out as well.

Send your submission with a brief covering letter, not with pages of explanations about the work. The sale will stand or fall by your pictures and/or words, never by the excuses you offer as to why certain pictures might not be too good. If they're not good enough, they won't sell.

Give your editor what he or she wants. Give them originality and sparkle, and present the whole package in the best way you can. Learn the rules and you'll be on your way to a good many picture sales.

But don't think that anyone is going to break those rules just for you. If your pictures don't measure up to what is required, there will always be another envelope right behind full of pictures that do. And there are no prizes for guessing which submission is going to make the sale.

MAGAZINES

The British magazine market is vast. Anyone who doubts that has only to look at the racks of periodicals in any major newsagent. And this is only the tip of the iceberg, the largest section of the consumer press. Beneath the surface there is the trade press, controlled circulation magazines and many smaller publications that are never seen on general sale. At the last count more than 8,000 magazines were being published on a regular basis in Britain.

In this section you will find detailed listings of magazines which are looking for freelances. Some pay a lot, others are less generous, but all have one thing in common – they are here because they need freelance contributions on a regular basis and they are willing to pay for them.

When you come to start looking at these listings in detail, you might be surprised by the number of magazines of which you have never heard. Don't let that put you off. What the newcomer to freelancing often fails to realise is that there are as many, if not more, trade magazines or small specialist titles as there are major consumer publications, and very few of these are ever seen on general sale.

Trade magazines, as the term implies, are aimed at people whose business is making money from the particular subject concerned. As such, their requirements are usually totally different to their consumer counterparts.

As an example, consider boating. A consumer magazine on that subject will be aimed at the boat owner or enthusiast and could contain features on boats and the way they are handled. A trade magazine on the same subject is likely to be more interested in articles about the profits being made by the boating industry and pictures of shop displays of boating accessories.

Trade magazines do not necessarily have a separate section to themselves. If the subject is a common one, such as the example above in which there are both trade and consumer publications, they have been listed for your convenience under a common heading. Despite that, however, there *is* a section specifically for trade. This contains trade magazines that have no consumer counterparts, as well as magazines whose subject is actually trade itself and trading in general.

As you go through these listings, therefore, it is important for you to realise that there is a very real difference between the two sides of the subject, but it is a difference which is explained under each publication's requirements. So don't ignore trade magazines of whose existence you were not previously aware. Very often such a magazine will have just as big a market for your pictures and the fees will be just as good, if not better, than those offered by the consumer press.

It is often a good idea for the freelance to aim at some of the more obscure publications listed here, be they trade magazines or the smaller hobbyist magazines. Simply because they are a little obscure they may not have been noticed by other freelances and, as such, your sales potential may well be higher even if fees paid by some of these publications are relatively low.

When you are looking through the entries, don't stop at the section on illustrations. Read what the magazine needs in the way of text too. A publication that might appear to have a very small market for individual pictures often has a larger potential for illustrated articles, and all you need to do to make a sale is add a few words.

You will also find that many publications talk about needing mainly commissioned work. Don't be misled by this. The commissions are given to freelances and, although this means they won't consider your work on spec, they could well be interested in giving you a commission if you can prove you are worth it. That's where previous experience comes in. When trying for commissions, you should always have examples of previously published work to show an editor.

Many of the larger magazines employ a specific editor to deal with picture submissions and with photographers. They may go under various titles – picture editor, art editor, art director – but this is the person directly responsible for picture selection and for commissioning photographers for specific jobs. This, therefore, is the person you should approach when sending pictures or seeking photographic assignments. When sending written material though – illustrated or not – your approach is best made direct to the editor.

The magazine market is one of the largest available to the freelance. You might not receive as large a fee per picture as you would from, say, the calendar market, or for certain sales that might be made on your behalf by an agency, but what this field does offer is a *steady* income, especially once you have made a breakthrough with one or more titles.

There are so many magazines, covering so many different subjects, that freelances who have their wits about them would be hard put *not* to find one to which their own style and interests can be adapted. Make yourself known to a few chosen magazine editors, let them see that you can turn out good quality work on the right subject, at the right time, and there is no reason why this market shouldn't make you a good, regular income, either part time or full time.

New Listings, Changes & Deletions

The following is designed to alert readers to possible new markets as well as to important changes that have taken place since the last edition of the *Handbook*.

'New Listings' includes magazines that have been launched since the last edition appeared as well as established titles that appear in the *Handbook* for the first time. 'Title Changes' lists publications that have changed their names (previous titles in brackets). 'Deletions' lists publications that appeared in the previous edition but are omitted from this one. Publications under this heading have not necessarily ceased publication – they may have been deleted because they no longer offer a worthwhile market for the contributor.

To find the page number for any particular magazine, refer to the main index at the back of the book.

New Listings

A Place in the Sun
All Out Cricket
BBC Parenting
BBC Wildlife
Celebrity Homes
Children Now
Gardenlife
GoMini
Everything Spain
The Falconers & Raptor Conservation Magazine
Farm Life
Fishing News
Forest Machine Journal
Ice
Italia UK
Jaguar Heritage
K9 Magazine
Landscape
Living France
Moto Magazine
Nuts
Olive
Portugal
Spanish Magazine
Sporting Shooter
TotalMG
Tractor & Farming Heritage
Viva España
Zoo Weekly

Title Changes

BD (Building Design)
f2 (Freelance Photographer)
Froots (Folk Roots)
H&E Naturist Monthly (H&E Monthly)
Rooms, Rooms, Rooms (Rooms & Living Magazine)
Walk (The Rambler)

Deletions

Active Life
Animal Action
Animal Life
BBC Good Food

BT Today
Bang
CCC
Classic Racer
Clean Air
Country
Diversity Today
Fashion Extras
Electronics World
GPMU Journal
Galaxy Publications
Gardening Which?
Hampshire
Holiday Which?
Housing
J17
MG World
19
Nurseryman & Garden Centre
Peak District Magazine
Pony
Soho
Tractor & Farm Machinery Trader
Travel Photography
Truck
Scotland Magazine
Whisky Magazine
World Hockey Online

Subject Index

Only magazines are included in this index, but it should be noted that many of these subjects are also required by agencies, book publishers and card and calendar publishers.

Separate subject indexes for book publishers and picture agencies appear in the appropriate sections, on pages 170 and 197 respectively.

To find the page number for any magazine, refer to the main index at the back of the book.

Agriculture

The Countryman
Crops
Dairy Farmer
Eurofruit Magazine
Farm Business/Farm Life
Farmers Guardian
Farmers Weekly
Poultry World
Tractor & Farming Heritage
World Tobacco

Aircraft

Aeroplane
Air International
Airforces Monthly
Airliner World
Aviation News
Defence Helicopter
Flight International
Flyer
Flypast
Jane's Defence Weekly
Pilot
Today's Pilot

Arts/Crafts

Best of British
Classic Stitches
Crafts Beautiful
Furniture & Cabinetmaking
Good Woodworking
Knitting
The Lady
Popular Crafts
Practical Crafts
This England
Woodcarving
Woodturning
Woodworker

Birds

BBC Wildlife
Bird Watching
Birds Illustrated
Birdwatch
The Falconers & Raptor Conservation Magazine
Parrots
Racing Pigeon Pictorial

Boats/Nautical

Boat International
Canal Boat & Inland Waterways
Canal & Riverboat
Classic Boat
Containerisation International
Cruise Traveller
International Boat Industry
Jet Skier & Personal Watercraft
Marine Engineers Review
Motor Boat and Yachting
Motor Boats Monthly
RYA Magazine
Regatta
Sailing Today
Sportsboat & RIB Magazine
Traditional Boats & Tall Ships
Water Craft
Waterways World
Yachting Monthly
Yachting World
Yachts and Yachting

Buildings

Architecture Today
BD
Build It
Country Homes and Interiors
The English Home
FX
Glass Age

House Beautiful
House Builder
House & Garden
Icon
Local Government News
Municipal Journal
Period Living & Traditional Homes
Planning
RIBA Journal
SelfBuild & Design
Stadium & Arena Management
World of Interiors

Business

Accountancy Age
Business Life
CA Magazine
Computer Weekly
Director
EN
The Economist
Export Times
Financial Management
MEED
Marketing
People Management
Real Business

Celebrities

Bella
Best
Celebrity Homes
Closer
Condé Nast Customer Publishing
Glamour
Heat
Hello!
Highbury Customer Publications
Mizz
More!
Now
OK!
Radio Times
Red
Saga
Sneak
The Stage
Sugar
TV Times
Woman
Woman and Home

Children

BBC Parenting
The Brownie
Children Now
Guiding Magazine
Mother & Baby
New Baby
Nursery World
Prima Baby
Right Start
Scholastic Magazines
Scouting
She
Woman Alive

Domestic/Farm Animals

Dairy Farmer
Dogs Today
Farm Business
Farmers Guardian
Horse Magazine
Horse and Rider
K9 Magazine
The Lady
Our Cats
Your Cat
Your Dog

Fashion

Arena
Attitude
Bella
Best
Company
Condé Nast Customer Publishing
Drapers
Elle
Esquire
Essentials
FHM
Front
GQ
Good Housekeeping
Harpers & Queen
Hello!
The Lady
Loaded
Manchester Life
Marie Claire
Maxim
Mizz

Flowers/Plants

Food/Drink

Glamour/Erotic

Homes/Interiors

Woman and Home
World of Interiors

Industry

Chemistry & Industry
Director
Education in Chemistry
The Engineer
Engineering
Financial Management
Industrial Diamond Review
People Management
Planning
Post Magazine
Professional Engineering
Sign World
Urethanes Technology
Utility Week
Works Management

Landscapes

Amateur Photographer
Best of British
Bird Watching
Buckinghamshire Countryside
Camping Magazine
Cheshire Life
Christian Herald
Cotswold Life
Country Homes & Interiors
Country Life
Country Walking
The Countryman
Cumbria
Dalesman
Dorset
Dorset Life
The Great Outdoors
Hertfordshire Countryside
The Lady
Lancashire Life
Lincolnshire Life
Outdoor Photography
Photography Monthly
Practical Photography
The Scots Magazine
Somerset Life
Sussex Life
TGO – The Great Outdoors
This England
Trail
Trout and Salmon
Walk
Waterways World
Woman Alive
Yorkshire Life

Military

Air International
Airforces Monthly
Defence Helicopter
Jane's Defence Weekly

Motor Vehicles

A&S Publishing
Auto Express
Autocar
The Automobile
Automotive Management
Boys Toys
CCC
Classic American
Classic Cars
Classic & Sports Car
Classics
Commercial Motor
Company Car
Driving Magazine
Evo
4x4
Fleet News
GoMini
Ice
Jaguar
Jaguar Heritage
Land Rover Monthly
Land Rover Owner
Maxpower
Motor Trader
Motoring & Leisure
Motorsport
911 & Porsche World
Octane
Performance Ford
Redline
Revs
Sports Car Classics
Street Machine
Top Gear Magazine
TotalMG
Triumph World
Truck and Driver
VW Motoring

Motorcycles

Back Street Heroes
Bike
Classic Bike
The Classic Motor Cycle
Dirt Bike Rider
Moto Magazine
Motor Cycle News
Motorcycle Voyager
Redline
Ride
Scootering
Superbike
Two Wheels Only

Pop/Rock

Blues and Soul
Echoes
Heat
Kerrang!
Keyboard Player
Loaded
Metal Hammer
MixMag
Mojo
New Musical Express
Q
Rhythm
Sneak
Smash Hits
Total Guitar

Railways

British Railway Modelling
Engineering in Miniature
Entrain
Heritage Railway
International Railway Journal
Rail
Rail Express
Railnews
Railway Magazine
Steam Railway
Traction

Sport

Adrenalin
All Out Cricket
Athletics Weekly
Badminton
Boat International
Boxing Monthly
Cycle Sport
Cycling Plus
Cycling Weekly
Darts World
Dirt Bike Rider
Dive
Esquire
F1 Racing
Fighters
First Down
FourFourTwo
Front
GQ
Golf Monthly
Golf Weekly
Golf World
Highbury Customer Publications
Horse & Hound
Ice
International Rugby News
Loaded
Martial Arts Illustrated
Match
Maxim
Men's Health
Motor Boats Monthly
Motor Cycle News
Motorsport
Mountain Biking UK
The Non-League Paper
Nuts
Redline
Regatta
Rugby World
Running Fitness
Shooting Gazette
Shooting Times & Country Magazine
Ski & Board
The Skier & Snowboarder Magazine
Snooker Scene
Snowboard UK
Sports Boat & RIB Magazine
Stadium & Arena Management
Swimming Magazine
Target Sports
Today's Golfer
Two Wheels Only
Windsurf Magazine
The Wisden Cricketer
World Illustrated
Yachts and Yachting
Zoo Weekly

Travel

A Place in the Sun
Business Life
Business Traveller
Coach & Bus Week
Condé Nast Customer Publishing
Condé Nast Traveller
Cruise Traveller
Everything France
Everything Spain
Food & Travel
France
French Magazine
Geographical
Good Housekeeping
Greece
Highbury Customer Publications
Italy
The Lady
Living France
The Middle East
Motorcycle Voyager
Motorhome Monthly
Motoring & Leisure
Portugal
Saga Magazine
Spain
Spanish Magazine
Travel
The Traveller
Viva España
Wanderlust
Woman and Home
Yours

Wildlife

Amateur Photographer
BBC Wildlife
Bird Watching
Birds Illustrated
Birdwatch
Country Life
The Countryman
Cumbria
Dalesman
Devon Today
Digital Photographer
The Falconers & Raptor Conservation Magazine
The Field
Geographical
The Lady
Natural World
Outdoor Photography
Photography Monthly
The Scottish Sporting Gazette
The Shooting Gazette
Shooting Times and Country Magazine
Sporting Shooter

Angling

ANGLER'S MAIL
IPC Media Ltd, King's Reach Tower, Stamford Street, London SE1 9LS.
Tel: 020 7261 5778. Fax: 020 7261 6016. E-mail: tim_knight@ipcmedia.com
Editor: Tim Knight.
Weekly publication with news and features for followers of coarse and sea fishing in the UK.
Illustrations: Colour. Digital media preferred. Topical news pictures of successful anglers with their catches. Captions should give full details concerning weight and circumstances of capture. Covers: pictures of anglers with exceptional specimen fish or catches.
Text: Features on coarse and sea fishing topics only. Up to 800 words.
Overall freelance potential: Minimal for non-angling freelances.
Editor's tips: Contributors really need knowledge and experience of the subject; pictures and text seen from non-anglers are rarely acceptable.
Fees: By agreement.

ANGLING TIMES
EMAP Active Ltd, Bushfield House, Orton Centre, Peterborough PE2 5UW.
Tel: 01733 232600. Fax: 01733 465844. anglingtimes@emap.com
Editor: Richard Lee.
Weekly newspaper format publication covering all types of angling: coarse, sea and game. Includes news, features and general instruction.
Illustrations: Colour. General angling images, especially newsworthy catches, action and scenics. Covers: "stunning" action shots featuring anglers in the environment.
Text: Illustrated features on all aspects of the hobby. Up to 800 words.
Overall freelance potential: Very good. High percentage used each week.
Fees: By agreement.

COARSE FISHERMAN
Metrocrest Ltd, 2 Harcourt Way, Meridian Business Park, Leicester LE19 1WP.
Tel: 0116 289 4567. E-mail: info@conceptdesignltd.co.uk
Editor: Stuart Dexter.
Monthly magazine covering all aspects of coarse fishing.
Illustrations: Colour. Pictures of anglers in action or riverside/lakeside scenes where coarse angling takes place. Covers: colour pictures showing anglers displaying particularly fine catches.
Text: Articles of 1,000–2,000 words, most usually first person accounts of angling experiences.
Overall freelance potential: Excellent scope for angling specialists.
Fees: Pictures from £10 upwards. £25 per 1,000 words for text.

FLY FISHING AND FLY TYING
Rolling River Publications Ltd, Aberfeldy Road, Kenmore, Perthshire PH15 2HF.
Tel/fax: 01887 830526.
Editor: Mark Bowler.
11 issues a year for the fly fisherman and fly-tyer.
Illustrations: Colour. Shots of fly fishermen in action, scenics of locations, flies and fly-tying, and appropriate insect pictures.
Text: Illustrated articles on all aspects of fly fishing.

Are you working from the latest edition of The Freelance Photographer's Market Handbook? It's published on 1 October each year. Markets are constantly changing, so it pays to have the latest edition

Overall freelance potential: Fairly good.
Editor's tips: Make an effort to avoid bland backgrounds, especially at water sides.
Fees: Colour from £24–£58; covers £50. Text £50 per 1,000 words.

IMPROVE YOUR COARSE FISHING
EMAP Active Ltd, Bushfield House, Orton Centre, Peterborough PE2 5UW.
Tel: 01733 237111. Fax: 01733 465658.
Editor: Kevin Wilmot.
Monthly, inspirational, "hints and tips" style magazine for coarse fishing enthusiasts.
Illustrations: Colour. Photographs depicting all aspects of coarse fishing.
Text: Ideas for illustrated features from experienced angling writers always considered. 2,500 words; submit a synopsis first.
Overall freelance potential: Limited; much of the editorial content is produced in-house.
Editor's tips: Always query the editor before submitting.
Fees: £50 per picture unless supplied with article; articles £100 – £200 inclusive of pictures.

SEA ANGLER
EMAP Active Ltd, Bushfield House, Orton Centre, Peterborough PE2 5UW.
Tel: 01733 465702. Fax: 01733 465658. E-mail: steve.diggle@emap.com
Editor: Mel Russ. **Designer:** Steve Diggle.
Monthly magazine dealing with the sport of sea angling from both boat and beach.
Illustrations: Colour. Good sea fishing and shore fishing pictures, and scenic coastline pictures from around the country. Proud angler with excellent catch. Covers: Head shots of individual sea fish and anglers with a good fish (must be a fresh catch).
Text: Instructional features, fishing expeditions, match articles, etc. 1,000 words.
Overall freelance potential: 50 per cent of published material comes from freelance sources.
Fees: By negotiation; good rates for the right kind of material.

TROUT AND SALMON
EMAP Active Ltd, Bushfield House, Orton Centre, Peterborough PE2 5UW.
Tel: 01733 237111. Fax: 01733 465820. E-mail: sandy.leventon@emap.com
Editor: Sandy Leventon.
Monthly magazine for game fishermen.
Illustrations: Colour. Photographs of trout or salmon waters, preferably with an angler included in the picture. Close-up and action shots to illustrate particular techniques. Captioned news pictures showing anglers with outstanding catches. Covers: attractive pictures of game fishing waters, always with an angler present.
Text: Instructional illustrated articles on all aspects of game fishing.
Overall freelance potential: Excellent for those who can produce the right sort of material.
Fees: Pictures inside according to use. Cover shots, £80. Text according to length.

TROUT FISHERMAN
EMAP Active Ltd, Bushfield House, Orton Centre, Peterborough PE2 5UW.
Tel: 01733 237111. Fax: 01733 465658. E-mail: mark.sutcliffe@emap.com
Editor: Mark Sutcliffe.
Monthly magazine for the trout fishing enthusiast.
Illustrations: Colour. Photographs depicting any aspect of angling for trout – outstanding catches, angling locations, techniques, flies and equipment.
Text: Illustrated articles on all aspects of trout fishing, around 1,500 words.
Overall freelance potential: Excellent scope for top quality material.
Editor's tips: Too much angling photography is dull and uninteresting; an original and lively approach would be welcome.
Fees: On a rising scale according to size of reproduction or length of text.

Animals & Wildlife

BBC WILDLIFE
Origin Publishing Ltd, 14th Floor, Tower House, Fairfax Street, Bristol BS1 3BN.
Tel: 0117 314 8371. Fax: 0117 934 9008. E-mail: wandasowry@originpublishing.co.uk
Editor: Sophie Stafford. **Art Editor:** Simon Bishop. **Picture Researcher:** Wanda Sowry.
Heavily-illustrated monthly for readers with a serious interest in wildlife and environmental matters.
Illustrations: Colour. Top-quality wildlife and environmental photography of all kinds, mostly to illustrate specific features. Contact picture researcher in the first instance with details of subjects and coverage available.
Text: Feature suggestions welcomed from contributors who have a genuine knowledge of their subject.
Overall freelance potential: Only for the very best quality work.
Fees: Pictures from £45 (under quarter-page) to £130 (dps); covers £200.

BIRD WATCHING
EMAP Active Ltd, Bretton Court, Bretton, Peterborough PE3 8DZ.
Tel: 01733 282605. Fax: 01733 465376. E-mail: sue.begg@emap.com
Editor: David Cromack. **Picture Researcher:** Sue Begg.
Monthly magazine devoted to bird watching and ornithology.
Illustrations: Colour. Top quality photographs of birds in the wild, both in the UK and overseas. Prefer to use pictures that illustrate specific aspects of bird behaviour. Also, landscape shots of British bird-watching sites. Potential contributors are asked to always send a list of subjects available in the first instance.
Text: Illustrated features on all aspects of birds and bird watching.
Overall freelance potential: Excellent scope for wildlife specialists.
Fees: By negotiation.

BIRDS ILLUSTRATED
Buckingham Press, 55 Thorpe Park Road, Longthorpe, Peterborough PE3 6LJ.
Tel: 01733 566815. E-mail: editor@buckinghampress.com
Editor: David Cromack.
Quarterly subscription-only magazine showcasing all aspects of bird life, birding, wildlife art and photography.
Illustrations: Colour. Transparencies preferred, but digital images accepted on CD. "Classic Images" feature requires pictures that are exceptional in aesthetic terms or which show unusual bird behaviour. Proposals for word and picture packages on individual species, birdwatching locations or bird behaviour are welcome. Also readers' pictures section.
Text: Articles on places to see birds, individual species or groups of birds, up to 3,000 words. Gallery-type profiles of bird photographers and artists, profiles of birding personalities.
Overall freelance potential: Excellent scope for wildlife specialists.
Fees: Relatively low at present while the magazine builds its subscription base. No fees paid for readers' gallery.

BIRDWATCH
Solo Publishing Ltd, B403A The Chocolate Factory, 5 Clarendon Road, London N22 6XJ.
Tel: 020 8881 0550.
Editor: Dominic Mitchell. **Picture Editor:** Steve Young.
Monthly for all bird watchers. Includes a strong emphasis on the photographic side of the hobby.
Illustrations: Colour. Digital media preferred. Good photographs of British and European birds in their natural habitat. Those with collections of such material should send lists of subjects available.
Text: Well-illustrated features on bird watching topics, including practical articles on bird

photography. 1,000–1,200 words, but send a synopsis first.
Overall freelance potential: Average.
Fees: According to use.

DOGS TODAY
Pet Subjects Ltd, Town Mill, Bagshot Road, Chobham, Surrey GU24 8BZ.
Tel: 01276 858880. Fax: 01276 858860. E-mail: dogstoday@btconnect.com
Editor: Beverley Cuddy.
Monthly magazine for the pet dog lover.
Illustrations: Colour. Digital media preferred. News pictures or shots showing dogs in action, in specific situations, and interacting with people (especially children). Will also consider exciting or amusing photo sequences and pictures of celebrities with their dogs. No simple dog portraits unless displaying a strong element of humour or sentiment. Shots of crossbreeds always needed.
Text: General illustrated features about dogs. Should be positive and have a "human interest" feel.
Overall freelance potential: Excellent for the right material.
Fees: According to use.

THE FALCONERS & RAPTOR CONSERVATION MAGAZINE
PW Publishing Ltd, Arrowsmith Court, Station Approach, Broadstone, Dorset BH18 8PW.
Tel: 0870 224 7810. Fax: 0870 224 7850. E-mail: steve@pwpublishing.ltd.uk
Editor: Peter Eldrett. **Art Editor:** Stephen Hunt.
The only magazine devoted to falconry and birds of prey.
Illustrations: B&W and colour. Digital media preferred. Usually only required to illustrate specific articles. Covers: Striking images of birds of prey.
Text: Articles on falconry and related topics. 1,000–5,000 words.
Overall freelance potential: Little scope for individual photographs, but complete illustrated articles always welcome.
Fees: By negotiation.

K9 MAGAZINE
K9 Media Solutions, I-Centre, Oakham Business Park, Mansfield, Notts NG18 5BR.
Tel: 08700 114 115. E-mail: mail@k9magazine.com
Editor: Ryan O'Meara.
Quarterly magazine plus extensive website (www.k9magazine.com), described as the only lifestyle magazine for British dog lovers.
Illustrations: Colour. Digital media preferred. High quality dog images – breeds, puppies, dogs with people, dogs in action, etc. Submit low-res samples via e-mail in the first instance. Some commissions available to experienced animal photographers.
Text: Illustrated features on aspects of dog behaviour and dog ownership.
Overall freelance potential: Very good.
Fees: By negotiation.

NATURAL WORLD
The Wildlife Trusts, The Kiln, Waterside, Mather Road, Newark, Nottinghamshire NG24 1WT.
Tel: 0870 0367711. Fax: 0870 0360101.
Editor: Deb Bright.
The magazine of The Wildlife Trusts, concerned with all aspects of wildlife and countryside conservation in the UK. Published three times per year.
Illustrations: Colour. Interesting shots of British mammals, amphibians, insects, flowers and trees. Subjects must be wild; no pets or zoo animals.
Text: Short photo-features on wildlife or conservation topics particularly connected with local Wildlife Trusts. Around 300 words.
Overall freelance potential: Limited.
Fees: £35 minimum.

OUR CATS
Our Dogs Publishing Co. Ltd, 5 James Leigh Street, Manchester M1 5NF.
Tel: 0870 7311 6505. Fax: 0870 731 6501. E-mail: editorial@ourcats.co.uk
Editor: Christine Stalker.
Fortnightly publication aimed at the serious cat breeder and exhibitor and all cat lovers.
Illustrations: B&W and colour. Newsy photographs of interest to serious cat lovers. All pictures must be accompanied by informative captions.
Text: Limited scope for knowledgeable features.
Overall freelance potential: Limited to the coverage of serious cat matters.
Editor's tips: If the subject concerns cats, take a chance and submit it.
Fees: By negotiation.

VETERINARY PRACTICE
A E Morgan Publications Ltd. Editorial: PO Box 618, Norwich NR7 0QT.
Tel/fax: 01603 708930. E-mail: bluefoxfilms@themag.fsnet.co.uk
Editor: Chris Cattrall.
Monthly newspaper for veterinary surgeons in general practice.
Illustrations: B&W and colour. Pictures of veterinary surgeons engaged in activities either connected with, or outside, their professional work.
Text: Features particularly concerned with veterinary practice. 800–1,500 words.
Overall freelance potential: Limited.
Fees: By agreement.

YOUR CAT
BPG (Stamford) Ltd, Roebuck House, 33 Broad Street, Stamford, Lincs PE9 1RB.
Tel: 01780 766199. Fax: 01780 766416. E-mail: s.parslow@bournepublishinggroup.co.uk
Editor: Sue Parslow.
Monthly magazine for all cat lovers. Covers every type of cat including the household moggie and pedigree cats.
Illustrations: Colour. Mostly by commission to accompany features as below. Some scope for interesting, unusual or humorous single pictures.
Text: Illustrated news items and features on the widest variety of topics relating to cats: famous cats, cats in the news, readers' cats, rare cats, cats that earn a living, etc. Also authoritative articles on practical matters: behaviour, grooming, training, etc.
Overall freelance potential: Reasonable; the magazine is heavily illustrated.
Fees: By negotiation.

YOUR DOG
BPG (Stamford) Ltd, Roebuck House, 33 Broad Street, Stamford, Lincs PE9 1RB.
Tel: 01780 766199. Fax: 01780 766416.
Editor: Sarah Wright.
Monthly magazine for "the everyday dog owner", with the emphasis on care and training.
Illustrations: Colour. Top quality pictures showing dogs and their owners in a practical context, i.e. walking, training, grooming; dogs in the news; amusing pictures. For covers pictures must be of the highest technical quality.
Text: Illustrated news stories, practical features, and articles on any interesting canine subject, i.e. working dogs, dog charities, celebrities and their dogs, etc. Always contact editor before submitting.
Overall freelance potential: Fair.
Editor's tips: Make sure that pictures are recent and not just something dug up from the back of the filing cabinet.
Fees: According to size of reproduction and by negotiation.

Architecture & Building

ARCHITECTURE TODAY
Architecture Today plc, 161 Rosebery Avenue, London EC1R 4QX.
Tel: 020 7837 0143. Fax: 020 7837 0155.
Editors: Ian Latham, Dr Mark Swenarton.
Independent monthly for the architectural profession.
Illustrations: Mainly colour. Most photography is commissioned, but interesting pictures of current architectural projects are always of interest on spec.
Text: Illustrated articles of genuine interest to a professional readership; submit ideas only first. 800–2,000 words.
Overall freelance potential: Limited scope for specialists.
Editor's tips: Potential contributors must contact the editors before submitting anything.
Fees: £100 per 1,000 words; photography by arrangement.

BD
CMP Information, Ludgate House, 245 Blackfriars Road, London SE1 9UY.
Tel: 020 7921 8216. Fax: 0207921 8244.
Editor: Robert Booth.
Weekly newspaper for architects and architectural technicians.
Illustrations: Mostly colour. News pictures may be considered on spec but most photography commissioned to illustrate major stories and features. Photographers should have a proven record in architectural photography and a demonstrable understanding of what it should capture.
Text: News pieces and features on all aspects of building design, by those with real understanding of the subject matter. Always make contact before submitting.
Overall freelance potential: Good for those with the requisite expertise.
Fees: Pictures variable according to use etc. Text around £160 per 1,000 words.

BATHROOMS & KITCHENS
Quantum Publishing, Quantum House, 19 Scarbrook Road, Croydon CR9 1LX.
Tel: 020 8565 4200. Fax: 020 8565 4278.
Editor: Phillipa Turrell.
Monthly trade journal for bathroom, bedroom and kitchen specialist retailers, builders' merchants, distributors, manufacturers, installers, builders, developers, architects, etc.
Illustrations: Colour. Pictures of bathroom and kitchen units, bedroom furniture and fittings, appliances, sinks, taps, worktops, tiles, floor and wall coverings, ceilings, blinds, etc.
Text: Only after prior consultation. Up to 1,000 words usually.
Overall freelance potential: Fairly good for the contributor with specialised expertise in the subject.
Fees: Good; on a rising scale according to the size of reproduction or length of article.

BUILD IT
Inside Communications Ltd, 1 Canada Square, 19th Floor, Canary Wharf, London E14 5AP.
Tel: 020 7772 8300. Fax: 020 7772 8599. E-mail: catherine_monk@mrn.co.uk
Editor: Catherine Monk.
Monthly devoted to the self-build market – those people building a one-off home or converting old barns, chapels, etc.

Illustrations: Colour only. Medium and large format only. Commissions available to experienced photographers to cover architecture, renovations and interiors. Some interest in stock photographs of housing and interior decoration subjects.
Text: Authoritative features on building, landscaping and interior design, plus specialised articles on finance, legal issues, weatherproofing, etc.
Overall freelance potential: Excellent for the experienced contributor in the architecture and interiors field.
Fees: £180 per 1,000 words for text; good rates for photographers, commissioned shoots negotiable.

BUILDERS' MERCHANTS JOURNAL
Faversham House Group, Faversham House, 232A Addington Road, South Croydon CR2 8LE.
Tel: 020 8651 7100. Fax: 020 8651 7117. E-mail: fionarussellhorne@fav-house.com
Editor: Fiona Russell Horne.
Monthly business to business magazine for the builders merchants industry – wholesale distributors of building products, including heating, bathroom and kitchen fixtures.
Illustrations: Mostly colour. Always interested in unusual photography of merchants' yards, computers, showrooms and vehicles. Ongoing requirement for shots of house building/refurbishment work. Possible scope for creative still life shots of items such as bricks, blocks, timber, etc. Commissions also available, depending on geographic location – write in with details of experience and rates.
Text: Limited scope for freelance articles on suitable subjects – send business card and samples of published work in the first instance.
Overall freelance potential: Limited.
Editor's tips: Most commissions here tend to be rather mundane, usually involving quite general shots of a merchant's yard. Need photographers who can provide a more creative approach. Write in the first instance – do not telephone.
Fees: Photographs by negotiation. Text around £125 per 1,000 words.

BUILDING SERVICES
The Builder Group PLC, 7th Floor, Anchorage House, 2 Clove Crescent, London E14 9BE.
Tel: 020 7560 4000. Fax: 020 7560 4020. E-mail: karen.fletcher@buildergroup.co.uk
Editor: Karen Fletcher. **Art Editor:** Jason Harris.
Monthly publication for engineers and senior management involved with installing heating, air conditioning, ventilation, lighting, lifts, hot and cold water systems etc. into buildings.
Illustrations: B&W and colour. Good quality pictures of building services. Pictures used for caption stories and for stock. Covers: colour, usually commissioned.
Text: No scope.
Overall freelance potential: Good, since very few pictures of this subject are offered.
Fees: By negotiation.

FX
ETP Ltd, Rosebery House, 41 Springfield Road, Chelmsford, Essex CM2 6JJ.
Tel: 01245 491717. Fax: 01245 499110.
Editor: Antonia Ward. **Art Director:** Patrick Myles.
Monthly interior design business magazine for the retail, hotel and commercial sectors. Aimed at architects, designers and their clients.
Illustrations: Mainly colour. By commission only; experienced architectural and interiors photographers with fresh ideas always welcome.
Text: Articles on commercial design matters and related business issues, only from those with real expertise in these areas.
Overall freelance potential: Good for the experienced worker.
Editor's tips: The magazine is very receptive to original ideas. Articles should be hard-hitting and possibly contentious.
Fees: Photography around £200–£250 per day. £160 per 1,000 words.

GLASS AGE
CMP Information Ltd, Anchorage House, 2 Clove Crescent, London E14 2BE.
Tel: 020 7560 4246. Fax: 020 7560 4017.
Editor: Dominic Bentham.
Monthly magazine for the flat glass and fenestration industries. Aimed at builders, architects, glaziers, shopfitters, glass merchants, stained glass artists and all glass-related workers.
Illustrations: B&W and colour. Particularly interested in pictures of glass in new buildings. Detailed captions essential.
Text: Features on glass in construction.
Overall freelance potential: Good opportunities for high quality architectural photography.
Editor's tips: Make contact before submitting any material.
Fees: On a rising scale according to the size of reproduction or length of feature.

H & V NEWS
EMAP Trenton, 19th Floor, Leon House, 233 High Street, Croydon CR0 9XT.
Tel: 020 8649 9665. Fax: 020 8277 5434.
Editor: Adam Northcroft.
Weekly for those who purchase or specify heating, ventilating and air conditioning equipment.
Illustrations: B&W only inside. Action pictures of installations and equipment in use, preferably with human interest. Covers: colour pictures of relevant subjects.
Text: News stories, installation stories regarding heating, ventilating and air conditioning equipment, stories on companies and people. 200–300 words. Longer features by negotiation.
Overall freelance potential: Good scope for newsworthy material.
Editor's tips: The more current the information supplied the better its chance of success.
Fees: £12 per 100 words; pictures by negotiation.

HOUSE BUILDER
House Builder Publications, 56-64 Leonard Street, London EC2A 4JX.
Tel: 020 7608 5130. Fax: 020 7608 5131. E-mail: allison.heller@house-builder.co.uk
Editor: Ben Roskrow.
Monthly journal of the House Builders Federation. Aimed at key decision makers, managers, technical staff, marketing executives, architects and local authorities.
Illustrations: Colour. Digital media preferred. Some scope for housebuilding coverage, but only by prior consultation with the editor.
Text: Features on marketing, land and planning, government liaison, finance, materials, supplies, etc. Always to be discussed before submission. 1,000 words.
Overall freelance potential: Around 50 per cent comes from freelances.
Editor's tips: Authoritative articles and news stories only. No PR "puffs".
Fees: £150 per 1,000 words; pictures by agreement.

ICON
Media Ten Ltd, National House, High Street, Epping, Essex CM16 4BD.
Tel: 01992 570030. Fax: 01992 570031. E-mail: marcus@icon-magazine.co.uk
Editor: Marcus Fairs. **Art Editor:** Alexander Boxill.
Monthly magazine covering architecture and design, aimed at both professionals and interested consumers.
Illustrations: B&W and colour. Top quality architectural and design photography, mostly by commission. Submit ideas and samples in the first instance. Also runs a regular monthly showcase, "Icon Hang", for individual photographer's portfolios.
Text: Suggestions considered, but contributors must really know their subject.
Overall freelance potential: Fair.
Editor's tips: Potential contributors should really study the magazine first in order to "tune in" to what it is trying to do.
Fees: By negotiation.

LANDSCAPE
Wardour Communications Ltd, Elsley House, Great Titchfield Street, London W1P 8BB.
Tel: 020 7016 2555. E-mail: joe@wardour.co.uk
Editor: Joe Gardiner.
Official magazine of The Landscape Institute. Aimed at professionals either producing or commissioning landscape architecture and designed to showcase the best work in the field.
Illustrations: Colour. Mostly by commission only; always happy to hear from photographers who can offer high-level skills in architectural work.
Text: Ideas for features will be considered.
Overall freelance potential: Good scope for experienced workers.
Editor's tips: Requirements are very specific, so in the first instance submit only a couple of samples as an indication of style.
Fees: By negotiation.

PRESTIGE INTERIORS
(Three separate titles covering CORPORATE, HIGH STREET, and HOTEL AND RESTAURANT interiors)
Albatross Publications, PO Box 523, Horsham, West Sussex RH12 4WL.
Tel: 01293 871201. Fax: 01293 871301.
Editor: Carol Andrews.
Quarterly publications covering interior design in the three commercial sectors specified above. Aimed at managers concerned with interiors in the fields of hotels and restaurants, office administration, retail and catering, and the designers serving them.
Illustrations: Colour only. Pictures of interesting new interiors and developments, especially striking examples of good (or bad) design and decor, lighting, and specific problems encountered. Pictures only accepted as part of an illustrated feature.
Text: News stories, and profiles of relevant individual projects, but always contact the editor with suggestions first.
Overall freelance potential: Fair.
Editor's tips: Remember that these are professional publications for business people and interior designers.
Fees: By negotiation.

RIBA JOURNAL
The Builder Group, Anchorage House, 2 Clove Crescent, London E14 2BE.
Tel: 020 7560 4120. Fax: 020 7560 4191.
Editor: Amanda Baillieu.
Monthly magazine of the Royal Institute of British Architects. Covers general aspects of architectural practice as well as criticisms of particular buildings, profiles and interviews.
Illustrations: Mostly colour. Pictures of buildings, old, new and refurbished. Covers: colour pictures connected with main feature inside. Best to send list of subjects initially.
Text: Illustrated features on architectural subjects and criticisms of particular buildings.
Overall freelance potential: Fair.
Fees: By arrangement.

SELFBUILD & DESIGN
Waterways World Ltd. Editorial: The Mill House, Bache Mill, Diddlebury, Shropshire FY7 9JX.
Tel/fax: 01584 841417. E-mail: r.stokes@easynet.co.uk
Editor: Ross Stokes.
Monthly practical consumer magazine covering self-build housing, including conversions and major extensions.
Illustrations: Colour. Striking photographs of recently completed self-builds (interiors and exteriors), particularly those of an innovative design or in unusual or visually appealing locations. Coverage of new builds by celebrities also welcomed.

Text: Authoritative and well illustrated articles covering all aspects of building and renovation, including brief items of a quirky, amusing or informative nature. Telephone to discuss ideas before submission.
Overall freelance potential: Good.
Fees: By negotiation.

STADIUM & ARENA MANAGEMENT
Alad Ltd. Editorial: 4 North Street, Rothersthorpe, Northants NN7 3JB.
Tel: 01604 832149. E-mail: mark.webb@tesco.net
Editor: Mark Webb.
Bi-monthly, international news magazine covering all aspects of stadium and arena design, construction and management.
Illustrations: Colour. Digital media preferred. Photographs of new stadia or arenas in the UK and Europe, both under construction and in active use (sport being played, performers on stage).
Text: News items always considered.
Overall freelance potential: Fair.
Editor's tips: Always make contact before undertaking a shoot; it may be possible to link the pictures to a feature story.
Fees: By negotiation.

Arts & Entertainment

BROADCAST HARDWARE INTERNATIONAL
The Hardware Magazine Company Ltd, 80 Hazel Drive, Woodley, Reading RG5 3SA.
Tel: 0118 9262787. Fax: 0118 9269928. E-mail: david-j-sparks@compuserve.com
Editor: David Sparks.
Bi-monthly magazine for the television broadcast industry, aimed at senior engineers.
Illustrations: B&W and colour. Photographs of television broadcast studios, control rooms, outside broadcast vehicles and operations – for general feature illustration. Covers: normally by commission.
Text: Technical aspects of television production and post-production. 2,000–2,500 words.
Overall freelance potential: Quite good.
Editor's tips: Phone with ideas in the first instance.
Fees: Negotiable.

CLUB MIRROR
Alchemy Media Solutions Ltd, Rosedale House, Rosedale Road, Richmond TW9 2SZ.
Tel: 020 8939 9026. E-mail: editorial@clubmirror.co.uk
Editor: Sean Ferris.
Published 10 times a year for officials, committee members and stewards of registered clubs throughout the UK; proprietary club owners and managers; and discotheque owners and managers.
Illustrations: Colour. Interior pictures of new clubs, new club openings, interesting general pictures of club activities.
Text: Articles on new club openings, new clubs planned, news stories on clubs, special features on successful clubs. Also features on the club trade, catering services etc.
Overall freelance potential: Good; 90 per cent from freelance sources.
Fees: By arrangement.

HEAT
EMAP Performance Network, Endeavour House, 189 Shaftesbury Avenue, London WC2H 8JG.
Tel: 020 7295 5000. Fax: 020 7817 8847. E-mail: clara.massie@emap.com
Editor: Mark Frith. **Picture Editor:** Clara Massie.
Popular entertainment weekly with news, reviews and heavy celebrity content.

Illustrations: Colour; Interested in hearing from photographers covering live events throughout the UK. Assignments available to shoot performances and behind-the-scenes coverage. Some scope for stock pictures of contemporary music and the entertainment industries, and paparazzi-type material.
Text: No scope.
Overall freelance potential: Good.
Fees: By negotiation.

RADIO TIMES
BBC Worldwide Publishing, Woodlands, 80 Wood Lane, London W12 0TT.
Tel: 020 8433 2000. Fax: 020 8433 3160.
Editor: Gill Hudson. **Picture Editor:** Patricia Taylor.
Weekly TV and radio listings magazine, containing news and features on mainly BBC productions and personalities.
Illustrations: Mostly colour. Coverage of broadcasting events, BBC productions, and TV personalities, usually by commission.
Text: Commissioned features on TV personalities or programmes of current interest.
Overall freelance potential: Fair for commissioned work.
Fees: Various.

THE STAGE
The Stage Newspaper Ltd, 47 Bermondsey Street, London SE1 3XT.
Tel: 020 7403 1818. Fax: 020 7357 9287.
Editor: Brian Attwood.
Weekly newspaper for professionals working in the performing arts and the entertainment industry.
Illustrations: B&W and colour. News pictures concerning people and events in the theatre and television worlds.
Text: Features on the theatre and light entertainment. 800 words.
Overall freelance potential: Limited.
Fees: Pictures by agreement, text £100 per 1,000 words.

TV TIMES
IPC Media Ltd, King's Reach Tower, Stamford Street, London SE1 9LS.
Tel: 020 7261 7000. Fax: 020 7261 7888.
Editor: Mike Hollingsworth. **Art Director:** Penny Miles. **Picture Editor:** Elaine McCluskey.
Weekly television programme listings magazine, plus features on major programmes.
Illustrations: Colour. Usually commissioned or requested from specialist sources. Mainly quality colour portraits or groups specific to current programme content.
Text: Articles on personalities and programmes.
Overall freelance potential: Between 50 and 75 per cent each week is freelance, but mostly from recognised contributors.
Fees: Negotiable.

Aviation

AEROPLANE
IPC Country & Leisure Media, King's Reach Tower, Stamford Street, London SE1 9LS.
Tel: 020 7261 5849. Fax: 020 7261 5269. E-mail: aeroplane_monthly@ipcmedia.co.uk
Editor: Michael Oakey.
Monthly aviation history magazine, specialising in the period 1909–1960. Occasional features on modern aviation.
Illustrations: Colour; B&W archive material. Photographs for use in their own right or for stock.

Main interests – veteran or vintage aircraft, including those in museums; preserved airworthy aircraft; unusual pictures of modern aircraft. Action shots preferred in the case of colour material – air-to-air, ground-to-air, or air-to-ground. Covers: high quality air-to-air shots of vintage or veteran aircraft. Transparencies 6x6cm minimum.
Text: Short news stories concerning preserved aircraft, new additions to museums and collections, etc. Not more than 300 words.
Overall freelance potential: Most contributions are from freelance sources, but specialised knowledge and skills are often necessary.
Editor's tips: The magazine is always in the market for sharp, good quality colour images of preserved aircraft in the air.
Fees: Colour photographs: full page £80; centre spread £100; covers £180. B&W from £10 upwards.

AIR INTERNATIONAL
Key Publishing Ltd, PO Box 100, Stamford, Lincolnshire PE9 1XQ.
Tel: 01780 755131. Fax: 01780 757261. E-mail: malcolm.english@keypublishing.com
Editor: Malcolm English.
Monthly general aviation magazine covering both modern military aircraft and the civil aviation industry. Includes some historical topics. Aimed at both enthusiasts and industry professionals.
Illustrations: Mostly colour. Topical single pictures or picture stories on aviation subjects worldwide, eg aircraft in active war zones, airliners in new livery, new aircraft at Heathrow, etc. Overseas material welcomed. Air show coverage rarely required.
Text: Illustrated features on topics as above, from writers with in-depth knowledge of the subject. Length variable.
Overall freelance potential: Very good for suitable material.
Editor's tips: Remember the magazine is read by professionals and is not just for enthusiasts.
Fees: B&W from £10; colour based on page rate of £75. Covers, up to £120 for full-bleed sole reproduction. Text £50 per 1,000 words.

AIRFORCES MONTHLY
Key Publishing Ltd, PO Box 100, Stamford, Lincolnshire PE9 1XQ.
Tel: 01780 755131. Fax: 01780 751323. E-mail: afm@keypublishing.com
Editor: Alan Warnes.
Monthly magazine concerned with modern military aircraft.
Illustrations: Mostly colour. Interesting, up-to-date pictures of military aircraft from any country. Must be current; archive material rarely used.
Text: Knowledgeable articles concerning current military aviation. No historical matter.
Overall freelance potential: Good for contributors with the necessary knowledge and access.
Fees: £25 minimum for colour; £10 minimum for B&W; covers £120. Text by negotiation.

AIRLINER WORLD
Key Publishing Ltd, PO Box 100, Stamford, Lincs PE9 1XQ.
Tel: 01780 755131. Fax: 01780 757261. E-mail: tony.dixon@keypublishing.com
Editor: Tony Dixon.
Heavily-illustrated monthly for civil aviation enthusiasts.
Illustrations: Colour, some B&W. Always interested in topical photos covering the commercial airline scene, including business jets – new aircraft being rolled out, new liveries, new airlines, airport developments, etc. International coverage. Some archive material used; send stock lists.

Text: Will consider ideas for articles on any civil aviation theme, around 2,000 words. Contributors must have in-depth knowledge of their subject.
Overall freelance potential: Excellent.
Fees: Pictures from £20; text £50 per 1,000 words.

AIRPORT WORLD
Insight Media Ltd, 26-30 London Road, Twickenham TW1 3RW.
Tel: 020 8831 7507. Fax: 020 8891 0123. E-mail: joe@insightgrp.co.uk
Editor: Joe Bates.
Bi-monthly trade journal published for the Airports Council International, circulated to airport operators worldwide.
Illustrations: Colour. Recent photographs taken in airports and airport terminals in any part of the world – must be high quality pictures with a creative approach. Before submitting photographers should first send details of airports they have on file.
Text: No scope.
Overall freelance potential: Fair.
Fees: By negotiation.

AIRPORTS INTERNATIONAL
Key Publishing Ltd, PO Box 100, Stamford, Lincs PE9 1XQ.
Tel: 01780 755131. Fax: 01780 757261. E-mail: tom.allett@keypublishing.com
Editor: Tom Allett.
Published nine times a year, dealing with all aspects of airport construction, management, operations, services and equipment worldwide.
Illustrations: Colour. Photographs related to airport operational affairs. Particularly interested in high quality images for cover use, and coverage of "exotic" overseas locations. Always contact the editor before submitting.
Text: Possible scope for overseas material, depending on region; Middle East, Asia-Pacific, South America and Africa of particular interest.
Overall freelance potential: Fair.
Fees: By negotiation.

AVIATION NEWS
HPC Publishing, Drury Lane, St Leonards on Sea, East Sussex TN38 9BJ.
Tel: 01424 720477. Fax: 01424 443693. ISDN: 01424 721727. E-mail:editor@aviation-news.co.uk
Editor: Barry Wheeler.
Monthly magazine covering aviation in general, both past and present. Aimed at both the industry and the enthusiast.
Illustrations: Colour; B&W archive material. Photographs of all types of aircraft, civil and military, old or new. Captioned news pictures of particular interest, but no space exploration or aircraft engineering.
Text: News items about current aviation matters. Historical contributions concerning older aircraft.
Overall freelance potential: About 45 per cent is contributed by freelances.
Fees: On a rising scale according to size of reproduction or length of text.

DEFENCE HELICOPTER
The Shephard Press Ltd, 111 High Street, Burnham, Bucks SL1 7JZ.
Tel: 01628 604311. Fax: 01628 669808. E-mail: ad@shephard.co.uk
Editor: Andrew Drwiega.
Bi-monthly publication concerned with military and public service helicopters.
Illustrations: Mainly colour. Pictures of military and public service (police, coastguard, emergency services, etc) helicopters anywhere in the world. Must be accurately captioned. Covers: high quality colour pictures of appropriate helicopters. Should preferably be exclusive and in upright format. No "sterile" pictures; must be action shots.

Text: News stories and features on helicopters in service use and helicopter technology. Up to 1,500 words.
Overall freelance potential: Good.
Fees: By negotiation.

FLIGHT INTERNATIONAL
Reed Business Information Ltd, Quadrant House, The Quadrant, Sutton, Surrey SM2 5AS.
Tel: 020 8652 3842. Fax: 020 8652 3840.
Editor: Murdo Morrison. **Production Editor:** Graeme Osborn.
Weekly aviation magazine with worldwide circulation, aimed at aerospace professionals in all sectors of the industry.
Illustrations: Mostly colour; digital only by prior arrangement. Weekly requirement for news pictures of aviation-related events. Feature illustrations on all aspects of aerospace, from airliners to satellites. Covers: clean, uncluttered pictures of aircraft – civil and military, light and business. Medium format preferred.
Text: News items always welcomed. Features by prior arrangement only; submit ideas in the first instance.
Overall freelance potential: Limited for those without contacts in the industry.
Editor's tips: News material should be submitted on spec. Pictures should always be as new as possible or have a news relevance.
Fees: B&W, £19.61; colour, £56.38 up to 30 sq.in., £65.93 to £106.93 30–60 sq. in.; £223.30 for cover. News reports, minimum £7.07 per 100 words; commissioned features by negotiation.

FLYER
Seager Publishing Ltd, 9 Riverside Court, Lower Bristol Road, Bath BA2 3DZ.
Tel: 01225 481440. Fax: 01225 481262. E-mail: nick@flyermag.co.uk
Editor: *TBA*.
Monthly magazine for private pilots.
Illustrations: Mostly colour. Attractive and striking photographs of light aircraft of the type commonly used by the private pilot. Details of material available should be sent first, rather than speculative submissions.
Text: News items and illustrated articles from those with proper knowledge of the subject.
Overall freelance potential: Limited – mainly provided by established contributors.
Editor's tips: All contributors should have a genuine understanding of the flying scene.
Fees: By negotiation.

FLYPAST
Key Publishing Ltd, PO Box 100, Stamford, Lincs PE9 1XQ.
Tel: 01780 755131. Fax: 10780 757261. E-mail: flypast@keypublishing.com
Editor: Ken Ellis.
Monthly magazine devoted to aviation heritage.
Illustrations: Mostly colour. Photographs of interesting old aircraft or aircraft collections from anywhere in the world, but always contact the editor before submitting.
Text: Articles on collections, museums, aircraft operators and personal accounts of past flying experiences.
Overall freelance potential: Good for those with access to suitable material.
Fees: £20 for colour; £10 B&W. Text £50 per 1,000 words.

PILOT
Archant Specialist, The Mill, Bearwalden Business Park, Wendens Ambo, Essex CB11 4GB.
Tel: 01799 544200. Fax: 01799 544201. E-mail: dave.calderwood@pilotweb.co.uk
Editor: Dave Calderwood.
Monthly publication for the general aviation (i.e. business and private flying) pilot.
Illustrations: Mostly colour. Digital media preferred. Pictures on topics associated with

this field of flying.
Text: Features, preferably illustrated, on general aviation. 2,000–4,000 words.
Overall freelance potential: Excellent. Virtually all of the editorial matter in the magazine is contributed by freelances.
Editor's tips: Read a copy of the magazine before submitting and study style, content, subject and coverage.
Fees: £150–£800 for features. Pictures inside £30; covers, £250.

TODAY'S PILOT
Key Publishing Ltd, PO Box 100, Stamford, Lincs PE9 1XQ.
Tel: 01780 755131. Fax: 01780 757261.E-mail: dave.unwin@keypublishing.com
Editor: David Unwin.
Monthly aimed at both private and commercial pilots, those learning to fly, and general aviation enthusiasts.
Illustrations: Colour. Digital media preferred. Will consider any news-based or unusual photographs likely to be of interest to the readership.
Text: Always interested in well-illustrated, authoritative articles on any aspect of private or commercial flying, ranging from travelogues to technical pieces. Submit suggestions only in the first instance
Overall freelance potential: Good scope for illustrated articles.
Fees: By negotiation.

Boating & Watersport

BOARDS
Yachting Press Ltd, 196 Eastern Esplanade, Southend-on-Sea, Essex SS1 3AB.
Tel: 01702 582245. Fax: 01702 588434.
Editor: Bill Dawes.
Monthly magazine devoted to boardsailing and windsurfing.
Illustrations: Mostly colour. Good clear action shots of boardsailing or windsurfing; pictures of attractive girls in a boardsailing context; any other visually striking material relating to the sport. Covers: good colour action shots always needed.
Text: Articles and features on all aspects of the sport.
Overall freelance potential: Very good for high quality material.
Editor's tips: Action shots must be clean, clear and crisp.
Fees: By negotiation.

BOAT INTERNATIONAL
Edisea Ltd, Ward House, 5–7 Kingston Hill, Kingston upon Thames, Surrey KT2 7PW.
Tel: 020 8547 2662. Fax: 020 8547 9731.
Editor: Amanda McCracken.
Monthly glossy magazine focusing on the top, luxury level of sailing and power vessels.
Illustrations: Colour. Top quality transparencies only. Will consider images of world class yacht racing and luxury cruising. 35mm acceptable for action shots, but larger formats preferred for static subjects.
Text: Mostly staff produced or commissioned from top writers in the field.
Overall freelance potential: Excellent for the best in boating photography and marine subjects.
Editor's tips: Only the very best quality is of interest.
Fees: By negotiation.

BOATING BUSINESS
Mercator Media, The Old Mill, Lower Quay, Fareham, Hants PO16 0RA.
Tel: 01329 825335. Fax: 01329 825220. E-mail: editor@boatingbusiness.co.uk

Editor: Peter Nash.
Monthly magazine for the leisure marine trade.
Illustrations: Colour. News pictures relating to the marine trade, especially company and overseas news. Some scope for commissioned work.
Text: Features on marine trade topics; always consult the editor first.
Overall freelance potential: Limited.
Fees: Photographs from £20; text £100 per 1,000 words.

CANAL & RIVERBOAT
A E Morgan Publications Ltd. Editorial: PO Box 618, Norwich NR7 0QT.
Tel: 01603 708930. Fax: 01603 708934. E-mail: bluefoxfilms@themag.fsnet.co.uk
Editor: Chris Cattrall.
Monthly publication aimed at inland waterway enthusiasts and canal holidaymakers.
Illustrations: Mostly colour. Photographs of all inland waterway subjects. Covers: colour pictures of attractive waterways subjects, preferably with an original approach.
Text: Illustrated articles on canals, rivers, boats and allied subjects.
Overall freelance potential: Good, especially for material with an original approach.
Fees: By negotiation.

CANAL BOAT & INLAND WATERWAYS
Romsey Publishing Company, 4 The Courtyard, Denmark Street, Wokingham, Berks RG40 2AZ.
Tel: 01189 771677. Fax: 01189 772903. E-mail: canalboat@goring.co.uk
Editor: Emrhys Barrell.
Monthly for serious enthusiasts of Britain's inland waterways, including rivers, lakes and canals.
Illustrations: Colour. Photographs required specifically for cover use. Should capture aspects such as the vivid colours of the boats, tranquillity of the waterways, scenic splendours beyond the towpath, and seasonal elements. Composition needs to take into account the upright cover format and the position of the magazine's logo. 35mm acceptable though medium format preferred.
Text: Generally provided by dedicated enthusiasts.
Overall freelance potential: Excellent for covers; little scope elsewhere.
Editor's tips: Refer to one or two recent covers to check if your picture really suits.
Fees: From £80–£120 for covers.

CLASSIC BOAT
IPC Country & Leisure Group, Leon House, 233 High Street, Croydon CR9 1HZ.
Tel: 020 8726 8000. Fax: 020 8774 0943. E-mail: cb@ipcmedia.com
Editor: Dan Houston. **Art Editor:** Peter Smith.
Monthly magazine for the enthusiast interested in traditional or traditional-style boats from any part of the world. Emphasis on sailing boats, but also covers traditional power boats, steam vessels and modern reproductions of classic styles.
Illustrations: Mostly colour. Digital media accepted, but transparencies preferred. Pictures to accompany features and articles. Single general interest pictures with 100 word captions giving full subject details. Particular interest in individual boat photo essays. Covers: spectacular sailing images, but exceptional boat building shots may be used. Upright format with space for logo and coverlines.
Text: Well-illustrated articles covering particular types of boat and individual craft, combining well-researched historical background with hard practical advice about restoration and maintenance. Some scope for humorous pieces and cruising articles involving classic boats. Always send a detailed

synopsis in the first instance.
Overall freelance potential: Good for those with specialist knowledge or access.
Editor's tips: Contributors' notes available on request. Well-documented and photographed practical articles do best.
Fees: £90-£100 per page pro rata; covers £200.

INTERNATIONAL BOAT INDUSTRY
IPC Country & Leisure (Marine) Ltd, King's Reach Tower, Stamford Street, London SE1 9LS.
Tel: 020 7261 5000. Fax: 020 7261 5731. E-mail: kim_hollamby@ipcmedia.com
Group Editor: Kim Hollamby.
Business publication dealing with the marine leisure industry worldwide. Eight issues a year.
Illustrations: Colour. Pictures of boat building and moulding, chandlery shops, showrooms, new boats and equipment. Also marinas.
Text: News items about the boat industry are always of interest.
Overall freelance potential: Good for those in touch with the boat trade.
Editor's tips: This is strictly a trade magazine – general pictures of cruising or racing are not required.
Fees: Linear scale – £100 per page down.

JET SKIER & PERSONAL WATERCRAFT
CSL Publishing Ltd, 72A Regent Street, Cambridge CB2 1DP.
Tel: 01223 460490. Fax: 01223 315960. E-mail: editor@jetskier.co.uk
Editor: Craig Barnett.
Monthly magazine devoted to small, powered water craft and related sports activity. Features Jet Skis, Wetbikes and other personal watercraft.
Illustrations: Mostly colour. Spectacular action shots and pictures of unusual individual craft and uses. Events coverage usually by commission.
Text: Some scope for illustrated articles from those with good knowledge of the subject. Submit ideas only in the first instance.
Overall freelance potential: Good.
Fees: By negotiation.

MOTOR BOAT & YACHTING
IPC Media Ltd, King's Reach Tower, Stamford Street, London SE1 9LS.
Tel: 020 7261 5333. Fax: 020 7261 5419. E-mail: mby@ipcmedia.com
Editor: Tom Isitt. **Art Editor:** Jason Keens.
Monthly magazine for owners and users of motor cruisers.
Illustrations: Colour. Pictures of motor cruisers at sea, harbour scenes, workboats. Covers: Pictures of people having fun on motor boats at sea. Also good harbour scenes, showing exceptional composition and/or lighting.
Text: Features on interesting, unusual or historic motor boats; first-person motor boat cruising accounts; technical motor boating topics. 1,500–2,500 words.
Overall freelance potential: Around 40 per cent of features and 20 per cent of pictures are freelance contributed.
Fees: Good; on a rising scale according to size of reproduction or length of article.

MOTOR BOATS MONTHLY
IPC Media, Room 220, King's Reach Tower, Stamford Street, London SE1 9LS.
Tel: 020 7261 7256. Fax: 020 7261 7900. E-mail: motor_boats_monthly@ipc.co.uk
Editor: Hugo Andreae.
Monthly magazine for all motorboating enthusiasts, but mainly aimed at owners of boats of up to 60 feet. Covers all aspects, from top level powerboat racing to inland waterway cruising.
Illustrations: Colour. News pictures, motor boat action, and shots of cruising locations, both in UK and overseas.

Text: Illustrated articles on any motorboat-related topic, UK and worldwide.
Overall freelance potential: Fairly good.
Fees: On a rising scale according to size of reproduction or length of text.

PRACTICAL BOAT OWNER
IPC Magazines Ltd, Westover House, West Quay Road, Poole, Dorset BH15 1JG.
Tel: 01202 440820. Fax: 01202 440860. E-mail: pbo@ipcmedia.com
Editor: Sarah Norbury. **Art Editor:** Kevin Slater.
Monthly magazine for yachtsmen, sail and power.
Illustrations: Colour. Up to date pictures of harbours and anchorages. Covers: Action shots of cruising boats up to about 40ft (preferably sail) showing people enjoying themselves. Must have strong colours.
Text: Features and associated illustrations of real use to the people who own boats. Subjects can cover any boating facet on which readers might take action, from raising the money to buying a boat, through insurance to navigation, seamanship, care and maintenance. No narrative yarns.
Overall freelance potential: About 75 per cent bought from contributors.
Fees: On a rising scale according to size of reproduction or length of feature.

RYA MAGAZINE
Royal Yachting Association, RYA House, Ensign Way, Hamball, Southampton SO31 4YA.
Tel: 0845 3450400. E-mail: deborah.cornick@rya.org.uk
Editor: Deborah Cornick.
Quarterly publication for personal members of the RYA, affiliated clubs and class associations.
Illustrations: Colour. Digital media preferred. Pictures of boats, yachting events and personalities, used either in their own right or as illustrations for reports and articles. Covers: seasonal/topical shots of yachting subjects.
Text: Reports and articles on yachting.
Overall freelance potential: Moderate.
Fees: By arrangement.

REGATTA
Amateur Rowing Association, 6 Lower Mall, London W6 9DJ.
Tel: 020 8237 6700. Fax: 020 8237 6749. E-mail: sophie.mackley@ara-rowing.org
Editor: Sophie Mackley.
Covers rowing and sculling – competitive, recreational and technical. 10 editions annually.
Illustrations: Mostly colour. Any coverage of the subject considered, especially action pictures of rowing and rowing in scenic settings.
Text: Short, illustrated articles on all aspects of rowing. Technical topics such as coaching, training and boat-building.
Overall freelance potential: Good.
Fees: By arrangement with editor.

SAILING TODAY
Madforsport Ltd, Swanwick Marina, Lower Swanwick, Southampton SO31 1ZL.
Tel: 01489 585225. Fax: 01489 565054. E-mail: feedback@sailingtoday.co.uk
Editor: John Goode. **Art Editor:** Julian Dace.
Practical monthly for active sail cruising enthusiasts.
Illustrations: Colour. Dynamic action shots of people involved in active sailing situations. Ideally

compositions should be closely cropped in to focus on the sailor(s) involved, who should be clearly enjoying themselves. Scope for location photo shoots and step-by-step boat improvement projects.
Text: Well-illustrated features on boat improvements and cruising round the British Isles. Should have a modern, upbeat and original approach.
Overall freelance potential: Good.
Fees: By negotiation.

SPORTSBOAT & RIB MAGAZINE
CSL Publishing Ltd, 72A Regent Street, Cambridge CB2 1DP.
Tel: 01223 460490. Fax: 01223 315960. E-mail: sue@sportsboat.co.uk
Editor: Sue Baggaley.
Monthly publication covering sports boats from 14–30 feet.
Illustrations: Mostly colour. Digital submission preferred. Top quality action shots of small sports boats. Also stylish pictures that show boats as glamorous and exciting. Commissions may be available to illustrate major features. Covers: colour action shots with plenty of impact.
Text: Illustrated articles on all aspects of sports boats and waterskiing will always be considered. 500–3,000 words.
Overall freelance potential: Excellent.
Fees: By negotiation.

TRADITIONAL BOATS & TALL SHIPS
Poundbury Publishing Ltd, Prospect House, Peverell Avenue East, Poundbury, Dorchester DT1 3WE.
Tel: 01305 266360. Fax: 01305 262760. E-mail:tallships@poundbury.co.uk
Editor: Stephen Swann.
Bi-monthly for enthusiasts of traditional sailing boats, with an emphasis on tall ships and other larger sea-going vessels.
Illustrations: Mainly colour (prints and digital media acceptable); archive B&W. Always interested in striking photographs of traditional vessels under full sail. Must have excellent definition, light and colour for often large-scale reproduction. Detailed captions also essential.
Text: Well-illustrated articles on traditional sailboats, including restoration projects and historical features.
Overall freelance potential: Excellent; the magazine relies on freelance contributors.
Editor's tips: Pictures that come with a story or interesting context stand the best chance of being used.
Fees: From £20–£90 depending on size of reproduction.

WATER CRAFT
Pete Greenfield Publishing, Bridge Shop, Gweek, Helston, Cornwall TR12 6UD.
Tel: 01326 221424. Fax: 01326 221728. E-mail: watercraft@netmatters.co.uk
Editor: Pete Greenfield.
Bi-monthly magazine devoted to traditional small boats and boat building.
Illustrations: Colour. Photographs mainly required as part of complete feature packages, but interesting or unusual singles and sequences considered if accompanied by detailed caption information.
Text: Well-illustrated features on suitable subjects
Overall freelance potential: Limited at present; much is produced by regular contributors.
Fees: Around £80 per published page inclusive of pictures.

WATERWAYS WORLD
Waterways World Ltd, 151 Station Street, Burton-on-Trent DE14 1BG.
Tel: 01283 742951. Fax: 01283 742957. E-mail: hugh.potter@wwonline.co.uk
Editor: Hugh Potter.
Monthly magazine that covers all aspects of canal and river navigations (not lakes) in Britain and

abroad. Aimed at inland waterway enthusiasts and holiday boaters.
Illustrations: Colour. Pictures of inland waterway subjects, eg interesting buildings; locks, preferably with boating activity if on a navigable waterway; canal scenes. No close-ups or artistic shots. Covers: canal or river scenes with boating activity prominently in the foreground; medium format transparencies preferred.
Text: Features on inland waterways, 500–2,000 words. Send sae or e-mail for contributors' guide.
Overall freelance potential: Around 20 per cent contributed.
Fees: Pictures £20 minimum; cover £75.

WINDSURF MAGAZINE
Arcwind Ltd, The Blue Barn, Tew Lane, Wootton, Woodstock, Oxon OX7 1HA.
Tel: 01993 811181. Fax: 01993 811481.
Editor: Mark Kasprowicz.
Published ten times a year. Aimed at the enthusiast and covering all aspects of windsurfing.
Illustrations: Mostly colour. Sequences and singles of windsurfing action. Top quality shots always considered.
Text: Illustrated articles on any aspect of windsurfing.
Overall freelance potential: Excellent.
Fees: £5–£15 for B&W; up to £35 for full-page colour; £60 for centre-spread; £60 for covers.

YACHTING MONTHLY
IPC Media Ltd, Room 2215, King's Reach Tower, Stamford Street, London SE1 9LS.
Tel: 020 7261 6040. Fax: 020 7261 7555.
Editor: Paul Gelder. **Art Editor:** Holly Ramsay.
Monthly magazine for cruising yachtsmen.
Illustrations: Colour. Digital media or film. News pictures for immediate use; general cruising and location pictures for stock; pictures illustrating seamanship, navigation and technical subjects. Covers: top quality shots of active cruising; people working boats; cruising boats at sea; yachts in harbour.
Text: Articles relevant to cruising yachtsmen, and short accounts of cruising experiences. 1,000–2,250 words.
Overall freelance potential: Around 40 per cent comes from outside contributors.
Fees: Dependent upon size of reproduction or length of feature. Normally around £50–£110 for colour; £200 for covers. Text from £75 per 1,000 words.

YACHTING WORLD
IPC Media Ltd, King's Reach Tower, Stamford Street, London SE1 9LS.
Tel: 020 7261 7787. Fax: 020 7261 6818. E-mail: ywpictures@ipcmedia.com
Editor: Andrew Bray. **Picture Editor:** Vanda Woolsey.
Monthly magazine for informed yachtsmen.
Illustrations: Colour. Digital media preferred. Pictures of general yachting techniques or types of boat; pictures of events and occasions; location shots and mood pictures. Major feature photography commissioned from known specialists. Covers: top quality pictures of yachts in 35-55ft range – action pictures on board, at sea.
Text: Informative or narrative yachting articles; technical yachting features; short humorous articles; and news. 1,000–1,500 words and 2,000–2,500 words. Send for writers' guidelines.
Overall freelance potential: Around 30 per cent comes from freelances.
Editor's tips: Contributors must know the subject and know the market. The most successful photographers we use are the ones who work the hardest.
Fees: Inside pictures according to size, from £35–£280 (dps), covers £585. Text up to £148 per 1,000 words.

YACHTS & YACHTING
Yachting Press Ltd, 196 Eastern Esplanade, Southend-on-Sea, Essex SS1 3AB.
Tel: 01702 582245. Fax: 01702 588434. E-mail: photos@yachtsandyachting.com
Editor: Gael Pawson.
Fortnightly publication covering all aspects of racing, including dinghies and offshore racers.
Illustrations: Colour. Pictures of racing dinghies, yachts and general sailing scenes. Covers: colour action shots of relevant subjects.
Text: Features on all aspects of the race sailing scene. 1,000–2,000 words.
Overall freelance potential: Quite good.
Fees: Negotiable.

Business

ACCOUNTANCY AGE
VNU Business Publications, 32–34 Broadwick Street, London W1A 2HG.
Tel: 020 7316 9000. Fax: 020 7316 9250. E-mail: accountancy_age@vnu.co.uk
Editor: Damien Wild.
Weekly publication for qualified accountants.
Illustrations: Colour. Digital media or film. All commissioned, but new photographers are always welcome.
Text: News and features coverage for accountants. Synopsis preferred in first instance. 1,200 words.
Overall freelance potential: Fairly good for commissioned photography. About 50 per cent of the features come from freelances.
Editor's tips: To gain acceptance, articles must contribute something which cannot be provided by the in-house staff.
Fees: By agreement.

CA MAGAZINE
Institute of Chartered Accountants of Scotland, CA House, 21 Haymarket Yards, Edinburgh EH12 5BH.
Tel: 0131 343 7500. Fax: 0131 343 7505. E-mail: scraig@icas.org.uk
Editor: Rob Outram. **Art Editor:** Steven Creig.
Scottish financial and management magazine incorporating monthly journal of The Institute of Chartered Accountants of Scotland.
Illustrations: B&W and colour. Digital media preferred. Creative and innovative images which can be related to the subject and which attract readers' attention.
Text: Articles on accounting and auditing, company law, finance, taxation, management topics, company/personal profiles, the financial and management scene in the UK and overseas, investment, computer science, etc. Length: 1,200–3,000 words.
Overall freelance potential: Fair for business specialists.
Fees: By arrangement.

DIRECTOR
Director Publications Ltd, 116 Pall Mall, London SW1Y 5ED.
Tel: 020 7766 8950. Fax: 020 7766 8840. E-mail: director-ed@iod.co.uk
Editor: Joanna Higgins. **Picture Editor:** Jane Moss.
Monthly journal for members of the Institute of Directors.
Illustrations: B&W and colour. Top quality portraits of company chairmen or major business personalities. Covers: colour portraits or top quality business/industry subjects. More creative,

avant-garde illustrations also used.
Text: Interviews; management advice; company profiles; business controversies; EC affairs.
Overall freelance potential: Good.
Fees: By negotiation.

EN
Entrepreneur Business Publishing, Portland Buildings, 127-129 Portland Street, Manchester M1 4PZ.
Tel: 0161 236 2782. Fax: 0161 236 2783.
Editor: Scott McCubbin.
Glossy business monthly for entrepreneurs, with separate editions for the North West and Yorkshire regions, aimed at owner-managed companies with turnover between £0.5m–£40m.
Illustrations: B&W and colour. Captioned news pictures about developments in private businesses as above. General business/industrial photography by commission, mainly portraiture but some general business/industrial work.
Text: Topical articles of interest to business people in the region – hard-edged, readable, jargon-free. Newsy items only.
Overall freelance potential: Quite good for the freelance with a professional and creative approach.
Editor's tips: Prefer a creative, even off-the-wall, style. Happy to consider newcomers as long as they are thoroughly professional and reliable.
Fees: By negotiation.

EXPORT TIMES
Highbury Business, Nexus House, Azalea Drive, Swanley, Kent BR8 8HY.
Tel: 01322 660070. Fax: 01322 666408.
Editor: Russell Flanders.
Monthly newspaper covering all aspects of UK exporting.
Illustrations: B&W and colour. Captioned news pictures covering foreign trade, overseas development, and everyday life and work overseas.
Text: News stories or short features about exporting.
Overall freelance potential: Limited; most material comes from regular contributors.
Editor's tips: Always best to write first. If going on a trip abroad, make contact beforehand not upon your return.
Fees: £140 per 1,000 words; pictures according to size of reproduction.

FINANCIAL MANAGEMENT
Chartered Institute of Management Accountants, 26 Chapter Street, London SW1P 4NP.
Tel: 020 7663 5441. Fax: 020 8849 2458.
Editor: Ruth Prickett.
Monthly publication for financial managers.
Illustrations: B&W and colour. Regular profile photography to accompany business-related articles.
Text: Occasional freelance market for articles on management/accountancy subjects.
Overall freelance potential: Good.
Fees: By agreement.

MARKETING
Haymarket Business Publications Ltd, 174 Hammersmith Road, London W6 7JP.
Tel: 020 8267 4208. Fax: 020 8267 4504.
Editor: Craig Smith. **Art Director:** Gene Cornelius.
Weekly publication for marketing management, both client and agency.
Illustrations: Colour. Commissioned coverage of subjects relating to marketing. Experienced business photographers should contact the art editor.

Text: News and features with a marketing angle and objective case histories.
Overall freelance potential: Limited; for business specialists only.
Editor's tips: Photographers must be able to work accurately to a brief.
Fees: Negotiable.

MIDDLE EAST ECONOMIC DIGEST (MEED)
EMAP Communications, 33-39 Bowling Green Lane, London EC1R 0DA.
Tel: 020 7470 6200. Fax: 020 7831 9537. E-mail: hassan.yusuf@meed.com
Editor: Tom Everett-Heath. **Art Director:** Hassan Yusuf.
Weekly business journal covering the affairs of Middle Eastern countries.
Illustrations: Colour; prints and digital accepted. Pictures of current major construction projects in the Middle East and stock shots of important personalities (politicians, leading businessmen) in the region. Recent general views of particular locations occasionally used. Covers: colour pictures of contemporary Middle East subjects, preferably with an obvious business flavour. Also, high-quality colour abstracts.
Text: Specialist articles on relevant business matters.
Overall freelance potential: Limited.
Fees: On a rising scale according to size of reproduction or length of text.

PEOPLE MANAGEMENT
Personnel Publications Ltd, 17 Britton Street, London EC1M 5TP.
Tel: 020 7880 6223. Fax: 020 7336 7635. ISDN: 020 7608 2865. claireh@ppltd.co.uk
Editor: Steve Crabb. **Picture Researcher:** Claire Handley.
Fortnightly magazine of the Institute of Personnel and Development. Covers all aspects of staff management and training.
Illustrations: Colour. Photographs of people at work in business and industry, particularly any depicting staff education and training. Detailed lists of subjects available welcomed. Some commissions may be available to experienced workers – contact picture researcher to show photographic portfolios.
Text: Ideas for articles always welcome; submit a short written proposal first.
Overall freelance potential: Quite good – a lot of stock pictures are used. Contributions here might also be used in Supply Management, a similar title produced by the same team for the Chartered Institute of Purchasing and Supply.
Fees: By negotiation.

POST MAGAZINE
Incisive Media Plc, Haymarket House, 28-29 Haymarket, London SW1Y 4RX.
Tel: 020 7484 9700. Fax: 020 7930 2238.
Editor: Jonathan Swift. **Art Editor:** Nicky Brown.
Weekly publication covering insurance at home and abroad.
Illustrations: Colour. Pictures of traffic, houses, offices, building sites, damage (including fire and motoring accidents), shipwrecks or aviation losses, etc. Also political and industry personalities.
Text: News and features on insurance, including life assurance, general insurance, reinsurance, pensions, financial services, savings, unit trusts, investment, marketing, technology, offices and personnel areas.
Overall freelance potential: Most news and features are contributed by freelances.
Fees: By negotiation.

PROMOTIONS & INCENTIVES
Haymarket Marketing Publications Ltd, 174 Hammersmith Road, London W6 7JP.
Tel: 020 8267 4152. Fax: 020 8267 4442.
Editor: Bhavna Mistry.
Monthly publication for brand managers, SP managers, incentive managers etc. Concerned with

incentive ideas for staff motivation and sales promotion campaigns, aids and general marketing themes.
Illustrations: B&W and colour. Digital media or film. Pictures limited to the marketing and/or promotions profession. Covers: highly creative colour pictures, usually linked to the main feature inside.
Text: Authoritatively written articles on technical aspects of the marketing and/or promotions profession. 1,500–2,000 words.
Overall freelance potential: Up to 30 per cent bought from freelances.
Editor's tips: Contact the magazine first.

Camping & Caravanning

CAMPING AND CARAVANNING
The Camping and Caravanning Club, Greenfields House, Westwood Way, Coventry CV4 8JH.
Tel: 02476 694995. Fax: 02476 694886.
Editor: Nick Harding.
Monthly magazine concerning all aspects of camping and caravanning.
Illustrations: Colour. Usually only required in conjunction with feature articles.
Text: Illustrated features on camping and caravanning in Britain, around 1,200 words. Contact the editor with ideas only in the first instance.
Overall freelance potential: Fair.
Fees: By agreement.

CAMPING MAGAZINE
Warners Group Publications plc, The Maltings, West Street, Bourne, Lincs PE10 9PH.
Tel: 01778 393313. Fax: 01778 425437.
Editor: Mike Cowton.
Monthly magazine covering all aspects of camping. Emphasises the range of activities that camping makes available.
Illustrations: Mainly colour. Photographs showing campers engaged in various activities; do not have to include a tent but must have an "outdoor" feel. Also landscapes and tourist attractions to illustrate specific area guides; assignments may be available. Covers: Strong images of campers obviously enjoying themselves on a family or lightweight camping holiday.
Text: Picture-led features that show camping as "a means to an end" and illustrate the range of people and lifestyles that camping embraces, travel features focusing on particular areas in the UK or the Continent. Always check with the editor before submitting.
Overall freelance potential: Excellent.
Editor's tips: Pictures should not be dominated by tents and camping clutter.
Fees: Text £90 per 1,000 words; pictures negotiable.

CARAVAN
IPC Focus Network, Leon House, 233 High Street, Croydon CR9 1HZ.
Tel: 020 8726 8000. Fax: 020 8726 8299. E-mail: steve_rowe@ipcmedia.com
Editor: Steve Rowe.
Monthly magazine for all caravanners.
Illustrations: Colour. Good general illustrations of touring and caravan-related subjects frequently needed to illustrate features. Some opportunities for commissioned work, though in-house photographers handle much of this.
Text: Well-illustrated accounts of touring in specific areas, or more general caravanning-related items with a human interest angle. Call or write with ideas first.
Overall freelance potential: Fair to good.
Fees: By negotiation.

CARAVAN INDUSTRY AND PARK OPERATOR
A.E.Morgan Publications Ltd, Stanley House, 9 West Street, Epsom, Surrey KT18 7RL.
Tel: 01372 741411. Fax: 01372 744493. E-mail: teamwork@ukonline.co.uk
Editor: David Ritchie.
Monthly publication for manufacturers, traders, suppliers and park operators in the caravan industry.
Illustrations: Mainly colour. News pictures of interest to the industry – new caravan park developments, new models, new dealer depots, etc.
Text: Company profiles on park owners and their businesses, traders and manufacturers. 900–1,200 words.
Overall freelance potential: Up to 30 per cent of the content comes from freelance contributors.
Fees: By agreement.

CARAVAN LIFE
Warners Group Publications Ltd, The Maltings, West Street, Bourne, Lincs PE10 9PH.
Tel: 01778 393313. Fax: 01778 425437. E-mail: mikelec@warnersgroup.co.uk
Editor: Michael Le Caplain.
Monthly caravanning magazine targeted at experienced caravanners.
Illustrations: Colour. Mostly commissioned work; scope only for photographers with experience of caravan and quality landscape photography.
Text: Approaches from experienced writers will be considered.
Overall freelance potential: Excellent if the contributor has writing flair and a pool of good ideas.
Fees: By negotiation.

MOTORHOME MONTHLY
Stone Leisure Ltd, Andrew House, 2a Granville Road, Sidcup, Kent DA14 4BN.
Tel: 020 8302 6150/6069 and 020 8300 2316. Fax: 020 8300 2315.
Editor: Bob Griffiths.
Monthly magazine about motorhomes and their use. Covers travel, lifestyle, etc.
Illustrations: Mostly colour. Photographs related to above subjects.
Text: Features on travel and motorhoming. 750–1,500 words with pix.
Overall freelance potential: Good.
Editor's tips: Preference for copy that requires a minimum of subbing or rewriting.
Fees: £20–£35 for illustrated articles.

PARK HOME & HOLIDAY CARAVAN
IPC Focus Network, Focus House, Dingwall Avenue, Croydon CR9 2TA.
Tel: 020 8774 0744. Fax: 020 8774 0939. E-mail: anne_webb@ipcmedia.com
Editor: Anne Webb. **Art Editor:** Waldemar Cheng.
Monthly covering residential park homes and caravan holiday homes.
Illustrations: Colour. Digital media preferred. Always interested in good photographs of park homes, static holiday caravans (not touring caravans), residential and holiday parks.
Text: Illustrated features on the above.
Overall freelance potential: Fair.
Fees: According to use.

PRACTICAL CARAVAN
Haymarket Publishing Ltd, 60 Waldegrave Road, Teddington, Middlesex TW11 8LG.
Tel: 020 8267 5629. Fax: 020 8267 5725. E-mail: practical.caravan@haynet.com
Editor: Alex Newby. **Art Editor:** Carl Golsby.
Monthly for caravanning holidaymakers.
Illustrations: Colour. Transparency only; medium format preferred. Mostly commissioned to accompany specific features, but interesting or unusual caravanning images may be considered on spec.

Text: Feature ideas and first-person stories always considered.
Overall freelance potential: Only for those with experience.
Fees: Commissions £250–£350 per day; other material negotiable.

PRACTICAL MOTORHOME
Haymarket Publishing Ltd, 60 Waldegrave Road, Teddington, Middlesex TW11 8LG.
Tel: 020 8267 5614. Fax: 020 8267 5725. E-mail: practical.motorhome@haynet.com
Editor: Carl Rodgerson. **Art Editor:** Martin Gannon.
Monthly for all motorhome holidaymakers and enthusiasts.
Illustrations: Colour. Transparency only; medium format preferred. Mostly commissioned to accompany specific features, but interesting or motorhome images may be considered on spec.
Text: Feature ideas and first-person stories always considered.
Overall freelance potential: Only for those with experience.
Fees: Commissions £250–£350 per day; other material negotiable.

Children & Teenage

BROWNIE
Warners Group Publications. Editorial: PO Box 48, Bexley, Kent DA5 1WB.
Tel/fax: 01322 400274. E-mail: mariontbrownie@aol.com
Editor: Marion Thompson.
Monthly publication for Brownies in the 7–10 age group.
Illustrations: Colour. Digital files preferred. Action pictures featuring Brownie activities and subjects.
Text: Articles with Brownie themes; 600-800 words. Also original, inexpensive craft ideas suitable for 7–10 year-olds, in step-by-step format with illustrations of each step; around 400 words.
Overall freelance potential: Around 10 per cent is contributed.
Fees: Pictures by arrangement; tend to be on the low side. Text £50 per 1,000 words.

GUIDING MAGAZINE
Girlguiding UK, 17-19 Buckingham Palace Road, London SW1W 0PT.
Tel: 020 7834 6242. Fax: 020 7828 5791. E-mail: guiding@girlguiding.org.uk
Editor: Wendy Kewley.
Monthly official magazine of The Guide Association.
Illustrations: Colour. Action pictures of Guiding subjects. Covers: Colour shots of Rainbows, Brownies, Guides, Rangers or Young Leaders in action and Guiders (adult leaders).
Text: Articles and activity ideas; freelances who feel they could contribute should contact magazine for more information.
Overall freelance potential: Suitable material from freelances always considered.
Fees: By arrangement.

MIZZ
IPC Media Ltd, Kings Reach Tower, Stamford Street, London SE1 9LS.
Tel: 020 7261 5118. Fax: 020 7261 6032. E-mail: claire_lewis-cole@ipcmedia.com
Editor: Sharon Christal. **Picture Editor:** Claire Lewis-Cole.
Fortnightly magazine aimed at girls in the 12–15 age group.
Illustrations: Colour. Youth celebrity pictures always of interest (young TV stars, boy/girl bands, etc). Most other photography by commission for specific features, but some scope for stock images that could illustrate "real life" situations encountered by teenage girls. Some scope for single captioned pictures of a humorous nature.
Text: Lively illustrated features on almost any topic that could be of interest to the the target age

group. Text should be informative as well as entertaining. A detailed synopsis should always be submitted in the first instance.
Overall freelance potential: Good for the experienced contributor.
Fees: By negotiation.

SCOUTING MAGAZINE
The Scout Association, Gilwell Park Chingford, London E4 7QW.
Tel: 020 8433 7100. Fax: 020 8433 7103. E-mail: scouting.magazine@scout.org.uk
Editor: Anna Sorensen.
Monthly publication offering practical programme and activity ideas for Scout Groups, plus articles of general interest to members of the Scout Movement as well as those involved in youth work and active lifestyles.
Illustrations: Colour. Pictures of Scouting activities, preferably action shots. Covers: colour action and head and shoulder shots of Beaver Scouts, Cub Scouts, Scouts, Venture Scouts, Explorer Scouts, Scout Network and Scout Fellowship members.
Text: Features on activities, competitions and interesting and unusual news stories suitable for a national readership. All material should be Scouting related or relevant to Scouting.
Overall freelance potential: A high proportion of pictures and text comes from Scout Association members.
Editor's tips: Note that where uniform is used, it should be the correct uniform; new uniforms were introduced from July 2001 and these are preferred in photos. Also, if pictures are of adventurous or hazardous activities, the correct safety rules must be seen to be observed and the correct safety equipment and precautions must be evident.
Fees: By agreement.

SNEAK
EMAP Performance Network, Mappin House, 4 Winsley Street, London W1W 8HF.
Tel: 020 7182 8885 (picture desk). Fax: 020 7182 8529. E-mail: vanessa.chandler@emap.com
Editor: Michelle Garnett. **Picture Editor:** Vanessa Chandler.
Celebrity weekly aimed at teenage girls.
Illustrations: Colour. Informal and paparazzi-style images of younger celebrities from the worlds of pop, film and TV. Emphasis on British rather than US stars.
Text: No scope.
Overall freelance potential: Good for those with access to suitable celebrities.
Fees: According to use and what is on offer.

SUGAR
Hachette Filipacchi (UK) Ltd, 64 North Row, London W1K 7LL.
Tel: 020 7150 7000. Fax: 020 7150 7001.
Editor: Nick Chalmers. **Art Director:** Deborah Peters.
Monthly for teenage girls.
Illustrations: Colour. Fashion, beauty, still-life and portraiture, all commissioned for specific features. Some scope for celebrity stock.
Text: No scope.
Overall freelance potential: Only for experienced specialists.
Fees: Basic rate £350 per day.

County & Country

BUCKINGHAMSHIRE COUNTRYSIDE
Beaumonde Publications, PO Box 5, Hitchin, Herts SG5 1GJ.
Tel: 01462 422014. Fax: 01462 422015. E-mail: sandra@buckscountryside.co.uk
Editor: Sandra Small.
Bi-monthly county magazine for the named area.
Illustrations: Mostly colour. People, places, and events in the county. Medium format required in the case of colour. Covers: colourful local countryside views.
Text: Topical articles, of a cultural nature, on any aspect of the county.
Overall freelance potential: Limited because much is supplied by regular freelance contributors.
Fees: By negotiation.

CHESHIRE LIFE
Archant Life, 3 Tustin Court, Portway, Preston PR1 8UR.
Tel: 01772 722022. Fax: 01772 760905. E-mail: patrick.o'neill@cheshirelife.co.uk
Editor: Patrick O'Neill.
Monthly up-market county magazine specialising in regional features.
Illustrations: Mainly colour. Prints and Pictures of the Cheshire region, mainly to accompany features on topics such as property, antiques, wildlife, society, arts and crafts, sport. Picture postcard scenes of Cheshire also of interest – landscapes, towns villages, heritage, etc.
Text: Articles and features on regional topics. Always consult the editor in the first instance.
Overall freelance potential: Good.
Fees: By negotiation.

COTSWOLD LIFE
Archant Life South, Cumberland House, Oriel Road, Cheltenham GL50 1BB.
Tel: 01242 216050. Fax: 01242 255116.
Publishing Editor: Peter Waters.
Monthly showcasing "the best of the Cotswolds".
Illustrations: Colour. Digital media or film. Pictures of local scenes and events, preferably with some life in them. Covers: Medium format colour of lively local scenes, with clear space at top for title logo.
Text: Illustrated articles of varying lengths, on local people, places, events, etc.
Overall freelance potential: Most material comes from regular freelance contributors but new contributors always considered.
Fees: Cover shots £50. Articles and other illustrations negotiable.

COUNTRY LIFE
IPC Media Ltd, Kings Reach Tower, Stamford Street, London SE1 9LS.
Tel: 020 7261 7058. Fax: 020 7261 5139.
Editor: Clive Aslet. **Art Director:** Steve Tydeman.
Weekly magazine for a general readership.
Illustrations: Colour. Pictures of British countryside, wildlife, interiors, country pursuits. Covers: Top quality pictures of landscapes, rural and urban. All formats acceptable.
Text: No scope.
Overall freelance potential: Limited; around 90 per cent of the magazine comes from regular suppliers.
Fees: Average; on a rising scale according to size of reproduction. Covers, £250.

COUNTRY QUEST
3 Brodog Court, Fishguard, Pembrokeshire SA65 9NF.
Tel: 01348 874445.
Editor: Beverly Davies. **Head of Content**: Catherine Collins.
Monthly country magazine for Wales and the border counties.
Illustrations: B&W and colour. Photographs focusing on the history, buildings, people and culture of the region.
Text: Illustrated articles on the above subjects, usually around 1,500 words.
Overall freelance potential: Very good; all contributions are freelance.
Fees: Variable, depending on what is offered.

COUNTRY WALKING
EMAP Active Ltd, Bretton Court, Bretton, Peterborough PE3 8DZ.
Tel: 01733 264666.Fax: 01733 282653. E-mail: jonathan.manning@emap.com
Editor: Jonathan Manning.
Monthly magazine for all walkers who enjoy great days out in the countryside.
Illustrations: Colour. Pictures depicting walkers in attractive locations, who must be wearing proper outdoor gear. Also top quality landscapes of suitable parts of the country, historic locations, landscapes with elements of walking interest (eg. stile, path), nature and wildlife. Covers: seasonal pictures of very attractive landscape settings. Medium format preferred.
Text: Well-illustrated articles and features on any walking or countryside topics. Strong emphasis on inspiration and entertainment and capturing the essence of why people walk.
Overall freelance potential: Fair, but much is produced by regulars.
Editor's tips: The emphasis is always on getting enjoyment from walking and the countryside.
Fees: By negotiation.

THE COUNTRYMAN
Countryman Publishing Ltd. Editorial office: Sheep Street, Burford, Oxon OX18 4LS.
Tel: 01993 824424. Fax: 01993 822012. E-mail: editorial@thecountryman.co.uk
Editor: Bill Taylor. **Picture Editor:** Andy Duncan.
Monthly covering all matters of countryside interest other than blood sports.
Illustrations: Mainly colour. Sequences of pictures about particular places, crafts, customs, farming practices, kinds of wildlife, etc. Must be accompanied by ample caption material. Only limited scope for single stock pictures.
Text: Well-illustrated articles of 800–1,000 words, on such subjects as mentioned above. Must be accurate, and usually based on the writer's own experience. Contact editor at editorial office.
Overall freelance potential: Excellent; almost all photographs, and most articles, are from freelance contributors.
Fees: £30 upwards for photographs. Text according to length and merit.

CUMBRIA
Dalesman Publishing Company Ltd, Stable Courtyard, Broughton Hall, Skipton, North Yorkshire BD23 3AZ.
Tel: 01756 701381. Fax: 01756 701326. E-mail: editorial@dalesman.co.uk
Editor: Terry Fletcher. **Picture Editor:** Paul Jackson.
Monthly countryside magazine for Cumbria and the surrounding area.
Illustrations: Colour. Attractive shots of landscapes, rural characters, wildlife, country pursuits and local heritage.
Text: Illustrated articles on any aspect of Lakeland country life. 800–1,200 words.
Overall freelance potential: Excellent.
Fees: Half-page £20; full-page £30; covers £100.

DALESMAN
Dalesman Publishing Company Ltd, Stable Courtyard, Broughton Hall, Skipton, North Yorkshire BD23 3AZ.
Tel: 01756 701381. Fax: 01756 701326. E-mail: editorial@dalesman.co.uk
Editor: Terry Fletcher. **Picture Editor:** Paul Jackson.
Monthly countryside magazine for Yorkshire.
Illustrations: Colour. Attractive shots of local landscapes, rural characters, wildlife, country pursuits and heritage.
Text: Illustrated articles on any aspect of rural Yorkshire life. 800–1,200 words.
Overall freelance potential: Excellent.
Fees: Half-page £20; full-page £30; covers £100.

DEVON TODAY
Westcountry Publications Ltd, Heron Road, Sowton, Exeter EX2 7NF.
Tel: 01392 442211. Fax: 01392 442473. E-mail: devontoday@westcountrypublications.co.uk
Editor: Jan Waldron.
Glossy monthly for the county of Devon.
Illustrations: Mainly colour. Images to illustrate features about life in Devon, especially plants and wildlife. Submit only lists of subjects in the first instance.
Text: Illustrated features on lifestyle topics including fitness, health treatments, travel and leisure. Submit ideas and samples of previously published work in the first instance.
Overall freelance potential: Limited for pictures as the magazine has a regular photographer.
Fees: By negotiation.

DORSET
Poundbury Publishing Ltd, Prospect House, Peverell Avenue East, Poundbury, Dorchester DT1 3WE.
Tel: 01305 266360. Fax: 01305 262760. E-mail:bridget@ poundbury.co.uk
Editor: Bridget Swann.
Monthly for people who like to explore the Dorset region.
Illustrations: Colour. Good stock photographs of the region: people, places, natural history, culture and heritage.
Text: Local news and illustrated articles on subjects as above, around 1,200 words.
Overall freelance potential: Good.
Fees: Pictures from £25–£45; text £100 per 1,000 words.

DORSET LIFE
Dorset County Magazines Ltd, 7 The Leanne, Sandford Lane, Wareham, Dorset BH20 4BY.
Tel: 01929 551264. Fax: 01929 552099
Editor: John Newth.
Monthly magazine for the Dorset area.
Illustrations: B&W and colour. Interesting and original photographs, but usually required as part of an article, not in isolation. Covers: prefer medium format transparencies of local scenes, suitable for upright reproduction. Must be original.
Text: Well-illustrated articles on any topic relating to Dorset, around 1,000 words.
Overall freelance potential: Most contributions come from regular freelance contributors but new contributors always considered.
Fees: According to size of reproduction and length of text.

THE FIELD
IPC Media, King's Reach Tower, Stamford Street, London SE1 9LS.
Tel: 020 7261 5198. Fax: 020 7261 5358. E-mail: rebecca_hawtrey@ipcmedia.com
Editor: Jonathan Young. **Art Editor:** Rebecca Hawtrey.
Monthly publication concerned with all rural and country sports interests.

Illustrations: Colour. Good pictures illustrating relevant articles as below.
Text: Illustrated features on country and country sporting subjects, such as shooting, fishing, gundogs etc. Length according to article, in the range 1,000–2,000 words.
Overall freelance potential: Around 80 per cent comes from outside contributors, most of whom are specialists.
Fees: According to merit.

HERTFORDSHIRE COUNTRYSIDE
Beaumonde Publications, PO Box 5, Hitchin, Herts SG5 1GJ.
Tel: 01462 422014. Fax: 01462 422015. E-mail: sandra@hertscountryside.co.uk
Editor: Sandra Small.
Monthly county magazine for the named area.
Illustrations: B&W and colour. People, places, and events in the county. Medium format required in the case of colour. Covers: colourful local countryside views.
Text: Topical articles, of a cultural nature, on any aspect of the county.
Overall freelance potential: Limited because much is supplied by regular freelance contributors.
Fees: By negotiation.

LANCASHIRE LIFE
Archant Life, Oyston Mill, Strand Road, Preston PR1 8UR.
Tel: 01772 722022. Fax: 01772 736496. E-mail: anthony.skinner@lancashirelife.co.uk
Editor: Tony Skinner.
Monthly up-market county magazine specialising in regional features.
Illustrations: Mainly colour. Pictures of the Lancashire region, mainly to accompany features. Pictures of nationally known personalities with a Lancashire connection. Covers: top quality regional scenes; medium format preferred.
Text: Articles and features on regional topics. Always consult the editor in the first instance.
Overall freelance potential: Good; around 40 per cent is from freelance sources.
Editor's tips: The magazine is not interested in the merely parochial.
Fees: By negotiation.

LINCOLNSHIRE LIFE
County Life Ltd, PO Box 81, Lincoln LN1 1HD.
Tel: 01522 527127. Fax: 01522 560035. E-mail: editorial@lincolnshirelife.co.uk
Editor: Judy Theobald.
Monthly magazine, dealing with county life past and present from the Humber to the Wash.
Illustrations: B&W and colour. Pictures of people and places within the county of Lincolnshire. No current social events. Covers: portrait format colour pictures of local landscapes, architecture, animals, people, street scenes, etc. 35mm acceptable, but medium format preferred. Submissions for annual calendar also accepted.
Text: Features on people and places within the appropriate area. No more than 1,600 words. Contact editor first to discuss.
Overall freelance potential: Fifty per cent of the magazine comes from freelance sources.
Fees: £50 for covers, other material by agreement.

MANCHESTER LIFE
Life Magazines, Oyston Mill, Strand Road, Preston PR1 8UR.
Tel/fax: 0161 626 8812.
Editor: Louise Taylor.
Monthly covering the scene in and around Manchester.
Illustrations: Colour. Always interested in strong images of the more fashionable end of life in Manchester – people, events, places – plus interesting shots of up-market fashion, local shopping, new developments and the Manchester "villages". Commissions possible.
Text: Short illustrated features on topics likely to be of interest to the readership. Intelligent but

possibly slightly irreverent in approach. Up to 700 words.
Overall freelance potential: Good.
Fees: According to use and nature of material.

NORTH EAST TIMES COUNTY MAGAZINE
Chris Robinson (Publishing) Ltd, 5-11 Causey Street, Gosforth, Newcastle-upon-Tyne NE3 4DJ.
Tel: 0191 284 9994. Fax: 0191 284 9915. E-mail: info@accentmagazines.co.uk
Editor: Alison Conlon.
Monthly up-market county magazine.
Illustrations: Colour. Any general interest pictures connected with the North East of England.
Text: Features on fashion, property, motoring, wining and dining, sport, etc. all with North East connections. Around 750 words with two pictures.
Overall freelance potential: Fully committed to freelances.
Fees: By agreement.

THE SCOTS MAGAZINE
D. C. Thomson and Co. Ltd, 2 Albert Square, Dundee DD1 9QJ.
Tel: 01382 223131. Fax: 01382 322214. E-mail: mail@scotsmagazine.com
Editor: John Methven. **Picture Editor:** Ian Neilson.
Monthly magazine for Scots at home and abroad, concerned with Scottish subjects.
Illustrations: Mostly colour. Scottish scenes, but avoid the obvious. Non-Highland subjects particularly welcome. Scenics with one or more figures preferred to "empty pictures". Ongoing requirement for good vertical scenes for possible front cover use.
Text: Features on all aspects of Scottish life past and present. 1,500–2,500 words.
Overall freelance potential: Around 80 per cent of the magazine comes from freelances.
Editor's tips: Do not cover sport, politics, household, beauty or fashion.
Fees: Variable.

SCOTTISH FIELD
Craigcrook Castle, Craigcrook Road, Edinburgh EH4 3PE.
Tel: 0131 312 4550. Fax: 0131 312 4551. E-mail: editor@scottishfield.co.uk
Editor: Archie Mackenzie.
Monthly magazine reflecting the quality of life in Scotland today for Scots at home and abroad.
Illustrations: Mainly colour. Varied subjects of Scottish interest; must be accompanied by appropriate text.
Text: Illustrated features with a Scottish dimension. 850–1,200 words. Submit only ideas initially, rather than completed articles.
Overall freelance potential: There are only limited openings for new contributors.
Editor's tips: Market study is essential.
Fees: Negotiable.

SOMERSET LIFE
Archant Life, Unit 22, Midsomer Enterprise Park, Radstock Road, Midsomer Norton BA3 2BB.
Tel: 01761 408173. Fax: 01761 419308. E-mail: info@somersetmag.co.uk
Publishing Editor: Peter Waters.
Monthly magazine for the Somerset area.
Illustrations: Mainly colour. Interesting and original photographs of the area, but usually required

 turn to page 9

as part of an article. Medium format transparencies for d.p.s. features and covers.
Text: Well-illustrated articles on any topic relating to Somerset, around 1,000 words.
Overall freelance potential: Most material comes from regular freelance contributors but new contributors always considered.
Fees: According to size of reproduction and length of text.

SUSSEX LIFE
Sussex Life Ltd, 28 Teville Road, Worthing, West Sussex BN11 1UG.
Tel: 01903 218719. Fax: 01903 820193.
Editor: *TBA.*
Monthly county magazine.
Illustrations: B&W and colour. Digital files or film. Stock photographs always welcomed, but complete illustrated articles are preferred. Covers: medium format transparencies of Sussex scenes, usually depicting landscapes, but houses, activities, interiors and personalities from Sussex also welcome.
Text: Well illustrated features on any topic relevant to the county. 1,000–2,000 words.
Overall freelance potential: Quite good.
Fees: 1,000-word article plus pics, £25.

TGO – THE GREAT OUTDOORS
SMG Magazines, 200 Renfield Street, Glasgow G2 3PR.
Tel: 0141 302 7700. Fax: 0141 302 7799.
Editor: Cameron McNeish.
Monthly magazine for walkers in the UK. Covers hill and mountain walking, and related topics.
Illustrations: Colour. Material required for stock – mostly landscapes featuring walkers; no towns or churches. Plus pictures to illustrate features. Covers: colour pictures in upright format considered independently of internal content. Photographs of walkers, backpackers and fell walkers in landscape settings. Must be modern, well-equipped people in photos; action shots preferred.
Text: Features on the subjects mentioned above. 2,000 words.
Overall freelance potential: Most of the magazine comes from freelance sources.
Editor's tips: Too many freelances send material which is outside the scope of the magazine – not interested in low level rambling.
Fees: Articles, £150–£450 depending on length and number of illustrations; covers, around £200.

THIS ENGLAND
This England International Ltd, PO Box 52, Cheltenham, Gloucestershire GL50 1YQ.
Tel: 01242 537900. Fax: 01242 537901.
Editor: Roy Faiers.
Quarterly magazine on England, mainly its people, places, customs and traditions. Aimed at those who love England and all things English.
Illustrations: Mostly colour. Town, country and village scenes, curiosities, craftsmen at work, nostalgia, patriotism. Prefer people in the picture, but dislike modernity etc. Pictures for stock or use in their own right.
Text: Illustrated articles on all things traditionally English. 1,000–1,500 words.
Overall freelance potential: Around 50 per cent comes from freelance sources.

TRAIL
EMAP Active Ltd, Bretton Court, Bretton, Peterborough PE3 8DZ.
Tel: 01733 264666. Fax: 01733 282653. E-mail: trail@emap.com
Editor: Guy Procter.
Monthly magazine aimed at the more adventurous walker, plus rock climbers and mountain bikers.
Illustrations: Colour. Well-composed pictures of walkers, backpackers, climbers and mountain

bikers in attractive and dramatic landscapes, UK or overseas, high viewpoints preferred. Walkers seen close up should be wearing proper outdoor gear. Covers: "stunning" colour shots as above.
Text: Illustrated articles on any aspect of hill walking, backpacking and overseas trekking, including diet, fitness, etc. Always discuss ideas with the editor in the first instance.
Overall freelance potential: Very good for high quality material.
Editor's tips: It is essential that people in pictures be wearing proper walking/climbing clothes and shoes – no jeans and trainers.
Fees: From £25–£150 (DPS). Text £80 per 1,000 words.

WALK
The Ramblers' Association, 2nd Floor, Camelford House, 87-90 Albert Embankment, London SE1 7TW.
Tel: 020 7339 8500. Fax: 020 7339 8501. E-mail: denisen@london.ramblers.org.uk
Editor: Christopher Sparrow. **Picture Editor:** Denise Noble.
Quarterly journal for members of the Ramblers' Association.
Illustrations: Colour. Scenic views of the countryside, preferably but not necessarily with ramblers in shot. Also pictures of difficulties encountered when walking in the countryside, eg damaged bridges, locked gates, obstructed footpaths, etc.
Text: Little scope for text as most articles are commissioned.
Overall freelance potential: Quite good for pictures.
Fees: By agreement.

YORKSHIRE LIFE
Life Magazines. Editorial: PO Box 26, Welburn, York YO60 7EH.
Tel/fax: 01653 619541.
Editor: Sarah Todd.
Monthly up-market county magazine for Yorkshire.
Illustrations: Mainly colour. Pictures of the Yorkshire region, mainly to accompany features. Pictures of nationally known personalities with a Yorkshire connection, and local society events, but most by commission. Covers: top quality regional scenes; medium format preferred.
Text: Articles and features on regional topics, from those with a truly professional approach. Always consult the editor in the first instance.
Overall freelance potential: Fair.
Fees: By negotiation.

Cycling & Motorcycling

BACK STREET HEROES
Inside Communications Ltd, One Canada Square, Canary Wharf, London E14 5AP.
Tel: 020 7772 8300. Fax: 020 7772 8585. E-mail: bsh-magazine@yahoo.com
Editor: Stu Garland.
Monthly magazine for custom bike enthusiasts.
Illustrations: Colour. Pictures of individual customised or one-off machines, and coverage of custom bike meetings and events. The style of photography must be tailored to fit the style of the magazine.
Text: Limited freelance market.
Overall freelance potential: Good for those who can capture the flavour and style of the custom bike scene.
Editor's tips: This is something of a lifestyle magazine, and it is essential that the stylistic approach be absolutely right.
Fees: By negotiation.

BIKE
EMAP Automotive Ltd, Media House, Lynchwood, Peterborough PE2 6EA.
Tel: 01733 468000. Fax: 01733 468196. E-mail: bike@emap.com
Editor: Tim Thompson.
Monthly motorcycling magazine aimed at all enthusiasts in the 18–80 age group.
Illustrations: Colour. Digital media preferred. Interesting or unusual topical pictures always required for news section. Sporting pictures for file. Top quality action pictures, "moody" statics and shots that are strong on creative effects. Reportage/documentary shots of events/people.
Text: Interesting or unusual news items. Scope for features on touring, personalities, icons etc; 1,000–3,000 words.
Overall freelance potential: Good for those with experience.
Editor's tips: Always looking for new photographers and styles.
Fees: By agreement.

CLASSIC BIKE
EMAP Automotive Ltd, Media House, Lynchwood, Peterborough PE2 6EA.
Tel: 01733 468465. Fax: 01733 468466. E-mail: classic.bike@emap.com
Editor: Hugo Wilson.
Monthly magazine dealing with thoroughbred and classic motorcycles from 1896 to 1980.
Illustrations: Colour. Pictures of rallies, races, restored motorcycles.
Text: Technical features, histories of particular motorcycles, restoration stories, profiles of famous riders, designers etc. 500–2,000 words.
Overall freelance potential: Most photography is freelance.
Editor's tips: Contact the editor before submitting.
Fees: By agreement and on merit.

THE CLASSIC MOTORCYCLE
Mortons Motorcycle Media Ltd, PO Box 99, Horncastle, Lincs LN9 6LZ.
Tel: 01507 525771. Fax: 01507 575772. E-mail: tcm@classicmotorcycle.co.uk
Group Editor: Gerard Kane.
Monthly magazine covering veteran, vintage and post-war motor cycles and motorcycling.
Illustrations: Mostly colour. Pictures that cover interesting restoration projects, unusual machines, personalities with a background story, etc. Covers: colour pictures, usually a well-restored and technically interesting motor cycle, always related to editorial.
Text: Features on subjects detailed above. 1,500–2,500 words.
Overall freelance potential: Around 50 per cent of the magazine comes from freelances, but much of it is commissioned.
Editor's tips: Potential contributors must have a good technical knowledge of the subject.
Fees: Good; on a rising scale according to size of reproduction or length of article.

CYCLE SPORT
IPC Focus Network, Focus House, Dingwall Avenue, Croydon CR9 2TA.
Tel: 020 8774 0703. Fax: 020 8774 0952. E-mail: robert_garbutt@ipcmedia.com
Editor: Robert Garbutt.
Monthly devoted to professional cycle sport, offering a British perspective on this essentially Continental sport.
Illustrations: Colour. High quality, topical photographs relating to professional cycle racing.
Text: Illustrated features on the professional scene, but always query the editor before submitting. 1,500–4,000 words.
Overall freelance potential: Good for those with access to the professional scene, but most coverage comes from specialists based on the Continent.
Editor's tips: Most interested in "the news behind the news".
Fees: Pictures according to nature and use. Text £100–£200 per 1,000 words.

CYCLING PLUS
Future Publishing Ltd, Beauford Court, 30 Monmouth Street, Bath BA1 2BW.
Tel: 01225 442244. Fax: 01225 732310. E-mail: warren.rossiter@futurenet.co.uk
Editor: Tony Farrely. **Art/Picture Editor:** Warren Rossiter.
Monthly magazine aimed at recreational cyclists, concentrating on touring and leisure/fitness riding. Some racing coverage.
Illustrations: Mainly colour. Digital media preferred. Photographs that capture the excitement and dynamics of cycle sport. Speculative submissions welcomed; commissions also available.
Text: Little freelance scope; most is produced by a team of regular writers.
Overall freelance potential: Good for photographers.
Fees: By negotiation.

CYCLING WEEKLY
IPC Media Ltd, Focus House, Dingwall Avenue, Croydon CR9 2TA.
Tel: 020 8774 0703. Fax: 020 8774 0952. E-mail: cycling@ipcmedia.com
Editor: Robert Garbutt.
News-based weekly magazine covering all aspects of cycling; aimed at the informed cyclist.
Illustrations: Colour. Digital media preferred. Good photographs of cycle racing, plus any topical photographs of interest to cyclists. Covers: striking colour photographs of cycle racing; must be current.
Text: Well-illustrated articles on racing and technical matters. Around 1,500 words.
Overall freelance potential: Fairly good.
Fees: According to use.

DIRT BIKE RIDER
L&M Newspapers. Editorial: Editorial: 12 Victoria Street, Morcambe, Lancs LA4 4AG.
Tel: 01524 842157.
Editor: Sean Lawless.
Monthly covering all forms of off-road motorcycle sport, aimed at competitors and those who aspire to compete. Bi-monthly devoted to motorcycle racing from its beginnings to the present day.
Illustrations: Colour. Current pictures of off-road events, bikes and riders. Archive shots of motorcycle racing of all periods, and coverage of the current classic and vintage racing scene.
Text: Illustrated features on all aspects of off-road motorcycling and racing. Contact editor with suggestions in the first instance.
Overall freelance potential: Good.
Fees: Negotiable.

MOTO MAGAZINE
4130 Publishing Ltd, PO Box 1300, Dorchester, Dorset DT1 1FN.
Tel: 01305 251263. E-mail: moto@4130.com
Editor: Rob Walters.
Bi-monthly magazine covering motocross from an international perspective.
Illustrations: Colour and B&W. Will consider any topical and relevant images on spec. Has two regular photographers covering main events but commissions may be available.
Text: Possible scope for features on leading riders - contact editor with suggestions.
Overall freelance potential: Quite good for specialists.
Fees: By negotiation.

MOTOR CYCLE NEWS
EMAP Automotive Ltd, Media House, Lynchwood, Peterborough PE2 6EA.
Tel: 01733 468000. Fax: 01733 468028. E-mail: mcn@emap.com
Editor: Marc Potter.

Weekly tabloid for all road-riding and recreational motorcyclists. Also covers motorcycle sport.
Illustrations: Mostly colour. Rarely use on-spec material, but frequently require freelances for assignments. Seek competent photographers with keen news sense, able to work closely to a given brief yet able to incorporate their own visual ideas. Successful applicants are added to a nationwide contact list and may be approached to cover stories at any time.
Text: Illustrated news stories on all aspects of motorcycling always considered. Lively tabloid style required.
Overall freelance potential: Good.
Editor's tips: Assignments are often at short notice and to tight deadlines – photographers who can work quickly and flexibly stand the best chance of success. Commission fees include copyright assignment to MCN, though permission for re-use by the photographer is rarely denied.
Fees: Single pictures from £50; day rate £200 plus expenses.

MOTORCYCLE VOYAGER
Bridge House, 7-9 Church Road, Lawrence Hill, Bristol BS5 9JJ.
Tel: 0117 954 7012. E-mail: info@motorcyclevoyager.com
Editor: Peter Jump.
Monthly focusing on motorcycle travelling.
Illustrations: Colour. Most pictures used within specific features as below.
Text: Well-illustrated articles and stories about travelling by motorcycle in any part of the world. Will be considered on spec but best to submit ideas in the first instance.
Overall freelance potential: Very good.
Editor's tips: It is more important that contributors are practising bike riders rather than experienced journalists.
Fees: By negotiation.

MOUNTAIN BIKING UK
Future Publishing Ltd, Beauford Court, 30 Monmouth Street, Bath BA1 2BW.
Tel: 01225 442244. Fax: 01225 822790. E-mail: tym.manley@futurenet.co.uk
Editor: Tym Manley.
Monthly magazine devoted to the sport of mountain biking.
Illustrations: Mostly colour. Spectacular or unusual shots of mountain biking, action pictures that convey a sense of both movement and height. General coverage of events and individual riders may be of interest.
Text: Well-illustrated articles that show good knowledge of the sport.
Overall freelance potential: Good scope for individual and original photography.
Fees: By negotiation.

RIDE
EMAP Automotive, Media House, Lynchwood, Peterborough Business Park, Peterborough PE2 6EA.
Tel: 01733 468081. Fax: 01733 468092.
Editor: Stefan Bartlett. **Art Editor:** Nick Lemon.
Monthly magazine for the motorcycling enthusiast.
Illustrations: Colour. Commissions available to produce coverage for road tests and general features, but only for those with prior experience of motor sport or similar action photography. Contact the art editor to show portfolio.
Text: Little scope.
Overall freelance potential: Limited, but increasing.
Editor's tips: The magazine is looking to expand its nationwide network of photographers, for reader shots, news pictures etc.
Fees: Around £250 per day.

SCOOTERING
PO Box 99, Horncastle, Lincs LN9 6LZ.
Tel/fax: 01507 524004.
Editor: Andy Gillard.
Monthly magazine for motor scooter enthusiasts.
Illustrations: Mostly colour. Pictures of motor scooters of the Lambretta/Vespa type – shows, meetings, "runs", racing, special paint jobs, "chopped" scooters, etc. Covers: usually staff-produced, but a good freelance shot might be used.
Text: Original ideas welcomed. Contributors should be aware of the particular lifestyle and terminology attached to the scooter scene.
Overall freelance potential: Good scope for those who know the current scooter scene and its followers.
Editor's tips: Be aware that the readers have a very good knowledge of this specialised subject.
Fees: By negotiation.

SUPERBIKE
IPC Focus Network, Leon House, 233 High Street, Croydon CR9 1HZ.
Tel: 020 8726 8000. Fax: 020 8726 8499.
Editor: Kenny Pryde.
Monthly for sports motorcycle enthusiasts. Specialising in new model tests and old model reviews, motorcycle Grand Prix, World Superbike and UK racing scene.
Illustrations: Colour. Pictures of unusual motorcycles, road-racing, drag-racing and other sports pictures of unusual interest or impact; crash sequences; motorcycle people.
Text: Features of general or specific motorcycle interest. Editorial style is humorous, irreverent. 1,500–3,000 words.
Overall freelance potential: Around 30 per cent of the magazine is contributed from outside sources.
Fees: Dependent on size and position in magazine.

TWO WHEELS ONLY
Haymarket Motorcycle Publications Ltd, Somerset House, Somerset Road, Teddington TW11 8RL.
Tel: 020 8267 8568. Fax: 020 8267 8561.
Editor: Bertie Simmonds.
Wide-ranging glossy monthly for all motorcycling enthusiasts. Covers road bikes, racing, touring and scooters.
Illustrations: Mainly colour. Digital files preferred. Any strong and interesting images connected with any aspect of motorcycling and the biking lifestyle – unusual bikes or biking situations, good race action, celebrities with bikes, etc. Most major feature photography is handled by a regular team but commissions may be available to those with experience.
Text: Limited scope, but original ideas considered.
Overall freelance potential: Good for the specialist.
Editor's tips: Images from the sidelines of the motorcycling scene may be of more interest than action or straight shots of bikes.
Fees: Negotiable, depending on what is offered.

Electronics & Computing

COMPUTER WEEKLY
Reed Business Information, Quadrant House, The Quadrant, Sutton, Surrey SM2 5AS.
Tel: 020 8652 8642. Fax: 020 8652 8979.
Editor: Hooman Bassirian.
Weekly news magazine aimed at IT directors.

Illustrations: B&W and colour. News pictures, plus general shots of people involved in computer usage situations for general illustration purposes.
Text: Illustrated features on professional and business applications and issues in information technology. Length around 1,200 words.
Overall freelance potential: Main scope is for specialists.
Fees: By negotiation.

PRACTICAL WIRELESS
PW Publishing Ltd, Arrowsmith Court, Station Approach, Broadstone, Dorset BH18 8PW.
Tel: 0870 224 7810. Fax: 0870 224 7850. E-mail: steve@pwpublishing.ltd.uk
Editor: Rob Mannion. **Art Editor:** Stephen Hunt.
Monthly magazine covering all aspects of radio of interest to the radio amateur and enthusiast.
Illustrations: B&W and colour. Digital media preferred. Usually only required to illustrate specific articles. Covers: radio-related subjects, B&W or colour.
Text: Articles on amateur radio or short wave listening, or on aspects of professional radio systems of interest to the enthusiast. 1,000–5,000 words.
Overall freelance potential: Little scope for individual photographs, but complete, illustrated articles always welcome.
Fees: By negotiation.

PRO SOUND NEWS
CMP Information, 7th Floor, Ludgate House, 245 Blackfriars Road, London SE1 9UR.
Tel: 020 7921 8319. Fax: 020 7921 8302. E-mail: david.robinson@cmpinformation.com
Editor: Dave Robinson.
Monthly news magazine for professionals working in the European sound production industry. Covers recording, live sound, post-production, mastering and broadcasting.
Illustrations: Colour. News pictures on all aspects of the industry, from equipment manufacture to live sound shows and concert performances to recording studios.
Text: Illustrated news items and features (800–1,000 words) on any aspect of the industry, but always check with the editor before submitting.
Overall freelance potential: Good for those with contacts in the audio and music business.
Fees: £140 per 1,000 words for text; photographs from £25.

RADIO ACTIVE
PW Publishing Ltd, Arrowsmith Court, Station Approach, Broadstone, Dorset BH18 8PW.
Tel: 01202 659910. Fax: 01202 659950. E-mail: elaine.richards@btinternet.com
Editor: Elaine Richards.
Monthly magazine for anyone interested in the world of two-way communications.
Illustrations: B&W and colour. Pictures connected with the world of radio and communications including ships, aircraft and vehicles.
Text: Features on radio systems. News and reviews of equipment, clubs, etc. 1,000–2,000 words.
Overall freelance potential: Between 50 and 75 per cent comes from freelances.
Editor's tips: The magazine is always on the lookout for features on new and novel uses for radio communications. Visual articles on all aspects of communications welcome.
Fees: £40 per published page.

SHORT WAVE MAGAZINE
PW Publishing Ltd, Arrowsmith Court, Station Approach, Broadstone, Dorset BH18 8PW.
Tel: 0870 224 7810. Fax: 0870 224 7850. E-mail: steve@pwpublishing.ltd.uk
Editor: Kevin Nice. **Art Editor:** Stephen Hunt.
Monthly magazine covering all aspects of radio of interest to the short wave listener and enthusiast.
Illustrations: B&W and colour. Usually only required to illustrate specific articles. Covers: radio-related subjects; B&W or colour.
Text: Articles on short wave listening, or on aspects of professional radio systems of interest to the

enthusiast. 1,000–5,000 words.
Overall freelance potential: Little scope for individual photographs, but complete illustrated articles always welcome.
Editor's tips: Free author's guide available on request.
Fees: By negotiation.

WHAT HI-FI?
Haymarket Magazines Ltd, 38-42 Hampton Road, Teddington, Middlesex TW11 0JE.
Tel: 020 8943 5000. Fax: 020 8943 5798.
Editor: Clare Newsome.
Monthly magazine with emphasis on equipment reviews.
Illustrations: Colour. News pictures from hi-fi shows, providing they are submitted quickly after the show. Commissioned photography to illustrate articles. As well as photographing equipment, the magazine looks for photographers who can take pix of readers, industry figures and hi-fi dealers to illustrate appropriate features (especially outside London).
Text: No scope.
Overall freelance potential: Fair.
Editor's tips: Photographers should be able to inject life into essentially boring black boxes.
Fees: Commissions usually £350 per day.

WHAT SATELLITE TV
Highbury Leisure, 53-79 Highgate Road, London NW5 1TW.
Tel: 020 7331 1000. Fax: 020 7331 1241. E-mail: alex.lane@wvip.co.uk
Editor: Alex Lane.
Monthly magazine for satellite TV system buyers and users. Contains tests on receivers and dishes, general features, programme listings, reviews and the latest satellite news.
Illustrations: B&W and colour. Photographs of satellite systems in situ, family/people shots with equipment in use.
Text: Technical topics, plus programme reviews and personality pieces. 500–1,200 words.
Overall freelance potential: Around 50 per cent from such sources.
Fees: By agreement.

Equestrian

EQUESTRIAN TRADE NEWS
Equestrian Management Consultants Ltd, Stockeld Park, Wetherby, West Yorkshire LS22 4AW.
Tel: 01937 582111. Fax: 01937 582778.
Editor: Elizabeth Peplow.
Monthly publication for business people and trade in the equestrian world.
Illustrations: B&W and colour. Pictures covering saddlery, feedstuffs, new riding schools and business in the industry. Also new pictures of people connected with the industry, eg people retiring, getting married, etc.
Text: Features on specialist subjects and general articles on retailing, marketing and business. 1,000 words.
Overall freelance potential: Around 50 per cent comes from freelances.

Editor's tips: Only stories with a business angle will be considered. No scope for general horsey or racing material.
Fees: Text, £25 per 1,000 words; pictures by arrangement.

HORSE
IPC Media Ltd, King's Reach Tower, Stamford Street, London SE1 9LS.
Tel: 020 7261 7969. Fax: 020 7261 7979. E-mail: amanda_gee@ipcmedia.com
Editor: Amanda Gee.
Monthly aimed at the leisure rider.
Illustrations: Colour. All photography by commission only to illustrate specific features. Experienced workers should send an introductory letter with examples of previously published work.
Text: No scope.
Overall freelance potential: Limited and only for the experienced equestrian specialist.
Fees: By negotiation.

HORSE & HOUND
IPC Country & Leisure Media, King's Reach Tower, Stamford Street, London SE1 9LS.
Tel: 020 7261 6514. Fax: 020 7261 5429. E-mail: alex_medhurst@ipc.co.uk
Editor: Lucy Higginson. **Picture Editor:** Alex Medhurst (Miss).
Weekly news magazine covering all equestrian sports.
Illustrations: Colour. Prints accepted, digital media preferred. News and feature pictures considered on spec for immediate use or for stock, covering racing, point-to-pointing, showjumping, eventing, polo, hunting, driving and showing. Commissions available to experienced equestrian/countryside photographers; make appointment with the picture editor to show portfolio.
Text: Possible opportunities for those with knowledge and experience of the above disciplines.
Overall freelance potential: Good for those who can show skill in this field; enquiries from photographers are encouraged.
Fees: Single pictures according to size of reproduction. Commission rates £200 per day (all rights); £135 per day (first use).

HORSE AND RIDER
D. J. Murphy (Publishers) Ltd, Headley House, Headley Road, Grayshott, Surrey GU26 6TU.
Tel: 01428 601020. Fax: 01428 601030.
Editor: Alison Bridge.
Monthly magazine aimed at adult horse-riders.
Illustrations: Colour. Off-beat personality shots and pictures for photo stories illustrating equestrian subjects, eg plaiting up, clipping, etc. Also general yard pictures, riding pictures, people and horses. Covers: horse's heads.
Text: Illustrated instructional features on stable management, grooming, etc. 1,500 words.
Overall freelance potential: Good for freelances who show an understanding of the market.
Editor's tips: Material must be technically accurate – riders must be shown wearing the correct clothes, especially hats; horses must be fit and correctly tacked.
Fees: Pictures £25–£60. Text £65 per 1,000 words.

Farming

CROPS
Reed Farmers Publishing Group, Quadrant House, The Quadrant, Sutton, Surrey SM2 5AS.
Tel: 020 8652 4080. Fax: 020 8652 8928.
Editor: Charles Abel.
Fortnightly magazine catering exclusively for the arable farmer.

Illustrations: Colour. News pictures depicting anything of topical, unusual or technical interest concerning crop farming and production. Captions must be precise and detailed.
Text: Limited scope for short topical articles written by specialists.
Overall freelance potential: Good for farming specialists.
Fees: By negotiation.

DAIRY FARMER
CMP Information Ltd, Sovereign Way, Tonbridge, Kent TN9 1RW.
Tel: 01732 377273. Fax: 01732 377543. E-mail: phollinshead@cmpinformation.com
Editor: Peter Hollinshead.
Monthly journal for dairy farmers.
Illustrations: Colour. Digital media preferred. Captioned pictures for use as fillers, technical or possibly historical. Also humourous or unusual pictures concerning the dairy industry. Some assignments to visit farms available.
Text: In-depth, technical features to help dairy farmers run their businesses more profitably.
Overall freelance potential: Limited, but open to suggestions.
Fees: By arrangement.

FARM LIFE/FARM BUSINESS
Grove House Publishing, Hendal Oast, Hendal Farm, Groombridge, Kent, TN3 9NU.
Tel: 01892 861664. Fax: 01892 861667. E-mail: cedric@farmbiz.fsnet.co.uk
Editor: Cedric Porter.
Monthly magazine covering both business and consumer aspects of farming and country living/ Business fortnightly for larger farm operators and their customers.
Illustrations: Colour. Mainly to illustrate stories and features as below. Some scope for stock images of agricultural subjects, farm produce and food retailing. Limited scope for captioned news pictures.
Text: Illustrated features emphasising the positive side of contemporary farming – new approaches and opportunities, solutions to problems, farmers diversifying or otherwise invigorating the countryside. Hard news stories and features concerning the business and marketing side of agriculture. No "soft" material about farm or countryside life.
Overall freelance potential: Main scope is in the monthly magazine.
Editor's tips: Most interested in positive and unusual stories that are not getting exposure elsewhere.
Fees: By negotiation.

FARMERS GUARDIAN
CMP Information Ltd, Unit 4, Fulwood Park, Caxton Road, Fulwood, Preston PR2 9NZ.
Tel: 01772 799413. E-mail: teveson@cmpinformation.com
Editor: Elizabeth Falkingham. Picture **Editor:** Theresa Eveson.
Weekly news publication for all farmers, with the emphasis on commerce.
Illustrations: Colour. Current farming news pictures accompanied by stories or extended captions. Stock pictures used to illustrate general items and features – send lists in the first instance.
Text: News items always of interest.
Overall freelance potential: Fair.
Fees: According to use.

FARMERS WEEKLY
Reed Business Information, Quadrant House, The Quadrant, Sutton, Surrey SM2 5AS.
Tel: 020 8652 4913. Fax: 020 8652 4005. E-mail: farmers.weekly@rbi.co.uk
Editor: Stephen Howe.
Weekly publication covering all matters of interest to farmers.
Illustrations: Colour. News pictures relating to the world of farming and picture stories on technical aspects. Some opportunities for assignments.

Text: Tight, well-written copy on farming matters and anything that will help farmers run their business more efficiently.
Overall freelance potential: Good.
Fees: By negotiation.
Editor's tips: News pages are started on Monday and close for press on Wednesday afternoon, so news material should be submitted during that period. Copy and pics can be received by e-mail.

POULTRY WORLD
Reed Business Information, Quadrant House, The Quadrant, Sutton, Surrey SM2 5AS.
Tel: 020 8652 4020. Fax: 020 8652 4042. E-mail: poultry.world@rbi.co.uk
Editor: Graham Cruikshank.
Monthly publication aimed at the UK, EU and worldwide commercial poultry industries. Covers egg production as well as chickens, turkeys, ducks and geese. Includes Pure Breeds section.
Illustrations: Colour. Prints or digital preferred. News pictures and good general stock relating to the poultry industry, both in UK and overseas.
Text: News stories and ideas for features always considered; breeding, processing, packing, marketing, etc.
Overall freelance potential: Limited.
Fees: By negotiation.

TRACTOR & FARMING HERITAGE
Mortons Heritage Media, Newspaper House, Morton Way, Horncastle, Lincs LN9 6JR.
Tel: 01507 529300. Fax: 01507 529495. E-mail: pkelly@mortons.co.uk
Editor: Peter Kelly.
Monthly magazine celebrating the farm tractor and its development.
Illustrations: Mainly colour; archive B&W. Images of interesting individual machines, restoration projects, tractor rallies and events. Detailed captions about individual machines and their history always essential. Also archive pictures depicting farm life and machinery from WW1 to the 1960s.
Text: Well-illustrated articles on relevant subjects always considered.
Overall freelance potential: Very good.
Fees: By negotiation.

Food & Drink

DECANTER
IPC Media Ltd, 1st Floor, Broadway House, 2-6 Fulham Broadway, London SW6 1AA.
Tel: 020 7610 3929. Fax: 020 7381 5282. E-mail: yvonne_eschoe@decantermagazine.com
Editor: Amy Wislocki. **Art Editor:** Lee Osborne. **Picture Researcher:** Yvonne Eschoe.
Monthly magazine for the serious wine enthusiast, featuring producer and regional profiles, tastings, and related food and travel features.
Illustrations: Mainly colour. Stock images of wine-producing regions often needed to illustrate features. Send details of coverage available in the first instance.
Text: Illustrated articles on topics as above; submit synopsis first.
Overall freelance potential: Fair.
Editor's tips: Pictures may be simply attractive travel images of the region, not necessarily specifically wine-related.
Fees: By negotiation.

FLAVOUR
Quantum Business Media, Quantum House, 19 Scarbrook Road, Croydon CR9 1LX.
Tel: 020 8565 4459. Fax: 020 8565 4465. E-mail: tomi@qpp.co.uk
Editor: Tom Innes.

Monthly magazine for bar professionals – those running or supplying the bar trade.
Illustrations: Colour. Mostly by commission. Some opportunities for assignments covering individual venues, location reports, company profiles and products. Contact the editor with details of previous experience and area covered.
Text: Features on individual bars, companies and products. Commissions available to writers who have some knowledge of the industry.
Overall freelance potential: Limited.
Editor's tips: The London area is well covered; best opportunities are in the regions.
Fees: By negotiation.

HOTEL & RESTAURANT MAGAZINE
Quantum Business Media, Quantum House, 19 Scarbrook Road, Croydon CR9 1LX.
Tel: 020 8565 4200. Fax: 020 8565 4480. E-mail: davidf@quantumbusinessmedia.com
Editor: Matthew Moggridge. **Art Director:** David Foster.
Monthly magazine for the UK hotel and restaurant trade.
Illustrations: Mainly colour. Digital media preferred. Mostly commissioned to accompany specific features. Much emphasis on design and "creative" photography.
Text: Illustrated features on areas of development, profiles of individual restaurateurs, hoteliers and their establishments. Coverage from outside London particularly welcome, but always contact the art director first.
Overall freelance potential: Good for the more experienced worker.
Editor's tips: The magazine deals with restaurants and hotels from the medium to the top end of the market and there is no interest in fast food outlets etc.
Fees: By negotiation.

ITALIA UK
Italia UK Limited, St Martins Studios, Greenbank Road, Ashton-on-Mersey, Sale, Manchester M33 5PN.
Tel: 0161 976 1212/1313. Fax: 0161 976 2888. E-mail: gr@italiauk.net
Editor: Glenn Routledge.
Anglo-Italian publication distributed through catering and food retail outlets.
Illustrations: Colour. Digital preferred. Images of Italian food, drink, restaurants, travel and culture. Send details of subjects available in the first instance.
Text: Will always consider quality restaurant reviews (with pictures) from main UK cities, and general feature suggestions.
Overall freelance potential: Average.
Editor's tips: Bear in mind readership is pro-Italian and already has a reasonable knowledge of Italy.
Fees: By negotiation.

OLIVE
BBC Worldwide Publishing, Woodlands, 80 Wood Lane, London W12 0TT.
Tel: 020 8433 1769 2000. Fax: 020 8433 3499.
Editor: Christine Hayes. **Creative Director**: Elizabeth Galbraith.
Monthly food and travel magazine for a young, upmarket readership.
Illustrations: Colour. Almost all by commission to illustrate major features. Experienced workers should make an an appointment to show portfolio to the creative director. Those with relevant stock collections should send lists.
Text: Will consider ideas from experienced contributors, especially for travel-related material, but no on spec submissions.
Overall freelance potential: Opportunities for specialists only.
Fees: By negotation.

PUBLICAN
Quantum Business Media, Quantum House, 19 Scarbrook Rd, Croydon CR9 1LX.
Tel: 020 8565 4200. Fax: 020 8565 4465. E-mail: lorna@qpp.co.uk
Editor: Lorna Harrison.
Weekly independent newspaper for publicans and pub companies throughout the UK.
Illustrations: Colour. Topical pictures concerning pubs and publicans, brewery and pub company management, and the drinks trade generally. Must be newsworthy or have some point of unusual interest, and preferably include people. Call before submitting.
Text: News items and picture stories about publicans – humorous, unusual, or controversial. Stories that have implications for the whole pub trade, or that illustrate a problem; original ways of increasing trade. News items up to 250 words; features around 500–800 words, but discuss proposal before submitting.
Overall freelance potential: Good for original material, especially from outside London and the South East.
Editor's tips: Forget charity bottle smashes, pub openings, and pictures of people pulling or holding pints – hundreds of these are received already.
Fees: On a rising scale according to size of reproduction or length of text.

RESTAURANT MAGAZINE
The Restaurant Game, 9 Carnaby Street, London W1F 7NJ.
Tel: 020 7434 9190. Fax: 020 7434 4517. E-mail: magazine@therestaurantgame.com
Editor: Chris Maillard. **Picture Editor:** Laurie Fletcher.
Fortnightly magazine for the restaurant trade, with coverage ranging from top London restaurants to high street operations. Also designed to appeal to serious food lovers and restaurant-goers.
Illustrations: Colour. Mostly by commission to shoot food, interiors, portraiture, reportage, still life and travel. Some scope for those with in-depth stock collections on suitable subjects. On-spec opportunities for coverage of restaurant openings, events and informal shots of trade personalities.
Text: Will consider ideas on any relevant subject.
Overall freelance potential: Good for experienced freelances.
Fees: By negotiation.

SCOTTISH LICENSED TRADE NEWS
Peebles Media Group, Berguis House, Clifton Street, Glasgow G3 7LA.
Tel: 0141 331 1022. Fax: 0141 331 1395.
Editor: Patrick Duffy.
Fortnightly publication for Scottish publicans, off-licensees, hoteliers, caterers, restaurateurs, drinks executives, drinks companies.
Illustrations: B&W only. News pictures connected with the above subjects.
Text: News and features of specific interest to the Scottish trade.
Overall freelance potential: Limited.
Fees: By agreement.

WAITROSE FOOD ILLUSTRATED
John Brown Citrus Publishing, The New Boathouse, 136-142 Bramley Road, London W10 6SR.
Tel: 020 7565 3000. Fax: 020 7565 3076.
Editor: William Sitwell. **Art Editor:** Kerry Wakefield. **Picture Editor:** Tabitha Hawkins.
Picture-led monthly concentrating on the "culture of food" as well as recipes and cookery.
Illustrations: Colour; transparency only. Very high quality food photography, plus coverage of food producers, gourmet travel, restaurants and chefs. Much commissioned from established specialists; those with suitable skills should submit examples of previous work with sae for return. Limited use of top quality specialist stock; send lists to picture editor. Commissions for interior/food shots for

restaurant reviews around the UK are frequently sought.
Text: Scope for well-experienced food and drink writers.
Overall freelance potential: Excellent, but only for the experienced worker in the field.
Fees: By negotiation.

WINE & SPIRIT INTERNATIONAL
Wilmington Publishing Ltd, 6-14 Underwood Street, London N1 7JQ.
Tel: 020 7549 2566. Fax: 020 7549 2550. E-mail: wineandspirit@wilmington.co.uk
Editor: Richard Woodard.
Monthly trade magazine for the international wine and spirit industry. Aimed at buyers, importers, producers and retailers.
Illustrations: Colour. Pictures relevant to the industry. Covers: vertical format shots of wine and spirit subjects.
Text: Features on sales marketing and production in the wine and spirits industry worldwide. By commission only but ideas welcome; submit a synopsis first.
Overall freelance potential: Good; around 60 per cent comes from freelance sources.
Fees: Negotiable for pictures; text around £150 per 1,000 words.

Gardening

BBC GARDENERS WORLD
BBC Worldwide Publishing, Room AG167, 80 Wood Lane, London W12 0TT.
Tel: 020 8433 3959. Fax: 020 8433 3986. E-mail: abigail.dodd@bbc.co.uk
Editor: Adam Pasco. **Creative Director:** Abigail Dodd. **Art Editor:** Guy Bennington.
Monthly magazine for gardeners at all levels of expertise.
Illustrations: Colour. Digital files or film. No speculative submissions. Photographers with specialist gardening collections should send lists of material available. Commissions may be available to photograph individual gardens; the editor will always be pleased to hear from photographers who can bring potential subjects to his attention. Also photographers prepared to set up small studios with lights on location: good studio, portrait and reportage photography also commissioned.
Text: All text is commissioned.
Overall freelance potential: Mainly for specialists.
Editor's tips: Always looking for interesting "real" gardens for possible coverage. Small gardens, patios and container gardening of particular interest.
Fees: By negotiation.

THE ENGLISH GARDEN
Romsey Publishing Group, Jubilee House, 2 Jubilee Place, London SW3 3TQ.
Tel: 020 7751 4800. Fax: 020 7751 4848. E-mail: theenglishgarden@romseypublishing.com
Editor: Janine Wookey.
Picture-led monthly featuring the most attractive gardens in Britain, from cottage gardens to stately homes.
Illustrations: Colour. Digital media preferred. Pictures mainly required as part of complete feature packages as below. Some scope for library shots illustrating specific types of garden, plant or tree – send lists of subjects available.
Text: High-quality, exclusive features on individual gardens accompanied by a good selection of pictures (8–10 published within each feature). Can be considered on spec but best to discuss with the editor first.
Overall freelance potential: Very good for top quality material.

Editor's tips: Most interested in beautiful, idyllic gardens that readers can either visit or just fantasise about.
Fees: By negotiation and according to use.

THE GARDEN
RHS Publications, 4th Floor, Churchgate, New Road, Peterborough PE1 1TT.
Tel: 01733 775775. Fax: 01733 775819. E-mail: thegarden@rhs.org.uk
Editor: Ian Hodgson.
Monthly Journal of the Royal Horticultural Society. Publishes articles on plants and specialist aspects and techniques of horticulture.
Illustrations: Colour. Top quality photographs of identified plants, general horticultural subjects and specific gardens.
Text: Some freelance market; submit suggestions first.
Overall freelance potential: Some potential opportunities.
Fees: £40–£100 according to size of reproduction; cover £150.

GARDEN ANSWERS
EMAP Active Ltd, Bretton Court, Bretton, Peterborough PE3 8DZ.
Tel: 01733 264666. Fax: 01733 282695.
Editor: Nicola Dela-Croix. **Art Editor:** Andrew Flitcroft.
Monthly magazine for the enthusiastic gardener.
Illustrations: Colour. Digital media preferred. Little scope for speculative submissions, but the art editor is always interested in receiving lists of subjects available from photographers. Do not send transparencies unless requested.
Text: Experienced gardening writers may be able to obtain commissions.
Overall freelance potential: Limited to the experienced gardening contributor.
Editor's tips: Practical gardening pictures are required, rather than simple shots of plants. Must be accompanied by detailed and accurate captions.
Fees: By arrangement.

GARDEN NEWS
EMAP Active Ltd, Bretton Court, Bretton, Peterborough PE3 8DZ.
Tel: 01733 264666. Fax: 01733 282695.
Editor: Sarah Page.
Weekly consumer newspaper for gardeners.
Illustrations: Colour. Pictures of general horticultural subjects. Practical photographs to illustrate gardening techniques, top quality colour portraits of trees, shrubs, flowers and vegetables, and coverage of quality small/medium sized gardens. Medium format material preferred.
Text: Short practical features of interest to gardeners. 600–800 words.
Overall freelance potential: Fair.
Fees: By agreement.

GARDEN TRADE NEWS
The Garden Communication and Media Company, 4th Floor, Churchgate, New Road, Peterborough PE1 1TT.
Tel: 01733 7775700. Fax: 01733 775900. E-mail: info@gardentradenews.uk.com
Editor: Mike Wyatt.
Monthly business publication containing news, features and advice for retailers, wholesalers, manufacturers and distributors of horticultural products.
Illustrations: Colour. Digital media preferred. Pictures to illustrate news items or features.
Text: Illustrated news stories or articles concerning garden centres, nurseries and garden shops. Maximum 600 words.
Overall freelance potential: Limited.
Fees: £12.50 per 100 words; pictures from £17.50–£50 according to size of reproduction.

GARDENLIFE
Seven Publishing Ltd, 7 St Martin's Place, London WC2N 4HA.
Tel: 020 7747 7000. E-mail: mlovering@7publishing.co.uk/jkraus@7publishing.co.uk
Editor: Tiffany Daneff. **Art Director:** Monique Lovering. **Picture Researcher:** Jenny Kraus.
Glossy monthly aimed at "lifestyle gardeners" in the 30–45 age group.
Illustrations: Colour. Scope for stock images and commissions. Photographers with specialist collections should contact picture researcher with details of what they have to offer. Opportunities for experienced garden/plant photographers to gain commissions – contact art director by post or e-mail in the first instance, with details of experience and/or samples of previously published work.
Text: Possible scope for experienced gardening journalists.
Overall freelance potential: Good for garden specialists.
Fees: Stock images according to use; commissions by negotiation according to brief.

GARDENS ILLUSTRATED
BBC Worldwide Publishing, Woodlands, 80 Wood Lane, London W12 0TT.
Tel: 020 8433 2000. Fax: 020 8433 2680.
Editor: Clare Foster. **Art Director:** Sian Lewis.
Ten issues per year. Heavily-illustrated magazine with a practical and inspirational approach.
Illustrations: Colour. Usually commissioned, but high quality submissions may be considered on spec. Photography should have a narrative and journalistic slant rather than just pretty pictures of gardens. The gardens should be depicted in relation to the landscape, houses and the people who own or work them. Coverage from outside UK welcome.
Text: Scope for experienced gardening writers – submit samples of previously published work first.
Overall freelance potential: Very good for the right material.
Editor's tips: Material previously featured elsewhere is not of interest.
Fees: By negotiation.

GARDENS MONTHLY
Highbury Leisure Publishing, Berwick House, 8-10 Knoll Rise, Orpington, Kent BR6 0PS.
Tel: 01689 887200. Fax: 01689 876847. E-mail: hgriffin@highburyleisure.co.uk
Editor: Helen Griffin. **Art Editor:** Konrad Manning
Monthly aimed at gardeners of all levels, with an emphasis on easy to achieve success.
Illustrations: Colour. Digital preferred. Stock images of gardening subjects often needed – send detailed list of subjects available in the first instance.
Text: Short, well-illustrated articles on gardening and garden design ideas always considered; submit suggestions first.
Overall freelance potential: Fair.
Fees: From £15, to £100 for full page or cover.

HORTICULTURE WEEK
Haymarket Publishing Ltd, 174 Hammersmith Road, London W6 4JP.
Tel: 020 8267 4977. Fax: 020 8267 4987. E-mail: hortweek@haynet.com
Editor: Graham Clarke. **Art Editor:** Sue Lamb.
Weekly news magazine for commercial growers of ornamental plants and those employed in landscape work, garden centres, public parks and gardens.
Illustrations: Colour. Captioned news and feature pictures relating to commercial horticulture, landscaping, public parks, garden centres. Stock botanical images often needed – send details of material available. Some commissions available.
Text: Short news items about happenings affecting the trade. Longer articles may be considered – discuss ideas with the editor. 500–1,500 words.
Overall freelance potential: Limited.
Fees: By arrangement.

PROFESSIONAL LANDSCAPER & GROUNDSMAN
Albatross Publications, PO Box 523, Horsham, West Sussex RH12 4WL.
Tel: 01293 871201. Fax: 01293 871301.
Editor: Carol Andrews.
Quarterly magazine for landscapers, contractors, foresters, environmental designers, groundsmen and local authorities. Covers both hard and soft landscape creation.
Illustrations: B&W and colour. Pictures depicting subjects as below, usually only accepted as part of a complete illustrated feature.
Text: Well-illustrated articles or case histories dealing with technical or practical landscaping matters, horticulture, and general environmental and conservation issues. 1,200–1,500 words.
Overall freelance potential: Limited.
Fees: By negotiation.

General Interest

BEST OF BRITISH
Ian Beacham Publishing, Bank Chambers, 27a Market Place, Market Deeping, Lincs PE6 8EA.
Tel/fax: 01778 342814. E-mail: mail@british.fsbusiness.co.uk
Editor: Ian Beacham.
Monthly magazine covering all aspects of British heritage, but with a strong emphasis on 1940s/1950s/1960s.
Illustrations: Mainly colour; B&W for nostalgia images from 1950s/60s. Digital media preferred. Top quality coverage of all British heritage subjects, from landscapes and museums to craftspeople and collectors; send details of material available in the first instance.
Text: Illustrated articles offering a positive view of aspects of Britain, past and present. Also profiles of people with unusual passions, humorous pieces about the British people and interviews with celebrities about aspects of Britain they love. Submit ideas or an outline first.
Overall freelance potential: Excellent.
Editor's tips: Pictures with good captions are always more interesting than those without. Material should always reflect a positive view of Britain. Nostalgic pictures always welcome. See website at www.bestofbritishmag.co.uk.
Fees: By negotiation with editor.

BIZARRE
IFG Ltd, 9 Dallington Street, London EC1V 0BQ.
Tel: 020 7687 7000. Fax: 020 7687 7096. E-mail: rebecca-deruvo@dennis.co.uk
Editor: Alex Godfrey. **Picture Editor:** Rebecca de Ruvo.
Monthly devoted to strange phenomena, weird behaviour, unusual experiences, cults and conspiracies, bizarre humour. Heavily illustrated, including special 10-page photo section.
Illustrations: Mostly colour. Will consider pictures depicting anything that broadly falls within the above parameters, "the more unique the better". Prefer material that has not been previously published.
Text: Little freelance scope unless the contributor is a genuine expert in a specific subject.
Overall freelance potential: Very good.
Editor's tips: Always call first with details of what you have to offer.
Fees: By negotiation and dependent on what is being offered.

CHOICE
1st Floor, 2 King Street, Peterborough PE1 1LT.
Tel: 01733 555123. E-mail: editorial@choicemag.co.uk
Editor: Norman Wright. **Art Editor:** Gill Shaw.

General interest monthly for the over-50s.
Illustrations: Colour. Photographs mainly used to illustrate specific features. Photography, especially of people, occasionally commissioned all over the UK; send cards or tearsheets in the first instance. Top quality British travel shots may be of interest, but send lists of subjects/locations available in the first instance.
Text: Ideas for articles on any suitable topic always welcome, especially when accompanied by relevant photos. Contact editor in the first instance.
Overall freelance potential: Good.
Fees: By negotiation.

CONDÉ NAST CUSTOMER PUBLISHING
Vogue House, Hanover Square, London W1R 0AD.
Tel: 020 7499 9080 (switchboard); 020 7152 3015 (pictures). E-mail: apepper@condenast.co.uk
Group Picture Editor: Alex Pepper.
Contract publishing division of Condé Nast. Produces titles for corporate clients such as HSBC, Harrods and the Savoy Group.
Illustrations: Mainly colour. Opportunities for experienced photographers to obtain commissions in the fields of fashion, portraiture, travel, music and popular culture. Contact picture editor by e-mail with details of previous experience and examples of work.
Text: N/A.
Overall freelance potential: Scope for photographers producing the highest quality work.
Fees: By negotiation.

DESIRE
Moondance Media Ltd, PO Box 282, London SW4 0QQ.
Tel: 020 7820 8844. Fax: 020 7820 9944.
Editor: Ian Jackson.
Bi-monthly magazine providing erotic entertainment for both men and women.
Illustrations: B&W and colour. Digital media preferred. Quality erotic photography of all kinds, especially portraying couples. Both single pictures and sets.
Text: Features celebrating sex and sensuality as a mutual, shared experience; study the magazine before submitting.
Overall freelance potential: Good.
Editor's tips: Seek material that is a cut above the usual standard of the more explicit top shelf. Prospective contributors can obtain a free copy of the magazine on request by enclosing four 1st class stamps.
Fees: Negotiable, but "competitive".

FORUM
Northern & Shell Plc, Northern & Shell Tower, PO Box 381, City Harbour, London E14 9GL.
Tel: 020 7308 5090. Fax: 020 7308 5075.
Editor: Elizabeth Coldwell. **Art Director:** Mark Chambers.
Monthly magazine dealing with all aspects of sex, eg social, medical, problematical, political, relationships, etc. Aimed at intelligent, aware, educated men and women.
Illustrations: B&W only. Pictures are used only to illustrate articles. Must be tasteful rather than explicit; subject matter can be anything from fetishes to problems with love and marriage.
Text: Factual, social and medical features with a keen sex relevance. No porn.
Overall freelance potential: Nearly all material comes from freelance sources.
Editor's tips: Study recent issues and submit only a synopsis or outline in the first instance.
Fees: By arrangement, but reasonably good.

HIGHBURY CUSTOMER PUBLICATIONS
Jordan House, 47 Brunswick Place, London N1 6EB.
Tel: 020 7608 6500. E-mail: tony.french@hhc.co.uk

Picture Editor: Tony French.
Customer publishing division of Highbury House Communications. Publications include specialist magazines, for corporate customers in finance, sport, business travel, technology, luxury goods and media.
Illustrations: Mostly colour; some B&W. Colour pictures to illustrate a wide range of the products. Major subjects of interest include industry, travel, sport and celebrities. B&W archive material of foreign countries, royalty and politicians. Send a few samples plus lists of subjects available, or make an appointment to show portfolio.
Text: Possible scope for specialist writers – contact relevant editor.
Overall freelance potential: Good.
Fees: Variable according to use, from £45 upwards.

READER'S DIGEST
The Reader's Digest Association Ltd, 11 Westferry Circus, Canary Wharf, London E14 4HE.
Tel: 020 7715 8000. Fax: 020 7715 8714.
Editor-in-Chief: Katherine Walker. **Picture Researcher:** Donna Clews.
British edition of the monthly magazine for a general interest readership.
Illustrations: Mostly colour. Digital media preferred. Pictures to illustrate specific general interest features. Some commission possibilities for experienced specialist workers.
Text: High quality features on all topics.
Overall freelance potential: Limited opportunities for new freelance contributors.
Fees: By agreement.

SAGA MAGAZINE
Saga Publishing Ltd, The Saga Building, Enbrook Park, Folkestone, Kent CT20 3SE.
Tel: 01303 771523. Fax: 01303 776699.
Editor: Emma Soames. **Art Editor:** Paul Hayes-Watkins.
Monthly, subscription-only, general interest magazine aimed at readers over 50.
Illustrations: Colour. Photography is mainly commission only, but some top quality photo features sometimes accepted.
Text: Will consider wide range of articles – human interest, "real life" stories, intriguing overseas interest (not travel), celebrity interviews, some natural history – all relevant to 50+ readership.
Overall freelance potential: Limited, but possible for carefully-targeted ideas exclusive to UK.
Fees: Good, but by negotiation.

WORLD ILLUSTRATED
World Illustrated Ltd, 29-31 Saffron Hill, London EC1N 8SW.
Tel: 020 7421 6000. Fax: 020 7421 6006. E-mail: charles.taylor@photoshot.com
Editor: Charles Taylor. **Picture Editor:** Tim Bishop.
Picture-led magazine depicting aspects of the world through photographs. Also sells prints of published images with commission paid to photographer.
Illustrations: B&W and colour. Digital media preferred. High-quality photo essays and photojournalism from all parts of the world. Major regular themes include news, reportage, travel, people, events and sport.
Text: Only a small amount used in support of images.
Overall freelance potential: Good for really top-quality material.
Editor's tips: Sets of images need to tell a story and have contemporary relevance.
Fees: By negotiation.

YOURS
EMAP Esprit Ltd, Bretton Court, Peterborough PE3 8DZ.
Tel: 01733 264666. Fax: 01733 465266.
Editor: Valery McConnnell. **Assistant Editor:** Sharon Reid.
Monthly publication aimed at the over-50s. Aims to be entertaining as well as informing the retired

generation of their rights and entitlements. It also campaigns on behalf of retired people.
Illustrations: Colour (plus B&W pictures from the past). Good stock shots of mature people engaged in a variety of activities, or depicted in varying moods (happy, worried, thoughtful, etc), always needed for general illustration purposes. The latter should be model-released. Send list of subjects and a few samples first.
Text: Positive stories about older people's achievements and general features likely to be of particular interest to an older readership. 750–1,000 words.
Overall freelance potential: Good.
Fees: By negotiation.

Health & Medical

DOCTOR/HOSPITAL DOCTOR
Reed Healthcare, Quadrant House, The Quadrant, Sutton, Surrey SM2 5AS.
Tel: 020 8652 8723. Fax: 020 8652 8701. E-mail: aimee.blumsom@rbi.co.uk
Editors: Charles Creswell/Mike Broad. **Picture Editor:** Aimee Blumsom.
Weekly newspapers for GPs and hospital doctors respectively.
Illustrations: Colour. Digital media preferred. News pictures of interest to the medical profession: health ministers, conferences, and GPs, consultants and hospitals in the news. Also portraits of doctors and surgeons, plus stock shots of hospital exteriors, waiting rooms, signs, surgical staff, A&E wards, etc. Some commissions available; contact picture desk and be prepared to show portfolio.
Text: News stories always welcomed.
Overall freelance potential: Good.
Fees: Pictures according to use, text £120 per 1,000 words.

GP
Haymarket Medical Ltd, 174 Hammersmith Road, London W6 7JP.
Tel: 020 8267 4849. Fax: 020 8267 4866. ISDN: 020 7413 4200.
Editor: Bronagh Miskelly. **Picture Editor:** Jason Lancy.
Weekly newspaper for family doctors.
Illustrations: Colour. Pictures of general practitioners involved in news stories, and clinical/scientific pictures for features.
Text: News stories, up to 400 words, preferably by prior arrangement with the news editor, Features by prior arrangement with the features editor.
Overall freelance potential: The paper uses a lot of pictures from freelances.
Fees: By negotiation, but around £200-£300 per 1,000 words, and £100 for half-day photographic session.

H & E NATURIST MONTHLY
New Freedom Publications Ltd, Burlington Court, Carlisle Street, Goole, East Yorkshire DN14 5EG.
Tel: 01405 769712. Fax: 01405 763815. E-mail: editorhenaturist@btconnect.com
Editor: Mark Nisbet.
Monthly naturist/nudist magazine.
Illustrations: Mainly colour; some B&W. Digital media preferred. Attractive photos of naturists in landscapes, on beaches, in countryside. Couples and singles, male and female, any age from 16 –70. Also travel and scenic shots used.
Text: Illustrated articles up to 1,500 words about naturist lives and resorts, and off the beaten track naturism.
Overall freelance potential: Excellent.
Editor's tips: Contributors' guidelines are available on request.
Fees: Cover £100– £150; £15–£20 per quarter page inside.

HEALTH & FITNESS
Highbury Lifestyle Publishing, 1-3 Highbury Station Road, London N1 1SE.
Tel: 020 7226 2222. Fax: 020 7288 7578.
Editor: Mary Comber.
Glossy monthly covering all aspects of fitness, health and nutrition, aimed at women.
Illustrations: Colour. Captioned news pictures, and photographs for use in illustrating articles and features. Covers: outstanding and striking colour shots, usually featuring an obviously healthy young woman in close-up.
Text: Articles and features on suitable topics, with an appeal to women generally. Always query the editor before submitting.
Overall freelance potential: Good.
Fees: By negotiation.

HERE'S HEALTH
EMAP Esprit, Greater London House, Hampstead Road, London NW1 7EJ.
Tel: 020 7874 0200. Fax: 020 7874 0201.
Editor: Sarah Wilson.
Monthly publication covering anything that relates to alternative health, from vitamin and mineral supplements to ecology and conservation. Accent is on the practical. Aimed at people who want to help themselves to total health: physical, mental and spiritual.
Illustrations: Colour. Digital media preferred. Mainly commissioned to illustrate specific features on the above; send examples of work to art editor.
Text: Features on all forms of alternative medicine, therapies, travel, food.
Overall freelance potential: Fair.
Editor's tips: Look at a recent issue to see if your work is appropriate.
Fees: On a rising scale, according to quality and size.

PULSE
CMP Information Ltd, Ludgate House, 245 Blackfriars Road, London SE1 9UR.
Tel: 020 7921 8102. Fax: 020 7921 8248. E-mail: mcollard@cmpinformation.com
Editor: Phil Johnson. **Picture Editor:** Marie Louise Collard.
Weekly newspaper for family doctors covering all aspects of general practice medicine.
Illustrations: Colour. Digital media preferred. Topical pictures with captions, involving GPs or illustrating relevant news stories. Commissions available for high quality portraiture, especially outside the London area. Pictures are also commissioned for the Pulse Picture Library, a specialist collection of life and medicine in general practice.
Text: News and topical features about GPs.
Overall freelance potential: Good, especially for portrait specialists.
Editor's tips: Most interested in photographers who can produce original and creative portrait work.
Fees: Negotiable. Around £150 per day for commissions.

Hobbies & Craft

BRITISH RAILWAY MODELLING
Warners Group Publications plc, The Maltings, West Street, Bourne, Lincs PE10 9PH.
Tel: 01778 391027. Fax: 01778 425437. E-mail: johne@warnersgroup.co.uk
Editor: John Emerson.
Monthly magazine for model railway enthusiasts at all levels. Covers only British railway subjects.
Illustrations: Mostly colour. Top quality coverage of serious model railway layouts and interesting, unusual or historical models. Also good archive pictures of real railway subjects to back up

modelling features. Some commissions may be available to those who can show real competence in this field. 35mm acceptable but larger formats preferred.
Text: Well-illustrated features on layouts or single models, which incorporate a very high standard of both modelling and photography.
Overall freelance potential: Limited to those with suitable expertise; the magazine is always open to freelance approaches.
Editor's tips: Photographers must be able to shoot small items in detail whilst maintaining perfect sharpness and depth of field.
Fees: £15–£50 per picture depending on size of reproduction. Text around £25–£35 per published page (most pages carry only a small amount of text since pictures dominate).

CLASSIC STITCHES
D C Thomson & Company Ltd, 80 Kingsway East, Dundee DD4 8SL.
Tel: 01382 575120. Fax: 01382 452491. E-mail: editorial@classicstitches.com
Editor: Bea Neilson.
Bi-monthly embroidery magazine which looks at the work of designers, their homes and lifestyles. Includes project-based features.
Illustrations: Mainly colour. Photography generally required only to accompany features, though feature ideas are often generated by photographs. Commissions available to experienced workers to shoot still life and room sets.
Text: Illustrated embroidery-related articles and specific projects, up to 1,000 words. Look at previous issues for style.
Overall freelance potential: Good; 70% of content is freelance.
Editor's tips: Make sure any submissions are relevant. For photographs, lighting and focus are paramount.
Fees: By negotiation.

CLOCKS
Splat Publishing Ltd, 8 Elizabeth House, Royal Elizabeth Yard, Dalmeny EH29 9RT.
Tel: 0131 312 3200. Fax: 0131 331 3213.
Editor: John Hunter.
Monthly magazine for clock enthusiasts generally, those interested in building, repairing, restoring and collecting clocks and watches.
Illustrations: B&W and colour. Digital media preferred. Pictures of anything concerned with clocks, eg public clocks, clocks in private collections or museums, clock movements and parts, people involved in clock making, repairing or restoration. Detailed captions essential. Covers: colour as detailed above.
Text: Features on clockmakers, repairers or restorers; museums and collections; clock companies. 1,000–2,000 words.
Overall freelance potential: Around 90 per cent of the magazine is contributed by freelances.
Editor's tips: Pictures unaccompanied by textual descriptions of the clocks, or articles about them, are rarely used.
Fees: By arrangement.

COLLECT IT!
Essential Publishing Ltd, The Tower, Phoenix Square, Colchester, Essex CO4 9PE.
Tel: 01206 851117. Fax: 01206 796922. E-mail: charlotte@essentialpublishing.co.uk
Editor: Charlotte Barber.
Monthly for collectors in all fields, concentrating on "affordable" collectable objects ranging from Royal Doulton china to toys and wine labels.
Illustrations: Colour. Mostly by commission to illustrate specific collections around the country, with most opportunities for photographers outside the South East Region.

Text: Original ideas always considered. Submit an outline and a sample picture in the first instance.
Overall freelance potential: Excellent.
Fees: By negotiation.

CRAFTS BEAUTIFUL
Aceville Publications Ltd, 25 Phoenix Court, Hawkins Road, The Hythe, Colchester, Essex CO1 1TH.
Tel: 01206 505975. Fax: 01206 505985. E-mail: editorial@crafts-beautiful.com
Editor: Lynn Martin.
Glossy monthly covering all types of arts and crafts. Aimed primarily at women, beginners to experts.
Illustrations: Colour. Commissions available to illustrate specific features. Medium or larger format equipment essential. Send samples of work in the first instance.
Text: Step-by-step illustrated features dealing with crafts which appeal to women, i.e. cross stitch, decoupage, silk painting, etc. 1,500–2,000 words.
Overall freelance potential: Good for those with suitable expertise.
Fees: Photography by negotiation. Features around £80 per 1,200 words.

ENGINEERING IN MINIATURE
TEE Publishing Ltd, The Fosse, Fosse Way, Radford Semele, Leamington Spa CV31 1XN.
Tel: 01926 614101. Fax: 01926 614293. E-mail: info@teepublishing.com
Editor: Chris Deith.
Monthly magazine concerned with model engineering and working steam models.
Illustrations: B&W only inside. Photographs only used in conjunction with specific news items or articles. No stock photos required. Covers: colour of model steam locomotives, engines or other model engineering subjects. A4 portrait format.
Text: Well-illustrated articles and features on all aspects of model engineering and serious modelling, and on full size railways and steam road vehicles. Must be of a serious and technical nature.
Overall freelance potential: Some 80 per cent of contributions come from freelances.
Editor's tips: Ideally engines depicted should be true steam-operated, not electric steam outline. There is no coverage of model railways below "0" gauge, or of plastic models.
Fees: Negotiable.

FURNITURE & CABINETMAKING
GMC Publications Ltd, 86 High Street, Lewes, East Sussex BN7 1XN.
Tel: 01273 477374. Fax: 01273 402849. E-mail: coline@thegmcgroup.com
Editor: Colin Eden-Eadon.
Monthly magazine for the serious furniture maker.
Illustrations: Colour. Mostly by commission to illustrate step-by-step projects and features on individual craftsmen – write with details of experience and samples of work. Good stock shots of fine furniture often required to illustrate specific styles. Topical single pictures may be considered if accompanied by detailed supporting text.
Text: Ideas for illustrated features always welcome. Submit a synopsis and one sample picture in the first instance.
Overall freelance potential: Good for experienced workers.
Fees: £25 per single picture inside; illustrated articles £50–£70 per page.

GIBBONS STAMP MONTHLY
Stanley Gibbons Publications, 7 Parkside, Christchurch Road, Ringwood, Hampshire BH24 3SH.
Tel: 01425 472363. Fax: 01425 470247. E-mail: hjefferies@stanleygibbons.co.uk
Editor: Hugh Jefferies.
Monthly magazine for stamp collectors.

Illustrations: Mainly colour. Digital media preferred. Pictures inside only as illustrations for articles. Covers: colour pictures of interesting or unusual stamps relating to editorial features.
Text: Features on stamp collecting. 500–3,000 words.
Overall freelance potential: Most of the editorial comes from freelance contributors.
Fees: From £40 per 1,000 words.

GOOD WOODWORKING
Future Publishing Ltd, Beauford Court, 30 Monmouth Street, Bath BA1 2BW.
Tel: 01225 442244. Fax: 01225 732398.
Editor: Phil Davy. **Art Editor:** Ollie Alderton.
Four weekly magazine for the serious amateur woodworker.
Illustrations: Mostly colour. By commission only. Assignments available to cover specific projects – contact the art editor.
Text: Ideas and suggestions welcome, but writers must have good technical knowledge of the subject. Commissions available to interview individual woodworkers.
Overall freelance potential: Good for those with experience of the subject.
Fees: Photography by negotiation. Text around £150 per 1,000 words.

KNITTING
Guild of Master Craftsman Publications Ltd, 86 High Street, Lewes, East Sussex BN8 4TH.
Tel/fax: 01273 400425. E-mail chrispics@aol.com
Editor: Christine Richardson.
Bi-monthly magazine for hand knitting enthusiasts.
Illustrations: Colour. Medium format transparencies preferred, but 35mm or digital images accepted. Seek interesting, unusual and colourful images of people knitting from around the world. Must be accompanied by detailed captions, up to 500 words.
Text: Will consider features on knitting, yarn or spinning related subjects, accompanied by about 10 pictures. Ideas always welcomed.
Overall freelance potential: Good.
Fees: By negotiation.

MODEL BOATS
Highbury Leisure Publishing Ltd, Berwick House, 8–10 Knoll Rise, Orpington, Kent BR6 0PS.
Tel: 01689 886677. Fax: 01689 886666.
Editor: John Cundell.
Monthly magazine that covers any facet of model boating plus occasional material on full-size subjects of interest to modellers.
Illustrations: B&W and colour. All model boating subjects, including regattas. Sharp colour prints preferred. Covers: colour transparencies of model boating subjects. Medium format preferred, but will consider 35mm if vertical format.
Text: News items, illustrated articles and plans on wide range of ship and boat modelling, eg scale, electric, internal combustion, steam, sail, etc. Other maritime subjects considered if there is some connection with modelling. Up to 3,000 words.
Overall freelance potential: Good; 30 per cent bought from outside contributors.
Editor's tips: Send sae with a request for a contributor's guide before submitting. Prints should be well captioned.
Fees: Approximately £20 per published page.

MODEL ENGINEER
Nexus Special Interests Ltd, PO Box 310, Hemel Hempstead, Hertfordshire HP3 8XL.
Tel/fax: 01442 269366. E-mail: mike.chrisp@nexusmedia.com
Editor: Mike Chrisp.
Fortnightly magazine aimed at the serious model engineering enthusiast.
Illustrations: B&W and colour. Digital files or film. No stock shots required; all pictures must be

part of an article. Covers: medium format transparencies depicting models of steam locomotives and traction engines; metalworking equipment and home workshop scenes; some full size vintage vehicles.
Text: Well-illustrated articles from specialists.
Overall freelance potential: Considerable for the specialist.
Fees: Negotiable.

PARROTS
Imax Ltd, 12 Riverside Business Centre, Brighton Road, Shoreham-by-Sea, West Sussex BN43 6RE.
Tel: 01273 464777. Fax: 01273 463999. E-mail: jlc@imaxweb.co.uk
Editor: John Catchpole.
Monthly magazine for the parrot enthusiast.
Illustrations: Colour. High quality photographs of specific types of parrots and parakeets. Must be well-posed and well lit, showing clear details of plumage. Full and accurate caption information (preferably including scientific names) also essential. Limited scope for amusing pictures involving parrots.
Text: Articles aimed at the parrot enthusiast. Amusing parrot stories.
Overall freelance potential: Good for top-quality material.
Editor's tips: Do not submit unidentified generic pictures of the "parrot on a branch" variety, or shots taken from long distances in zoos or bird parks. Only properly thought out, close-up shots will be considered.
Fees: Dependent on quality.

POPULAR CRAFTS
Highbury Leisure Publications, 8-10 Knoll Rise, Orpington, Kent BR6 0PS.
Tel: 01689 886673. Fax: 01689 886666. E-mail: dmoss@highburyleisure.co.uk
Editor: Debbie Moss.
Monthly magazine for everyone interested in crafts.
Illustrations: Colour. Digital media preferred. Pictures used as illustrations for features, or with news items. Covers: colour pictures linked with feature inside.
Text: Illustrated articles on all types of crafts. Should have a strong practical bias, helped by step-by-step pictures, or should be interesting profiles of craftspeople. 500–2,000 words. Also 100-word news items.
Overall freelance potential: Around 85 per cent of the magazine is contributed.
Fees: Approximately £50 per published page.

PRACTICAL CRAFTS
Traplet Publications Ltd, Traplet House, Pendragon Close, Malvern WR14 1GA.
Tel: 01684 588500. Fax: 01684 594586. E-mail: practicalcraft@traplet.com
Editor: Michelle Powell.
Monthly "how to do it" crafts magazine with the emphasis on practical hobby-craft projects.
Illustrations: Colour. Invariably in conjunction with specific articles as below.
Text: Well-illustrated "step-by-step" crafts projects. Submit suggestions and/or examples of previous work in the first instance.
Overall freelance potential: Good for the experienced worker in this field.
Fees: By negotiation.

PRACTICAL FISHKEEPING
EMAP Active Ltd, Bretton Court, Bretton, Peterborough PE3 8DZ.
Tel: 01733 264666. Fax: 01733 465246. E-mail:karen.young@emap.com
Editor: Karen Youngs.
Monthly magazine for all tropical freshwater, marine, pond and coldwater fishkeepers, aimed at every level from hobbyist to expert.

Illustrations: Colour. Pictures of all species of tropical, marine and coldwater fish, plants, tanks, ponds and water gardens. Fish diseases, pond and tank maintenance, and pictures of things that have "gone wrong" are especially welcome. Prefer to hold material on file for possible future use.
Text: Emphasis on instructional articles on the subject. 1,000–2,000 words.
Overall freelance potential: Most is supplied by contributors with a specific knowledge of the hobby, but freelance material is considered on its merit at all times.
Editor's tips: Telephone first to give a brief on the intended copy and/or photographs available. Caption all fish clearly and get names right.
Fees: Negotiable.

THE ROUTER
GMC Publications, 86 High Street, Lewes, East Sussex BN7 1XN.
Tel: 01273 477374. Fax: 01273 487692.
Editor: Stuart Lawson.
Bi-monthly for router machine tool users, both hobbyists and professionals.
Illustrations: Colour. Detailed illustrations of the use of the tool and its application to projects, mostly as part an article package or by commission to illustrate the work of writers. For the latter, photographers must have the ability to take detailed technical shots of wood and metal parts, as well as headshots.
Text: Will always consider well-illustrated articles covering use of the router, techniques and tips, and individual projects.
Overall freelance potential: Fair for those with a good understanding of this type of work.
Editor's tips: Most pictures are close-up and well-detailed so photographers need to have the skill to achieve this.
Fees: By negotiation.

TEDDY BEAR SCENE
Warners Group Publications plc, The Maltings, West Street, Bourne, Lincs PE10 9PH.
Tel: 01778 393313. Fax: 01778 394748.
Editor: Kathy Martin.
Bi-monthly for collectors of teddy bears and other "furry friends".
Illustrations: Colour. Pictures of interesting individual bears or of specialist collectors, supported by detailed captions or a story.
Text: Well-illustrated features on notable bear makers or collectors. Raise ideas with the editor in the first instance.
Overall freelance potential: Fair.
Editor's tips: Always on the lookout for fresh and original contributions.
Fees: From £25 per page; negotiable for special material.

TODAY'S FISHKEEPER
PS Magazines, 6-7 The Rickyard, Clifton Reynes, Olney, Bucks MK4 5LQ.
Tel/fax: 01234 714784.
Editor: Christina Evatt.
Monthly fishkeeping magazine dealing with tropical, freshwater, marine and coldwater fish; water gardening, aquarium keeping and allied subjects, eg amphibians, conservation, etc.
Illustrations: Colour. Any picture connected with indoor or outdoor keeping of pet fish, reptiles and amphibians, and water gardening. Not fishing or angling.
Text: Features on the keeping of indoor or outdoor fish, aquatic plants, expeditions, conservation

and herpetological subjects. 500 – 2,000 words.
Overall freelance potential: Reasonable; over 50 per cent comes from outside contributors.
Fees: By arrangement.

TREASURE HUNTING
Greenlight Publishing, The Publishing House, 119 Newland Street, Witham, Essex CM8 1NF.
Tel: 01376 521900. Fax: 01376 521901. E-mail: greg@acguk.com
Editor: Greg Payne.
Monthly magazine for metal detecting and local history enthusiasts.
Illustrations: Colour prints preferred. Digital media preferred. Usually only as illustrations for features detailed below, but captioned news pictures may be of interest. Covers: colour pictures of people using metal detectors in a countryside or seaside setting.
Text: Illustrated news stories and features on individual finds, club treasure hunts, lost property recovery, local history, etc. However, fees nominal.
Overall freelance potential: Approximately 50 per cent of the magazine comes from freelances.
Editor's tips: Advisable to telephone the magazine before attempting a cover.
Fees: Covers, £55; news items £10 per 1,000 words; features £15 per 1,000 words.

WOODCARVING
Guild of Master Craftsman Publications Ltd, 86 High Street, Lewes, East Sussex BN7 1XN.
Tel: 01273 477374. Fax: 01273 487692. E-mail: stuartl@thegmcgroup.com
Editor: Stuart Lawson.
Magazine published six times per year and aimed at both amateur and professional woodcarvers.
Illustrations: Colour. Mostly to illustrate specific articles, but some scope for news pictures and shots of interesting pieces of work accompanied by detailed captions. Covers: striking colour shots of exceptional woodcarvings or woodcarvers in action, relating to article inside.
Text: Illustrated articles on all aspects of serious woodcarving, including profiles of individual craftsmen.
Overall freelance potential: Good for the right material.
Fees: £25 for one-off reproductions inside. £60 per published page for articles, including photos.

WOODTURNING
Guild of Master Craftsman Publications Ltd, 86 High Street, Lewes, East Sussex BN7 1XN.
Tel: 01273 477374. Fax: 01273 486300. E-mail: gmcwt@aol.com
Editor: Mark Baker.
Monthly magazine aimed at both amateur and professional woodturners.
Illustrations: Colour. Mostly to illustrate specific articles, but some scope for unusual or interesting single pictures with full captions. Covers: striking colour shots of turned items, relating to article inside.
Text: Illustrated articles on all aspects of woodturning, including profiles of individual craftsmen.
Overall freelance potential: Good for the right material.
Fees: £25 for one-off reproductions inside. £50 per published page for articles, including photos.

WOODWORKER
Highbury Leisure, Berwick House, 8-10 Knoll Rose, Orpington, Kent BR6 0PS.
Tel: 01689 886656.
Editor: Mark Ramuz.
Monthly magazine for all craftspeople in wood. Readership includes schools and woodworking

businesses, as well as individual hobbyists.
Illustrations: Colour. Pictures relating to wood and wood crafts, mostly as illustrations for features. Covers: colour pictures of fine furniture. 35mm acceptable but medium format preferred.
Text: Illustrated features on all facets of woodworking crafts. 1,500 words.
Overall freelance potential: Good, about 75 per cent bought from outside contributors.
Editor's tips: Clear, concise authoritative writing in readable, modern style essential.
Fees: Negotiable, but around £50–55 per published page.

Home Interest

BBC GOOD HOMES
BBC Worldwide Publishing, Woodlands, 80 Wood Lane, London W12 0TT.
Tel: 020 8433 2000. Fax: 020 8433 2691.
Editor: Lisa Allen. **Art Director:** Georgia Hibberdine.
Glossy monthly aimed at people who love their homes and love to decorate. Maintains some links with BBC TV programmes on home topics.
Illustrations: Colour. Top quality photography of interiors, gardens, home products, etc, all by commission. Photographers who have previously worked on top quality homes publications should write with details of their experience.
Text: No scope.
Overall freelance potential: Limited to those experienced in producing the highest standard of work.
Editor's tips: Not interested in hearing from photographers who have not done editorial interiors work before, no matter how skilled in other fields.
Fees: Standard day rate £450.

CELEBRITY HOMES
Merricks Media Ltd, Cambridge House South, Henry Street, Bath BA1 1JT.
Tel: 01225 786885.
Editor: Lynette Peck. **Picture Editor:** Kerri Littlefield.
Interior design monthly offering practical ways to emulate the homes of the rich and famous. Some coverage of gardening, travel and beauty.
Illustrations: Colour. Limited scope for freelances seeking commissions. Most interested if freelances can come up with offers of exclusives to cover particular celebrities and their homes.
Text: Little scope unless an exclusive is on offer.
Overall freelance potential: Limited.
Fees: By negotiation.

COUNTRY HOMES & INTERIORS
Southbank Publishing Group, King's Reach Tower, Stamford Street, London SE1 9LS.
Tel: 020 7261 6451. Fax: 020 7261 6895.
Editor: Rhoda Parry. **Art Director:** Patrick Grabham.
Monthly magazine concerning up-market country homes, interiors and allied subjects.
Illustrations: Colour. Top quality coverage of architecture, interiors, gardens and landscapes. Mostly by commission, but speculative submissions of picture features on specific country houses or gardens, or other country-based topics, may be considered if of the highest quality. No market for single pictures. Covers: always related to a major feature inside.
Text: Top level coverage of country home and lifestyle subjects, only by commission.
Overall freelance potential: Excellent for photographers who can provide the right sort of material.
Fees: Negotiable from a minimum of £100.

ELLE DECORATION
Hachette Filipacchi (UK) Ltd, 17-19 Berners Street, London W1T 3LN.
Tel: 020 7150 7000. Fax: 020 7070 3407.
Editor: Rachel Loos. **Art Director:** Andrea Lynch.
Monthly interior decoration magazine aimed at a trend-setting readership.
Illustrations: Mostly colour. By commission only, but always interested in hearing from photographers experienced in this field.
Text: Ideas for features always of interest.
Overall freelance potential: Plenty of scope for the experienced freelance.
Editor's tips: Particular projects must always be discussed in detail beforehand to ensure that the magazine's specific styling requirements are observed.
Fees: Photography according to commission.

THE ENGLISH HOME
Romsey Publishing Group, Jubilee House, 2 Jubilee Place, London SW3 3TQ.
Tel: 020 7751 4800. Fax: 020 7751 4848. E-mail: charlottec@romseypublishing.com
Editor: Charlotte Coward-Williams.
Bi-monthly home interest title emphasising traditional English style.
Illustrations: Colour. Mainly by commission. Opportunities for experienced architectural and interiors photographers to obtain assignments. Suggestions, with sample pictures, of suitable homes or places to feature always welcome.
Text: Illustrated features on traditional English homes, decoration, UK travel, and style. Submit ideas in the first instance.
Overall freelance potential: Good.
Fees: By negotiation.

HOME
Highbury Leisure Publishing Ltd, Berwick House, 8–10 Knoll Rise, Orpington, Kent BR6 0PS.
Tel: 01689 887259. Fax: 01689 896847. E-mail: home@highburyleisure.co.uk
Editor: Jocelyn Garside.
Glossy monthly concentrating on individual homes and interior design, but also covering all home interest topics.
Illustrations: Colour. By commission only to illustrate features – mainly houses/interiors work and still life/product photography. Also gardening.
Text: Well-illustrated features on individual homes and decorating possibilities. Most interested in homes that have been decorated in very personal, creative style by the occupants. Write in with suggestions first.
Overall freelance potential: Very good; many contributions are freelance.
Fees: By negotiation.

HOMES & GARDENS
IPC Media Ltd, King's Reach Tower, Stamford Street, London SE1 9LS.
Tel: 020 7261 5000. Fax: 020 7261 6247. E-mail: natasha_evans@ipcmedia.com
Editor: Deborah Barker. **Art Director:** Caroline Harrington. **Picture Editor:** Natasha Evans.
Monthly glossy magazine devoted to quality interior design and related matters.
Illustrations: Colour. High quality commissioned coverage of interior decoration, design, architecture, gardens, furnishings, food and travel. Emphasis on homes decorated in a tasteful style, up-market and attractive rather than wacky. Ideas for coverage always welcome.
Text: Heavily-illustrated features as above.
Overall freelance potential: Good for really top quality work.
Editor's tips: Out of London material particularly welcome.
Fees: By negotiation.

HOMESTYLE
Essential Publishing, The Tower, Phoenix Square, Colchester, Essex CO4 9HU.
Tel: 01206 851117. Fax: 01206 849078. E-mail: sally@essentialpublishing.co.uk
Editor: Sally Narraway.
Monthly magazine concerned with home and home improvement projects.
Illustrations: Colour. Digital files or film. Commissions available for experienced workers in the home or DIY fields.
Text: Scope for contributors who can write knowledgeably and enjoyably on specific subjects – crafts, home, interior design, etc. Illustrated features on one particular project are required for regular "Open House" feature, but submit ideas only in the first instance. Celebrity "at home" features also considered.
Overall freelance potential: Very good for those with some experience in the field.
Fees: By negotiation.

HOUSE & GARDEN
Condé Nast Publications Ltd, Vogue House, Hanover Square, London W1S 1JU.
Tel: 020 7499 9080. Fax: 020 7629 2907.
Editor: Susan Crewe. **Art Director:** Fiona Hayes. Picture Coordinater: Katie Burton.
Monthly glossy magazine devoted to high quality homes and associated subjects.
Illustrations: Colour; transparency or print only. Almost entirely by commission. Photographs of interior decoration, architecture, furnishings, food and wine, and gardens. Complete picture features depicting a house or apartment of interest and quality.
Text: Features on subjects as above, invariably commissioned.
Overall freelance potential: Reasonable scope for experienced architectural and interiors photographers to obtain commissions. Some scope for non-commissioned features on houses, gardens and food.
Fees: By negotiation.

HOUSE BEAUTIFUL
National Magazine Company Ltd, 72 Broadwick Street, London W1F 9EP.
Tel: 020 7439 5642. Fax: 020 7437 6886.
Editor: Kerryn Harper. **Art Editor:** Hilde Bovang. **Picture Researcher:** Pascale Rowan.
Monthly magazine with the emphasis on practical home decorating ideas.
Illustrations: Colour. Usually by commission. Photographs of houses, interior decoration, furnishings, cookery and gardens. Complete picture features depicting houses and interiors of interest.
Text: Features on subjects as above, invariably commissioned, but possible scope for speculative features on suitable subjects.
Overall freelance potential: Quite good for experienced contributors in the home interest and interiors field.
Fees: By negotiation.

IDEAL HOME
Southbank Publishing Ltd, King's Reach Tower, Stamford Street, London SE1 9LS.
Tel: 020 7261 6474. Fax: 020 7261 6697.
Editor: Susan Rose. **Picture Editor:** Warren Filmer.
Monthly devoted to interiors and decorating.
Illustrations: Colour; print and Major feature photography always by commission; make appointment to show portfolio. Some scope for good general home style and decorating images for stock and general illustration.
Text: No scope.

Overall freelance potential: Very good for experienced workers.
Editor's tips: Research past issues to see what subjects have already been covered and to anticipate the types of issues likely to be covered in the future.
Fees: By negotiation.

INSPIRATIONS
Highbury-SPL Publishing Ltd, Berwick House, 8–10 Knoll Rise, Orpington, Kent BR6 0PS..
Tel: 01689 887200. Fax: 01689 896847.
Editor: Andrée Frieze.
Monthly creative homes magazine with the emphasis on creative ideas.
Illustrations: Colour. By commission only; studio and location assignments available to experienced interiors photographers.
Text: No freelance scope.
Overall freelance potential: Good for the experienced worker in this field.
Fees: By negotiation.

PERFECT HOME
Brooklands Magazines, Medway House, Lower Road, Forest Row, East Sussex RH18 5HE.
Tel: 01342 828700. Fax: 01342 828701.
Editor: Sarah Giles.
Monthly magazine for anyone interested in home improvements.
Illustrations: Colour. Pictures to accompany articles and features on interior decoration, home improvements, gardens, etc. Usually commissioned.
Text: Suggestions from experienced contributors always considered.
Overall freelance potential: Possibilities for experienced contributors in this field, but much is produced by regulars.
Fees: By negotiation.

PERIOD LIVING & TRADITIONAL HOMES
EMAP East, Mappin House, 4 Winsley Street, London W1W 8HF.
Tel: 020 7343 8775. Fax: 020 7343 8710. E-mail: period.living@emap.com
Editor: Sharon Parsons. **Art Editor:** Lorna Wood.
Monthly magazine featuring homes from any period pre-1939, and traditional-style living.
Illustrations: Colour. Commissions available to experienced architectural and interiors photographers, who should show portfolios in the first instance.
Text: No scope.
Overall freelance potential: Good.
Fees: By negotiation.

ROOMS, ROOMS, ROOMS
Essential Publishing Ltd, The Tower, Phoenix Square, Colchester, Essex CO4 9PE.
Tel: 01206 851117. Fax: 01206 796022.
Editor: Sarah Gallagher.
Home interest/interior design monthly with the emphasis on home improvement.
Illustrations: Colour. Will consider original photography of attractive homes, both location and studio work with set builds, for stock and future use. Commissions available for studio set work and location houses and interiors – send examples of work in the first instance.
Text: Suggestions always welcome.
Overall freelance potential: Good.
Editor's tips: Always looking for homes to feature, and will usually commission whoever finds them.
Fees: By negotiation.

25 BEAUTIFUL HOMES
Southbank Publishing Ltd, King's Reach Tower, Stamford Street, London SE1 9LS.
Tel: 020 7261 5015. Fax: 020 7261 6680. E-mail: john_smigielski@ipcmedia.com
Editor: John Smigielski.
Interior design magazine featuring 25 individual homes per issue. 13 issues a year.
Illustrations: Colour. Digital or medium format transparency. Top quality interiors photography illustrating specific homes. Always looking for homes to feature: initially send a selection of recce snaps showing each room, plus an exterior shot, with brief details about the home and its owners; a commission to produce a full feature may follow.
Text: Features as above.
Overall freelance potential: Very good for the experienced interiors photographer.
Fees: Fee for complete feature package of words and pictures normally around £1,200.

THE WORLD OF INTERIORS
The Condé Nast Publications Ltd, Vogue House, Hanover Square, London W1R 0AD.
Tel: 020 7499 9080. Fax: 020 7493 4013. E-mail: mszemberg@msmail.condenast.co.uk
Editor-in-Chief: Rupert Thomas. **Art Director:** Malgosia Szemberg.
Monthly magazine showing the best interior decoration of all periods and in all countries.
Illustrations: Mainly colour, occasional B&W. Subjects as above. Extra high standard of work required.
Text: Complete coverage of interesting houses; occasionally public buildings, churches, shops, etc. 1,000–2,000 words.
Overall freelance potential: Much of the work in the magazine comes from freelances.
Fees: Negotiable.

Industry

ELECTRICAL TIMES
Highbury Business Communications, Media House, Azalea Drive, Swanley, Kent BR8 8HU.
Tel: 01322 660070. E-mail: b.sedacca@highburybiz.com
Editor: Boris Sedacca.
Monthly publication for electrical contractors in the public and private sectors, wholesalers, architects, commercial and industrial users of electricity and the electricity supply industry.
Illustrations: Colour. Pictures of new technical products, site installation work, electrical-related exhibitions, personalities, equipment, etc.
Text: Some openings for business-related articles on the electrical industry. 750–1,000 words.
Overall freelance potential: Limited.
Fees: By negotiation.

ENERGY IN BUILDINGS & INDUSTRY
Pinede Publishing Ltd, PO Box 825, Guildford, Surrey GU4 8WQ.
Tel/fax: 01483 452854. E-mail: mark.thrower@btinternet.com
Editor: Mark Thrower.
Monthly magazine concerned with the use and conservation of energy in large buildings and the industrial environment.
Illustrations: Colour. Pictures of relevant and interesting installations.
Text: Some scope for writer/photographers who have good knowledge of the energy business.
Overall freelance potential: Limited unless contributors have connections within the field.
Fees: £30–£40 per picture; £140 per 1,000 words for text.

ENGINEERING
Gillard Welch Ltd, Oakfield House, 478 Station Road, Dorridge, Solihull, West Midlands B93 8HE.
Tel: 01564 771772. Fax: 01564 774776.
Editor: Jonathan Ward.
Monthly magazine dealing with all areas of manufacturing engineering from a design viewpoint.
Illustrations: Colour. Photographs depicting all aspects of design in industrial engineering, from aerospace and computers to energy management and waste disposal. Much from manufacturers but some by commission. Covers: Abstract and "artistic" photography.
Text: Short illustrated news items up to major design features. 250–2,000 words.
Overall freelance potential: Good for commissioned work.
Fees: £100 per published page for text. Covers £300–£400. Other commissioned photography around £120 per day.

EUROPEAN RUBBER JOURNAL
Crain Communications Ltd, 34 Southwark Bridge Road, London SE1 9EU.
Tel: 020 7457 1400. Fax: 020 7457 1440. E-mail: dshaw@crain.demon.co.uk
Editor: David Shaw.
Published 11 times per year for the rubber producing, processing and using industries.
Illustrations: B&W and colour. Pictures of rubber and rubber applications of a technical nature, eg tyres, belting, etc. Also news and people pictures. Covers: graphically striking colour pictures of rubber-related subjects. Human interest would help as well as technical content. Vertical format.
Text: Features on new applications of rubber and new product stories; new equipment, materials, processes information; business, marketing, personnel and technical news. Features up to 2,000 words.
Overall freelance potential: Limited, but around 5–10 per cent of the publication comes from freelances.
Editor's tips: All contributions must have a high news value or have sound technical content.
Fees: By arrangement.

INDUSTRIAL DIAMOND REVIEW
20th Floor, Wembley Point, 1 Harrow Road,Wembley, Middlesex HA9 6DE.
Tel: 020 8422 5891. E-mail: martin.jennings@idr-online.com
Editor: Martin Jennings.
Quarterly publication designed to promote a wider and more efficient use of diamond tools, i.e. grinding wheels, drill bits, saw blades, etc. in all branches of engineering.
Illustrations: B&W and colour. Pictures of any type of diamond tool in action.
Text: Case histories on the use of diamond tools in engineering, mining, etc. Up to 2,000 words for finished feature.
Overall freelance potential: Excellent but highly specialised.
Editor's tips: Technical case histories are welcome, but check acceptance with editor before submitting material. Potential contributors are requested to consult the editor before pursuing any possible editorial leads.
Fees: Excellent; by arrangement.

INDUSTRIAL FIRE JOURNAL
Hemming Information Services, No 8, The Old Yarn Mills, Westbury, Sherborne, Dorset DT9 3RG.
Tel: 01935 816030. Fax: 01935 817200. E-mail: aylene@kennedycommunications.co.uk
Editor: Aidan Turnbull.
Quarterly magazine concerning firefighting in the industrial sector.
Illustrations: Colour. Pictures of anything concerning or involving firefighting services in an industrial context, including firefighting personnel in action. Covers: powerful colour images of the same.

Text: No scope for non-specialists.
Overall freelance potential: Fair.
Editor's tips: Seek editor's agreement before submitting. No photos of ordinary car fires or firefighters/engines at domestic home/high street fires. Look for racy, exciting and explicit shots to interest and educate a readership of fire professionals who've "seen it all before".
Fees: Negotiable, but generally good. Up to £200 for a really good cover picture.

MANUFACTURING CHEMIST
Polygon Media Ltd, Tubs Hill House, London Road, Sevenoaks, Kent TN13 1BY.
Tel: 01732 470025. Fax: 01732 470070. E-mail: hayshford@wilmington.co.uk
Editor: Hilary Ayshford.
Monthly journal for the pharmaceutical industry. Read by senior management involved in research, development, manufacturing and marketing of pharmaceuticals.
Illustrations: Colour. Digital files preferred. Pictures of any aspect of the pharmaceutical industry. 35mm acceptable, but digital format preferred.
Text: Features on any aspect of the pharmaceutical industry as detailed above. 1,000–2,000 words.
Overall freelance potential: Approximately 30 per cent is contributed by freelances.
Fees: Text, £170 per 1,000 words for features, £15 per 100 words for news stories; pictures by agreement.

MARINE ENGINEERS' REVIEW
Institute of Marine Engineering, Science & Technology, 80 Coleman Street, London EC2R 5BJ.
Tel: 020 7382 2600. Fax: 020 7382 2670. E-mail: mer@imarest.org
Editor: Patrik Wheater.
Monthly publications for marine engineers.
Illustrations: Colour. Interesting topical photographs of ships and marine machinery.
Text: Articles on shipping and marine engineering, including naval and offshore topics.
Overall freelance potential: Good, but enquire before submitting.
Fees: By negotiation.

NEW CIVIL ENGINEER
EMAP Construct, 151 Rosebery Avenue, London EC1R 4GB.
Tel: 020 7505 6666. Fax: 020 7505 6667. E-mail: nceedit@construct.emap.com
Editor: Anthony Oliver.
Weekly news magazine for professional civil engineers.
Illustrations: Colour. Digital files preferred. Up-to-date pictures depicting any civil engineering project. Must be well captioned and newsworthy.
Text: By commission only.
Overall freelance potential: Limited.
Fees: On a rising scale according to size of reproduction or length of text.

NEW DESIGN
Gillard Welch Ltd, Icon House, Jury Street, Warwick CV34 4EW.
Tel: 01564 771772. Fax: 01564 774776.
Editor: Steve Welch.
Monthly for professional designers and manufacturers, covering developments in industrial and product design.
Illustrations: Colour. Photographs depicting new or current product, industrial and interior design, including architecture, theatre, textile, medical and transport design. Pictures should either have a news angle or be particularly strong images in their own right that might be used for covers.
Text: Illustrated news stories or features on any aspect of contemporary commercial design.
Overall freelance potential: Good.
Fees: Dependent on use, up to £300–£400 for covers.

PROFESSIONAL ENGINEERING
Professional Engineering Publishing, Institution of Mechanical Engineers, 1 Birdcage Walk, London SW1H 9JJ.
Tel: 020 7973 1299. Fax: 020 7973 0462. E-mail: pe@pepublishing.com
Editor: John Pullin.
Fortnightly publication for members of the Institution of Mechanical Engineers and decision-makers in industry.
Illustrations: Colour. Pictures of relevant people, locations, factories, processes and specific industries.
Text: Features with a general engineering bias at a fairly high management level, eg management techniques, new processes, materials applications, etc. 1,500 words maximum.
Overall freelance potential: Limited, and usually commissioned specifically.
Fees: Not less than around £200 per 1,000 words; pictures by agreement.

ROUSTABOUT MAGAZINE
Roustabout Publications, Suite 5, International Base, Greenwell Road, East Tullos, Aberdeen AB1 4AX.
Tel: 01224 876582. Fax: 01224 879757.
Managing Editor: Ann Duguid.
Monthly for oil industry personnel working on and off shore in the North Sea. Also covers Houston, Norway & business news.
Illustrations: Colour. All pictures must be directly related to the international oil and gas industry. Minimum transparency size: 6x6cm.
Text: Articles related to the international oil and gas industry. 600–1,000 words.
Overall freelance potential: Limited because of extremely specialised subject.
Fees: By arrangement.

SIGN WORLD
A. E. Morgan Publication Ltd, Stanley House, 9 West Street, Epsom, Surrey KT18 7RL.
Tel: 01372 741411. Fax: 01372 744493.
Editor: Mike Connolly.
Monthly publication dealing with sign manufacturing and allied industries.
Illustrations: Mainly B&W (also colour by arrangement). Only as illustrations to features.
Text: Features on new technological developments in the sign manufacturing industry. Information on relevant contracts at home and abroad. Usually 1,000–1,500 words, or by arrangement.
Overall freelance potential: Open to development for freelances with the right ideas or specialist knowledge
Editor's tips: Sample copies available – phone for details.
Fees: About £100 per 1,000 words; pictures by agreement.

URETHANES TECHNOLOGY
Crain Communications Ltd, 34 Southwark Bridge Road, London SE1 9EU.
Tel: 020 7457 1400. Fax: 020 7457 1440. E-mail: dreed@crain.demon.co.uk
Editor: David Reed.
Bi-monthly publication for the polyurethane producing, processing, and using industries.
Illustrations: B&W and occasional colour. Pictures of production, equipment, and application of polyurethane materials. Also news pictures and shots of trade personalities. Covers: top quality and graphically striking medium format colour of polyurethane-related subjects.
Text: Features on new applications of polyurethanes; new products; new equipment and processing. Business, marketing, personnel and technical news items. Up to 2,000 words.
Overall freelance potential: Good scope for those with access to the industries involved.
Fees: By arrangement.

UTILITY WEEK
Reed Business Information Ltd, Quadrant House, The Quadrant, Sutton, Surrey SM2 5AS.
Tel: 020 8652 3806. Fax: 020 8652 8906.
Editor: Chris Bennett.
Weekly business magazine for the four major supply utilities: electricity, gas, telecommunications and water.
Illustrations: Colour. News pictures concerning the major utilities. Possible scope for good stock coverage of industry subjects. Commissions available to experienced portrait and business/industry workers.
Text: Contributors with expert knowledge always welcomed. Submit details of experience in the first instance.
Overall freelance potential: Very good for industrial specialists.
Fees: By negotiation.

WORKS MANAGEMENT
Findlay Publications Ltd, Franks Hall, Horton Kirby, Kent DA4 9LL.
Tel: 01322 860000. Fax: 01322 420395.
Managing Editor: Paddy Baker. **Art Editor:** Neil Young.
Monthly publication for managers and engineers who directly control or perform the works management function in selected manufacturing concerns.
Illustrations: Mainly colour. Occasional need for regional coverage of managers and workers in realistic work situations in factories. Mostly pictures are used only to illustrate features.
Text: Illustrated features of interest to management, eg productivity, automation in factories, industrial relations, employment law, finance, energy, maintenance, handling and storage, safety and welfare. Around 1,500 words.
Overall freelance potential: Up to 30 per cent is contributed by freelances.
Fees: By agreement.

WORLD TOBACCO
DMG World Media, Queensway House, 2 Queensway, Redhill, Surrey RH1 1QS.
Tel: 01737 855221. Fax: 01737 855467. E-mail: georgegay@uk.dmgworldmedia.com
Editor: George Gay.
Bi-monthly aimed at international manufacturers, dealers and suppliers to the tobacco processing and manufacturing industries.
Illustrations: B&W and colour. Digital media preferred. Pictures of tobacco growing, processing or manufacture from any part of the world.
Text: Limited scope depending on the country.
Overall freelance potential: Fair.
Editor's tips: Pictures from remote parts of the world are particularly welcome.
Fees: By arrangement.

Local Government & Services

CHILDREN NOW
Haymarket Publishing Ltd, 174 Hammersmith Road, London W6 7JP.
Tel: 020 8267 4767. Fax: 020 8267 4728.
Editor: Stovin Hayter.
Weekly publication covering the children's service sector, family support, primary healthcare, children's trust, school nurses and Sure Start.
Illustrations: B&W and colour. Pictures of young people aged 13–21, involved in group activities of a formal or informal nature, inter-generational groups, positive images of children. Lists of specialities welcomed.

Text: Small proportion of copy is from freelance contributors.
Overall freelance potential: Limited.
Fees: According to use.

FIRE AND RESCUE
Hemming Information Services, No 8, The Old Yarn Mills, Sherborne, Dorset DT9 3RG.
Tel: 01935 816030. Fax: 01935 817200. E-mail: aylene@kennedycommunications.co.uk
Editor: Aidan Turnbull.
Quarterly magazine for all involved in municipal firefighting and emergency services.
Illustrations: Colour. Good shots of firefighting and emergency services personnel in action. Also pictures of major fires, accidents, vehicle crashes, extrications, fire and accident victims. Coverage of paramedic intervention, specific injuries and unusual rescues also appreciated but discuss with the editor first. Covers: powerful colour images of the same.
Text: Scope only for those with expert knowledge of the subject.
Overall freelance potential: Fair.
Editor's tips: Seek editor's agreement before submitting. No photos of ordinary car fires or firefighters/engines at domestic home/high street fires. Prefer racy, exciting and explicit shots to interest and educate a readership of fire professionals who've "seen it all before".
Fees: Negotiable, but generally good. Up to £200 for a really good cover picture.

FIRE PREVENTION AND FIRE ENGINEERS JOURNAL
Fire Protection Association, Bastille Court, 2 Paris Garden, London SE1 8ND.
Tel: 01608 812508. Fax: 01608 812501. E-mail: ahayes@thefpa.co.uk
Editor: Anna Hayes.
Monthly technical publication on fire safety. Aimed at fire brigades, fire equipment manufacturers, architects, insurance companies, and those with responsibility for fire safety in public sector bodies, commerce and industry.
Illustrations: B&W and colour. Digital media preferred. Pictures of large and small fires to illustrate reports. Pictures showing different types of occupancy (offices, commercial premises, warehouses, etc) also welcome.
Text: Technical articles and news items on fire prevention and protection. Features 1,000–2,000 words.
Overall freelance potential: Good pictures of fires and unusual fire safety experiences are always welcome.
Fees: Pictures, negotiable from £15. Text, negotiable from £110 per 1,000 words.

LEGAL ACTION
The Legal Action Group, 242 Pentonville Road, London N1 9UN.
Tel: 020 7833 2931. Fax: 020 7837 6094. E-mail: vwilliams@lag.org.uk
Editor: Valerie Williams.
Monthly publication for lawyers, advice workers, law students and academics.
Illustrations: B&W only. Pictures of lawyers and judges, especially other than the standard head and shoulders shot. Plus stock pictures to illustrate features covering a wide range of subjects (eg housing, police, immigration, advice services).
Text: Features on legal services and professional issues, including the courts. High technical detail required. Also information for news and feature material that can be written in-house.
Overall freelance potential: Always interested in hearing from photographers holding suitable material.
Fees: By negotiation.

LOCAL GOVERNMENT NEWS
B&M Publications (London) Ltd, PO Box 13, Hereford House, Bridle Path, Croydon CR9 4NL.
Tel: 020 8680 4200. Fax: 020 8667 1685. E-mail: tom@lgn.co.uk
Editor: Tom Idle.

Monthly news magazine for professional officers, middle to higher grade, in technical departments of local authorities, officers in water authorities and professional civil servants in relevant government departments.
Illustrations: Colour. Digital files or film. Pictures of architectural and building projects, road schemes, urban design, housing projects, national and local politicians and news pictures with local government angle.
Text: Features on any local government related story with exception of those dealing with education or social service policy matters. 750–1,000 words.
Overall freelance potential: More than 50 per cent of material comes from freelance sources.
Fees: By negotiation.

MUNICIPAL JOURNAL
Hemming Group Ltd, 32 Vauxhall Bridge Road, London SW1V 2SS.
Tel: 020 7973 6400. Fax: 020 7233 5051.
Editor: Michael Burton.
Weekly publication for senior local government officers, councillors, Whitehall departments and academic and other institutions.
Illustrations: B&W and colour. News pictures; relevant personalities, vehicles, buildings, etc; general stock shots of local government subjects and situations to illustrate features.
Text: Features on local government issues. 750–1,000 words.
Overall freelance potential: Very good.
Fees: Good; on a rising scale according to the size of reproduction or length of feature.

PLANNING
Haymarket Business Publications Ltd, 174 Hammersmith Road, London W6 7JP
Tel: 020 7413 4328. Fax: 020 7413 4013.
Editor: Huw Morris. Group **Art Editor:** Kate Harkus.
Weekly news magazine for all involved with town and country planning and related issues. Official journal of the Royal Town Planning Institute.
Illustrations: B&W and colour. News pictures always of interest, on specific planning issues. Also good generic shots of subjects planning touches on, eg conservation, transport, rivers, waste disposal, housing, energy, industry, retailing, etc. Some commissions available to illustrate major features.
Text: Illustrated news stories and longer features from contributors with good knowledge of planning issues, up to 1,500 words. Must be relevant to planners. Always contact the art editor before submitting.
Overall freelance potential: Good for genuinely relevant topical material.
Editor's tips: Photos can be of general or specific interest.
Fees: Photography according to use or assignment; text £100 per 1,000 words.

POLICE REVIEW
Jane's Information Group, First Floor, 180 Wardour Street, London W1F 8FY.
Tel: 020 8276 4701. Fax: 020 7287 4765.
Editor: Catriona Marchant. **Art Editor:** Fleur Valois.
Weekly news magazine for the police service.
Illustrations: B&W and colour. Digital files or film. All aspects of the police service. Particular interest in up-to-date news pictures covering the previous seven days. Some commissioned work available, with a need for more photographers to carry out regional work. Contact first to show portfolio.
Text: Limited scope because of specialist subject matter, but will consider any subject of contemporary interest to police officers, 1,000–1,500 words.
Overall freelance potential: Good.
Editor's tips: The magazine is published on Friday with a Tuesday morning deadline for news

pictures. Photographs for features should be good photojournalism and reportage; not interested in "publicity-style" photos.
Fees: Negotiable, minimum £50.

SCHOLASTIC MAGAZINES
Scholastic Ltd, Villiers House, Clarendon Avenue, Leamington Spa CV32 5PR.
Tel: 01926 887799. Fax: 01926 883331.
Design/Picture Editor: Sally King.
Range of monthly publications for teachers in primary and nursery education.
Illustrations: Colour. News pictures and good, unposed pictures of school children from 3-12 years, in classroom and other school situations. Covers: Colour pictures as above but often commissioned. Pictures are stored within a large in-house library. Now filing digitally and will accept Kodak Photo-CD or JPEGs on CD-ROM as long as originals available if required.
Text: No scope.
Overall freelance potential: Good.
Fees: By agreement.

THE TEACHER
National Union of Teachers, Hamilton House, Mabledon Place, London WC1H 9BD.
Tel: 020 7380 4708. Fax: 020 7383 7230. E-mail: teacher@nut.org.uk
Editor: Mitch Howard.
Official magazine of the National Union of Teachers. Published eight times a year.
Illustrations: B&W and colour. Digital media preferred. News pictures concerning any educational topic, especially those taken in schools and colleges. Coverage of union activities, personalities, demonstrations, etc.
Text: Short articles and news items on educational matters.
Overall freelance potential: Limited; interested in good pictures though.
Editor's tips: Consult the editor before submitting.
Fees: According to use.

YOUNG PEOPLE NOW
Haymarket Publishing Ltd, 174 Hammersmith Road, London W6 7JP.
Tel: 020 8267 4707. Fax: 020 8267 4728.
Editor: Steve Barrett.
Weekly publication for youth workers, social workers, careers officers, teachers, counsellors and others working in the youth affairs field.
Illustrations: B&W and colour. Pictures of young people aged 13–21, involved in group activities of a formal or informal nature, street activities, relationships with police, inter-generational groups, positive images of young people. Lists of specialities welcomed.
Text: Small proportion of copy is from freelance contributors.
Overall freelance potential: Occasional news pictures and one or two features using freelance photos per issue.
Fees: According to use.

Male Interest

ARENA
EMAP Elan Men's Group, 189 Shaftesbury Avenue, London WC2H 8JG.
Tel: 020 7437 9011. Fax: 020 7520 6500. E-mail: editorial@arenamag.co.uk
Editor: Anthony Noguera. **Art Director:** Tom Usher.
Monthly general interest magazine for fashion-conscious men in the 20–40 age group.
Illustrations: Mainly colour; some high-quality B&W. By commission only, to illustrate features on

fashion, design, sport, travel, etc. Photographers with an original approach always welcome.
Text: Features and profiles aimed at the intelligent and style-conscious man. Up to 3,000 words.
Overall freelance potential: Fairly good, but only for the experienced contributor.
Fees: Photography by negotiation; text around £200 per 1,000 words.

ATTITUDE
Northern & Shell PLC, Northern & Shell Tower, City Harbour, London E14 9GL.
Tel: 020 7308 5090. Fax: 020 7308 5384. E-mail: adam.mattera@nasnet.co.uk
Editor: Adam Mattera. **Fashion Editor:** Luke Day. **Art Director:** Lisa Kilpatrick.
Monthly style magazine aimed primarily, but not exclusively, at gay men.
Illustrations: Mostly colour. Mostly by commission to illustrate specific features. Some opportunities for experienced fashion and style workers (contact fashion editor). Also some scope for travel, reportage and popular culture material.
Text: Ideas for features – human interest, travel, celebrities – always considered; submit an outline first. Should appeal to a gay readership even if written from a "straight" perspective.
Overall freelance potential: Fair.
Fees: £100 per page for photography; text £150 per 1,000 words.

BOYS TOYS
Freestyle Publications Ltd, Alexander House, Ling Road, Poole, Dorset BH12 4NZ.
Tel: 01202 735090. Fax: 01202 733969.
Editor: *TBA*. **Art Editor:** Duncan Madden.
Monthly for young men, covering all lifestyle topics but with an emphasis on desirable products and technology.
Illustrations: Mainly colour. Mostly commissioned in the fields of sport, fashion, motoring, technology and portraiture. Portfolios can be viewed in London. On spec material also considered if it fits the magazine's style.
Text: Ideas always considered.
Overall freelance potential: Excellent.
Fees: By negotiation.

CLUB INTERNATIONAL
Paul Raymond Publications Ltd, 2 Archer Street, London W1D 7AW.
Tel: 020 7292 8000. Fax: 020 7734 5030. E-mail: mattb@pr-org.co.uk
Editor: Matt Berry.
Popular glamour monthly for men.
Illustrations: Colour; 35mm Kodachrome preferred. Requires top quality glamour sets of very attractive girls (aged 18 – 25).
Text: Articles on sexual or humorous topics, or factual/investigative pieces. 1,000–2,000 words.
Overall freelance potential: Most of the published glamour material comes from freelances, but they are normally experienced glamour photographers.
Editor's tips: Study the magazine to appreciate style. As well as being very attractive, girls featured must look contemporary and fashionable.
Fees: £650 for glamour sets. Text up to £200 per 1,000 words.

ESCORT
Paul Raymond Publications Ltd, 2 Archer Street, London W1D 7AW.
Tel: 020 7292 8000. Fax: 020 7292 8042. E-mail: escort@pr-org.co.uk
Editor: James Hundleby.
Monthly glamour magazine; less sophisticated than the other Paul Raymond publications, Men Only and Club International.
Illustrations: Colour; 35mm Kodachrome preferred. Looks for glamour sets of "normal, healthy, girl-next-door" types. Each issue contains about 10 glamour sets running to 2–5 pages each.

Text: Purely "readers' contributions".
Overall freelance potential: Good.
Fees: £400+ for glamour sets, or from £25 per picture.

ESQUIRE
The National Magazine Company Ltd, 72 Broadwick Street, London W1F 9EP.
Tel: 020 7439 5000. Fax: 020 7439 5675. E-mail: henny.manley@natmags.co.uk
Editor: Simon Tiffin. **Art Director:** Alex Breuer. **Picture Editor:** Henny Manley.
Up-market general interest monthly for intelligent and affluent men in the 25–44 age group.
Illustrations: Mainly colour. Top-quality material only, invariably by commission. Mostly portraiture, fashion and photojournalism.
Text: Scope for "name" writers only.
Overall freelance potential: Good for photographers, but restricted to those experienced at the highest level of magazine work.
Fees: By negotiation.

FHM
EMAP Elan Men's Group, Mappin House, 4 Winsley Street, London W1W 8HF.
Tel: 020 7436 1515. Fax: 020 7312 8191.
Editor: David Davies. **Photo Director:** Marsha Arnold. **Picture Editor:** Regina Wolek.
Monthly lifestyle and fashion magazine for young men.
Illustrations: Mainly colour. Main feature and fashion photography always by commission. Stock images relating to subjects of major interest (sports, travel, adventure, cars, sex) often required – send details of coverage available.
Text: Will consider interesting short items of interest to a young male readership, and feature ideas from experienced workers.
Overall freelance potential: Good for the experienced contributor.
Fees: By negotiation.

FRONT
Highbury Lifestyle, The Publishing House, Highbury Station Road, London N1 1SE.
Tel: 020 7288 7541. Fax: 020 7288 7576. E-mail: adrian.callaghan@hcc.co.uk
Editor: Eoin McSorley. **Picture Editor:** Adrian Callaghan.
Monthly for 18-24 year old men.
Illustrations: Colour. Wide range of stock pictures always required – glamour, sex, sport, music, fashion, reportage, etc – plus "weird and bizarre" images of all kinds. Some commissions available; make appointment to show portfolio.
Text: Little scope.
Overall freelance potential: Good.
Fees: By negotiation.

GQ
Condé Nast Publications Ltd, Vogue House, Hanover Square, London W1R 0AD.
Tel: 020 7499 9080. Fax: 020 7629 2093.
Editor: Dylan Jones. **Art Editor:** Paul Solomans. **Picture Editor:** James Mullinger.
Up-market general interest magazine for men in the 20–45 age group.
Illustrations: Mainly colour. Top-quality illustrations for articles on a range of topics, invariably by commission.
Text: Top level investigative, personality, fashion and style features, plus articles on other subjects likely to be of interest to successful and affluent men.
Overall freelance potential: Only for the contributor experienced at the top level of magazine work.
Editor's tips: See from the magazine itself what sort of style and quality is required.
Fees: By negotiation.

ICE
Ice Media International, Centre 500, 500 Chiswick High Road, London W4 5RG.
Tel: 020 8956 2442. Fax: 020 8956 2430. E-mail: darren.halford@icemagazine.co.uk
Editor: Darren Halford. **Picture Editor:** Adrian Callaghan.
Monthly magazine for young men.
Illustrations: Colour. Glamour, sport, cars etc, usually by commission. Also photo stories on any spectacular or unusual subject that might appeal to young men.
Text: Ideas for features on topics as above always considered.
Overall freelance potential: Best for quality photo stories.
Editor's tips: If you think you have something of possible interest, e-mail a couple of JPEGs first.
Fees: By negotiation.

LOADED
IPC Media Ltd, King's Reach Tower, Stamford Street, London SE1 9LS.
Tel: 020 7261 5562. Fax: 020 7261 5557.
Editor: Martin Daubney. **Picture Editor:** Sam Riley.
General interest monthly for men in their 20s. Covers music, sport, humour, fashion and popular culture in a down-to-earth and irreverent manner.
Illustrations: Mainly colour. Mostly by commission to accompany features, but speculative submissions always considered. Submit only dupes or photocopies in the first instance.
Text: Fashion features, reportage (clubs, drugs, crime, etc), interviews, humour and "anything off the wall".
Overall freelance potential: Always open to fresh and original photography and ideas.
Fees: By negotiation.

MAXIM
Dennis Publishing Ltd, 30 Cleveland Street, London W1P 5FF.
Tel: 020 7907 6410. Fax: 020 7907 6439. E-mail: editorial@maxim-magazine.co.uk
Editor: Greg Gutfield. **Picture Editor:** Catherine Costelloe.
General interest lifestyle magazine aimed at sophisticated men in the 25–44 age group. More practical and less "aspirational" than other men's magazines.
Illustrations: Mostly colour. Commissioned coverage of male fashion, grooming, sport, cars, etc – make appointment to show portfolio. Also some high quality reportage work on topical issues, colour or B&W.
Text: Limited scope, but ideas from experienced contributors always considered.
Overall freelance potential: Good for the experienced worker.
Editor's tips: An original approach could pay off.
Fees: Variable according the nature of the work.

MAYFAIR
Paul Raymond Publications Ltd, 2 Archer Street, London W1D 7AW.
Tel: 020 7292 8000. Fax: 020 7437 8788.
Editor: David Spenser. **Art Editor:** Nick Barclay.
Glamour-based monthly for men.
Illustrations: Colour; 35mm preferred. Only top quality material can be accepted. Glamour sets taken in up-market surroundings and real-life locations, such as a luxury furnished flat. Outdoor material needs strong sunlight.
Text: Sex fiction and journalistic non-fiction only.
Overall freelance potential: Best scope is for the non-glamour material – most glamour is produced by regulars.
Editor's tips: For glamour thought should be given to the erotic use of clothing and suggestion of sex appeal or sexual situation, together with striking but simple colour co-ordination. Always call before submitting.
Fees: £250–£1,000 for glamour sets, or dependent on use. Covers: £150 and up.

MEN ONLY
Paul Raymond Publications Ltd, 2 Archer Street, London W1D 7AW.
Tel: 020 7292 8000. Fax: 020 7734 5030. E-mail: menonly@pr-org.co.uk
Editor: Pierre Perron.
Sophisticated erotic monthly for men.
Illustrations: Colour; 35mm preferred. Imaginative glamour sets featuring "the most beautiful women". Models must be young, fresh, athletic and natural. Sets welcomed from new photographers as well as established contributors. Also picture-led supporting features.
Text: Laid-back humour, sport, male interests etc.
Overall freelance potential: Excellent.
Editor's tips: Attention to detail in clothes and make-up, a wide variety of poses, and imaginative locations will always set you apart. New ideas and faces always welcome.
Fees: £500–£1,000 for glamour sets. Other pictures by negotiation.

MEN'S HEALTH
Rodale Press Ltd, 72 Broadwick Street, London W1F 9EP.
Tel: 020 7339 4400. Fax: 020 7339 4444.
Editor: Morgan Rees. **Art Director:** Gary Mears.
Magazine published 10 times per year and covering sports, fitness, grooming and other aspects of male lifestyle.
Illustrations: Mainly colour. Mostly by commission, though possible scope for good generic stock shots of fitness etc. subjects.
Text: Articles on male lifestyle subjects, especially health and fitness. Write with ideas and details of experience in the first instance.
Overall freelance potential: Only for the experienced contributor.
Fees: By negotiation.

NUTS
IPC Media Ltd, King's Reach Tower, 1 Stamford Street, London SE1 9LS.
Tel: 020 7261 5395. Fax: 020 7261 5480. E-mail: john_gooch@ipcmedia.com
Editor: Phil Hilton. **Picture Editor:** John Gooch.
Weekly general interest magazine for young men.
Illustrations: Colour. Always interested in "amazing, spectacular and extreme" images for "True Stories" picture feature section – single pictures or series of pictures used over double-page spreads, usually 4–5 per issue. Must have obvious appeal to the target market, anything from spectacular sports shots to unusual animal pics. Also relevant news pictures (sport, celebrities) which have not been seen elsewhere. Limited opportunities for commissioned work, but will consider approaches from experienced photographers working in suitable areas.
Text: Little scope.
Overall freelance potential: Excellent.
Fees: Dependent on the individual image and how it is used, as well as on level of exclusivity.

PENTHOUSE
Sapphire Multimedia Ltd, PO Box 297, Surrey KT11 3WB.
Tel: 01932 589490. Fax: 00932 589499. E-mail: bryan.francis@sapphiremultimedia.com
Editor: Deric Botham.
Sophisticated monthly devoted to erotic photography and other male interests.
Illustrations: Mainly colour. Very high-quality erotic photography of all kinds considered, sets or singles, in all formats. Images should be positive, intelligent and not demeaning to women. Some scope for reportage work on sex-based or other male interest subjects.
Text: Little scope.
Overall freelance potential: Very good for the right material.
Editor's tips: Think about fresh ways of depicting sex and eroticism for grown-ups.
Fees: Negotiable dependent on what is offered.

REFRESH
Swan Publishing Ltd, 4-5 Greenwich Quay, Clarence Road, London SE8 3EY.
Tel: 020 8469 9700. Fax: 020 8469 9703. E-mail: refresh@swanpublishing.co.uk
Editor: David Tickner.
Monthly magazine for affluent gay men.
Illustrations: Colour. Digital media preferred. Mostly by commission, but opportunities often available. Main scope is for fashion shoots, both studio and location. Some portraiture, interiors and travel. E-mail samples with a CV in the first instance.
Text: Ideas for features always considered.
Overall freelance potential: Good – always looking to broaden the range of photographers used.
Fees: By negotiation.

ZOO WEEKLY
EMAP Performance Network, Endeavour House, 189 Shaftesbury Avenue, London WC2H 8JG.
Tel: 020 7208 3797. Picture desk: 020 7208 3728. E-mail: steve.nash@emap.com
Editor: Paul Merrill. **Features Editor:** Mark Dinning. **Picture Editor:** Steve Nash.
Weekly general interest magazine for young men.
Illustrations: Colour. Always need topical, unusual and visually striking images for the magazine's "Snapped" section – several double-page spreads per issue displaying spectacular or unusual images of all kinds. Also unusual or exclusive sports images. Commissions in relevant areas may be available.
Text: Will consider ideas for topical features and real life stories. Material should have a laddish/humorous approach but be backed with genuine knowledge of the subject. Submit suggestions to features editor in the first instance.
Overall freelance potential: Excellent.
Fees: Negotiable, dependent on the nature of images and their exclusivity.

Motoring

A&S PUBLISHING
A&S Publishing Co Ltd, Messenger House, 35 St Michael's Square, Gloucester GL1 1HX.
Tel: 01452 307181. Fax: 01452 307170. E-mail: sarah.heppenstall@aandspublishing.com
Managing Editor: Sara Vielvoye. **Group Art Editor:** Sarah Heppenstall.
Publisher of specialist motoring titles, most devoted to a particular marque or model. Titles published include Classic Ford, Fast Ford, Mini Magazine, Retro Cars and Total Vauxhall.
Illustrations: Mainly colour. Mainly by commission. Will consider approaches from experienced and competent car photographers – contact art editor in the first instance. Pictures of unusual or particularly interesting cars of the right type may be considered on spec.
Text: Little scope, but suggestions considered.
Overall freelance potential: Fair.
Fees: By negotiation.

AUTO EXPRESS
Dennis Publishing, 30 Cleveland Street, London W1T 4JD.
Tel: 020 7631 1433. Picture library: 020 7907 6137. Fax: 020 7917 5556.
Editor: David Johns. **Picture Manager:** Kathy Farrell.
Popular weekly magazine, aimed at the average motorist rather than the car enthusiast.

Illustrations: Colour. Digital media preferred. Hard news pictures and topical motoring subjects with impact may be considered on spec, but most is by commission.
Text: Features on any motoring topic, to appeal to a general readership. May be practical but should not be too technical. 1,000–2,000 words. Always submit a synopsis in the first instance.
Overall freelance potential: Limited for the non-specialist.
Editor's tips: Although a popular non-technical title, accuracy is essential.
Fees: Photographs according to size of reproduction. Text usually £200 per 1,000 words.

AUTOCAR
Haymarket Publishing Ltd, 60 Waldegrave Road, Teddington, Middlesex TW11 8LG.
Tel: 020 8267 5630. Fax: 020 8267 5759. E-mail: steve.hopkins@haynet.com
Editor: Steve Sutcliffe. **Art Editor:** Steve Hopkins.
High quality general interest motoring weekly. Includes road tests, new car descriptions, international motor sport, motor shows, etc.
Illustrations: Colour. Mostly by commission for top quality general car coverage, test reports, performance cars, industry picture stories and portraits – submit CV/portfolio to the Art Editor. Always interested in scoop pictures of pre-production models under test or any other exclusive motor industry photo items.
Text: Illustrated features on motoring subjects, by prior arrangement with the editor. 1,000–2,000 words.
Overall freelance potential: Good for those with experience.
Editor's tips: Technical accuracy and full information on the cars featured is essential. Familiarise yourself with the magazine first; too much material received is unsuitable.
Fees: Features by negotiation.

THE AUTOMOBILE
Enthusiast Publishing Ltd. Editorial: Helens Lodge, Helens Gate, Rickmansworth WD3 5DH.
Fax: 01923 284379. E-mail: mhlbowler@boltblue.com
Editor: Michael Bowler.
Monthly publication featuring veteran, vintage, and pre-1950s motor vehicles.
Illustrations: Colour. Not much scope for single pictures unless of particular interest. The main requirement is for well-illustrated articles concerning any pre-1950s motor vehicle; not only cars but also commercial vehicles. Also limited room for coverage of race meetings, exhibitions or other events at which old motor vehicles are present.
Text: Informative illustrated articles as above. Of particular interest are good restoration features, with both "before" and "after" pictures showing what can be achieved.
Overall freelance potential: Although limited there is scope for illustrated features – consult the editor before starting on feature.
Editor's tips: Do not submit material concerning post-1950s vehicles.
Fees: By negotiation.

CAR & ACCESSORY TRADER
Haymarket Autosport Publications, Somerset House, Somerset Road, Teddington, Middlesex TW11 8RT.
Tel: 020 8943 5906. Fax: 020 8943 5993.E-mail: cat.eds@haynet.com
Editor: *TBA*. **Assistant Editor:** Daniel Anderson.
Monthly magazine for traders involved in the selling of car parts and accessories.
Illustrations: B&W and colour. Captioned news pictures concerning new products, openings of new premises, handover of sales awards, etc. Much is commissioned. Covers: excellent relevant photographs considered.
Text: Varied subjects of interest to the trade, by commission only.
Overall freelance potential: About 50 per cent of contributions are from freelance sources.
Fees: £100 per £1,000 words. Photographs negotiable.

CLASSIC & SPORTS CAR
Haymarket Magazines Ltd, Somerset House, Somerset Road, Teddington, Middlesex TW11 8RT.
Tel: 020 8267 5399. Fax: 020 8267 5318.
Editor: James Elliott.
Monthly magazine covering mainly post-1945 classic cars, generally of a sporting nature. Strong coverage of the owners' scene.
Illustrations: Colour; B&W archive material. Digital files or film. Mainly interested in coverage of club or historic car gatherings, unless staff photographer is present. Feature photography always commissioned.
Text: Articles of interest to the classic car enthusiast and collector, up to 2,500 words.
Overall freelance potential: Small, as much material is staff produced.
Editor's tips: Always get in touch before submitting.
Fees: According to merit.

CLASSIC AMERICAN
Trader Media Group, Optimum House, Clippers Quay, Salford Quays, Manchester M5 2XP.
Tel: 0161 836 4406. Fax: 0161 872 6238. E-mail: clasam@aol.com
Editor: Ben Klemenzson. **Art Editor:** Tony Crowther.
Monthly magazine concerning American cars mainly of the '50s, '60s and '70s.
Illustrations: Mainly colour. Striking or unusual pictures of classic US vehicles. However, much of the photography is commissioned from regulars or staff-produced.
Text: Illustrated articles on specific cars or bikes and their owners, plus features on other aspects of American-style youth culture such as clothing, music, sport, etc. 1,000–2,000 words. Always check with the editor before submitting.
Overall freelance potential: Car coverage welcome, but best scope is for lifestyle features.
Fees: Pictures by negotiation. £150 per 1,000 words for text.

CLASSIC CARS
EMAP Automotive Ltd, Media House, Lynchwood, Peterborough Business Park, Peterborough PE2 6EA.
Tel: 01733 468000. Fax: 01733 468888. E-mail: classic.cars@emap.com
Editor-in-Chief: Martyn Moore.
Glossy, heavily-illustrated monthly covering classic cars of all eras.
Illustrations: Colour. Will consider on-spec images of classic cars of all types, especially ones that are in regular use, and informal, reportage-style coverage of classic car gatherings around the country. Major feature photography mostly handled by a team of regulars.
Text: Limited scope, but suggestions considered.
Overall freelance potential: Very good for the right sort of material.
Editor's tips: Make an effort to place cars in an interesting setting – not just on the driveway. Detailed captions and a contact number for each car's owner are essential.
Fees: On a rising scale according to size of reproduction, up to £150 for a full-bleed page.

CLASSICS
Highbury Leisure Publishing Ltd, Berwick House, 8–10 Knoll Rise, Orpington, Kent BR6 0PS.
Tel: 01689 889276. Fax: 01689 876438. E-mail: classics@splpublishing.co.uk
Editor: Tim Morgan.
Four-weekly practical magazine for classic car owners.
Illustrations: Colour. Digital media preferred. Captioned pictures of newsworthy cars and events, including relevant motorsport coverage, always considered on spec. Also scope for commissions to do photo shoots of featured cars; send samples of previous work in the first instance.
Text: Well-illustrated features about restoring classic cars; reports from events.
Overall freelance potential: Good.
Editor's tips: Look at mag carefully before submitting work, particularly the editorial profile and

style. Always interested in hearing about cars which might make a good feature subject. Send a sample shot with some details about the car and a commission to shoot may be offered.
Fees: Pictures, typically £100 per feature; £120 per 1,000 words; commissioned photography, £200 per day.

COMPANY CAR
DMG World Media, Queensway House, 2 Queensway, Redhill, Surrey RH1 1QS.
Tel: 01737 768611. Fax: 01737 855207. E-mail: companycar@uk.dmgworldmedia.com
Editor: Tony Meredith.
Monthly magazine for companies running in excess of ten cars. Aimed at main board directors and senior executives/managers.
Illustrations: Colour. Exclusive and newsworthy pictures relating to fleet sales or fleet cars. Covers: topical colour pictures, including new car launches; medium format required.
Text: Features on car management or cost. Exclusive material only. 1,000–1,500 words plus 2/3 pictures.
Overall freelance potential: Most photography supplied by PR sources.
Fees: Negotiable.

DRIVING MAGAZINE
Safety House, Beddington Farm Road, Croydon CR0 4XZ.
Tel: 0845 345 5151. Fax: 020 8665 5565. E-mail: drivingmagazine@driving.org
Editor: Graham Fryer.
Bi-monthly road safety publication for advanced drivers, road safety educationists and driving instructors.
Illustrations: Colour (prints or digital preferred). Pictures of home or overseas motorists/driving school vehicles in unusual surroundings or circumstances. Humorous incidents, traffic accidents of an unusual nature, unusual road signs, humorous signs or those in extraordinary positions.
Text: Features on road safety, driver training occasionally accepted. 500–2,000 words.
Overall freelance potential: Modest.
Fees: Photographs from £15–£20, variable according to subject and quality.

EVO
Evo Publications Ltd, Tower Court, Irchester Road, Wollaston, Wellingborough NN29 7PJ.
Tel: 020 7907 6310. Fax: 01933 663367. E-mail: eds@evo.co.uk
Editor: Peter Tomalin. **Art Editor:** Chee-Chiu Lee.
Glossy monthly covering the high-performance end of the car market.
Illustrations: Colour. Digital preferred. All by commission. Interested in hearing from freelances who can produce good action photography of cars on the move, preferably with an individual and "cutting edge" style. Some portrait work also available.
Text: No scope.
Overall freelance potential: Good for the experienced car photographer.
Fees: By negotiation.

FLEET NEWS
EMAP Automotive Ltd, Media House, Lynchwood, Peterborough Business Park, Peterborough PE2 6EA.
Tel: 01733 468000. Fax: 01733 468296. E-mail: fleetnews@.emap.com
Editor: John Maslen.
Weekly newspaper aimed at those responsible for running company car and light commercial vehicle fleets.
Illustrations: Colour. Captioned news pictures concerning company car operations, handover of car fleets to companies, appointments in the trade, etc.
Text: News, articles on business car management and related subjects.

Overall freelance potential: Excellent.
Editor's tips: Always write or e-mail first.
Fees: Negotiable.

4x4
IPC Focus Network, Leon House, 233 High Street, Croydon CR9 1HZ.
Tel: 020 8726 8374. Fax: 020 8726 8398.
Editor: John Carroll.
Monthly magazine devoted to four-wheel-drive vehicles.
Illustrations: Colour. Pictures of new vehicles, travel and other "off road" events. Must be captioned with full details of driver, event and location.
Text: Illustrated articles concerning four-wheel-drive vehicles and off-road activities. 1,000–2,000 words.
Overall freelance potential: Limited, but there is room for new contributors.
Fees: By negotiation.

GOMINI
A&S Publishing Ltd, Messenger House, 35 St Michael's Square, Gloucester GL1 1HX.
Tel: 01452 317770. Fax: 01452 307170. E-mail: chris.anderson@aandspublishing.com
Editor: Chris Anderson. **Art Editor:** Bonnie Coupland.
Monthly magazine devoted solely to the "New Mini".
Illustrations: Colour. All by commission. Will consider approaches from car photographers with experience, especially those who have worked for performance-oriented titles.
Text: Possible scope for experienced car journalists.
Overall freelance potential: Limited.
Fees: By negotiation.

JAGUAR
Haymarket Publishing Ltd, 60 Waldegrave Road, Teddington, Middlesex TW11 8LA.
Tel: 020 8267 5947. Fax: 020 8267 5916. E-mail: jaguar-magazine@haynet.com
Editor: Jonathan Evans.
Glossy general interest quarterly for owners of Jaguar cars.
Illustrations: Colour. High quality commissioned photography of Jaguar cars, travel and general lifestyle subjects, plus coverage of Jaguar F1 racing. Opportunities only for experienced workers with medium format equipment.
Text: Strongly-illustrated articles on travel and lifestyle subjects. All work is by commission, no unsolicited work is accepted.
Overall freelance potential: Good for experienced workers, though limited by the publishing frequency.
Fees: Photography by negotiation. Articles around £400; pictures, £600.

JAGUAR HERITAGE
Ardent Media Ltd, Aldbury House, Dower Mews, Berkhamsted, Herts HP4 2BL.
Tel: 01442 866944. E-mail: francoisprins@jaguarheritagemag.com
Editor: François Prins.
Concentrates on the history of the Jaguar company and of individual cars bearing the Jaguar, Daimler or Lanchester marques. Published monthly in association with the Jaguar Daimler Heritage Trust.
Illustrations: Colour; archive B&W. Most interested in coverage of individual classic models that are still in good running order, especially if they have an interesting story attached. Will also consider interesting older photographs, from 1896 on, though a good deal of material is sourced from the Heritage Trust archive. Commission available to experienced car photographers.
Text: Feature packages about unusually interesting classics and restoration projects always of

considerable interest. Submit suggestions and ideas in the first instance.
Overall freelance potential: Good.
Fees: Pictures according to use; text usually £100 per 1,000 words.

LAND ROVER MONTHLY
Milebrook Ltd, The Publishing House, 19d Woolpit Business Park, Woolpit, Suffolk IP30 9UP.
Tel: 01359 240066. Fax: 01359 244221. E-mail: hq@lrm.co.uk
Managing Editor: Richard Howell-Thomas.
Monthly magazine for Land Rover enthusiasts.
Illustrations: Colour. Digital media preferred. Little scope for individual photographs unless accompanied by extended captions or background text.
Text: Well-illustrated articles on all matters relating to Land Rover, Range Rover, Discovery and Freelander vehicles; travel/adventure stories, features on interesting individual vehicles and off-roading personalities, competition and club event reports. Limited scope for vehicle test reports.
Overall freelance potential: Excellent for those who can add words to their pictures, and have good knowledge of Land Rover products.
Fees: By negotiation.

LAND ROVER OWNER
EMAP Automotive Ltd, Media House, Lynchwood, Peterborough Business Park, Peterborough PE2 6EA.
Tel: 01733 468000. Fax: 01733 468238.
Editor: John Pearson.
Magazine for Land Rover owners and enthusiasts. 13 issues a year.
Illustrations: Mostly colour. Interesting or unusual pictures of Land Rovers, Range Rovers, Freelanders, Defenders and Discoverys. Celebrities pictured with such vehicles.
Text: Illustrated articles on overland expeditions using Land Rovers. Length 1,000 words, plus around six pictures.
Overall freelance potential: Good.
Fees: Text, £100 per 1,000 words; pictures by negotiation.

MAXPOWER
EMAP Automotive Ltd, Media House, Lynchwood, Peterborough Business Park, Peterborough PE2 6EA.
Tel: 01733 468000. Fax: 01733 468001. E-mail: roger.payne@emap.com
Editor: Roger Payne.
Monthly for young men heavily involved with fast cars and modifying them.
Illustrations: Colour. Pictures of smart and well-modified cars; also "sheds" (particularly badly modified cars). Also picture stories of likely interest to the target readership, including coverage of car gatherings.
Text: Ideas for features of interest to "lads" in their twenties always considered.
Overall freelance potential: Good for those in touch with this scene.
Editor's tips: Freelances need to be able to recognise the particular type of "cool" car that is featured here, and be aware of the general mood of the magazine.
Fees: Picture stories around £200–£300; single pictures according to use.

MOTOR TRADER
Highbury Business Communications, Media House, Azalea Drive, Swanley, Kent BR8 8HU.
Tel: 01322 660070. Fax: 01322 616378. E-mail: c.hutchinson@highburybiz.co.uk
Editor: Curtis Hutchinson.
Weekly trade newspaper, controlled circulation and subscription, read by dealers & manufacturers in the car and component industries, garage owners, body shop workers.
Illustrations: B&W and colour. News pictures on anything connected with the motor trade.
Text: News and features relevant to the motor trade and industry. 300–1,000 words.

Overall freelance potential: Good for those in touch with the trade.
Editor's tips: This is the trade's only weekly newspaper; it is particularly interested in hard news. Call to discuss with editor or deputy before submitting material.
Fees: Negotiable.

MOTORING & LEISURE
Csma Ltd, Britannia House, 21 Station Street, Brighton BN1 4DE.
Tel: 01273 744744. Fax: 01273 744761.
Editor: David Arnold.
Monthly journal of the Civil Service Motoring Association, covering motoring, travel and leisure activities.
Illustrations: Colour. Digital media preferred. General car-related subjects and Continental travel.
Text: Illustrated articles on motoring, travel, camping and caravanning. 750–1,000 words.
Overall freelance potential: Limited.
Fees: By arrangement.

MOTORSPORT
Haymarket Specialist Publications Ltd, Somerset House, Somerset Road, Teddington TW11 8RT.
Tel: 020 8267 5256. Fax: 020 8267 5222 E-mail: motorsport@haynet.com
Editor: Paul Fearnley.
Monthly devoted to motorsport and sports cars, both old and new.
Illustrations: Colour; B&W archive material. Will consider coverage of classic or vintage sports car meetings and racing, but always contact magazine before attending an event. Archive collections always of interest.
Text: No scope.
Overall freelance potential: Fair.
Fees: From around £35 upwards.

911 & PORSCHE WORLD
CH Publications Ltd, PO Box 75, Tadworth, Surrey KT20 7XF.
Tel: 01737 814311. Fax: 01737 814591.
Editor: Chris Horton.
Magazine published nine times a year and devoted to Porsche or Porsche-derived cars.
Illustrations: Mostly colour. All commissioned, with opportunities for those who have original ideas and can produce top quality car photography.
Text: Ideas for articles always of interest; write with details in the first instance.
Overall freelance potential: Very good for specialist coverage.
Fees: Photography by arrangement; around £100 per 1,000 words.

OCTANE
Octane Media Ltd, Isis Way, Minerva Business Park, Lynch Wood, Peterborough PE2 6QR.
Tel: 01733 392890. Fax: 01733 236671. E-mail: rob@octane-magazine.co.uk
Editor: Robert Coucher. **Art Editor:** Rob Gould.
Monthly covering both contemporary high-performance cars and prestige classics from all eras.
Illustrations: Colour; historic B&W. Mostly by commission with good opportunities for experienced car photographers. Possible on-spec scope for picture stories covering specific events such as meets, rallies, races, etc. Relevant archive material also of interest.
Text: Suggestions always considered.
Overall freelance potential: Good.
Fees: By negotiation.

PERFORMANCE FORD
Unity Media Communications Ltd, Becket House, Vestry Road, Sevenoaks, Kent TN14 5EJ.
Tel: 01732 748000. Fax: 01732 748001.
Editor: Ben Birch.
Monthly magazine devoted to Ford and Ford-based vehicles, with the emphasis on high-performance road use.
Illustrations: Colour. Pictures to illustrate features, or topical single pictures of particular quality, i.e. prototypes, one-offs, etc. Medium format transparencies preferred.
Text: Illustrated articles on maintenance and modification of Ford-based cars. Personality profiles with a direct relevance to Ford products.
Overall freelance potential: Fair.
Editor's tips: Always raise ideas with the editor before submitting material.
Fees: Pictures according to size of reproduction; text £120 per 1,000 words.

REDLINE
Future Publishing, Beauford Court, 30 Monmouth Street, Bath BA1 2BW.
Tel: 01225 442244. Fax: 01225 822793. E-mail: tim.durant@futurenet.co.uk
Editor: Dan Lewis. **Art Editor:** Tim Durant.
Motoring monthly for young men who want to get the best out of their modified cars.
Illustrations: Colour. Exciting and dramatic pictures of modified cars, sporting and speed events, unusual vehicles and fast lifestyles. Commissions available for car shoots, also some glamour; make appointment with the art editor.
Text: Will always consider suggestions for illustrated articles on suitable subjects, such as touring trips, unusual events, weird car-based experiences, etc.
Overall freelance potential: Moderate.
Editor's tips: Although photographers should know how to light and shoot cars, non-specialists are welcome if they can produce something exciting and different.
Fees: Single pictures £25–£250; page rate ££50–£125; day rate £150–£300.

REVS
EMAP Automotive Ltd, Media House, Lynchwood, Peterborough Business Park, Peterborough PE2 6EA.
Tel: 01733 468000. Fax: 01733 468179. E-mail: nigel.grimshaw@emap.com
Editor: Nigel Grimshaw.
Lively monthly aimed at car modification enthusiasts, offering a combination of inspiration, information and entertainment.
Illustrations: Colour. Mostly by commission to a tight brief. Happy to hear from photographers who are prepared to experiment with the magazine to produce something different. The odd on-spec shot may be considered if it is right for the target market.
Text: Always interested in hearing from writers who understand the field and its ethos, and who can produce good entertaining copy.
Overall freelance potential: Very good for those who can produce exciting, top quality work.
Editor's tips: Photographers need to be able to produce exciting action as well as having a good eye for statics and details.
Fees: By negotiation.

SPORTS CAR CLASSICS
Trinity Publications Ltd, 1st Floor, Edward House, 92-93 Edward Street, Birmingham B1 2RA.
Tel: 0121 233 8712. Fax: 0121 233 8715. E-mail: sportscarclassic@aol.com
Editor: Frank Westworth. **Assistant Editor:** Dan Shaw.
Monthly devoted to classic sports cars from the 1950s onwards.
Illustrations: Colour; historic B&W. Pictures mainly used to illustrate features on individual cars, especially those in regular daily use or being raced/rallied, restorations and modifications. Commissions possible.

Text: Illustrated features on topics as above, with the emphasis on the relationship between car and owner.
Overall freelance potential: Good for the right subject matter.
Fees: By negotiation.

STREET MACHINE & AMERICAN CAR WORLD
CH Publications Ltd, PO Box 75, Tadworth, Surrey KT20 7XF.
Tel: 01737 814311. Fax: 01529 300235.
Editor: Richard Nicholls.
Monthly magazine covering custom cars and hot rods based on pre-1975 vehicles, British or American; and American cars, standard and modified, up to present day.
Illustrations: Colour. Newsy and well-captioned single pictures depicting happenings on the UK custom and American car scene. Other pictures usually as part of a story/picture package on subjects detailed below. Prefers British-sourced material.
Text: Well-illustrated features on completed cars, step-by-step illustrated material on how to do it, track tests of modified cars and coverage of shows and events. Always phone or write first to discuss ideas.
Overall freelance potential: Good for the right sort of material.
Editor's tips: Not interested in front-wheel drive or post-1980 vehicles.
Fees: £50 for news items; text £125 per 1,000 words.

TOP GEAR MAGAZINE
BBC Magazines, Room AG192, Woodlands, 80 Wood Lane, London W12 0TT.
Tel: 020 8576 3721. Fax: 020 8576 3754.
Editor: Michael Harvey. **Picture Editor:** Pete Trafford.
General interest motoring magazine designed to complement the BBC TV programme of the same name.
Illustrations: Colour. All by commission and much from known specialists, but photographers with a fresh approach and a good portfolio are welcomed. Send samples and details of previous experience in the first instance, or call for appointment. Stock images of pre-1990 cars often needed to illustrate articles.
Text: Motoring-related features considered, preferably out of the ordinary.
Overall freelance potential: Quite good.
Fees: By negotiation.

TOTALMG
9 Publishing, PO Box 163, Bicester, Oxon OX25 4YS.
Tel: 01869 340061. E-mail: phil@9publishing.co.uk
Editor: Philip Raby.
Monthly for MG car enthusiasts, covering both classic and modern models.
Illustrations: Colour. All by commission only. Interested in hearing from professional car photographers who can offer something different. Write first enclosing samples of work.
Text: Ideas from professional motoring writers always welcome – apply in writing only.
Overall freelance potential: Good.
Editor's tips: Study the magazine before getting in touch.
Fees: Negotiable, but from around £150 for photo assignments, £100 per 1,000 words for text.

TRIUMPH WORLD
CH Publications Ltd, PO Box 75, Tadworth, Surrey KT20 7XF.
Tel: 01895 623612. Fax: 01895 623613. E-mail: triumphworld@chpltd.com
Editor: Tony Beadle.
Bi-monthly for Triumph car (not motorcycle) enthusiasts.
Illustrations: B&W and colour. Photographs of newsworthy or unusual Triumph cars, especially the "classics" such as Heralds, TRs, Spitfires and Stags. Some opportunities for experienced

photographers to produce commissioned work for major features.
Text: Illustrated articles likely to appeal to the dedicated enthusiast. Phone first to discuss ideas.
Overall freelance potential: Good.
Fees: Pictures by negotiation and according to use. Text £120 per 1,000 words.

VW MOTORING
Warners Group Publications plc, The Maltings, West Street, Bourne, Lincs PE10 9PH.
Tel: 01778 391000. Fax: 01778 423063.
Editor: Peter Rosenthal.
Monthly magazine for owners and enthusiasts of Volkswagen Audi, new and old, classic and custom, plus coverage of Skoda and Porsche.
Illustrations: B&W and colour. Digital media preferred. Relevant photo features and motorsport photography. Good quality 35mm transparency required for larger reproductions; crisp 6x4 colour prints OK for detail pics. Covers: VW or Audi vehicles in interesting settings.
Text: Features of interest to VW and Audi enthusiasts, especially DIY, rebuild projects, historical and technical subjects. In-depth knowledge of the subject more important than slick writing style, but must be accompanied by relevant photographic or illustrative material to publication standards.
Overall freelance potential: Mostly use regular contributors, but always open to appropriate material from freelance sources.
Fees: By agreement, on sight of material.

Music

BLUES & SOUL
Blues & Soul Ltd, 153 Praed Street, London W2 1RL.
Tel: 020 7402 6869. Fax: 020 7224 8227.
Editor: Bob Kilbourn.
Fortnightly publication covering soul, R&B, funk, fusion, jazz, house, garage, urban dance – all forms of black music excepting reggae.
Illustrations: B&W and colour. Digital media preferred. Will always consider original and exclusive pictures of black music performers.
Text: Small amount of scope for exclusive articles or interviews.
Overall freelance potential: Limited.
Editor's tips: Think of the readership, and the format, in order to produce something really striking and eye-catching.
Fees: By negotiation.

CLASSICAL MUSIC
Rhinegold Publishing Ltd, 241 Shaftesbury Avenue, London WC2H 8TF.
Tel: 020 7333 1742. Fax: 020 7333 1769. E-mail: classical.music@rhinegold.co.uk
Editor: Keith Clarke.
Fortnightly news and feature magazine for classical music professionals and the interested general public.
Illustrations: B&W and colour. Digital media preferred. Very limited scope as most pictures are supplied by promoters, etc, but always happy to look at portfolios, subject to appointment. Occasional urgent need for a musician or group in the news – most easily met if freelances can supply lists of photographs they hold.
Text: Short news items and news stories about events in the music/arts world, including politics and performance, up to 800 words. Longer background features about musicians, usually relating to a forthcoming event, up to 2,000 words. All work is commissioned.
Overall freelance potential: Limited for photographers, but most text is from commissioned freelance sources.
Fees: Pictures by negotiation; text from £100 per 1,000 words.

ECHOES
Notcarl Ltd, Unit LFB2, The Leather Market, Weston Street, London SE1 3HN.
Tel: 020 7407 5888. Fax: 020 7402 2929.
Editor: Chris Wells.
Weekly publication devoted to all aspects of black popular music.
Illustrations: Mostly colour. Outstanding photographs of popular black music performers, for immediate publication or for file.
Text: Little scope.
Overall freelance potential: Fair.
Fees: By negotiation.

FROOTS
Southern Rag Ltd, PO Box 337, London N4 1TW.
Tel: 020 8340 9651. Fax: 020 8348 5626. E-mail: froots@frootsmag.com
Editor: Ian Anderson.
Monthly publication concerned with folk and world roots music.
Illustrations: B&W and colour. Pictures to be used in conjunction with interviews, reviews of records or reports on events. Mostly commissioned.
Text: Interviews and reviews concerned with folk and world music.
Overall freelance potential: Limited for the contributor unknown in this field. The magazine favours its regular contributors.
Fees: By agreement.

KERRANG!
EMAP Performance Network, Mappin House, 4 Winsley Street, London W1W 8HF.
Tel: 020 7436 1515. Fax: 020 7312 8910. E-mail: kerrang@emap.com
Editor: Ashley Bird.
Weekly magazine covering a wide range of hard rock.
Illustrations: Mainly colour. Pictures of relevant bands. On-stage performance shots preferred, with the emphasis on action. Some posed shots and portraits of top performers also used.
Text: Little freelance market.
Overall freelance potential: Very good. The magazine is heavily illustrated.
Fees: According to size of reproduction.

KEYBOARD PLAYER
Bookrose Ltd, 100 Birkbeck Road, Enfield, Middlesex EN2 0ED.
Tel: 020 8245 5840. E-mail: stevemiller@keyboardplayer.fsnet.co.uk
Editor: Steve Miller.
Monthly magazine for players of all types of keyboard instrument. Covers pianos, organs, keyboards and synthesisers; and all forms of music, from pop to classical.
Illustrations: B&W and colour. Photographs of keyboard instruments and their players, preferably accompanied by a newsy caption. Covers: striking colour pictures of keyboard instruments.
Text: Articles of around 1,000 words on any topic of interest to keyboard players.
Overall freelance potential: Fairly limited, but scope is there for the right type of material.
Editor's tips: Run-of-the-mill pictures of players seated at their instruments will not be met with much enthusiasm – a strikingly different approach is required.
Fees: By negotiation.

METAL HAMMER
Future Publishing Ltd, 99 Baker Street, London W1V 6FP.
Tel: 020 7317 2600. Fax: 020 7486 5678. E-mail: jamie.hibbard@futurenet.co.uk
Editor: Jamie Hibbard. **Art Editor:** Sarah Athoe-Harvey.
Monthly for heavy metal and hard rock fans.

Illustrations: Mostly colour. Good action and group portrait photographs of hard rock or heavy metal performers – send lists of subjects available. Commissions available to experienced rock photographers.
Text: Illustrated articles, interviews and reviews. Submit suggestions only in the first instance.
Overall freelance potential: Excellent for those in touch with this scene.
Fees: By negotiation.

MIXMAG
EMAP Performance Network, Mappin House, 4 Winsley Street, London W1W 8HF.
Tel: 020 7436 1515; features: 020 7312 8167. Fax: 020 7312 8977. E-mail: mixmag@emap.com
Editor: Pauline Haldane. **Picture Editor:** Shona Wong.
Monthly covering the dance music and clubbing scene.
Illustrations: Colour. Photographs of clubs and clubbers throughout the country; portraits of musicians; photo features. Fresh young photographers always welcome.
Text: Reports from clubs nationwide; young writers welcome.
Overall freelance potential: Very good.
Editor's tips: Contributors don't have to have experience, just a good sense of what the dance scene is about.
Fees: By negotiation.

MOJO
EMAP Performance Network, Mappin House, 4 Winsley Street, London W1W 8HF.
Tel: 020 7312 8207. Fax: 020 7312 8296. E-mail: matt.turner@emap.com
Editor-in-Chief: Phil Alexander. **Picture Editor:** Matt Turner.
Monthly rock music magazine aimed at fans of all ages.
Illustrations: Mostly colour. Photographs of leading rock artists, both contemporary and from earlier eras. Archive material from the '50s, '60s and '70s always of interest. Good opportunities for commissioned work.
Text: In-depth profiles of individual artists and bands, but scope mainly for established writers.
Overall freelance potential: Good.
Editor's tips: Previously unpublished or unseen photographs, or those that have not been used for some years, are of particular interest.
Fees: According to use.

NEW MUSICAL EXPRESS
IPC Media Ltd, 25th Floor, King's Reach Tower, Stamford Street, London SE1 9LS.
Tel: 020 7261 5749. Fax: 020 7261 5185. E-mail: nmepics@ipcmedia.com
Editor: Conor McNicholas. **Art Director:** Rob Biddulph. **Picture Editor:** Marian Paterson.
Weekly tabloid covering all aspects of popular music and allied youth culture.
Illustrations: Mostly colour. All aspects of contemporary popular music, but see below.
Text: Scope for exclusive news stories or interviews with rock musicians, film stars, or other personalities of interest to a young and aware readership. Always write or phone with suggestions first.
Overall freelance potential: Good, but very dependent on subject matter.
Editor's tips: NME only covers those parts of the music scene considered worthwhile by the editorial team – study recent issues.
Fees: On a rising scale according to size of reproduction.

Q
EMAP Performance Network, Mappin House, 4 Winsley Street, London W1W 8HF.
Tel: 020 7436 1515. Fax: 020 7182 8547. E-mail: qpictures@emap.com
Editor: Paul Rees. **Picture Editor:** Steve Peck.
Monthly rock music magazine aimed at the 18–35 age group.

Illustrations: Mostly colour. Most pictures staff-produced or commissioned from a pool of regular contributors, but suitable stock pictures of relevant personalities will always be considered.
Text: Top quality profiles, interviews and feature articles of interest to a rock-oriented readership, invariably by commission.
Overall freelance potential: 50 per cent is commissions; good for library/stock shots.
Fees: By negotiation.

RHYTHM
Future Publishing Ltd, Beauford Court, 30 Monmouth Street, Bath BA1 2BW.
Tel: 01225 442244. Fax: 01225 732285. E-mail: louise.king@futurenet.co.uk
Editor: Louise King.
Monthly magazine for drummers and percussionists in the rock and pop music field.
Illustrations: Mostly colour. Interesting photographs relating to contemporary percussion instruments and their players, including the use of electronic and computer-aided equipment.
Text: Illustrated profiles, interviews and features about leading contemporary drummers and percussionists. Articles on technique and programming from knowledgeable contributors.
Overall freelance potential: Limited.
Fees: £110 per 1,000 words for text; photographs according to use.

SMASH HITS
EMAP Performance Network, Mappin House, 4 Winsley Street, London W1W 8HF.
Tel: 020 7182 8000. Fax: 020 7636 5792.
Editor: Lisa Smosarski. **Picture Editor:** Emma Thomas.
Fortnightly popular music magazine aimed at 9–14 year olds.
Illustrations: Colour. Posed, pin-up style photographs of performers who currently have a record in the charts, usually studio shots. Faces should be clearly shown.
Overall freelance potential: Very good for photographers in touch with the current pop music scene.
Fees: £40 upwards for any picture. £110-£150 for full page. Covers: £400 upwards.

TOTAL GUITAR
Future Publishing Ltd, Beauford Court, 30 Monmouth Street, Bath BA1 2BW.
Tel: 01225 442244. Fax: 01225 462986. E-mail: brad.merrett@futurenet.co.uk
Editor: Scott Rowley. **Art Editor:** Brad Merrett.
Monthly magazine for guitar players at all levels, concentrating on practical advice.
Illustrations: Mainly colour. Mostly commissioned to accompany features and reviews. Stock shots of well-known players and individual instruments always of interest; send lists first.
Text: Profiles and interviews with leading guitarists, and practical articles. Submit ideas only in the first instance.
Overall freelance potential: Limited.
Fees: By negotiation.

Parenting

BABY & YOU
Highbury Lifestyle, The Publishing House, Highbury Station Road, London N1 1SE.
Tel: 020 7226 2222. Fax: 020 7288 7578.
Editor: Amanda Burnley.
Monthly magazine devoted to the first year of life.
Illustrations: Colour. Interested in good stock images of young babies no more than one year old.

Commissions available for experienced workers to shoot covers, fashion, studio work and some reportage.
Text: Articles on relevant subjects. Submit synopsis in the first instance.
Overall freelance potential: Good.
Editor's tips: Most available stock tends to feature older babies; there is a real need for good images of the younger baby.
Fees: By negotiation.

BBC PARENTING
BBC Worldwide, Studio 210, The Bon Marché Centre, 241-251 Ferndale Road, London SW9 8BJ.
Tel: 020 7733 4955. Fax: 020 7733 7155. E-mail: bbcparentingmagazine@bbc.co.uk
Editor: Stephanie Cooper. **Art Editor:** Meg Georgeson.
Monthly for parents of children aged 1–12.
Illustrations: Colour. Scope for both commissioned work and for stock images covering childcare, education, family issues, fashion, food and leisure. Contact art editor in the first instance with details of experience or of coverage available.
Text: Suggestions for articles always considered.
Overall freelance potential: Fair.
Fees: By negotiation.

MOTHER & BABY
EMAP Esprit, Greater London House, Hampstead Road, London NW1 7EJ.
Tel: 020 7874 0200. Fax: 020 7347 1888.
Editor: Elena Dalrymple.
Monthly aimed at pregnant women and mothers of young children.
Illustrations: Mostly colour. High quality photographs of mothers with babies, or babies (under one year) on their own. Medium format preferred.
Text: Articles on all subjects related to pregnancy, birth, baby care and the early years.
Overall freelance potential: Limited, since the magazine is frequently overstocked.
Editor's tips: Only top quality pictures will be considered.
Fees: From £30 upwards for single pictures.

NURSERY WORLD
TSL Education Ltd, Admiral House, 66-68 East Smithfield, London E1W 1BX.
Tel: 020 7782 3120. Fax: 020 7782 3131. E-mail: liz.roberts@nursery-world.co.uk
Editor: Liz Roberts. **Picture Editor:** Margaret Clark.
Weekly publication on child care. Aimed at professional baby and child care workers such as teachers, nursery nurses and nannies.
Illustrations: B&W and colour. Digital media preferred. Pictures of babies and young children (up to five years old) involved in various activities in childcare settings. Covers: Studio shots of children, always linked to a feature inside.
Text: Features on child care, education, health, and any aspect of bringing up children, eg physical, intellectual, emotional etc. Ideas for nurseries and playgroups.
Overall freelance potential: Many features come from freelance contributors.
Fees: By arrangement.

PREGNANCY & BIRTH
EMAP Esprit Ltd, Greater London House, Hampstead Road, London NW1 7EJ.
Tel: 020 7874 0200. Fax: 020 7874 0201. E-mail: dani.corbett@emap.com
Editor: Kay McIntosh. **Art Editor:** Dani Corbett.
Monthly covering pregnancy from inception to birth.
Illustrations: Colour. Mostly by commission. Opportunities for experienced photographers to produce cover shots, mother and baby fashion, and "real life" material; contact art editor in the first instance. Always interested in hearing of good specialist stock collections.

Text: No scope.
Overall freelance potential: Good for experienced workers.
Editor's tips: Photographers need to be capable of working with real people rather than models.
Fees: By negotiation.

PRIMA BABY
National Magazine Company, 72 Broadwick Street, London W1F 9EP.
Tel: 020 7439 5000. Fax: 020 7312 4100.
Editor: Julia Goodwin. **Art Director:** Julian Barrett.
Glossy monthly covering pregnancy, babies and toddlers up to three years.
Illustrations: Mainly colour. Digital media preferred. Top quality pictures of babies and toddlers, with/without parents, in situations, engaged in activities, etc. Also pictures relating to aspects of childcare, health, food, fashion and home life. Must be warm, natural lifestyle images rather than posed "stock" shots. Write with details in the first instance. Some commissions available, mainly for food and fashion; call first to discuss possibilities.
Text: Limited freelance scope.
Overall freelance potential: Very good for quality material.
Fees: Variable; day rate around £350.

RIGHT START
McMillan Scott plc, 10 Savoy Street, London WC2E 7HR.
Tel: 020 7878 2338. Fax: 020 7379 6261. E-mail: lynette@rightstartmagazine.com
Editor: Lynette Lowthian.
Bi-monthly magazine for parents of pre-school and primary school age children, covering health, behaviour, education and family life.
Illustrations: B&W and colour. Mostly by commission but some scope for good stock coverage of children in educational and learning situations; send only lists or details of coverage available in the first instance.
Text: Opportunities for education and child care specialists. Approach with details of ideas and previous experience.
Overall freelance potential: Limited.
Fees: By negotiation.

Photography & Video

AV MAGAZINE
Quantum Business Media, 19 Scarbrook Rd, Croydon CR9 1LX.
Tel: 020 8565 4224. Fax: 020 8565 4282.
Editor: Peter Lloyd.
Monthly magazine for managers in industry and commerce, public services, government etc who use audiovisual communication techniques, eg slides, film, video, overhead projection and filmstrips, plus the new technologies of computer graphics and telecommunication.
Illustrations: B&W and colour. Pictures of programmes being shown to audiences, preferably supported by case history details; relevant news; new products or location shooting pictures. All must be backed with solid information. Covers: colour pictures of same, but check before submitting.
Text: Case histories of either shows, conferences or studies of a particular company's use of AV

techniques. Good location/conference stories always welcome. 1,000–2,500 words.
Overall freelance potential: Up to 25 per cent comes from freelances.
Fees: Text, £180-£200 per 1,000 words; pictures by agreement.

AMATEUR PHOTOGRAPHER
IPC Country & Leisure Group, King's Reach Tower, Stamford Street, London SE1 9LS.
Tel: 020 7261 5100. Fax: 020 7261 5404. E-mail: amateurphotographer@ipcmedia.com
Editor: Garry Coward-Williams.
Weekly magazine for all photographers, from beginners to experienced enthusiasts.
Illustrations: B&W and colour. Pictures to illustrate specific photo techniques and general photo features. Series ideas welcomed. General portfolios in B&W and colour. Send no more than 20 pictures, prints unmounted, slides in a plastic slide wallet.
Text: Technique articles on all types of photography. Picture captions on a separate sheet. 1,000–1,500 words.
Overall freelance potential: Good. Around half of photography comes from freelance sources.
Fees: £50 per published page, pictures and text.

BLACK & WHITE PHOTOGRAPHY
GMC Publications Ltd, 86 High Street, Lewes, East Sussex BN7 1XN.
Tel: 01273 477374. Fax: 01273 402849. E-mail: ailsam@thegmcgroup.com
Editor: Ailsa McWhinnie.
Monthly magazine devoted to showcasing the best in black and white photography.
Illustrations: B&W only. Features and portfolios showcasing the work of individual photographers, usually a cohesive body of work on a specific subject or theme. Regular "Reader Gallery" feature devotes two pages per reader/contributor. Photojournalistic work of particular interest, especially long-term projects produced over an extended period. Also step by step features showing all stages from a straight print to the final print. Digital techniques also covered. Little scope for single images.
Text: Illustrated articles on printing techniques, film/paper combinations, equipment choices, etc. Submit sample prints and synopsis in the first instance.
Overall freelance potential: Excellent for the dedicated B&W worker.
Fees: £100 for "Gallery" feature; other fees according to subject and use.

BRITISH JOURNAL OF PHOTOGRAPHY
Incisive Media, Haymarket House, 28-29 Haymarket, London SW1Y 4RX.
Tel: 020 7484 9700. Fax: 020 7484 9988. E-mail: bjp.editor@bjphoto.co.uk
Editor: Simon Bainbridge.
Weekly publication for professional and semi-professional photographers, technicians, etc., and all those engaged in professional photography.
Illustrations: B&W and colour. Portfolios along with some biographical notes about the photographer concerned.
Text: Interested in anything related to professional photography, particularly the more unusual and technical aspects.
Overall freelance potential: Good for bringing freelances to the attention of potential clients.
Editor's tips: Contributors do need to offer something special. Remember the magazine is aimed at those engaged in professional and semi-professional photography – technical features must therefore be of the highest calibre.

Fees: Portfolios not normally paid for; exposure in the magazine frequently leads to commissions elsewhere. Negotiable for text.

CAMCORDER USER
Highbury-WV, 53-79 Highgate Road, London NW5 1TW.
Tel: 020 7331 1000. Fax: 020 7331 1242.
Editor: Robert Hull. **Art Editor:** Steve Chamberlaine.
Monthly magazine for buyers and users of camcorders, with a practical bias.
Illustrations: B&W and colour. General shots of camcorders in use, shots to illustrate technique and advice features. Good colour pictures of camcorders in use at various locations especially welcomed, eg on the beach, at sports events, at social occasions, on expeditions. Also pictures of editing and post-production equipment in use. Spectacular location shots may also be considered.
Text: Technique articles on producing better video movies, tests on machines and accessories, action and application features, equipment reviews and personality interviews.
Overall freelance potential: Excellent. Around 50 per cent from such sources.
Fees: By agreement.

DIGITAL CAMERA MAGAZINE
Future Digital, Beauford Court, 30 Monmouth Street, Bath BA1 2BW.
Tel: 01225 442244. Fax: 01225 732295. E-mail: editor.dcm@futurenet.co.uk
Editor: Adam Evans.
Monthly for the mid-market of digital camera users, those mainly using digital compacts in the £400–£800 price range.
Illustrations: B&W and colour. Good single images required to illustrate seasonal subjects and topical events, for "Images with Impact" gallery section, and as examples of creative digital manipulations/compositions. Should be accompanied by detailed captions.
Text: Well-illustrated "how to" articles on digital photography and image editing. Contributors need to have some prior experience of producing such material.
Overall freelance potential: Good.
Editor's tips: Contributors should supply as much background detail about their images as they can.
Fees: Single images by negotiation and according to use; features £80 per published page.

DIGITAL PHOTO
EMAP Active Ltd, Bretton Court, Bretton, Peterborough PE3 8DZ.
Tel: 01733 264666. Fax: 01733 465246. E-mail: dp@emap.com
Editor: Jon Adams.
Monthly aimed at photographers keen to use their computer to enhance their pictures.
Illustrations: B&W and colour. Need for high-quality – technically and pictorially – original images that inspire readers to produce similar work. Ideally submissions should be accompanied by step-by-step screengrabs and words illustrating the thought processes and the stages involved in producing the work. Creative work always needed for the portfolio pages; require ten outstanding digitally manipulated images.
Text: Good potential for quality, step-by-step tutorials, but the final image must be outstanding and relevant. Contact editor in the first instance.
Overall freelance potential: Excellent for step-by-step tutorials.
Editor's tips: Look at and read the magazine first, then e-mail ideas and low-resolution JPEGs to illustrate. If submitting on CD always enclose high-quality inkjet prints too.
Fees: Negotiable, but typically £60 per page or £120 per 1,000 words.

DIGITAL PHOTOGRAPHER
Highbury Entertainment Ltd, Paragon House, St Peters Road, Bournemouth BH1 2JS.
Tel: 01202 299900. Fax: 01202 299955. E-mail: michaelr@paragon.co.uk
Editor: Michael Roscoe. **Picture Editor:** Janine Kay.

Digital photography magazine for the more advanced user, aimed at serious enthusiasts and professionals.
Illustrations: B&W and colour. Dgital submission preferred. Pictures mainly required to illustrate features on aspects of digital equipment, software and processes – little scope for single images in their own right. Opportunities best for photographers using digital for specialist subjects (landscape, wildlife, portraiture, etc) or those experienced in Photoshop techniques.
Text: Practical illustrated articles and features on topics as above.
Overall freelance potential: Good for those with well-developed skills in digital work.
Fees: Negotiable, depending on what is on offer.

DIGITAL PHOTOGRAPHY TECHNIQUES
Future Digital, Beauford Court, 30 Monmouth Street, Bath BA1 2BW.
Tel: 01225 442244. Fax: 01225 732295. E-mail: chris.bates@futurenet.co.uk
Editor: Dan Oliver. **Art Editor:** Chris Bates.
Monthly magazine concentrating on digital editing and manipulation techniques.
Illustrations: B&W and colour. Striking images that display digital editing skills and specific techniques, both single images with "before/after" illustrations and sequences demonstrating how effects were achieved.
Text: Fully-illustrated, step-by-step features on specific digital editing techniques.
Overall freelance potential: Excellent – all contributions are freelance.
Fees: By negotiation.

EOS MAGAZINE
Robert Scott Publishing Ltd, The Old Barn, Ball Lane, Tackley, Kidlington, Oxon OX5 3AG.
Tel: 01869 331741. Fax: 01869 331641. E-mail: editorial@eos-magazine.com
Editor: Angela August.
Quarterly magazine for users of Canon EOS cameras.
Illustrations: Mostly colour, but B&W considered. Digital media preferred. Top quality photographs of any subject taken with Canon EOS cameras. Should demonstrate some aspect of photographic technique or the use of equipment. Comparison shots always of interest.
Text: Contributions are welcomed.
Overall freelance potential: Very good.
Editor's tips: Up-to-date details of photo requirements available on request. Phone or E-mail to discuss ideas for written contributions.
Fees: Text: £90–£150 per 1,000 words (higher rates are for technique material which is comprehensive and well researched). Minimum fee for pictures is £10, but most are paid at between £15 and £50 depending on usage. Cover and dps, £100-£250.

EPHOTOZINE
Pixel House, PO Box 197, Worksop S80 1YZ.
Tel: 01909 488305. Fax: 01909 489451. E-mail: peter@ephotozine.com
Web: www.ephotozine.com
Editor: Peter Bargh.
Free online photography magazine aimed at photographers at all levels and covering all aspects.
Illustrations: B&W and colour. Digital media essential. Images of all types to illustrate all aspects of photography, from basic exposure and composition to advanced lighting and manipulation techniques. Always contact by e-mail before submitting. Large gallery section allows for uploading of images for feedback from other users.
Text: Well-illustrated features on any aspect of imaging – how-to articles, step-by-step techniques, comparison tests, etc. Submit suggestions only in the first instance.
Overall freelance potential: Excellent.
Fees: Negotiable according to use, or links to contributor's website, gallery or business may be offered in lieu of payment.

f2
Icon Publications Ltd, Maxwell Lane, Kelso, Roxburghshire TD5 7BB.
Tel: 01573 226032. Fax: 01573 26000. E-mail: iconmags@btconnect.com
Editor: David Kilpatrick.
Bi-monthly magazine for all involved in freelance photography, from serious amateurs to professionals.
Illustrations: B&W and colour. Digital files preferred. Mostly required to accompany and illustrate specific articles. Limited scope for outstanding single pictures and portfolios.
Text: Illustrated articles and features on all aspects of serious amateur and professional freelance photography.
Overall freelance potential: Very good.
Editor's tips: Always make contact before submitting.
Fees: Features £60 per page; single pictures up to £75; profiles/portfolios £150; Covers £75.

HOTSHOE INTERNATIONAL
World Illustrated Ltd, 29-31 Saffron Hill, London EC1N 8SW.
Tel: 020 7421 6000. Fax: 020 7421 6006. E-mail: hotshoe@photoshot.com
Editor: Charles Taylor.
Monthly for commercial photographers working in advertising, design and photojournalism.
Illustrations: B&W and colour. Digital submission preferred. Will consider anything that illustrates interesting uses of photography in commercial contexts. Also unusual or interesting images of photographers at work.
Text: Illustrated features on any aspect of commercial work, with the emphasis on the business angles.
Overall freelance potential: Very good for the right material.
Editor's tips: Contributions need to be of real interest to other working photographers.
Fees: By negotiation.

MARKET NEWSLETTER
Bureau of Freelance Photographers, Focus House, 497 Green Lanes, London N13 4BP.
Tel: 020 8882 3315. Fax: 020 8886 5174. E-mail: eds@thebfp.com
Editor: John Tracy.
Monthly journal of the BFP, mainly devoted to detailing markets for photography. For members only.
Illustrations: B&W and colour. Photographs required for "Pictures that Sell" feature – photographs taken by BFP members that have proven commercial success, having earned high fees and/or having sold to a wide range of markets.
Text: Photographer profiles in which a successful photographer outlines his or her freelance activities, or general features on aspects of selling photography, backed up with examples of successful pictures and hints and tips to encourage others. Around 1,000 words.
Overall freelance potential: Limited.
Fees: £30 for "Pictures that Sell", £100 for photographer profile/feature.

OUTDOOR PHOTOGRAPHY
GMC Publications, 86 High Street, Lewes, East Sussex BN7 1XN.
Tel: 01273 477374. Fax: 01273 478606. keithw@thegmcgroup.com
Editor: Keith Wilson.
Monthly devoted to the photography of all types of outdoor subject matter.
Illustrations: Mainly colour. Top-quality photographs of British landscapes, countryside, wildlife, gardens, architecture and travel abroad. Scope for good single images in the "Reader's Pictures" gallery section, but prefer packages of both words and pictures.
Text: Well-illustrated articles on all aspects of outdoor photography, accompanied by full background details on location or subject.

Overall freelance potential: Excellent; the magazine relies on freelances contributors.
Editor's tips: The magazine is seasonally-led, so subject matter needs to be relevant to the month of publication.
Fees: By negotiation.

PENTAX USER
Pixel House, PO Box 197, Worksop S80 1YZ.
Tel: 01909 489451. Fax: 01909 489451. E-mail: peter@pentaxuser.co.uk
Web: www.pentaxuser.co.uk
Editor: Peter Bargh.
Exclusive magazine for members of the Pentax User club. Features techniques reviews and how-to articles on all areas of photography with an emphasis on Pentax camera equipment.
Illustrations: B&W and colour. Film or digital accepted. Images mainly required for cover – any image that is taken on a Pentax, with space available to allow logo to appear top right and tasters bottom left. Other images usually only as part of a complete package of words and pictures.
Text: Well-illustrated articles on all aspects of photography with an emphasis on Pentax camera equipment. How-to articles on using modes of compacts and SLRs particularly sought after, along with techniques on using flash, lenses, filters etc. Please submit suggestions in writing in first instance. The editor will then phone or reply to discuss commission.
Overall freelance potential: Most of the magazine is based on articles from club members or freelances.
Fees: £50 per published page.

PHOTOGRAPHY MONTHLY
Archant Specialist, Barber House, Storeys Bar Road, Peterborough PE1 5YS.
Tel: 0845 650 1065. Fax: 01733 558623. E-mail: photography.monthly@photographymonthly.co.uk
Editor: Daniel Lezano.
Magazine for the general enthusiast, with the emphasis on helping readers improve their own photography.
Illustrations: B&W and colour. High quality photography of all types – action, portraits, still life, architecture, travel, wildlife, etc. Also images to illustrating photographic techniques, use of specific equipment, comparison shots, image manipulation, special film effects, etc.
Text: Mostly produced by regular contributors but ideas always considered.
Overall freelance potential: Excellent.
Fees: According to use, from £20–£100 per picture.

PRACTICAL PHOTOGRAPHY
EMAP Active Ltd, Bretton Court, Bretton, Peterborough PE3 8DZ.
Tel: 01733 264666. Fax: 01733 465246. E-mail: practical.photography@emap.com
Editor: Andrew James.
Monthly magazine aimed at all photographers, with news, interviews, equipment tests , etc. Growing ermphasis on digital imaging techniques.
Illustrations: B&W and colour. Photographs of any subject considered for general illustration and for the magazine's files. Images should have strong impact and be original, also illustrating some aspect of photographic technique – use of filters, shooting at the right time of day, camera viewpoint, etc. Colour and B&W portfolios regularly featured.
Text: Some potential, but contact editor or associate editor in the first instance. Will use writers who can offer something the staff writers can't.
Overall freelance potential: Excellent for pictures and digital techniques; fewer opportunities for words but ideas still welcome.
Editor's tips: Read the magazine and study the pictures; if you can produce comparable work, send it in.
Fees: Negotiable but typically £80 per page and £120 per 1,000 words.

PROFESSIONAL PHOTOGRAPHER
Archant Specialist, PO Box 78, Saffron Walden, Essex CB11 4GB.
Tel: 01799 544246. Fax: 01799 544201. E-mail: steve.hynes@professionalphotographer.co.uk
Editor: Terry Hope.
Monthly magazine for professional photographers.
Illustrations: B&W and colour. Digital submission preferred. Only with features as below.
Text: Techniques, equipment, business skills and general issues of interest to professional photographers. Check with the editor before submitting.
Overall freelance potential: Good – for the right material appropriately written.
Editor's tips: The magazine appeals to readers who find other magazines too superficial. It is therefore more important than ever that potential contributors study recent issues.
Fees: From £200 per article, words and pictures.

TOTAL DIGITAL PHOTOGRAPHY
Archant Specialist, The Mill, Bearwalden Business Park, Wendens Ambo, Saffron Walden, Essex CB11 4GB.
Tel: 01799 544200. Fax: 01799 544201. E-mail: tdp@archant.co.uk
Editor: William Cheung FPRS.
Monthly for all digital photography enthusiasts.
Illustrations: B&W and colour. Digital files preferred. Always keen to see excellent examples of digital imaging. Best opportunities with digitally-manipulated images.
Text: will consider proposals for articles about all aspects of digital imaging techniques and software, though most is staff-produced.
Overall freelance potential: Good.
Editor's tips: The magazine wants images that can inspire readers to produce similar efforts with their own work. Ideally contributors need to be able to show how their images were produced in a step-by-step manner.
Fees: Single pictures from £20–£75; other material by negotiation.

WHAT DIGITAL CAMERA
IPC Country & Leisure Group, King's Reach Tower, Stamford Street, London SE1 9LS.
Tel: 020 7261 7284. Fax: 020 7261 5398. E-mail: wdc@ipcmedia.com
Editor: Nigel Atherton.
Monthly consumer magazine for digital photography enthusiasts.
Illustrations: Mostly colour. Digital media preferred. Will consider original, creative, digital images, preferably digitally originated rather than manipulations from conventional film.
Text: Illustrated features about the techniques and applications of digital cameras, especially the use of the technology in work contexts.Contact editor with suggestions first.
Overall freelance potential: Fair.
Fees: Pictures by negotiation and according to use. Text £100 per 1,000 words.

Politics & Current Affairs

THE BIG ISSUE
1-5 Wandsworth Road, London SW8 2LN.
Tel: 020 7526 3200. Fax: 020 7526 3241.
Editor: Matt Ford. **Art Editor:** Charles Howgego.
Current affairs weekly sold in support of the homeless.
Illustrations: B&W and colour. Broad range of mainly news-based images covering politics, social issues and the arts. For hard news pictures contact the news desk; for general feature photography contact the art director.

Text: Suitable reportage-type features always considered. usually around 1,200 with with 2-3 illustrations.
Overall freelance potential: Very good for the right sort of material.
Fees: By negotiation.

THE ECOLOGIST
Unit 18, Chelsea Wharf, 15 Lots Road, London SW10 0QJ.
Tel: 020 7351 3578. Fax: 020 7351 3617. E-mail: design@theecologist.org
Editor: Zac Goldsmith. **Art Director:** Peter Bishop.
Monthly magazine covering all ecological and environmental topics.
Illustrations: Mainly colour. News pictures and images to illustrate features on current environmental or ethical concerns.
Text: News items and articles on relevant topical issues. Contributors must have good, in-depth knowledge of their subject.
Overall freelance potential: Fair.
Fees: According to use.

THE ECONOMIST
The Economist Newspaper Ltd, 25 St James's Street, London SW1A 1HG.
Tel: 020 7830 7000. Fax: 020 7830 7130. E-mail: celinadunlop@economist.com
Editor: Bill Emmott. **Picture Editor:** Celina Dunlop.
Weekly publication covering world political, business and scientific affairs.
Illustrations: Colour. Pictures of politicians, businessmen, social conditions (housing, health service, etc), major industries (coal, steel, oil, motor, agriculture, etc). Always prepared to keep digital images for stock.
Text: All staff-produced.
Overall freelance potential: Only for serious and experienced photojournalists. Commissions not available.
Editor's tips: Telephone picture editor in the first instance.
Fees: On a rising scale according to size of reproduction inside.

JANE'S DEFENCE WEEKLY
Jane's Information Group, Sentinel House, 163 Brighton Road, Coulsdon, Surrey CR5 2YH.
Tel: 020 8700 3700. Fax: 020 8763 1007. E-mail: jdw@janes.com
Editor: Peter Felstead. **News Editor:** Ian Kemp.
News magazine concentrating on developments in all military fields.
Illustrations: Mainly colour. Digital media preferred. News pictures of defence subjects worldwide – exercises, deployments, equipment, etc. Contact the news editor initially.
Text: News items and informed articles on the military, industrial and political aspects of global defence.
Overall freelance potential: Limited for those without contacts in the forces or defence industry, but work submitted here may also be published in the various annuals produced by the Jane's Information Group.
Fees: Photographs £40 inside; covers negotiable; text from £200 per 1,000 words.

JEWISH CHRONICLE
Jewish Chronicle Newspapers Ltd, 25 Furnival Street, London EC4A 1JT.
Tel: 020 7415 1616. Fax: 020 7405 9040. E-mail: jceditor@thejc.com
Editor: Ned Temko.
Weekly newspaper publishing news and features concerning, and of interest to, the British Jewish community.
Illustrations: B&W and colour. Any topical pictures related to the purpose stated above. Also material for the paper's wide range of supplements that deal with subjects such as holidays, fashion, interior decoration, regional development, etc.

Text: Features on topics detailed above. 600–2,500 words.
Overall freelance potential: At least 30 per cent of the content comes from freelance sources.
Fees: By negotiation.

LIBERAL DEMOCRAT NEWS
Liberal Democrats, 4 Cowley Street, London SW1P 3NB.
Tel: 020 7227 1361. Fax: 020 7222 7904. E-mail: ldn@libdems.org
Editor: Deirdre Razzall.
Weekly tabloid newspaper of the Liberal Democrats.
Illustrations: B&W and colour. Prints or digital media accepted (no transparencies). Pictures of Liberal Democrat activities around the country and general political news pictures.
Text: News and features: politics, current affairs.
Overall freelance potential: Limited.
Fees: By negotiation.

THE MIDDLE EAST
IC Publications Ltd, 7 Coldbath Square, London EC1R 4LQ.
Tel: 020 7713 7711. Fax: 020 7713 7970. E-mail: p.lancaster@africasia.com
Editor: Pat Lancaster.
Monthly publication directed at senior management, governmental personnel and universities. Covers Middle Eastern current affairs of a political, cultural and economic nature.
Illustrations: B&W and colour. Digital media preferred. Pictures of all topical Middle Eastern subjects, personalities and scenes.
Text: Features on Middle Eastern subjects or world subjects that relate to the area. 1,000–3,000 words.
Overall freelance potential: Most of the pictures come from freelances and around 75 per cent of the overall editorial.
Fees: B&W pictures £15–£35; covers by agreement. Text, from £80 per 1,000 words.

MILAP WEEKLY/NAVIN WEEKLY
Masbro Centre, 87 Masbro Road, London W14 0LR.
Tel/fax: 020 7385 8966
Editors: Ramesh Soni/Ramesh Kumar.
Weekly news publications for Indian, Pakistani and Bangladeshi people. Published in Hindi (Navin) and Urdu (Milap).
Illustrations: B&W only. News pictures concerning topical immigrant matters, pictures of leading Asian personalities.
Text: News stories; all matters of interest to immigrant Asian communities.
Overall freelance potential: Good for those in touch with relevant communities.
Fees: By negotiation.

NEW INTERNATIONALIST
55 Rectory Road, Oxford OX4 1BW.
Tel: 01865 728181. Fax: 01865 793152. E-mail: ni_ed@newint.org
Co-Editors: (UK) Katharine Ainger, Vanessa Baird, David Ransom, Dinyar Godrej.
Monthly magazine covering global issues from a mainly Southern (Africa, Asia, Latin American) perspective.

Illustrations: B&W and colour. Digital files or film. Pictures to illustrate news stories and topical features on subjects such as social justice, human rights, environmental issues, poverty, sustainable development, etc.
Text: Illustrated stories and features on relevant topics as above.
Overall freelance potential: Good.
Editor's tips: Each editor edits individually themed issues and is responsible for his/her own picture research.
Fees: Pictures, from a minimum of £40 to £250 for front cover.

PCS VIEW
The Public & Commercial Services Union, 160 Falcon Road, Clapham, London SW11 2LN.
Tel: 020 7801 2746. Fax: 020 7801 2822. E-mail: editor@pcs.org.uk
Editor: Sharon Breen.
Monthly publication for members of the PCS Union, the biggest civil service union. Also has large private sector membership.
Illustrations: Colour. News pictures of trade union activity, especially involving members of PCS. Other topical pictures of current affairs that may impinge on Union members may also be of interest.
Text: No scope.
Overall freelance potential: Good, 75 per cent of pictures come from outside contributors.
Fees: Good; on a rising scale according to size of reproduction.

Railways

ENTRAIN
Platform 5 Publishing, 3 Wyvern House, Sark Road, Sheffield S2 4HG.
Tel: 0114 255 2625. Fax: 0114 255 2471. E-mail: platfive@platfive.freeserve.co.uk
Editor: Peter Fox.
Monthly covering the contemporary British railway scene, aimed at both rail professionals and enthusiasts.
Illustrations: Colour. News pictures relating to current or planned UK rail operations, accompanied by detailed captions or stories. Stock material may be of interest – send detailed lists in the first instance.
Text: Feature suggestions always considered, but only from writers who have in-depth knowledge of their subject.
Overall freelance potential: Limited, as much is obtained from industry sources.
Editor's tips: Always contact editor before submitting as many stories may already be covered.
Fees: Pictures from £15; text £75 per page.

HERITAGE RAILWAY
Mortons Heritage Media, PO Box 43, Horncastle, Lincs LN9 6JR.
Tel: 01507 529300. Fax: 01507 529301.
Editor: Robin Jones.
Monthly magazine devoted to railway preservation – steam, diesel and electric.
Illustrations: Mainly colour. Captioned news pictures depicting restoration projects, restored locomotives on their first runs, special events etc, especially from less well-known lines and museums. Mainly UK-based but will also consider overseas coverage of locomotives with a British connection, especially really "stunning and attractive" pictures.
Text: Well-illustrated features on preservation and restoration topics; write with suggestions first.
Overall freelance potential: Very good.
Fees: By negotiation.

INTERNATIONAL RAILWAY JOURNAL
Simmons-Boardman Publishing Corporation, PO Box 8, Falmouth, Cornwall TR11 4RJ.
Tel: 01326 313945. Fax: 01326 211576. E-mail: irj@railjournal.com
Editor: David Briginshaw.
Monthly publication for the principal officers of the railways of the world (including metro and light rail systems), ministers and commissioners of transport, railway equipment manufacturers and suppliers.
Illustrations: B&W and colour. Digital media preferred. Pictures of new line construction projects, electrification projects, track or signalling improvements, new locomotives, passenger coaches and freight wagons. Interesting pictures of railway operations from far-flung corners of the world. No steam or nostalgia material. Covers: colour shots tied in with the theme of a particular issue.
Text: Features on any sizeable contracts for railway equipment; plans for railway developments, eg new line construction, track or signalling improvements; almost anything which involves a railway spending money or making improvements and techniques. No padding or speculation.
Overall freelance potential: Quite good for the right business-oriented material.
Fees: Rising scale according to size of pictures; text, £120 per 1,000 words.

RAIL
EMAP Active Ltd, Bretton Court, Bretton, Peterborough PE3 8DZ.
Tel: 01733 264666. Fax: 01733 282720. E-mail: rail@emap.com
Editor: Nigel Harris.
Fortnightly magazine dealing with modern railways.
Illustrations: Mostly colour, some B&W. Single photographs and up-to-date news pictures on any interesting railway topic in Britain, particularly accidents and incidents of all kinds. Covers: Colour shots with strong impact.
Text: Illustrated articles of up to 1,500 words on any railway topic. Check recent issues for style.
Overall freelance potential: Excellent.
Editor's tips: Topicality is everything for news coverage. For other pictures try to get away from straightforward shots of trains; be imaginative. Always looking for something different.
Fees: Pictures range from £25–£70; illustrated articles around £90–£150. Will pay more for high-impact special pics that give the magazine a commercial advantage.

RAIL EXPRESS
Foursight Publishing, 20 Park Street, King's Cliffe, Peterborough PE8 6XN.
Tel: 01780 470086. Fax: 01780 470060. E-mail: editors@railexpress.co.uk
Editors: Murray Brown, Philip Sutton.
Monthly magazine for modern railway enthusiasts.
Illustrations: Mainly colour (prints acceptable). Any good or unusual photographs of the contemporary railway scene, but really need to be of current and newsworthy interest (new locomotives, new liveries, etc). Some scope for historic diesel/electric coverage.
Text: Suggestions for articles welcome, from anyone with good background knowledge of the subject, especially traction. Consult with the editor first.
Overall freelance potential: The magazine features lots of photography and always needs more.
Editor's tips: Topicality is the key.
Fees: From basic rate of £20 per picture.

RAILNEWS
Railnews Ltd, East Side Offices, King's Cross Station, London N1 9AP.
Tel: 020 7278 6100. Fax: 020 7278 6145. E-mail: newsdesk@railnews.co.uk
Editor: David Harding.
Monthly newspaper for people in the rail industry, covering the modern railway scene in the UK.

Illustrations: B&W and colour prints. Digital media preferred. Railway news pictures, unusual pictures of events, operations, activities, with good captions.
Text: No scope.
Overall freelance potential: Good.
Editor's tips: Approach before submitting.
Fees: By negotiation.

RAILWAY MAGAZINE
IPC Country & Leisure Media Ltd, King's Reach Tower, Stamford Street, London SE1 9LS.
Tel: 020 7261 5821. Fax: 020 7261 5269. E-mail: railway@ipcmedia.com
Editor: Nick Pigott.
Monthly for all rail enthusiasts, covering both main line and heritage railways, modern and historic.
Illustrations: Mostly colour, digital preferred. News pictures concerning the current rail network, as well as images from recent heritage events, galas or rail tours. Also pictures of new liveries, new trains on test, accidents/derailments, and rare or unusual workings. Previously unpublished material from the 1940s onwards always of interest for historical features. Top quality non-news pictures may be used for spreads and/or occasional calendars. Captions should be supplied on individual slide mounts or prints, not on separate caption sheet. For digital e-mail thumbnails (10 images max) in first instance; CDs (50 images max) must have thumbnail sheet.
Text: Well-researched illustrated articles on any British railway topic, current or historic; discuss ideas with the editor first.
Overall freelance potential: Excellent.
Editor's tips: News pictures must be recent – no more than six weeks old.
Fees: From £15 minimum for news pictures, to £50+ for larger reproductions.

STEAM RAILWAY
EMAP Active Ltd, Bretton Court, Bretton, Peterborough PE3 8DZ.
Tel: 01733 264666. Fax: 01733 282720. E-mail: steam.railway@emap.com
Editor: Tony Streeter.
Four-weekly magazine for the steam railway enthusiast. Closely concerned with railway preservation.
Illustrations: Mostly colour. Accurately captioned photographs depicting steam trains and railways past and present, preserved railway lines, and railway museums (topical subjects especially welcomed).
Text: Illustrated articles on relevant subjects.
Overall freelance potential: Most of the content is contributed by freelances.
Editor's tips: Material should be lively, topical and newsworthy, although some nostalgic or historic material is accepted.
Fees: By arrangement.

TRACTION
Warners Group Publications, The Maltings, West Street, Bourne, Lincs PE10 9PH.
Tel: 01778 391160. Fax: 01778 425437. E-mail: davidb@warnersgroup.co.uk
Managing Editor: David Brown.
Monthly magazine dedicated to diesel and electric locomotives past and present.
Illustrations: Mostly colour; B&W archive material. Photographs of classic diesels and electrics operating on British railways from the 1940s to the present day. Particular interest in archive shots from the earlier eras up to the early 1970s. More contemporary material should have a newsworthy angle.
Text: Nostalgic features, which should ideally include some technical interest, always considered.
Overall freelance potential: Good.
Fees: From £15–£50 according to size of reproduction.

Religion

CATHOLIC HERALD
Herald House, 15 Lamb's Passage, Bunhill Row, London EC1Y 8TQ.
Tel: 020 7588 3101. Fax: 020 7256 9728. E-mail: editorial@catholicherald.co.uk
Editor: Luke Coppen.
Weekly newspaper reflecting on Catholicism/Christianity and its place in the wider world, plus church news.
Illustrations: Colour and B&W. Digital media preferred. Principal need for news photographs of events involving churches, clerics or prominent Catholics.
Text: Articles of up to 1,200 words on the social, economic and political significance of the church domestically and internationally, plus spiritual and reflective writings.
Overall freelance potential: Better for features than other material.
Fees: By arrangement but not high.

CATHOLIC TIMES
Gabriel Communications Ltd, First Floor, St James Buildings, Oxford Street, Manchester M1 6FP.
Tel: 0161 236 8856. Fax: 0161 236 8530.
Editor: Kevin Flaherty.
Weekly newspaper covering Catholic affairs.
Illustrations: B&W and colour. Topical pictures of Catholic interest. Also off-beat devotional shots.
Text: News stories and short features. 900 words maximum.
Overall freelance potential: Very good.
Fees: Text around £40 per 1,000 words; pictures by negotiation.

CHRISTIAN HERALD
Christian Media Centre Ltd, Garcia Estate, Canterbury Road, Worthing, West Sussex BN13 1EH.
Tel: 01903 821082. Fax: 01903 821081. ISDN: 01903 537308. E-mail: news@christianherald.org.uk
Editor: Russ Bravo.
Weekly tabloid aimed at evangelical Christians.
Illustrations: Colour preferred. Digital media preferred. News events, people shots.
Text: Guidelines for contributors available.
Overall freelance potential: Some freelance pictures and articles used every week.
Fees: Negotiable, but usually £10–£40.

CHURCH OF ENGLAND NEWSPAPER
20-26 Brunswick Place, London N1 6DZ.
Tel: 020 7417 5800. Fax: 020 7216 6410. E-mail: cen@parlicom.com
Editor: Colin Blakely.
Weekly newspaper covering Anglican news and views.
Illustrations: B&W and colour. Colour print and digital accepted. Will consider any news pictures that relate to the Church of England.
Text: News stories, plus features that relate Christian faith to politics, the arts and everyday life. Up to 1,000 words, but submit ideas only in the first instance.
Overall freelance potential: Good for those with Church connections.
Fees: £20 – £40 per published picture; text about £40 per 1,000 words.

CHURCH TIMES
G.J.Palmer & Sons Ltd, 33 Upper Street, London N1 0PN.
Tel: 020 7359 4570. Fax: 020 7226 3073. E-mail: news@churchtimes.co.uk
Editor: Paul Handley.
Weekly newspaper covering Church of England affairs.
Illustrations: B&W and colour. Digital media preferred. Up-to-the-minute news pictures of

Anglican events and personalities. Detailed captions essential.
Text: Short articles on current religious topics; up to 1,000 words.
Overall freelance potential: Fair.
Editor's tips: It is preferred that people in pictures are engaged in activities rather than just looking at the camera.
Fees: Photographs according to use, average £70; text £100 per 1,000 words.

WOMAN ALIVE
Christian Media Centre, Garcia Estate, Canterbury Road, Worthing, West Sussex BN13 1EH.
Tel: 01903 821082. Fax: 01903 821081. E-mail: womanalive@christianmedia.org.uk
Editor: Jackie Stead.
Monthly publication for women with church links.
Illustrations: B&W and colour. Stock pictures of family life and parenting, nature, scenic views, people in various situations (holidays, jobs, festive occasions), news events, plus novelty and fun items.
Text: Limited freelance market.
Overall freelance potential: Quite good.
Fees: Variable.

Science & Technology

CHEMISTRY & INDUSTRY
Society of Chemical Industry, 15 Belgrave Square, London SW1X 8PS.
Tel: 020 7235 3681. Fax: 020 7235 9410. E-mail: enquiries@soci.org
Editor: Simon Robinson.
Fortnightly science and business magazine covering chemistry and related sciences, and the chemical, healthcare, food, biotech, environment and water industries.
Illustrations: Mostly colour. Photographs of chemical factories, chemistry research and environmental pollution, food, plants, water, people and places.
Text: News stories and articles from contributors with the requisite technical background.
Overall freelance potential: Limited.
Editor's tips: Always contact the editor before preparing any submission.
Fees: £250 per 1,000 words for text; photographs by negotiation.

EDUCATION IN CHEMISTRY
The Royal Society of Chemistry, Burlington House, Piccadilly, London W1J 0BA.
Tel: 020 7437 8656. Fax: 020 7437 8883. E-mail: esc@rsc.org
Editor: Kathryn Roberts.
Bi-monthly publication for teachers, lecturers in schools and universities, concerning all aspects of chemical education.
Illustrations: Colour. Digital media preferred. Pictures that deal with chemistry in the classroom, laboratories or the chemical industry. Covers: Pictures relating to specific articles inside.
Text: Features concerned with chemistry or the teaching of it. Under 2,500 words.
Overall freelance potential: Limited.
Fees: By agreement.

FOCUS
Origin Publishing, 14th Floor, Tower House, Fairfax Street, Bristol BS1 3BN.
Tel: 0117 927 9009. Fax: 0117 934 9008. E-mail: sallypalmer@originpublishing.co.uk
Editor: Paul Parsons. **Features Editor:** Sally Palmer.
General interest monthly covering popular science, technology, space exploration, medicine and the environment. Aimed at young, upmarket men.

Illustrations: Colour. Transparencies preferred for features, digital acceptable for smaller pieces. Will consider colour photo essays on subjects as above. Also contributions for "Picture This" double-page spread, depicting an interesting or unusual aspect of contemporary life, science, gadgets and general interest.
Text: Interesting features on subjects above always considered. Submit a synopsis first.
Overall freelance potential: Fair.
Editor's tips: Only top quality material is considered; study the magazine before submitting.
Fees: Negotiable; generally good.

NEW SCIENTIST
Reed Business Information, 84 Theobalds Road, London WC1X 8RR.
Tel: 020 7611 1200. Fax: 020 7611 1250. E-mail: alison.lawn@newscientist.com
Editor: Jeremy Webb. **Art Editor:** Alison Lawn.
Weekly magazine about science and technology for people with some scientific or technical education and also for the intelligent layman.
Illustrations: B&W and colour. Pictures on any topic that can be loosely allied to science and technology. Particularly interested in news photographs related to scientific phenomena and events. Covers: usually connected with a feature inside.
Text: News and features on scientific/technical subjects that might appeal to a wide audience.
Overall freelance potential: A lot of freelance work used, but consult the magazine before submitting.
Fees: Photographs on a rising scale according to size of reproduction. Text £150 per 1,000 words.

T3
Future Publishing Ltd, 99 Baker Street, London W1U 6FP.
Tel: 020 7317 2686. Fax: 020 7317 2433. E-mail: t3@futurenet.co.uk
Editor: James Beechinor-Collins. **Art Editor:** Stuart James.
Monthly technology and gadget magazine aimed primarily at young men.
Illustrations: Colour. Always interested in pictures of new technology and new designs for consumer durables, especially exclusive shots of latest developments, pre-production models, new releases etc. Also general stock of any technology-related subject.
Text: Mainly staff produced but exclusive news items on new products always of interest.
Overall freelance potential: Fair
Fees: By negotiation. Will pay top rates for exclusives.

Sport

ADRENALIN
Media Cell Ltd, 10-16 Tiller Road, London E14 8PX.
Tel: 020 7987 6166. Fax: 020 7538 4999.
Editor: Michael Fordham.
Quarterly covering skate, surf and snow culture.
Illustrations: Colour. Top quality photography of relevant sports, plus reportage, lifestyle images, fashion and music. Some commissions available for location shoots; write first with details of experience.
Text: Ideas for illustrated features always considered.
Overall freelance potential: Excellent.
Fees: By negotiation.

AIR GUNNER
Romsey Publishing Company, 3 The Courtyard, Denmark Street, Wokingham, Berkshire RG40 2AZ.
Tel: 011897 71677. Fax: 011897 72903. E-mail: nigela@romseypublishing.com
Managing Editor: Nigel Allen.
Monthly magazine for all airgun enthusiasts.
Illustrations: Colour. Illustrated news items, and stock shots of small field animals (rats, rabbits) and pest species of birds (pigeons, magpies, crows). Covers: colour, usually commissioned, but a speculative picture might be used.
Text: Articles on any aspect of airgun use, 700–1,000 words, and accompanied by a good selection of transparencies.
Overall freelance potential: Good for file photos and well illustrated articles.
Fees: In the region of £50 per published page.

ALL OUT CRICKET
TriNorth Ltd, Unit 504, The Chandlery, 50 Westminster Bridge Road, London SE1 7QY.
Tel: 020 7953 7473. E-mail: aff@alloutcricket.co.uk/matt@alloutcricket.co.uk
Editors: Andy Afford, Matt Thacker.
Official magazine of the Professional Cricketer's Association. Published 10 times a year.
Illustrations: Colour. Assignments available to shoot individual cricketers or teams for profiles – submit details of experience and areas covered by e-mail in the first instance. No scope for stock images, which are supplied via agency contract.
Text: Suggestions for profiles and features always considered.
Overall freelance potential: Fair.
Fees: By negotiation.

ATHLETICS WEEKLY
Descartes Publishing, 83 Park Road, Peterborough PE1 2TN.
Tel: 01733 898440. Fax: 01733 898441. ISDN: 01733 349199.
E-mail: jason.henderson@athletics-weekly.co.uk
Editor: Jason Henderson.
Weekly news magazine for the competitive and aspiring athlete. Focuses on events and results.
Illustrations: Colour. Digital media preferred. Coverage of athletics events at grass roots level, such as area championships, rather than top events (the latter are supplied by agency photographers). Always interested in anything out of the ordinary, such as well-known athletes off the track or in unusual situations.
Text: No scope.
Overall freelance potential: Fair.
Editor's tips: Freelances aware of what is happening locally can often obtain coverage missed by the nationals and agencies – top athletes "dropping in" to take part in local events etc.
Fees: According to size of reproduction, from £15 – £30. Published pictures frequently gain extra sales via reader requests.

BADMINTON
Connect Sports Ltd, 14 Woking Road, Cheadle Hulme, Cheshire SK8 6NZ.
Tel: 0161 485 4790. Fax: 0161 485 2728.
Editor: William Kings.
The only magazine in the UK devoted to badminton. Published quarterly.
Illustrations: B&W and colour. Will consider good action coverage, sports fashion, health material.
Text: Little scope for writing on the sport itself, but will consider articles on sports fashion, health, fitness and diet. 750–1,000 words.
Overall freelance potential: Limited.
Fees: £25 for B&W; £50 for colour. Text by agreement.

BOXING MONTHLY
40 Morpeth Road, London E9 7LD.
Tel: 020 8986 4141. Fax: 020 8986 4145.
Editor: Glyn Leach.
Heavily illustrated publication for boxing enthusiasts, covering both professional and amateur boxing.
Illustrations: B&W and colour. Coverage of boxing at all levels, including the amateur scene.
Text: Knowledgeable articles, features, interviews, etc. on any aspect of the boxing scene. Always contact the editor in the first instance.
Overall freelance potential: Excellent scope for boxing specialists, and for good amateur boxing coverage.
Fees: By negotiation.

CLIMBER
Warners Group Publications plc, The Maltings, West Street, Bourne, Lincs PE10 9PH.
Tel: 01778 391117. Fax: 01778 394748.
Editor: Bernard Newman.
Monthly magazine dealing with world-wide climbing from Lakeland fells to Everest. Highly literate readership. Contributors range from "unknowns" to top climbers like Chris Bonington.
Illustrations: Mostly colour. First ascents and newsworthy events but, in the main, used only with text. Covers: action shots of climbers or dramatic mountain pictures.
Text: Features on rock climbing, Alpinism, high altitude climbing, mountain skiing (not downhill racing). 1,500–2,000 words.
Overall freelance potential: Good; 90 per cent of articles and 100 per cent of pictures come from freelances, but many are regulars.
Editor's tips: This is a specialist field and is full of good writer/photographers. There is potential for the freelance to break in, but the magazine is heavily commissioned and usually well stocked with material.
Fees: Variable.

DARTS WORLD
World Magazines Ltd, 28 Arrol Road, Beckenham, Kent BR3 4PA.
Tel: 020 8650 6580. Fax: 020 8650 4343. E-mail: dartsworld@blueyonder.co.uk
Editor: Tony Wood.
Monthly magazine for darts players and organisers.
Illustrations: B&W and colour. Pictures on any darts theme, action shots and portraits of leading players. Good colour material also required for the annual Darts Player.
Text: Features on all darts subjects.
Overall freelance potential: Most of the copy and pictures comes from freelances.
Editor's tips: The darts-playing environment is often dim and smoky, which can make it difficult to produce bright, interesting pictures. Photographers who can come up with colourful shots that catch the eye are welcomed.
Fees: Good, on a rising scale according to size of reproduction or length of feature.

DIVE
Dive International, 83-84 George Street, Richmond, Surrey TW9 1HE.
Tel: 020 8940 0555. Fax: 020 8332 9307. E-mail: simon@dive.uk.com
Editor: Simon Rogerson. **Art Editor:** Alistair Cook.
Monthly magazine for divers and underwater enthusiasts.

Illustrations: Colour. Top-quality underwater photography, usually published within photojournalistic features. Most interested in material that tells a story and involves people, with images showing divers in action.
Text: Features as above.
Overall freelance potential: Excellent for underwater specialists.
Editor's tips: Good quality material from British waters stands a good chance of being published, as this is harder to find than that from clearer waters abroad.
Fees: £150 per published page.

F1 RACING
Haymarket Publishing Ltd, 60 Waldegrave Road, Teddington TW11 8LG..
Tel: 020 8267 5806. Fax: 020 8267 5022. E-mail: eddie.judd@haynet.com
Editor: Matt Bishop. **Art Editor:** Alison Lane. **Picture Editor:** Eddie Judd.
Glossy monthly devoted to Formula One motor racing.
Illustrations: Mainly colour. All coverage of Formula One, past and present; those with collections of relevant material should send lists. Commissions available to experienced portrait and reportage photographers who can deliver high quality whatever the circumstances – contact picture editor to show portfolio.
Text: Will always consider ideas for any F1 related material, which should always be discussed with the editor before submission.
Overall freelance potential: Good.
Editor's tips: Write or e-mail first, don't phone.
Fees: Set rates, from £60 minimum to £230 full page, £320 dps, £400 cover.

FIGHTERS
Peterson Publications Ltd, Peterson House, Northbank, Berryhill Industrial Estate, Droitwich, Worcestershire WR9 9BL.
Tel: 01905 795564. Fax: 01905 795905.
Editor: Tim Ayling.
Monthly magazine for martial arts and similar disciplines.
Illustrations: B&W and colour. Coverage of events, clubs and individuals and any general martial arts interests.
Text: Features on martial arts events, profiles of clubs and individuals and any other martial arts interests. 500–3,500 words.
Overall freelance potential: Quite good.
Fees: By negotiation.

FIRST DOWN
Independent Magazines Ltd, Independent House, 191 Marsh Wall, London E14 9RS.
Tel: 020 7005 5041. Fax: 020 7005 5075. E-mail: firstdown@indmags.co.uk
Editor: Keith Webster.
Weekly newspaper covering American football, in the UK, Europe and USA.
Illustrations: Mostly colour. News pictures and personality portraits from the British scene.
Text: Short news items, match reports, and profiles or interview features.
Overall freelance potential: Quite good.
Fees: According to use.

FOURFOURTWO
Haymarket Leisure Magazines Ltd, 38-42 Hampton Road, Teddington, Middlesex TW11 0JE.
Tel: 020 8267 5339. Fax: 020 8267 5354. E-mail: 442pictures@haynet.com
Editor: Mat Snow. **Picture Editor:** Richard Lawrence.
Monthly magazine aimed at the adult soccer fan.
Illustrations: Mainly colour. Especially interested in exclusive or unusual shots of footballers and

football people. Always interested to know of good stock collections, both current and historic. Commissions possible for photographers with at least some sports experience – submit samples of work via e-mail in the first instance.
Text: Some scope for specialists.
Overall freelance potential: Quite good but best for specialists.
Fees: According to size of reproduction, based on page rate of £200. Text £100–£175 per 1,000 words.

GOLF MONTHLY
IPC Media Ltd, King's Reach Tower, Stamford Street, London SE1 9LS.
Tel: 020 7261 7237. Fax: 020 7261 7240. E-mail: golfmonthly@ipcmedia.com
Editor: Jane Carter. **Art Editor:** Chris Swales.
Monthly international consumer magazine for golfers.
Illustrations: Colour. Mainly for use as illustrations to articles. Small market for one-off pictures from golf tournaments of golf-related events.
Text: Illustrated features on instruction and other golf-related topics. Also in-depth profiles of leading world players. Around 2,000 words, but not critical.
Overall freelance potential: Most of the magazine is commissioned. Room for more material of the right type from freelances.
Editor's tips: This is an international magazine so material must have a wide appeal. No features of a parochial nature.
Fees: By agreement.

GOLF WEEKLY
EMAP Active Ltd, Bushfield House, Orton Centre, Peterborough PE2 5UW.
Tel: 01733 288034. Fax: 01733 288025. E-mail: peter.masters@emap.com
Editor: Peter Masters.
Weekly magazine featuring general news and tournament reports from the professional and top amateur end of the sport.
Illustrations: Colour. Prints accepted; digital media preferred. News pictures and general coverage from top amateur and professional tour events. All with detailed captions.
Text: Will always consider suggestions for illustrated features.
Overall freelance potential: Around 40% is from freelance sources.
Fees: According to size of reproduction or length of text.

GOLF WORLD
EMAP Active Ltd, Bushfield House, Orton Centre, Peterborough PE2 5UW.
Tel: 01733 237111. Fax: 01733 288025. E-mail: paul.ewen@emap.com
Editor-in-Chief: David Clarke. **Art Director:** Paul Ewen.
Monthly publication for golfers, covering all aspects of the sport.
Illustrations: Mostly colour. Unusual golfing pictures always of interest.
Text: Profiles of leading golfers and general or instructional features. 1,500–2,000 words.
Overall freelance potential: Around 20 per cent comes from freelance sources.
Fees: By agreement.

INTERNATIONAL RUGBY NEWS
Independent Magazines Ltd, Independent House, 191 Marsh Wall, London E14 9RS.
Tel: 020 7005 5077. Fax: 020 7005 5075. E-mail: intrugbynews@indmags.co.uk
Editor: Graeme Gillespie.
Monthly rugby magazine covering all levels of the sport.
Illustrations: Almost exclusively colour. Coverage at the top level is usually obtained from agency sources, so scope for the freelance is mostly at local and "grass roots" level, including school tournaments.
Text: Articles and local match reports may be considered, but always query the editor first.

Overall freelance potential: Fair.
Editor's tips: The different picture with really good action, at whatever level, will always be of interest.
Fees: By negotiation.

MARTIAL ARTS ILLUSTRATED
Martial Arts Ltd, 8 Revenue Chambers, St Peter Street, Huddersfield, West Yorkshire HD1 1EL.
Tel: 01484 435011. Fax: 01484 422177.
Editor: Bob Sykes.
Monthly magazine covering all forms of Oriental fighting and self-defence techniques.
Illustrations: B&W and colour. Single pictures or sets depicting well-known martial artists, club events, tournament action and aspects of technique.
Text: Well-illustrated articles on any relevant subject – profiles of leading figures and individual clubs, interviews, technique sequences and self-defence features.
Overall freelance potential: Excellent for those with access to the martial arts scene.
Editor's tips: Always write in the first instance with suggestions.
Fees: Should be negotiated before submission, as many contributions are supplied free of charge.

MATCH
EMAP Active Ltd, Bushfield House, Orton Centre, Peterborough PE2 5UW.
Tel: 01733 237111. Fax: 01733 288150.
Editor: Simon Caney.
Weekly publication looking at the whole spectrum of soccer. Aimed at readers in the 9–15 age group.
Illustrations: Colour. Good soccer action shots, generally featuring top players. Usually bought only after consultation with the editor. Covers: top quality colour action.
Text: Profiles and interviews concerning personalities in the soccer field. Length by arrangement.
Overall freelance potential: Limited – most is staff or agency produced.
Fees: By agreement.

THE NON-LEAGUE PAPER
Greenways Media Ltd, Tuition House, St George's Road, Wimbledon, London SW19 4DS.
Tel: 020 8971 4333. Fax:020 8971 4366. ISDN: 020 8605 2391. E-mail: nlp@greenwaysmedia.co.uk
Editor: David Emery. **Production Editor:** John Cleal.
Twice-weekly tabloid covering the non-league soccer scene, carrying mid-week match reports and previews every Friday and full match reports every Sunday.
Illustrations: Mainly colour. Digital files required. Always interested in hearing from capable football photographers able to produce regular coverage of their local teams, but must have the ability/facilities to send material direct via modem on the Saturday night. Submit details of experience and area covered in the first instance.
Text: No scope – all staff or agency produced.
Overall freelance potential: Much is produced by freelance regulars but replacements are often needed.
Fees: According to assignment and/or use.

RACING PIGEON PICTORIAL
The Racing Pigeon Publishing Co. Ltd, 127 High Street, Farnborough Village, Kent BR6 7AZ.
Tel: 01689 600006. Fax: 01689 811580.
Editor: Steve Dunn.
Monthly magazine for pigeon fanciers. Provides in-depth articles on methods, successful fanciers, scientific information, etc.
Illustrations: B&W and colour. Pictures to illustrate features, plus some one-off pictures of pigeons. Covers: colour pictures of pigeons, pigeon lofts, pigeon fanciers and related subjects.
Text: Features on subjects as above, from contributors with serious knowledge of the sport. 1,500 words.

Overall freelance potential: Around 10–15 per cent of the pictures come from freelance photographers. Articles are mostly by specialist writers.
Editor's tips: Short, colourful, exotic articles with good illustrations stand a reasonable chance.
Fees: £20 per published page minimum.

RUGBY WORLD
IPC Media Ltd, King's Reach Tower, Stamford Street, London SE1 9LS.
Tel: 020 7261 6823. Fax: 020 7261 5419.
Editor: Paul Morgan. **Art Editor:** Kevin Eason.
Britain's biggest selling monthly rugby magazine giving general coverage of Rugby Union.
Illustrations: Mostly colour. Digital media preferred. Main scope is for regional/local coverage, since the top level matches are covered by regulars. Photographs of Cup matches, County championships, personalities, off-beat shots, etc. Covers: colour action shots of top players.
Text: Dependent on quality and appeal.
Overall freelance potential: Good articles with different angles are always of interest.
Fees: On a rising scale according to size of reproduction or length of text.

RUNNER'S WORLD
Natmag-Rodale, 6th Floor, 33 Broadwick Street, London W1F 0DQ.
Tel: 020 7339 4400. Fax: 020 7339 4420.
Editor: Steven Seaton. **Art Editor:** Russell Fairbrother.
Monthly publication for running enthusiasts.
Illustrations: Mostly colour. Pictures relating to sports, recreational and fitness running. Consult art editor before submitting.
Text: Feature material considered, but only by prior consultation with the editor.
Overall freelance potential: Fair.
Fees: By agreement.

RUNNING FITNESS
Kelsey Publishing, 1st Floor, South Wing, Broadway Court, Broadway, Peterborough PE1 1RP.
Tel: 01733 347559. Fax: 01733 891342.
Editor: Paul Larkins.
Monthly magazine for active running enthusiasts, those who run for health or recreation.
Illustrations: Colour. Coverage of competitions and running events at local or regional level, off-beat pictures, and general stock shots of runners. Both racing and training pictures are welcome. Some scope for general atmospheric pictures incorporating runners and athletic-looking subjects in picturesque and inspirational settings. Possible commission scope for "fashion" features. Covers: usually by commission – interested in hearing from photographers who can bring a creative approach to the subject.
Text: Illustrated articles of a practical nature, giving advice on training, diet, etc., and on unusual or exciting running events worldwide 1,000–1,500 words. Features of an inspirational nature also welcome – well-written and illustrated pieces on elite athletes, or other sportspeople who run as part of their training. Discuss ideas with the editor first.
Overall freelance potential: Good.
Fees: From a minimum of £20 up to £80 for a full page; text £70 per 1,000 words.

SGB UK
Datateam Publishing Ltd, London Road, Maidstone ME16 8LY.
Tel: 01622 687031. Fax: 01622 757646. ISDN: 01732 771039 E-mail: sgb@datateam.co.uk
Editor: Alistair Phillips.
Monthly magazine for the UK sports retail trade.
Illustrations: B&W and colour. Topical pictures concerning the retail trade, usually to illustrate

specific news stories, features and new products.
Text: Illustrated features and news stories on anything to do with the sports retail industry, including manufacturer and retailer profiles etc.
Overall freelance potential: Limited.
Fees: Text, £150 per 1,000 words; pictures by negotiation.

THE SCOTTISH SPORTING GAZETTE
Country Pursuits Ltd, Roebuck House, 33 Broad Street, Stamford, Lincs PE9 1RB.
Tel: 01780 766199. Fax: 01780 754774. E-mail: mikebpgroup@talk21.com
Editor: Mike Barnes.
Annual publication to market Scottish shooting, fishing, stalking and allied services. Aimed at the upper income bracket in the UK, Europe and America.
Illustrations: B&W and colour. Digital media preferred. Pictures of shooting, fishing, stalking, live game animals, whisky production, antique Scottish weapons, tartans, castles and hunting lodges. Covers: exceptional colour pictures of game animals or action sporting shots.
Text: Features on shooting, fishing and stalking in Scotland or articles on other topics that are particularly Scottish, as above. 600–2,000 words.
Overall freelance potential: Good.
Editor's tips: Pictures and text must be unusual, not the normal anecdotes associated with this field. Material should have a good Scottish flavour. It does not have to be essentially sporting, but should be allied in some way.
Fees: Open to negotiation.

SCUBA WORLD
Freestyle Publications Ltd, Alexander House, Ling Road, Tower Park, Poole, Dorset BH12 4NZ.
Tel: 01202 735090. Fax: 01202 733969. E-mail: fraines@freepubs.co.uk
Editor: Frank Raines.
Monthly for recreational scuba divers, diving clubs, underwater photographers.
Illustrations: Colour. To accompany features as below. Covers: interesting shots showing a diver either underwater or on surface, or wrecks and marine life.
Text: Illustrated articles on UK diving and wreck sites, holiday destinations, aquatic life, underwater photography, equipment and topical subjects. 1,500–2,000 words.
Overall freelance potential: Very good; all contributions are freelance.
Fees: Between £40 and £100 per feature. Covers negotiable.

THE SHOOTING GAZETTE
BPG (Bourne) Ltd, Roebuck House, 33 Broad Street, Stamford, Lincolnshire PE9 1RB.
Tel: 01780 764974. Fax: 01780 754774. E-mail: mikebpgroup@talk21.com
Editor: Mike Barnes.
Britain's only monthly magazine covering exclusively game and rough shooting, wildlife, countryside.
Illustrations: Colour. Pictures for general illustration, including countryside scenes, hunting, shooting, fishing, farming, birds and animals – quarry and non-quarry species.
Text: Well-illustrated articles from those with specialist knowledge, and profiles or interviews. Up to 2,000 words.
Overall freelance potential: Good.
Fees: By negotiation.

SHOOTING TIMES & COUNTRY MAGAZINE
IPC Country & Leisure Media Ltd, King's Reach Tower, Stamford Street, London SE1 9LS.
Tel: 020 7261 6180. Fax: 020 7261 7179.
Editor: Robert Grey.
Weekly magazine concentrating on all aspects of quarry shooting (game, pigeon, rough shooting, wildfowling and stalking). Also covers clay shooting, other fieldsports and general country topics.

Illustrations: Colour. Good photographs of shooting subjects plus gundogs, wildlife, rural crafts, country food. Some scope for good generic photographs of British counties, showing known landmarks. Covers: shots should be vertical in shape with room for title at the top – medium format preferred but sharp 35mm acceptable.
Text: Illustrated features on all aspects of quarry shooting and general country topics as above. In the region of 900 words.
Overall freelance potential: Excellent; plenty of scope for new contributors.
Editor's tips: The magazine likes to keep pictures on file as it is not always possible to know in advance when a picture can be used. For features, remember that the readers are real country people.
Fees: Colour inside £10–£60 according to size; covers £70–£90. Features £40 per 500 words.

SKI & BOARD
The Ski Club of Great Britain, The White House, 57-63 Church Road, Wimbledon Village, London SW19 5SB.
Tel: 020 8410 2000. Fax: 020 8410 2001. E-mail: s&b@skiclub.co.uk
Editor: Arnie Wilson.
Published four times a year. Official journal of the Ski Club of Great Britain, covering the sport at all levels.
Illustrations: Colour. Pictures of holiday skiing, ski-touring, racing, and equipment. Shots illustrating snowcraft and particular techniques. Good, attractive pictures of ski resorts and ski slopes in season. Covers: good colour action with one or more skiers; 35mm acceptable but larger formats preferred. Good adventure/action pics. Gallery section.
Text: Some scope for general articles about skiing, and on techniques. Very interested in Adventure articles, especially with pics.
Overall freelance potential: Quite good.
Fees: By arrangement.

SKIER & SNOWBOARDER MAGAZINE
Mountain Marketing Ltd, PO Box 386, Sevenoaks, Kent TN13 1AQ.
Tel: 0845 310 8303. Fax: 01732 779266.
Editor: Frank Baldwin.
Published five times a year: July, Sep/Oct, Nov/Dec, Jan/Feb, Mar/Apr. Covers all aspects of skiing and snowboarding.
Illustrations: Colour. Good action pictures and anything spectacular, odd or humorous that summons up the spirit of skiing. Also a special "Photo File" section in which photographers can submit up to three favourite shots backed by text which tells the reader about the set-ups/techniques used, linked with a short biog of the photographer.
Text: Original ideas for illustrated features always welcome. Possible scope for resort reports and news items.
Overall freelance potential: Very good.
Fees: By negotiation.

SNOOKER SCENE
Cavalier House, 202 Hagley Road, Edgbaston, Birmingham B16 9PQ.
Tel: 0870 220 2125. Fax: 0121 452 1822. E-mail: clive.everton@talk21.com
Editor: Clive Everton.
Monthly publication for snooker players and enthusiasts.
Illustrations: B&W and colour. Digital media preferred. Snooker action pictures and coverage related to tournaments, or material of historical interest. Covers: Colour pictures on similar themes.
Text: Features on snooker and billiards. 250–1,000 words.
Overall freelance potential: Small.
Fees: By arrangement.

SNOWBOARD UK

Freestyle Publications Ltd, Alexander House, Ling Road, Tower Park, Poole, Dorset BH12 4NZ.
Tel: 01202 735090. Fax: 01202 733969. E-mail: snowboardUK@wannadoo.fr
Editor: Tom Copsey.
Magazine covering the sport of snowboarding. Published seven times a year during the winter sports season and once in the summer.
Illustrations: Colour. Digital files or film. Good action coverage of the sport always required; should be colourful and stylish. Interested in any freestyle or alpine shots from anywhere in the world.
Text: Short, heavily-illustrated articles on any aspect of the sport.
Overall freelance potential: Excellent; the magazine is very photo-based.
Editor's tips: The magazine, which also supplies shots to other publications, is keen to build up a pool of photographers who can be relied upon to produce quality coverage of the sport.
Fees: Variable; according to use and nature of material.

SPORTING SHOOTER

Romsey Publishing Group, Jubilee House, 2 Jubilee Place, London SW3 3TQ.
Tel: 020 7751 4909. Fax: 020 7751 4848. E-mail: charlie@sportingshooter.co.uk
Editor: Charlie Jacoby.
Monthly aimed at sports shooters and gamekeepers.
Illustrations: Will consider good stock images depicting pigeon, clay and pheasant shooting, deer stalking, gun dogs, gamekeeping and relevant wildlife. Some commissions possible to photograph specific features.
Text: also very interested in illustrated articles on shooting topics
Overall freelance potential: Good.
Editor's tips: The magazine has a very specific style so always call to discuss ideas first.
Fees: By negotiation.

SWIMMING MAGAZINE

41 Granby Street, Loughborough, Leicestershire LE11 3DU.
Tel: 01509 632230. Fax: 01509 632233. E-mail: swimmingtimes@swimming.org.uk
Editor: Peter Hassall.
Official monthly magazine of the Amateur Swimming Association and Institute of Swimming Teachers and Coaches. Covers all aspects of swimming including diving, synchro-swimming, water polo, etc.
Illustrations: B&W and colour. Digital media preferred. News pictures of swimmers at major events and any off-beat or particularly interesting shots of swimming-related activity.
Text: Human interest stories about individual swimmers.
Overall freelance potential: Limited.
Fees: Negotiable.

TARGET SPORTS

Peterson Publications Ltd, Peterson House, Northbank, Berryhill Industrial Estate, Droitwich, Worcestershire WR9 9BL.
Tel: 01905 795564. Fax: 01905 795905.
Editor: Richard Atkins.
Monthly publication for all target shooters – muzzle loading, (fullbore and smallbore, pistols and rifles, shotguns, archery, crossbows and airweapons).
Illustrations: Mainly colour, some B&W for technical illustration. Pictures of guns, firearms, bows and related equipment, technique, technical/engineering matters and pictures of general interest in the sport. Some opportunities for colour covers.

Text: General and technical instructional articles; reports of meetings. 500–2,500 words.
Overall freelance potential: Quite good.
Editor's tips: It is likely that only those with some knowledge of the subject will be in a position to supply the type of material required.
Fees: By negotiation.

TODAY'S GOLFER
EMAP Active Ltd, Bushfield House, Orton Centre, Peterborough PE3 5UW.
Tel: 01733 237111. Fax: 01733 288014. E-mail: paul.crawford@emap.com
Editor: Paul Hamblin. **Art Director:** Paul Crawford.
Monthly for golfing enthusiasts.
Illustrations: Colour. Stock shots of leading players and courses, and anything off-beat, considered on spec.
Text: Instructional material; player profiles; equipment features; course tests.
Overall freelance potential: Limited.
Fees: By negotiation.

THE WISDEN CRICKETER
Wisden Cricket Magazines Ltd, The New Boathouse, 136-142 Bramley Road, London W10 6SR.
Tel: 020 7565 3000. Fax: 020 7565 3055.
Editor: John Stern. **Art Director:** Nigel Davies.
Monthly publication aimed at all cricket lovers. Concentrates on the game at first-class and especially international level.
Illustrations: Mainly colour. Exceptional photographs of the above always considered.
Text: Scope for exclusive news stories and features. But check first before submitting. 400–2,500 words.
Overall freelance potential: Fair.
Fees: On a rising scale according to size of pictures or length and significance of article.

Trade

AM
EMAP Automotive Ltd, Media House, Lynchwood, Peterborough Business Park, Peterborough PE2 6EA.
Tel: 01733 468259. Fax: 01733 468350.
Editor: Steve Briers.
Fortnightly publication for the motor industry, mainly franchised dealers.
Illustrations: Colour. News photographs covering the motor trade generally. Some scope for commissions to photograph industry figures and premises.
Text: News items and news features of interest to industry executives.
Overall freelance potential: Good for those with contacts in the trade and local freelances.
Fees: By negotiation.

THE BOOKSELLER
VNU Entertainment Media UK Ltd, 5th Floor, Endeavour House, 189 Shaftesbury Avenue, London WC2H 8TJ.
Tel: 020 7420 6006. Fax: 020 7420 6103.
Editor: Nicholas Clee.
Weekly trade magazine for booksellers, publishers, librarians and anyone involved in the book industry. Covers trade trends and events, authors, etc.
Illustrations: B&W and colour. Digital media preferred. Pictures of bookshops and book-related

activities outside London. Busy book fairs, busy book shops, etc. Portraits of authors and book trade figures.
Text: Serious, humorous, analytical, descriptive articles connected with the book trade, plus author interviews.
Overall freelance potential: Only for those freelances who have good access to the book trade.
Fees: Variable; depends on material.

BRITISH BAKER
Quantum Business Media, Quantum House, 19 Scarbrook Road, Croydon CR9 1LX.
Tel: 020 8565 4285. Fax: 020 8565 4303. E-mail: sylviam@qpp.co.uk
Editor: Sylvia Macdonald.
Weekly business-to-business news magazine covering the entire baking industry.
Illustrations: Colour only. Interesting photographs relating to working bakeries, especially news items such as shop openings, promotions, charity events, etc. Also good stock shots of bakery products.
Text: Short news stories (300 words) or features (500–1,000 words) on any baking industry topic.
Overall freelance potential: Fair, for those who can supply relevant material.
Fees: £125 per 1,000 words for text; photographs by negotiation.

CABINET MAKER
CMP Information Ltd, Ludgate House, 245 Blackfriars Road, London SE1 9UY.
Tel: 020 7921 8433. Fax: 020 7921 8452.
Editor: Alison Gay. **Deputy Editor:** Andrew Kidd.
Weekly publication for all those in the furniture and furnishing trade and industry.
Illustrations: Colour. Freelances commissioned to cover news assignments in the trade. Some scope for pictures to illustrate features.
Text: Features about companies making furniture for sale to retailers and interior designers. Length from one to four pages (1,000 words plus three pictures makes two pages).
Overall freelance potential: Around 10 per cent contributed, including news coverage.
Editor's tips: Approach the editor or deputy editor for a brief before submitting.
Fees: By agreement.

CATERER & HOTELKEEPER
Reed Business Information Ltd, Fifth Floor, Quadrant House, The Quadrant, Sutton, Surrey SM2 5AS.
Tel: 020 8652 3221. Fax: 020 8652 8973. E-mail; mark.lewis@rbi.co.uk
Editor: Mark Lewis. **Art Editor:** Sarah Thompson. **Picture Librarian:** Hazel Bush.
Weekly magazine for the hotel and catering trade.
Illustrations: B&W and colour. News pictures relevant to hotel and catering establishments – openings, extensions, refurbishments, people, etc. Special interest in regional material. Commissions possible to cover establishments, equipment and food.
Text: Specialist articles of interest to the trade, by commission only.
Overall freelance potential: Mainly limited to those with connections within the trade.
Editor's tips: Also welcomes tip-offs concerning the industry, for which a fee of £15–£25 is paid.
Fees: On a rising scale according to size of reproduction or length of text.

CHEMIST & DRUGGIST
CMP Information Ltd, Sovereign House, Sovereign Way, Tonbridge, Kent TN9 1RW.
Tel: 01732 377487. Fax: 01732 367065. E-mail: chemdrug@cmpinformation.com
Editor: Charles Gladwin.
Weekly news publication for retail pharmacists; the pharmaceutical, toiletries and cosmetics industries; pharmaceutical wholesalers, etc.
Illustrations: B&W and colour. News pictures concerning individual retailers and retailing related

events, plus industry events relating to pharmaceutical companies.
Text: Local news stories relating to community pharmacy.
Overall freelance potential: Limited.
Fees: On a rising scale, according to contribution.

CONTAINERISATION INTERNATIONAL
Informa Business Publishing, 69-77 Paul Street, London EC2A 4LQ.
Tel: 020 7017 4820. Fax: 020 7017 4976.
Editor: Jane Boyes. **Art Editor:** Robert Evers.
Monthly business-oriented magazine on issues facing the international container transport industry.
Illustrations: Colour. Digital media preferred. Unusual pictures of container shipping activities, especially in exotic locations overseas, or interesting uses for containers inland.
Text: Well-researched and exclusive articles, preferably on some aspect of the container transport business not covered by staff writers. Around 2,000 words.
Overall freelance potential: Limited.
Fees: By agreement.

CONVENIENCE STORE
William Reed Ltd, Broadfield Park, Crawley, West Sussex RH11 9RT.
Tel: 01293 613400. Fax: 01293 610330. E-mail: sue.bell@william-reed.co.uk
Editor: Sonia Young.
Fortnightly magazine for independent neighbourhood retailers and convenience stores, and their wholesale suppliers.
Illustrations: Colour. Photographs usually to illustrate specific features; little scope for pictures on their own.
Text: Illustrated features or stories concerning late-night, local, food-based stores. Should ideally feature a retailer who is doing something a bit different, or who has been highly successful in some way.
Overall freelance potential: Modest.
Fees: By negotiation.

DRAPERS
EMAP Retail, 33-39 Bowling Green Lane, London EC1R 0DA.
Tel: 020 7812 3700. Fax: 020 7812 3760. E-mail: josephine.collins@emap.com
Editor: Josephine Collins. **Art Editor:** Heather Reeves.
Weekly news publication for clothing and textile retailers.
Illustrations: Colour. Digital media preferred. News pictures of interest to the clothing and fashion trade. Some scope for portraits and fashion shoots by commission.
Text: Features, fashion and news items of relevance to retailers in the fashion and textile fields.
Overall freelance potential: Limited for news; fair for commissioned work.
Editor's tips: Do not send unsolicited material – call the art editor first.
Fees: Good; on a rising scale according to size of illustration or length of feature.

EUROFRUIT MAGAZINE
Market Intelligence Ltd, 4th Floor, Market Towers, One Nine Elms Lane, London SW8 5NQ.
Tel: 020 7501 3700. Fax: 020 7498 6472. E-mail: maura@fruitnet.com
Editor: Maura Maxwell.
Monthly magazine of the European fresh fruit and vegetable trade. Aimed at producers, exporters, importers, merchants and buyers.
Illustrations: Colour. Subjects such as harvesting fruit, loading on to ships or lorries, quality checks on fruit, packing etc. Photographs accepted mostly for the magazine's own picture library.
Text: Topical features on fruit and vegetables, eg Chilean apples in Europe, French Iceberg lettuce, Egypt's expanding export range, Norway as an alternative market, etc. 1,250–2,000 words.

Overall freelance potential: Quite good. Some regular contributors, but scope for the freelance writer who can also supply pictures.
Editor's tips: It is best to work in close contact with the editorial department to get names of people who would be of interest to the publication.
Fees: Negotiable.

FISHING MONTHLY

Special Publications, Craigcrook Castle, Craigcrook Road, Edinburgh EH4 3PE.
Tel: 0131 312 4550. Fax: 0131 312 4551. E-mail: bkennedy@fishupdate.com
Editor: Bob Kennedy.
Monthly tabloid for the the UK and Irish commercial fishing industries, but with coverage extending to the rest of Europe.
Illustrations: B&W and colour. Digital media preferred. Captioned news pictures covering any subject relating to the UK, Irish and European fishing industries, including fish farming, processing, etc.
Text: Short illustrated news items, and longer features from contributors with suitable knowledge of the industry.
Overall freelance potential: Good, especially for those with connections in the fishing industry.
Fees: By negotiation.

FISHING NEWS

Informa Business Publishing, Telephone House, 69-77 Paul Street, London EC2A 4LQ.
Tel: 020 7017 4531. Fax: 020 7017 4536. E-mail: tim.oliver@informa.com
Editor: Tim Oliver.
Weely newspaper for the commercial fishing industry in Britain and Ireland.
Illustrations: B&W and colour. Captioned news pictures covering any subject relating to the UK or Irish fishing industries.
Text: Illustrated news stories always considered.
Overall freelance potential: Very good; a lot of photographs are used.
Fees: Standard £30 per picture.

FLORIST & WHOLESALE BUYER

Wordhouse Publishing Group Ltd, The Word House, Clifton Road, Kingston upon Thames, Surrey KT2 6PZ.
Tel: 020 8549 6549. Fax: 020 8549 6059. E-mail: info@theflorist.co.uk
Editor: Caroline Marshall-Foster.
Publication for retail florists, published 10 times a year.
Illustrations: Mainly colour. News pictures about the trade and other interesting pictures of floristry in the retail context, i.e. special displays, promotions, etc.
Text: Features on anything relating to floristry and retailing, shop profiles, practical aspects, advertising and promotion, etc.
Overall freelance potential: Limited.
Fees: Text, £80 per 1,000 words published; pictures by agreement.

FOOD TRADER FOR BUTCHERS

National Federation of Meat & Food Traders, 1 Belgrove, Tunbridge Wells, Kent TN1 1YW.
Tel: 01892 541412. Fax: 01892 535462. E-mail: graham@nfmft.co.uk
Editor: Graham Bidston.
Official magazine of the National Federation of Meat & Food Traders. Published 10 times a year.
Illustrations: Colour. Topical pictures related to news and issues in the meat and related food industry.

Text: Topical features on the food industry, primarily the meat trade. Up to 2,000 words.
Overall freelance potential: Fair for those in close contact with the trade.
Editor's tips: Only exclusive material will be considered.
Fees: By negotiation.

FORECOURT TRADER
William Reed Publishing Ltd, Broadfield Park, Crawley, West Sussex RH11 9RT.
Tel: 01293 613400. Fax: 01293 610330.
Editor: Meryl Bolton.
Monthly magazine for petrol station operators.
Illustrations: Colour. News pictures relating to petrol stations and the petrol sales business generally.
Text: News and features relating to all areas of petrol retailing.
Overall freelance potential: Fair.
Fees: Text, £120 per 1,000 words; pictures according to use.

FOREST MACHINE JOURNAL
PO Box 7570, Dumfries DG2 8YD.
Tel: 01387 880359. Fax: 01387 247945. E-mail: fmj.editor@virgin.net
Editor: Mark Andrews.
Monthly magazine covering all aspects of forestry and timber production – arboriculture, estate management, harvesting, haulage, and recreational use of forests/woodland.
Illustrations: Colour. Plenty of photographs used, but usually only as accompaniment to features on topics as below.
Text: Always seeking freelances to produce well-illustrated local stories on forestry topics, and for profiles of individual contractors etc. Write or e-mail the editor with suggestions and/or details of areas covered.
Overall freelance potential: Good for complete illustrated features.
Fees: £150 per published page.

HARDWARE & GARDEN REVIEW
Faversham House Group Ltd, Faversham House, 232A Addington Road, South Croydon CR2 8LE.
Tel: 020 8651 7100. Fax: 020 8651 7117. E-mail: hgr@fav-house.com
Editor: Susanna Clarke.
Monthly magazine for the independent hardware, housewares, garden centre and DIY trade.
Illustrations: B&W and colour. Digital media preferred. Trade news pictures and picture stories concerning particular stores and outlets.
Text: Illustrated articles on store redesign, and retailer profiles. Around 1,000 words.
Overall freelance potential: Fair.
Editor's tips: Articles should be exclusive in this field. Always send an outline in the first instance.
Fees: On a rising scale according to size of reproduction or length of text.

INDEPENDENT RETAIL NEWS
Highbury Business Communications, Media House, Azalea Drive, Swanley, Kent BR8 8HY.
Tel: 01322 611240. Fax: 0322 616375. E-mail: r.siddle@highburybiz.com
Editor: Richard Siddle.
Fortnightly publication for independent, convenience, licensed and CTN retailers. Assists them in being more profitable and aware of new products and campaigns.
Illustrations: Colour. Captioned news pictures and picture stories of interest to independent grocery and convenience store traders. Stock images to illustrate people buying goods in independent/corner stores, retail crime, under-age sales, bootlegging, national lottery sales, etc.
Text: Articles and stories relevant to small retailers.
Overall freelance potential: Fair.
Editor's tips: A sample copy of the magazine is available to potential contributors. Always phone

first with ideas.
Fees: Photographs according to how sourced, but up to £150 for features and £50-£100 for news stories. For commissioned features £170 per 1,000 words and negotiable for news stories.

MEAT & POULTRY NEWS
Yandell Publishing Ltd, PO Box 5121, Milton Keynes, Bucks MK15 8ZN.
Tel: 01908 613323. Fax: 01908 612579. E-mail: nicci.p@meatmag.com
Editor: Nicci Piggott.
Monthly journal for the whole meat and poultry trade.
Illustrations: Colour. Digital media preferred. Pictures relating to any current meat trade issue, including legislation, food scares, court cases, etc.
Text: Stories on current issues as above. Illustrated features of around 1,000 words on current food issues, research, technology, and profiles of individual businesses.
Overall freelance potential: Very good for those in a position to cover this industry.
Editor's tips: It is much preferred if material offered is exclusive.
Fees: £25 for pictures. £110 per 1,000 words for text. Higher rates may be payable for material of special interest.

THE SUBPOSTMASTER
National Federation of Subpostmasters, Evelyn House, Windlesham Gardens, Shoreham-by-Sea BN4 5AZ.
Tel: 01273 452324. Fax: 01273 465403.
Editor: John Willshaw.
Monthly journal of the Federation of Subpostmasters, with strong news content.
Illustrations: B&W, or colour prints. Captioned pictures of any subpostmaster in the news for any reason and national issues affecting subpostmasters.
Text: No freelance market.
Overall freelance potential: Limited.
Editor's tips: More interested in subjects with unusual hobbies, histories, etc. than in attack stories.
Fees: On a rising scale, according to the size of reproduction.

WORLD FISHING
Highbury Business, Media House, Azalea Drive, Swanley, Kent BR8 8HY.
Tel: 01322 660070. Fax: 01322 616324. E-mail: pilar.santamaria@nexusmedia.com
Editor: Pilar Santamaria-Gonzalez.
Monthly journal for the commercial fishing industry. Covers fisheries and related industries from an international perspective.
Illustrations: B&W and colour. Mainly to accompany specific articles, but some scope for scene-setting shots of commercial fishing activity in specific locations worldwide.
Text: Illustrated articles on any commercial fishing topic. Should always contain some international interest. Maximum 1,500 words.
Overall freelance potential: Good for those with connections in the industry.
Fees: By negotiation.

Transport

COACH AND BUS WEEK
EMAP Active Ltd, Bretton Court, Bretton, Peterborough PE3 8DZ.
Tel: 08700 623130. Fax: 01733 467770. E-mail: mark.williams@emap.com
Editor: Mark Williams.
Weekly news magazine covering coach and bus operations. Aimed at licensed coach, bus

and tour operators.
Illustrations: Colour. Pictures as illustrations to features mentioned below; coach and bus related news items. Places of interest to coach parties.
Text: Features on coach and bus operators, hotels, ferry operations, resorts and venues, anything that would be of interest to a coach party or an operator. Articles on subjects that an operator might find useful in their day-to-day business. Up to1,000 words.
Overall freelance potential: Always interested in seeing work from freelances.
Fees: By negotiation.

COMMERCIAL MOTOR
Reed Business Information Ltd, Quadrant House, The Quadrant, Sutton, Surrey SM2 5AS.
Tel: 020 8652 3302. Fax: 020 8652 8969. ISDN: 020 8652 4888. E-mail: steven.gale@rbi.co.uk
Editor: Brian Weatherley. **Art Editor:** Steve Gale.
Weekly publication devoted to the road haulage industry. Aimed at vehicle enthusiasts as well as industry readers.
Illustrations: Colour. Mostly commissioned; arrange to show portfolio to the art editor first. Stock photographs of commercial vehicles and all aspects of road haulage and road usage may be of interest – send lists of subjects available.
Text: Technical articles on road haulage topics, from expert contributors only.
Overall freelance potential: Very good.
Fees: Day rate around £250–£300 plus expenses. Other material by negotiation.

OLD GLORY
Mortons Heritage Media, PO Box 43, Horncastle, Lincs LN9 6JR.
Tel: 01507 529300. Fax: 01507 529301. E-mail: ctyson@mortons.co.uk
Editor: Colin Tyson.
Monthly devoted to industrial/commercial transport and machinery heritage and vintage restoration including traction engines, tractors, etc.
Illustrations: B&W and colour. Pictures of all forms of traction engines, tractors, buses, commercial vehicles, fairground machinery and maritime subjects such as old steamboats. News pictures of individual machines, restoration projects, etc. Detailed captions necessary including where and when picture taken. Covers: colourful pictures of traction engines in attractive settings.
Text: Illustrated articles on subjects as above.
Overall freelance potential: Excellent. A lot of scope for good colour material.
Fees: Generally £5–£15 for B&W; £15–£30 for colour.

ROADWAY
IRG Ltd, Hill House, Hill House Road, Norwich NR1 4BE.
Tel: 01603 627294. Fax: 01603 633638. E-mail: roadway@rha.net
Editor: John O'Hanlon.
Monthly news magazine for the road haulage industry. Official magazine of the Road Haulage Association.
Illustrations: Colour. Pictures of trucks on motorways, at depots etc. Should be newsworthy or of unusual interest.
Text: Articles on any aspect of the road haulage industry. Length by prior agreement with the editor.
Overall freelance potential: Limited.
Fees: By arrangement.

TRACTOR & MACHINERY
Kelsey Publishing Group. Editorial: 1 Longview Cottage, Bodle Street Green, East Sussex BN27 4RA.
Tel: 01323 833125. E-mail: peterlove@kelsey.co.uk
Editor: Peter Love.
Monthly magazine for tractor enthusiasts, covering classic, vintage and contemporary machines from all parts of the world.
Illustrations: Mainly colour. Digital media preferred. Pictures of tractors in the news, classic and vintage gatherings, unusual and interesting tractors, and related machinery. Captions must include details of type, model and year of tractor and name of driver. Contact editor before preparing a submission.
Text: Those who can add words to their images are welcomed.
Overall freelance potential: Good.
Fees: By arrangement.

TRUCK & DRIVER
Reed Business Information, Quadrant House, The Quadrant, Sutton, Surrey SM2 5AS.
Tel: 020 8652 3682. Fax: 020 8652 8988.
Editor: Dave Young. **Art Director:** Tim Noonan.
Monthly magazine for truck drivers.
Illustrations: Colour. Interesting individual trucks, unusual situations involving drivers and their vehicles, news items and some studio work.
Text: Commissioned features on anything of interest to truck drivers. Looks for freelances with ideas.
Overall freelance potential: Very good.
Fees: By negotiation.

Travel

A PLACE IN THE SUN
Brooklands Magazines Ltd, Medway House, Lower Road, Forest Row, East Sussex RH18 5HE.
Tel: 01342 828700. Fax: 01342 828701. E-mail: ann@brooklandsgroup.com
Editor: Ann Wallace.
Glossy monthly for prospective buyers of overseas property. Official magazine of the C4 TV series of the same name.
Illustrations: Colour. Mostly by commission, though some stock images are used. Will consider sets of images based around people moving or living abroad, or suggestions for subjects, which could lead to a full-scale commission. Other general commissions also possible – submit details of experience and a few samples in the first instance.
Text: Illustrated feature stories as above.
Overall freelance potential: Good for the more experienced worker.
Fees: By negotiation.

BUSINESS LIFE
Cedar Communications Ltd, Pegasus House, 37-42 Sackville Street, London W1S 3EH.
Tel: 020 7534 2400. Fax: 020 7534 2541. E-mail: businesslife@cedarcom.co.uk
Editor: Tim Hulse.
Monthly business travel magazine distributed on British Airways flights within Europe.
Illustrations: Colour. Digital media preferred. All aspects of business travel within Europe. Send details of specialities and coverage available in the first instance. Covers: colourful, graphic portrait

shots with a "different" angle.
Text: Little scope, but original ideas on European business travel always considered.
Overall freelance potential: Fair.
Fees: According to the nature of material and use.

BUSINESS TRAVELLER
Perry Publications Ltd, Nestor House, Playhouse Yard, London EC4V 5EX.
Tel: 020 7778 1534. Fax: 020 7778 0022. E-mail: editorial@businesstraveller.com
Editor: Tom Otley. **Art Editor:** Ian Ascott.
Monthly consumer publication aimed at the frequently travelling international and domestic business executive.
Illustrations: Colour. Digital media preferred. Pictures to illustrate destination features on a wide variety of cities around the world – request features list of upcoming destinations.
Text: Illustrated features on business travel, but only by prior consultation with the editor.
Overall freelance potential: Around 65 per cent of the magazine is contributed by freelances.
Editor's tips: Submit low-res digital or dupes in the first instance.
Fees: Pictures from £50 up to £180 for a full page; covers £250. Text, £200 per 1,000 words.

CONDE NAST TRAVELLER
The Condé Nast Publications Ltd, Vogue House, Hanover Square, London W1R 0AD.
Tel: 020 7499 9080. Fax: 020 7493 3758. E-mail: cntraveller@condenast.co.uk
Editor: Sarah Miller. **Director of Photography:** Caroline Metcalfe. **Picture Editor:** Lucy Perceval.
Heavily-illustrated glossy monthly for the discerning, independent traveller.
Illustrations: Colour and occasional B&W. Top quality photo-feature material covering all aspects of travel, from luxury hotels and food, restaurant interiors to adventure travel, ecological issues, and reportage, etc. Very stylish and striking B&W photography also sought. Always interested in hearing from experienced photographers who are planning specific trips.
Text: Mostly commissioned from top name writers.
Overall freelance potential: Very good for material of the highest quality.
Editor's tips: The magazine seeks to use material with an original approach. Particularly interested in hearing from photographers who can produce excellent work but who are not necessarily travel specialists.
Fees: Variable depending on what is offered, but top rates paid for suitable material.

CRUISE TRAVELLER
Marlin Publishing Ltd, 10 Crofton Avenue, Chiswick, London W4 3EW.
Tel: 020 8987 2750. E-mail: sue@cruisetraveller.co.uk
Editor: Sue Bryant.
Quarterly magazine and associated website (www.cruisetraveller.co.uk) for anyone interested in cruising and cruise holidays.
Illustrations: Colour. Stock images required of major cruise destinations and the cruising lifestyle, though much of the latter is supplied by cruise operators. Strong images also needed for cover shots, showing a cruise ship in an attractive location, at sea or in harbour.
Text: No scope.
Overall freelance potential: Limited.
Editor's tips: Do not submit straightforward images of cruise liners – these are easily obtained direct from operators.
Fees: By negotiation and according to use.

EVERYTHING FRANCE
Brooklands Magazines Ltd, Medway House, Lower Road, Forest Row, East Sussex RH18 5HE.
Tel: 01342 828719. Fax: 01342 828701. E-mail: jon@brooklandsgroup.com

Editor: Jon Stackpool.
13 issues a year devoted to all aspects of visiting or living in France.
Illustrations: Colour. Substantial need for good stock images of regional landscapes, towns, cities, historic buildings, people, homes, gardens, property, history, culture, food and drink.
Text: Illustrated features incorporating topics as above – regional tours, city portraits, people profiles (native French or expats), regional food and drink, heritage and property.
Overall freelance potential: Excellent.
Editor's tips: Contact editorial team for advance notice of upcoming features.
Fees: According to use and by negotiation.

EVERYTHING SPAIN
Brooklands Magazines Ltd, Medway House, Lower Road, Forest Row, East Sussex RH18 5HE.
Tel: 01342 828700. Fax: 01342 828701. E-mail: sarah@brooklandsgroup.com
Editor: Sarah Monaghan.
Monthly for a mature readership (40+) interested in property and life in Spain.
Illustrations: Colour. Will consider themed sets of images covering tourism and residence in Spain: cities, regions, touring, food and drink, traditions, people, property, and life in Spain for British expats. A theme is essential – sets of unconnected images will not be considered. Send e-mail with a few low-res samples in the first instance.
Text: Will always consider ideas for illustrated articles on any Spanish topic.
Overall freelance potential: Fair.
Fees: By negotiation.

FOOD & TRAVEL
Fox Publishing Ltd, 1st Floor, Lion House, Red Lion Street, Richmond, Surrey TW9 1RE.
Tel: 020 8332 9090. Fax: 020 8332 9991.
Editor: Nicki Symington. **Food Editor:** Vanessa Kendall. **Creative Director:** Angela Dukes.
Up-market monthly for affluent couples interested in long-haul travel, weekend breaks and eating out.
Illustrations: Colour. High quality food and travel photography, invariably produced on commission. Specialist photographers are advised to contact the appropriate editor (food editor for food photography; creative director for travel) with details of experience and ideas. Limited scope for travel stock material since most is commissioned.
Text: Ideas for articles always considered.
Overall freelance potential: Good for specialists; better for travel than for food.
Fees: By negotiation.

FRANCE MAGAZINE
Archant House, Oriel Road, Cheltenham, Gloucestershire GL50 1BB.
Tel: 01242 216050. Fax: 01242 216074. E-mail: editorial@francemag.com
Editor: Kate McNally. **Picture Editor:** Susan Buzzard.
Monthly magazine for Francophiles, with the emphasis on the real France.
Illustrations: Colour. Picture stories, and top quality individual pictures to illustrate articles, on French regions, annual events, cuisine, travel, arts, history, shopping, fashion, sport and property. Especially interested in destination, scenic, character and human interest shots, and mood pictures. Covers: pictures that capture the essence of France. Photographs also required for annual calendar – selected early in each new year.
Text: Lively and colourful illustrated features on the life, culture and history of France. Normally around 800–1,200 words, but up to 2,000 words considered. Factual accuracy essential.
Overall freelance potential: Excellent for top quality material.
Editor's tips: Regular "wants" lists and contributors' notes will be sent on request. Not much interested in accounts of family holidays.
Fees: Photographs from £25 up to £100 for cover or DPS. £100 per 1,000 words.

FRENCH MAGAZINE
Merricks Media Ltd, Cambridge House South, Henry Street, Bath BA1 1JT.
Tel: 01225 786800. Fax: 01225 786801. E-mail: edit@frenchmagazine.co.uk
Editor: Justin Postlethwaite.
Monthly magazine for regular travellers to France and those with, or seeking, property there.
Illustrations: Colour. Digital media preferred. Typical French images for general illustration purposes – historic sites, vineyards, food/restaurants, activities, and homes and interiors etc. Submit lists of subjects available in the first instance. Commissions may be available to photographers with medium format or high-end digital equipment.
Text: Well-illustrated articles always welcomed, especially on gastronomy, buying property and regional features. Around 1,0500 words plus 8-10 illustrations.
Overall freelance potential: Excellent.
Fees: Single pictures according to use; features from £150 per 1,000 words; packages negotiable.

GEOGRAPHICAL
Campion Interactive Publications Ltd, Unit 11, Pall Mall Deposit, 124–128 Barlby Road, London W10 6BL
Tel: 020 8960 6400. Fax: 020 8960 6004. E-mail: magazine@geographical.co.uk
Editor: Nick Smith.
Monthly magazine of the Royal Geographical Society. Covers a wide spread of topics including travel, culture, environment, wildlife, conservation, history and exploration.
Illustrations: Colour. Digital media accepted but transparencies preferred. Mainly looking for photo-stories on geographical topics – human, political, ecological, economic and physical. Relevant news pictures always considered.
Text: Well-illustrated articles on any geographical subject, written in an informative but accessible way.
Overall freelance potential: Excellent for the right type of material.
Fees: Negotiable, but in the region of £100 per published page. Single pictures according to use.

GREECE MAGAZINE
Merricks Media Ltd, Cambridge House South, Henry Street, Bath BA1 1JT.
Tel: 01225 786835. E-mail: greece.edit@merricksmedia.co.uk
Managing Editor: Diana Cambridge. **Assistant Editor:** Kate Collyns.
Bi-monthly for lovers of Greece, both holidaymakers and those considering property in the country.
Illustrations: Colour. Attractive stock images of Greek subjects, but especially holiday activities and food and drink. Send lists of coverage available.
Text: Illustrated features on subjects of interest to the visitor or potential home buyer. Submit ideas only in the first instance.
Overall freelance potential: Fair.
Fees: Pictures according to use; features negotiable.

ITALY
Poundbury Publishing Ltd, Prospect House, Peverell Avenue East, Poundbury, Dorchester DT1 3WE.
Tel: 01305 756391. Fax: 01305 262760. E-mail: editor@italymag.co.uk
Editor: Fiona Tankard (Italy). **Art Editor:** Paul Tutill (UK).
General interest monthly for lovers of all things Italian.
Illustrations: Colour. Stock images always required on all aspects of Italian life and culture – send detailed lists in the first instance.
Text: Illustrated articles always considered. Should focus on interesting but less well-known places and regions rather than the popular holiday destinations, or on aspects of Italian lifestyle, culture, crafts and history.
Overall freelance potential: Very good.

Editor's tips: In all cases, make first approach by e-mail to editor in first instance, with subject lists or ideas.
Fees: From £30 depending on size of reproduction. Text £100 per 1,000 words.

LIVING FRANCE
Archant Life, Archant House, Oriel Road, Cheltenham GL50 1BB.
Tel: 01242 216091. Fax: 01242 216094. E-mail: editorial@livingfrance.com
Editor: Lucy-Jane Cypher. **Assistant Editor:** Eleanor O'Kane.
Monthly magazine for Francophiles, with a bias towards those seeking property there.
Illustrations: Colour. General images of France – regions, countryside, cities, towns, villages, food and property. Submit subject lists to assistant editor in the first instance.
Text: Suggestions for articles always considered, but many subjects covered by regulars. Main scope for destination pieces, practical articles on living and working in France, articles on French history and culture. E-mail synopsis in the first instance.
Overall freelance potential: Good.
Fees: Individual pictures according to use; illustrated articles £250 for 1,000–2,500 words.

PORTUGAL
Merricks Media, Cambridge House South, Henry Street, Bath BA1 1JT.
Tel: 01225 786800. E-mail: chippisley@aol.com
Editor: Christina Hippisley.
Monthly magazine devoted to Portugal, with emphasis on the holiday homes market.
Illustrations: Colour. No scope for stock material, which is sourced within Portugal. Possible opportunities for photographers who are planning to visit the country on other business. Initial contact via e-mail or letter is requested.
Text: Always interested in well-illustrated articles on the country. Write with suggestions in the first instance.
Overall freelance potential: Good for complete articles.
Fees: By negotiation.

SPAIN
The Media Company Publications Ltd, 21 Royal Circus, Edinburgh EH3 6TL.
Tel: 0131 226 7766. Fax: 0131 226 4567. E-mail: nmccormack@btclick.com
Editor: Nicola McCormack. **Picture Editor:** Alex Aikman Smith.
Monthly magazine for lovers of Spain, especially those owning or aiming to buy property in the country or with an interest in the culture and history of Spain.
Illustrations: Colour. Commissions available to photographers resident in or visiting Spain. Stock images mostly sourced from agencies but photographers with in-depth collections may find it worthwhile to submit lists of subjects available.
Text: Ideas for illustrated features welcomed, on topics such as property, food and drink, travel and leisure activities. Submit outline first.
Overall freelance potential: Good.
Fees: Negotiable and dependent on what is on offer.

SPANISH MAGAZINE
Merricks' Media, Cambridge House South, Henry Street, Bath BA1 1JT.
Tel: 01225 786800. E-mail: lisa.mcgee@merricksmedia.co.uk
Editor: Lisa McGee.
Monthly magazine aimed at mature (40+) UK readers who are considering buying Spanish property or retiring to Spain.
Illustrations: Colour. Interested in hearing from photographers who can offer good stock coverage of regions, cities, activities, etc. Write in the first instance, with details of the coverage and subjects you can offer.

Text: Will consider illustrated features on Spanish property and expatriate life in Spain.
Overall freelance potential: Fair.
Fees: Pictures according to use, features by negotiation.

TRAVEL
River Publishing Ltd, Victory House, Leicester Square, London WC2H 7QH.
Tel: 020 7306 0304 (ext 347). Fax: 020 7306 0314. E-mail: smarking@riverltd.co.uk
Editor: Jane Knight. **Picture Editor:** Sam Marking.
Bi-monthly glossy aimed at up-market travellers. Published in association with The Sunday Times.
Illustrations: Colour. Will always consider high-quality travel material on spec, including especially striking single images for use in double-page spreads. Lists of stock material always of interest. Only limited scope for commissions.
Text: Will consider very high-quality illustrated travel features. Should include human interest story elements rather than simple travelogues.
Overall freelance potential: Good for top-quality work.
Fees: Negotiable and according to use.

TRAVELLER
WEXAS International Ltd, 45 Brompton Road, London SW3 1DE.
Tel: 020 7589 3315. Fax: 020 7581 1357. E-mail: traveller@wexas.com
Editor: Jonathan Lorie.
Quarterly publication containing narrative features on unusual and adventurous travel, usually in the developing countries of the world. Aimed at the independent traveller who prefers to travel off the beaten track.
Illustrations: Colour. High quality documentary travel pictures, usually from developing countries, rarely Europe or North America. Usually required as an integral part of illustrated articles as below, but there is also a six-page photo-essay (action/reportage). No tourist brochure-type shots.
Text: Well-illustrated travel articles from contributors with in-depth knowledge of the area/subject covered. Around 2,000 words, plus about 10 pictures. Unusual subject matter preferred, including coverage of world hot spots.
Overall freelance potential: Good, but limited by the magazine's frequency.
Editor's tips: Excellent photographic work is essential.
Fees: Photographs, From £50, full-page £80, £100 for cover. Text, £150 per 1,000 words.

VIVA ESPAÑA
Blendon Communications Ltd, 207 Providence Square, Mill Street, London SE1 2EW.
Tel: 020 7939 9888. Fax: 020 7939 9889. E-mail: df@blendoncom.com
Editor: George Sell. **Picture Editor:** Darren Fuller.
Bi-monthly glossy offering in-depth coverage of Spanish life and culture, plus large property section.
Illustrations: Colour. Images and picture-essays covering of all aspects of Spain – travel, people, lifestyle, heritage and culture, food and wine, the arts, sport and fashion. Property-related subjects especially of interest. Submit detailed list of subjects available in the first instance.
Text: Well-illustrated articles on any aspect of the country. Submit suggestions to the editor.
Overall freelance potential: Very good.
Fees: By negotiation and according to use.

WANDERLUST
Wanderlust Publications Ltd, PO Box 1832, Windsor, Berks SL4 1YT.
Tel: 01753 620426. Fax: 01753 620474.
Editor: Lyn Hughes. **Picture Editor:** Tor Mathews.
Bi-monthly for the "independent-minded" traveller. Aims to promote awareness of other cultures and the environment.
Illustrations: Colour transparency preferred; digital only by prior arrangement. Most required for

use in conjunction with features. Send a summary stock list in the first instance. Covers: always looking for simple, bold images that say "wanderlust", preferably ethnic people. Should be vertical or croppable to vertical.
Text: Well-illustrated features on independent and special interest travel at any level and in any part of the world. Contributors must have in-depth knowledge of their subject area and be prepared to cover both good and bad aspects. Short pieces up to 750 words; longer articles from 1,800–2,500 words.
Overall freelance potential: Excellent for complete packages of words and pictures.
Editor's tips: Don't send unsolicited originals; photocopies or prints will do as samples. Detailed "Notes for Contributors" and "Guidelines for Photographers" can be viewed on website: www.wanderlust.co.uk.
Fees: Photographs by negotiation and according to use; text £200 per 1,000 words.

Women's Interest

BELLA
H. Bauer Publishing Ltd, Academic House, 24-28 Oval Road, London NW1 7DT.
Tel: 020 7241 8000. Fax: 020 7241 8056.
Editor: Jayne Marsden. **Picture Editor:** Lizzie Rowe.
Weekly magazine for women, covering human interest stories, fashion, cookery and celebrities.
Illustrations: Mainly colour. Pictures of celebrities and royalty, off-beat pictures and curiosities considered on spec. Fashion and food, mostly commissioned.
Text: Some scope for exclusive human interest features and celebrity interviews. Always check with the editor first.
Overall freelance potential: Limited for speculative work.
Fees: By negotiation.

BEST
National Magazine Company, 72 Broadwick Street, London W1F 9EP.
Tel: 020 7439 5000. Fax: 020 7437 6886.
Editor: Louise Court. **Picture Editor:** Alison Thurston.
Weekly magazine for women, covering affordable fashion, health matters, cookery, home improvements, features etc.
Illustrations: Mainly colour. Scope for off-beat, general human interest and curiosity shots, and informal celebrity material. Commissioned coverage of fashion, food, features, etc.
Text: Articles with a practical slant, aimed at working women.
Overall freelance potential: Quite good.
Fees: Commissioned photography by negotiation; other material according to use.

CLOSER
EMAP Elan Network, Endeavour House, 189 Shaftesbury Avenue, London WC2H 8JG.
Tel: 020 7859 8685. Fax: 020 7859 8685. E-mail: carol.hendry@emap.com
Editor: Jane Johnson. **Picture Editor:** Caroline Ducker.
Weekly women's magazine with the emphasis on celebrities and true-life stories.
Illustrations: Colour. Mainly by commission. Opportunities for experienced photographers to shoot a range of celebrity material, from paparazzi street photography to studio work. Exclusive paparazzi material also considered on spec, but much is sourced from agencies. Photographers in all parts of the UK also needed to shoot portraits to illustrate true-life stories – submit details of experience and area of the country covered.
Text: True-life stories about ordinary people always wanted – submit brief details in the first instance.

Overall freelance potential: Good for those with some experience in these areas.
Fees: Photography by negotiation or according to job. True-life stories, up to £500.

COMPANY
National Magazine Company Ltd, 72 Broadwick Street, London W1V 2BP.
Tel: 020 7439 5000. Fax: 020 7439 5117.
Editor: Victoria White. **Picture Editor:** Ginny Henry.
Monthly magazine aimed at up-market young women in their twenties.
Illustrations: Colour. Photographs to illustrate features on fashion, beauty, relationships, careers, travel and personalities, invariably by commission.
Text: Articles on the above topics, of varying lengths. Also, more topical and "newsy" features.
Overall freelance potential: Fair scope for experienced contributors.
Fees: By negotiation.

COSMOPOLITAN
National Magazine Company Ltd, 72 Broadwick Street, London W1V 2BP.
Tel: 020 7439 5000. Fax: 020 7439 5016.
Editor: Sam Baker. **Art Editor:** David Dowding. **Picture Editor:** Joan Tinney.
Monthly magazine for women in the 18–34 age group.
Illustrations: Colour. Photographs to illustrate features on fashion, style and beauty, by commission only. Some top quality stock situation pictures may be used to illustrate more general features on emotional, sexual or social issues.
Text: Articles of interest to sophisticated young women. Always query the editor first
Overall freelance potential: Only for the experienced contributor to the women's press.
Fees: By negotiation.

ELLE
Hachette Filipacchi (UK) Ltd, 64 North Row, London W1K 7LL.
Tel: 020 7150 7000. Fax: 020 7150 7001.
Editor: Sarah Bailey. **Photography Director:** Duane Ashurst. **Picture Editor:** Giulia Carnera.
Up-market monthly magazine with the emphasis on fashion.
Illustrations: Mainly colour. Top quality coverage of fashion and style subjects, portraiture and still life, always by commission.
Text: Some scope for top quality feature articles and photojournalism, usually by commission and from established contributors.
Overall freelance potential: Good for contributors experienced at the top level of magazine journalism.
Fees: By negotiation.

ESSENTIALS
IPC Media Ltd, King's Reach Tower, Stamford Street, London SE1 9LS.
Tel: 020 7261 6970. Fax: 020 7261 5262.
Editor: Julie Barton-Breck. **Art Director:** Rebecca Brannigan.
Monthly mass-market magazine for women with the emphasis on practical matters.
Illustrations: Mainly colour. Health, interior decoration, travel, food, etc. Some commissioned work available.
Text: Practical articles, health, features of interest to women. Synopsis essential in first instance.
Overall freelance potential: Good for experienced contributors to quality women's magazines.
Fees: By negotiation.

GLAMOUR
The Condé Naste Publications Ltd, 6-8 Old Bond Street, London W1S 4PH.
Tel: 020 7499 9080. Fax: 020 7491 2551.
Editor: Jo Elvin. Picture Director: Lucy Slade.

Mid-market general interest monthly for the 18-32 age group.
Illustrations: Colour. Mostly by commission to shoot features, portraiture, still life and interiors; make an appointment to show portfolio. Possible but limited scope for stock, including celebrity material.
Text: Limited freelance opportunities.
Overall freelance potential: Only for the experienced worker.
Fees: By negotiation.

GOOD HOUSEKEEPING
National Magazine Company Ltd, National Magazine House, 72 Broadwick Street, London W1V 2BP.
Tel: 020 7439 5000. Fax: 020 7439 5591.
Editor: Lindsay Nicholson. **Picture Editor:** Maureen Elliott.
General interest magazine for up-market women. Concentrates on home and family life.
Illustrations: Mainly colour. Interiors, gardening, food, fashion, travel and reportage. Usually by commission to illustrate specific articles.
Text: Articles of interest to up-market women – interesting homes (with photos), gardening, personality profiles, emotional features, humorous articles, etc.
Overall freelance potential: Good scope for the highest quality material.
Fees: By negotiation.

HARPERS & QUEEN
National Magazine Company Ltd, 72 Broadwick Street, London W1V 2BP.
Tel: 020 7439 5000. Fax: 020 7439 5506.
Editor: Lucy Yeoman. **Art Director:** Sheila Jack. **Picture Editor:** Leanne Bracey.
Monthly glossy magazine featuring fashion, design, travel, interiors, beauty and health.
Illustrations: Colour and high-quality B&W. Top quality photography to illustrate subjects as above, only by commission.
Text: General interest features of very high quality. 1,500–3,000 words. Only by commission.
Overall freelance potential: Good for those who can produce the right material.
Fees: Good; on a rising scale according to length of feature.

HELLO!
Hello Ltd, Wellington House, 69/71 Upper Ground, London SE1 9PQ.
Tel: 020 7667 8700. Fax: 020 7667 8711. E-mail: pictures@hellomagazine.com
Editor: Ronnie Whelan. **Picture Editor:** Freddie Sloan.
Weekly magazine for women covering people and current events.
Illustrations: Mainly colour. Pictures and picture stories on personalities and celebrities of all kinds. People in the news and current news events. Off-beat pictures. Dramatic picture stories of bravery, courage or rescue.
Text: Interviews and/or reports to accompany photos.
Overall freelance potential: Excellent for quality material.
Editor's tips: The magazine has short lead times which it likes to exploit to the full – can include late stories in colour up to the Thursday of the week before publication.
Fees: By negotiation.

THE LADY
The Lady, 39–40 Bedford Street, Strand, London WC2E 9ER.
Tel: 020 7379 4717. Fax: 020 7836 4620.
Editor: Arline Usden. **Picture Researcher:** Rose Haire.
Weekly general interest magazine for women.
Illustrations: B&W and colour. Pictures only required to accompany particular articles. Covers: colour pictures of women 35–50 years; famous faces.

Text: Illustrated articles on British and foreign travel, the countryside, human interest, wildlife, pets, cookery, gardening, fashion, beauty, British history and commemorative subjects. 1,000–1,200 words.
Overall freelance potential: Excellent for complete illustrated articles.
Fees: Photographs £14 mono; £18 colour. Text from £80 per 1,000 words.

MARIE CLAIRE
European Magazines Ltd, 13th Floor, King's Reach Tower, Stamford Street, London SE1 9LS.
Tel: 020 7261 5240. Fax: 020 7261 5277.
Editor: Marie O'Riordan. **Creative Director:** Stuart Selner. **Picture Editor:** Luisa Nitrato-Izzo.
Fashion and general interest monthly for sophisticated women in the 25–35 age group.
Illustrations: Mainly colour. Top quality fashion, beauty, portraits, reportage, interiors, still life, etc, usually by commission.
Text: In-depth articles, features and profiles aimed at an intelligent readership. Up to 4,000 words.
Overall freelance potential: Very good for experienced contributors in this field.
Fees: By negotiation.

MORE!
EMAP Elan Ltd, Endeavour House, 189 Shaftesbury Avenue, London WC2H 8JG.
Tel: 020 7437 9011. Fax: 020 7208 3595.
Editor: Ali Hall. **Picture Director:** Katey Lee.
Fortnightly magazine for young women in the 18–24 age group.
Illustrations: Mainly colour. Up-to-date news pictures featuring celebrities, formal and informal. Fashion, beauty, health and pictures to illustrate specific articles, always by commission.
Text: Articles and features, often with a practical slant, of general interest to young women. Submit ideas only in the first instance.
Overall freelance potential: Quite good for quality material.
Editor's tips: No unsolicited features – commissions only.
Fees: By negotiation.

MS LONDON
Independent Magazines, Independent House, 191 Marsh Wall, London E14 9RS.
Tel: 020 7005 5000. Fax: 020 7005 2999.
Editor: Bill Williamson. Group **Art Editor:** Steve Bowling.
Weekly magazine for young, independent women working in London.
Illustrations: B&W and colour. Mostly fashion and portraits, some still life and reportage work. Covers: colour fashion and general interest subjects; medium format preferred.
Text: Off-beat, sharply-written features of interest to young, aware, working Londoners. 800–1,500 words.
Overall freelance potential: Around 90 per cent of the magazine comes from freelances.
Editor's tips: Best to send copies of recently-published work plus list of ideas before actual submission.
Fees: Approximately £120 per 1,000 words; pictures by agreement.

NOW
IPC Media Ltd, King's Reach Tower, Stamford Street, London SE1 9LS.
Tel: 020 7261 6146. Fax: 020 7261 6406.
Editor: Jane Ennis. **Picture Editor:** Francesca D'Avanzo.
Weekly entertainment for women with the focus on celebrities and "true-life" stories.
Illustrations: Colour. Digital media preferred. Topical coverage of current film and TV stars, both

formal and informal shots. Some commissions available to illustrate true-life stories and general features.
Text: Ideas for stories and interviews always considered.
Overall freelance potential: Limited.
Fees: Variable according to the material or assignment; top rates paid for good exclusives.

OK!
Northern & Shell plc, 4th Floor, Ludgate House, 245 Blackfriars Road, London SE1 9UX.
Tel: 020 7928 8000. Fax: 020 7579 4607. E-mail: sophie.mutter@express.co.uk
Editor: Nick McCarty. **Art Director:** Wayne Kirk. **Picture Editor:** Amanda Davis.
Weekly, picture-led magazine devoted to celebrity features and news pictures.
Illustrations: Colour. Shots of celebrities of all kinds considered on spec, especially exclusives or unpublished archive material. Commissions available to experienced photographers – contact picture editor.
Text: Exclusive stories/interviews with celebrities always of interest.
Overall freelance potential: Excellent for the right type of material.
Fees: Negotiable; depends on nature of the material or assignment.

PRIMA
National Magazine Company, 72 Broadwick Street, London W1F 9EP.
Tel: 020 7439 5000. Fax: 020 7312 4100. E-mail: jo.lockwood@natmags.co.uk
Editor: Maire Fahey. **Art Director:** Jacqueline Hampsey. **Picture Editor:** Jo Lockwood.
Picture Researcher: Matthew Brown.
General interest women's monthly with a strong emphasis on practical subjects. Major topics covered include cookery, gardening, crafts, health, fashion and homecare.
Illustrations: Colour only. Top quality work in the fields of food, fashion, still-life, interiors and portraiture, usually by commission. Some scope for good stock shots of family and domestic situations, food, pets, etc that could be used for general illustration purposes, but query needs before before submitting.
Text: Short, illustrated practical features with a "how-to-do-it" approach.
Overall freelance potential: The magazine relies heavily on freelances.
Fees: Commissioned photography in the region of £400 per day. Other fees according to use.

RED
Hachette Filipacchi (UK) Ltd, 64 North Row, London W1K 7LL.
Tel: 020 7150 7000. Fax: 020 7150 7001.
Editor: Trish Halpin. **Art Director:** Jonathan Whitelocke. **Picture Editor:** Sian Parry.
Sophisticated monthly aimed at women in their 30s.
Illustrations: Mainly colour. High quality commissioned photography covering fashion, interior design, food, fashion and celebrities, plus some photojournalistic work for general and investigative features. Telephone to make an appointment to drop off portfolio in the first instance. Little scope for stock material.
Text: Ideas always welcome from experienced writers.
Overall freelance potential: Good for the experienced worker.
Fees: By negotiation.

SHE
National Magazine Company, National Magazine House, 72 Broadwick Street, London W1V 2BP.
Tel: 020 7439 5000. Fax: 020 7439 5350.
Editor: Terry Tavner. **Picture Editor:** Abi Dillon.
General interest monthly for the 30-something woman.
Illustrations: Mainly colour. Most material by commission for specific articles; anything else only considered by appointment.
Text: Top quality features of interest to intelligent women; always query the editor first.

Overall freelance potential: Little unsolicited material used, but quite good for commissions.
Editor's tips: Please study the format before contacting magazine.
Fees: By arrangement.

THAT'S LIFE!
H.Bauer Publishing Ltd, 24-28 Oval Road, London NW1 7DT.
Tel: 020 7241 8000. Fax: 020 7241 8008. E-mail: jim.taylor@bauer.co.uk
Editor: Jo Checkley. **Picture Editor:** Jim Taylor.
Popular women's weekly concentrating on true-life stories and confessions.
Illustrations: Colour. Digital files preferred. Mostly commissioned shots of people to accompany stories; photographers who can produce good informal portrait work should write to the picture editor enclosing a couple of samples. Also limited opportunities in fashion, food and still life. Quirky and amusing "readers' pictures" always considered on spec – should be accompanied by a brief story or anecdote.
Text: Personal true-life stories always of interest – shocking, scandalous, embarrassing, tear-jerking, etc. Around 300 words. Contact the editor with suggestions first.
Overall freelance potential: Good.
Fees: Story shoots around £150; readers' pictures £25; other photography by negotiation. £200 for true stories.

WI HOME & COUNTRY
NFWI, 104 New Kings Road, Fulham, London SW6 4LY.
Tel: 020 7731 5777. Fax: 020 7736 4061. E-mail: h&ced@nfwi.org.uk
Editor: Susan Seager. **Designer:** Diane Lilley.
Monthly publication for Women's Institute members. Includes WI news and features, plus general articles of interest to women.
Illustrations: Mostly colour. Pictures of WI events etc.
Text: Features of general women's interest and rural conservation issues, commissioned in advance; ideas welcomed. 800–1,200 words.
Overall freelance potential: A small but regular amount bought each month.
Editor's tips: Always consult the editor before submitting.
Fees: By agreement.

WOMAN
IPC Media Ltd, King's Reach Tower, Stamford Street, London SE1 9LS.
Tel: 020 7261 6395. Fax: 020 7261 5997.
Editor: Carole Russell. **Picture Editor:** Emma Smith.
Weekly magazine devoted to all women's interests.
Illustrations: Mainly colour. Most pictures commissioned to illustrate specific features. Some scope for human interest shots which are dramatic, off-beat or unusual.
Text: Interviews with leading personalities, human interest stories. Other features mostly staff-produced. Submit a synopsis in the first instance.
Overall freelance potential: Only for experienced contributors in the field.
Fees: Good; on a rising scale according to size of reproduction or length of articles.

WOMAN & HOME
IPC Media Ltd, King's Reach Tower, Stamford Street, London SE1 9LS.
Tel: 020 7261 5176. Fax: 020 7261 7346.
Editor: Sue James. **Art Director:** Craig Mitchell. **Picture Researcher:** Louise Connolly.
Monthly magazine for all women concerned with family and home. Subjects covered include cookery, fashion, beauty, interior design, DIY, gardening, travel, topical issues and personality articles.
Illustrations: Mainly colour. All photography on above subjects commissioned from experienced freelances.
Text: Articles on personalities, either well-known or who lead interesting lives. 1,500 words.

Overall freelance potential: Very good for the experienced worker. Including regular contributors, about 50 per cent of the magazine is produced by freelances.
Fees: £120 per 1,000 words. Pictures by negotiation.

WOMAN'S OWN
IPC Media Ltd, King's Reach Tower, Stamford Street, London SE1 9LS.
Tel: 020 7261 5000. Fax: 020 7261 5346.
Editor: Elsa McAlonan. **Picture Editor:** *TBA*.
Weekly publishing articles and practical features of interest to women.
Illustrations: Mainly colour. Mostly commissioned to illustrate features on fashion, interior design, crafts, etc.
Text: Mostly staff-produced. Send a brief outline of any proposed feature in the first instance to the features editor.
Overall freelance potential: Fair for commissioned work, but much is produced by regulars.
Fees: Good; on a rising scale according to size of reproduction or length of article.

WOMAN'S WEEKLY
IPC Media Ltd, King's Reach Tower, Stamford Street, London SE1 9LS.
Tel: 020 7261 5000. Fax: 020 7261 6322.
Editor: Gilly Sinclair. **Art Editor:** Fiona Watson. **Picture Editor:** Sue De Jong.
General interest family-oriented magazine for women in the 35+ age group.
Illustrations: Colour. Mostly by commission to illustrate features on fashion, beauty, cookery, decoration, etc.
Text: Practical features on general women's topics, plus human interest stories and celebrity pieces.
Overall freelance potential: Fairly good for the experienced contributor.
Fees: By negotiation.

WOMEN'S HEALTH
Highbury Lifestyle Publishing, 1-3 Highbury Station Road, London N1 1SE.
Tel: 020 7226 2222. Fax: 020 7228 7579. E-mail: womenshealth@highburywv.com
Editor: Tracey Smith.
Lifestyle monthly incorporating health and nutrition elements rather than a dedicated fitness title.
Illustrations: Colour. Opportunities for commissions to shoot illustrations for health, fitness and food features. Also scope for stock on health and general women's lifestyle subjects.
Text: Will always consider suggestions for articles on women's health, lifestyles, relationships, nutrition.
Overall freelance potential: Fair.
Fees: Photography by agreement; text £160 per 1,000 words.

NEWSPAPERS

In this section we list the national daily and Sunday newspapers, and their associated magazine supplements. While the supplements may publish a wide range of general interest subject matter, the parent papers are obviously only likely to be interested in hard news pictures and stories of genuine interest to a nationwide readership.

News pictures

Despite the heavy presence of staff and agency photographers at major events, it is still perfectly possible for an independent freelance to get the shot that makes the front page. And when it comes to the unexpected, the freelance is often the only one on the spot to capture the drama.

If you think you have obtained a "hot" news picture or story, the best procedure is to telephone the papers most likely to be interested as soon as possible and let them know what you have to offer.

If they are interested, they will advise you how to get it to them it by the fastest convenient method.

Note that newspapers prefer to work from digital files and will not want to handle transparencies. They will, however, accept colour print or negative if that is all that is available.

In the listings that follow, as well as the main switchboard number you will find direct line telephone numbers which take you directly through to the picture desk of the paper concerned.

There should be little cause to use fax numbers for newspapers these days, but if you do it is advisable to always check the correct number for the department you want. Newspaper offices have numerous fax machines; the numbers listed here are necessarily general editorial numbers and if used without checking might delay your message getting to the department you need.

Other material

There is some scope for other material apart from hard news in most of the papers. Some use the occasional oddity or human interest item as a "filler", while in the tabloids there is always a good market for celebrity pictures.

Finally, of course, there is a market for top quality glamour material of the "Page 3" variety in several of the tabloids.

The supplements operate much like any other general interest magazine. Most of their content is commissioned from well-established photographers and writers, though some will accept exceptional photojournalistic features or exclusives on spec.

Fees

Fees paid by newspapers can vary tremendously according to what is offered and how it is used. However, it can be taken for granted that rates paid by the national papers listed here are good.

Generally, picture fees are calculated on standard rates based on the size of the reproduction, with the minumum fee you might expect from a national newspaper being around £65.

However, for material that is exclusive or exceptional the sky is almost literally the limit. If you think you have something very special and are prepared to offer it as an exclusive, make sure you negotiate a fee, and perhaps get several offers, before committing the material to anyone.

National Daily Newspapers

DAILY EXPRESS
Express Newspapers, Ludgate House, 245 Blackfriars Road, London SE1 9UX.
Tel: 020 7928 8000. Picture desk: 020 7922 7171. Fax: 020 7922 7976.
E-mail: macdesk@express.co.uk
Editor: Chris Williams. **Picture Editor:** Neil McCarthy.
SATURDAY
Picture Editor: Yvonne Irwin.

DAILY MAIL
The Daily Mail Ltd, Northcliffe House, Derry Street, London W8 5TT.
Tel: 020 7938 6000. Picture desk: 020 7938 6373. Fax: 020 7937 5560.
E-mail: dmpix@dailymail.co.uk
Editor: Paul Dacre. **Picture Editor:** Paul Silva.

DAILY MIRROR
Mirror Group Newspapers Ltd, Canary Wharf Tower, 1 Canada Square, London E14 5AP.
Tel: 020 7293 3000. Picture desk: 020 7293 3851. Fax: 020 7293 3983. Modem: 0800 216036.
ISDN: 020 7572 5802 (Foresight); 020 7572 5803 (Easy Transfer).
E-mail: picturedesk@mirror.co.uk
Editor: Richard Wallace. **Picture Editor:** Ian Down.

DAILY RECORD
The Scottish Daily Record and Sunday Mail Ltd, One Central Quay, Glasgow G3 8DA.
Tel: 0141 309 3000. Picture desk: 0141 309 3248. Fax: 0141 309 3835. ISDN: 0141 309 4879.
E-mail: s.nicol@dailyrecord.co.uk
Editor: Bruce Waddell. **Picture Editor:** Stuart Nicol.

DAILY SPORT
Sport Newspapers Ltd, 19 Great Ancoats Street, Manchester M60 4BT.
Tel: 0161 236 4466. Picture desk: 0161 238 8169. Fax: 0161 236 4535.
E-mail: paul.currie@sportnewspapers.co.uk
Editor: Dave Beevers. **Picture Editor:** Paul Currie.

DAILY STAR
Express Newspapers, Ludgate House, 245 Blackfriars Road, London SE1 9UX.
Tel: 020 7928 8000. Picture desk: 020 7922 7353. Fax: 020 7922 7960.
E-mail: rob.greener@dailystar.co.uk
Editor: Peter Hill. **Picture Editor:** Rob Greener.

THE DAILY TELEGRAPH
The Daily Telegraph Plc, 1 Canada Square, Canary Wharf, London E14 5DT.
Tel: 020 7538 5000. Picture desk: 020 7538 6369. Fax: 020 7538 7640.
E-mail: photo@telegraph.co.uk
Editor: Martin Newland. **Picture Editor:** Robert Bodman.
TELEGRAPH MAGAZINE
Editor: Daniella Agnelli. **Picture Editor:** Cheryl Newman.

FINANCIAL TIMES
The Financial Times Ltd, Number One Southwark Bridge, London SE1 9HL.
Tel: 020 7873 3000. Picture desk: 020 7873 3466. Fax: 020 7873 3073. ISDN: 020 7378 6642.
Modem: 020 7873 3948. E-mail: chris.lawson@ft.com
Editor: Andrew Gowers. **Picture Editor:** Chris Lawson.

THE GUARDIAN
119 Farringdon Road, London EC1R 3ER.
Tel: 020 7278 2332. Picture desk: 020 7239 9585. Fax: 020 7239 9951.
E-mail: pictures@guardian.co.uk
Editor: Alan Rusbridger. **Picture Editor:** Roger Tooth.
WEEKEND GUARDIAN
Editor: Katherine Viner. **Picture Editor:** Kate Edwards.

THE HERALD
200 Renfield Street, Glasgow G2 3QB.
Tel: 0141 302 7000. Picture desk: 0141 302 6668. Fax: 0141 302 7007. ISDN: 0141 302 2101 1826.
Modem: 0141 302 6663. E-mail: pictures@theherald.co.uk
Editor: Mark Douglas-Home. **Picture Editor:** Douglas Salteri.

THE INDEPENDENT
Independent News & Media Plc, Independent House, 191 Marsh Wall, London E14 9RS.
Tel: 020 7005 2000. Picture desk: 020 7005 2830. Fax: 020 7005 2086. ISDN: 020 7005 2424/2626
E-mail: picturedesk@independent.co.uk
Editor: Simon Kelner. **Picture Editor:** Lynn Cullen.
THE INDEPENDENT MAGAZINE
Editor: Lisa Markwell. **Picture Editor:** Nick Hall.

THE SCOTSMAN
The Scotsman Publications Ltd, 108 Hollyrood Road, Edinburgh EH8 8AS.
Tel: 0131 620 8620. Picture desk: 0131 620 8555. Fax: 0131 620 8615.
E-mail: pspics@scotsman.com
Editor: Iain Martin. **Picture Editor:** Alan Macdonald.

THE SUN
News Group Newspapers Ltd, 1 Virginia Street, London E1 9XP.
Tel: 020 7782 4000. Picture desk: 020 7782 4110/4116. Fax: 020 7782 4108.
E-mail: pictures@the-sun.co.uk
Editor: Rebekah Wade. **Picture Editor:** John Edwards.

THE TIMES
News International Newspapers Ltd, 1 Pennington Street, London E98 1TT.
Tel: 020 7782 5000. Picture desk: 020 7782 5877. Fax: 020 7782 5449.
E-mail: pictures@thetimes.co.uk
Editor: Robert Thomson. **Picture Editor:** Bob Kirwin.
THE TIMES MAGAZINE
Editor: Gill Morgan. **Picture Editor:** Graham Wood.

National Sunday Newspapers

THE INDEPENDENT ON SUNDAY
Independent News & Media Plc, Independent House, 191 Marsh Wall, London E14 9RS.
Tel: 020 7005 2000. Picture desk: 020 7005 2837/2828. Fax: 020 7005 2086.
E-mail: picturedesk@independent.co.uk
Editor: Tristan Davies. **Picture Editor:** Lynn Cullen.
THE SUNDAY REVIEW
Editor: Andrew Tuck. **Picture Editor:** Victoria Lukens.

THE MAIL ON SUNDAY
Northcliffe House, 2 Derry Street, Kensington, London W8 5TS.
Tel: 020 7938 6000. Picture desk: 020 7938 7017. Fax: 020 7938 6609.
E-mail: pix@mailonsunday.co.uk
Editor: Peter Wright. **Picture Editor:** Liz Cocks.
YOU MAGAZINE
Editor: Sue Peart. **Picture Editor:** Eve George.
NIGHT & DAY
Editor: Christena Appleyard. **Picture Editor:** Sara Mahon.

NEWS OF THE WORLD
News International Newspapers Ltd, Virginia Street, London E1 9XR.
Tel: 020 7782 4000. Picture desk: 020 7782 4421. Fax: 020 7782 4463.
ISDN: 020 7680 1010/7702 9140. E-mail: nowpicture@newsint.co.uk
Editor: Andy Coulson. **Picture Editor:** Paul Bennett.
SUNDAY MAGAZINE
Editor: Judy McGuire. **Picture Editor:** David Jester.

THE OBSERVER
The Observer Ltd, 119 Farringdon Road, London EC1R 3ER.
Tel: 020 7278 2332. Picture desk: 020 7713 4304. Fax: 020 7713 4250.
ISDN: 020 7713 7496. E-mail: obspics@observer.co.uk
Editor: Roger Alton. **Picture Editor:** Greg Whitmore.
OM Magazine
Editor: Allan Jenkins. **Picture Editor:** Jenny Ricketts.
OBSERVER FOOD MONTHLY
Editor: Nicola Jeal. **Picture Editor:** Greg Whitmore.
OBSERVER SPORT MONTHLY
Editor: Jason Cowley. **Picture Editor:** Greg Whitmore.

THE PEOPLE
Mirror Group plc, 1 Canada Square, Canary Wharf, London E14 5AP.
Tel: 020 7293 3000. Picture desk: 020 7293 3901. Fax: 020 7293 3810.
ISDN: 020 7572 5801 (Easy Transfer); 020 7513 2427 (Foresight).
E-mail: pictures@people.co.uk
Editor: Mark Thomas. **Picture Editor:** Paula Derry.
TAKE IT EASY
Editor: Maria Coole. **Picture Editor:** Mariana Felicio.

SCOTLAND ON SUNDAY
Barclay House, 108 Holyrood Road, Edinburgh EH8 8AS.
Tel: 0131 620 8620. Picture desk: 0131 620 8438. Fax: 0131 620 8491. ISDN: 0131 556 5379/1230.
E-mail: sspics@scotsman.com
Editor: John McLelland. **Executive Picture Editor:** Tony Marsh. **Assistant Editor, Pictures:** Kayt Turner.

SUNDAY EXPRESS
Express Newspapers, Ludgate House, 245 Blackfriars Road, London SE1 9UX.
Tel: 020 7928 8000. Picture desk: 020 7922 7171. Fax: 020 7922 7976.
E-mail: macdesk@express.co.uk
Editor: Martin Townsend. **Picture Editor:** Terry Evans.
SUNDAY EXPRESS MAGAZINE
Editor: Louise Robinson. **Picture Editor:** Andrea Whittaker.

SUNDAY HERALD
200 Renfield Street, Glasgow G2 3QB.
Tel: 0141 302 7000. Picture desk: 0141 302 7876. Fax: 0141 302 7815. ISDN: 0141 302 2103.
E-mail: sunday.pictures@sundayherald.com
Editor: Andrew Jaspan. **Picture Editor:** Elaine Livingstone.
SUNDAY HERALD MAGAZINE
Editor: Jane Wright. **Picture Editor:** Leanne Thompson.

THE SUNDAY MAIL
The Scottish Daily Record and Sunday Mail Ltd, 1 Central Quay, Glasgow G3 8DA.
Tel: 0141 309 7000. Picture desk: 0141 309 3434. Fax: 0141 309 3587.
ISDN: 0141 309 4884/4886. E-mail: a.hosie@sundaymail.co.uk
Editor: Allan Rennie. **Picture Editor:** Andy Hosie.

SUNDAY MIRROR
Mirror Group plc, 1 Canada Square, Canary Wharf, London E14 5AP.
Tel: 020 7293 3000. Picture desk: 020 7293 3335/6. Fax: 020 7510 6991.
E-mail: pictures@sundaymirror.co.uk
Editor: Tina Weaver. **Picture Editor:** Mike Sharp.
M CELEBS
Editor: Mel Brodie. **Picture Editor:** Jo Aspill.

THE SUNDAY POST
D. C. Thomson & Co Ltd, Courier Place, Dundee DD1 9QJ.
Tel: 01382 223131. Picture desk: 01382 575804. Fax: 01382 201064. ISDN: 01382 575935.
E-mail: mail@sundaypost.com
Editor: David Pollington. **News Editor:** Tom McKay. **Picture Editor:** Alan Morrison.
THE SUNDAY POST COLOUR MAGAZINE
Editor: Maggie Dun.

SUNDAY SPORT
Sport Newspapers Ltd, 19 Great Ancoats Street, Manchester M60 4BT.
Tel: 0161 236 4466. Picture desk: 0161 238 8169. Fax: 0161 236 4535.
E-mail: paul.currie@sportnewspapers.co.uk
Editor: Paul Carter. **Picture Editor:** Paul Currie.

THE SUNDAY TELEGRAPH
The Telegraph Plc, 1 Canada Square, Canary Wharf, London E14 5AR.
Tel: 020 7538 5000. Picture desk: 020 7538 7369. Fax: 020 7538 7918.
E-mail: stpics@telegraph.co.uk
Editor: Dominic Lawson. **Picture Editor:** Nigel Skelsey.
SUNDAY TELEGRAPH MAGAZINE
Editor: Lucy Tuck. **Picture Editor:** Hilary Kirby.

THE SUNDAY TIMES
Times Newspapers Ltd, 1 Pennington Street, London E1 9XW.
Tel: 020 7782 5000. Picture desk: 020 7782 5666. Fax: 020 7782 5563.
E-mail: pictures@sunday-times.co.uk
Editor: John Witherow. **Picture Editor:** Ray Wells.
THE SUNDAY TIMES MAGAZINE
Editor: Karen Robinson. **Picture Editor:** Aidan Sullivan.

BOOKS

Books represent a substantial and ever-growing market for the photographer. In an increasingly visual age the market for heavily illustrated books continues to expand, with hundreds of new titles being published every year.

In this section we list major book publishers, and specifically those companies that make considerable use of photographic material.

As well as regular publishers, also included here are book packagers. These are companies that offer a complete editorial production service and specialise in producing books that can be sold as finished packages to publishers internationally. The majority of their products are of the heavily illustrated type, and thus these companies can often present a greater potential market for photographic material than do the mainstream publishers.

Making an approach

In this field the difficulty for the individual freelance is that there is no easy way of knowing who wants what and when.

Obviously book publishers only require pictures of specific subjects when they are currently working on a project requiring such material. Much of the time they will rely heavily on known sources such as picture libraries, but this does not mean that there is not good scope for the individual photographer who has a good collection of material on particular subjects, or who may be able to produce suitable work to order.

The solution for the photographer, therefore, is to place details of what he or she has to offer in front of all those companies that might conceivably require material of that type.

The initial approach is simply to send an introductory letter outlining the sort of material that you can supply. A detailed list of subjects can be attached where appropriate.

There is little point however, in sending any photographs at this stage, unless it be one or two samples to indicate a particular style. And one should not expect an immediate response requesting that work be submitted; most likely the publisher will simply keep your details on file for future reference.

Preceding the listings of book publishers is a subject index that should assist in identifying the most promising markets for those areas in which you have good coverage.

In the listings that follow, the major areas of activity for each publisher are detailed under "Subjects". Of course, the larger companies publish on the widest range of subjects and therefore their coverage may be stated as "general", but in most entries you will find a list of specific subject areas. These are by no means a complete list of all the subjects handled by each publisher, but indicate those areas where the company is most active and therefore most likely to be in need of photographic material.

In some entries a "Contact" name is given. However, in a lot of cases it is not possible to give a specific name as larger book publishers usually have large numbers of editorial personnel with constantly shifting responsibilities for individual projects. In addition, many companies frequently use the services of freelance picture researchers. A general approach should therefore simply be addressed to the editorial director.

Rights and fees

Whereas the rights sold in the magazine world are invariably for UK use only, book publishers – and especially packagers – make a good deal of their profit from selling their products to other publishers in overseas markets.

It is therefore quite likely that when work is chosen for use in a particular book the publisher may at some stage request, in addition to British publishing rights, rights for other areas such as "Commonwealth", "North American", "French language", etc. These differing rights will, of course, affect the fees that the photographer receives – the more areas the book sells into, the higher the fees.

Other major factors affecting fees are the size of reproduction on the page and the quantity of the print-run.

Thus there is no easy way to generalise about the sort of fees paid in this field. On the whole, however, fees in book publishing are quite good and comparable with good magazine rates. For packages destined for the international co-edition market they can be substantially higher.

A word about names and imprints

The use by large publishers of a multiplicity of names for different divisions can be quite confusing.

Many famous publishing names, though still in existence, now belong to huge publishing conglomerates. Some are still run as separate companies, but others have effectively become "imprints".

Imprints are the names used by large publishers for specific sections of their list. Only relevant, illustrated imprints are listed here, and are generally cross-referenced to their parent company. Note, however, that in many cases an imprint may operate as a completely separate company.

Subject Index

Robert Hale Ltd
Headline Book Publishing
Frances Lincoln Ltd
New Holland Publishers
Octopus Publishing Group Ltd
Orion Publishing Group Ltd
Pan Macmillan
Piatkus Books
Quarto Publishing plc
Reader's Digest Association Ltd
Ryland, Peters & Small
Salamander Books Ltd
Sheldrake Press Ltd
Simon & Schuster
Souvenir Press Ltd

Gardening

Anness Publishing
Antique Collectors' Club Ltd
BBC Books
Boxtree
Breslich & Foss
Carroll & Brown Publishers
Kyle Cathie Ltd
Chrysalis Books Group
The Crowood Press
Dorling Kindersley
Focus Publishing
W. Foulsham & Co Ltd
Guild of Master Craftsman Publications Ltd
Headline Book Publishing
Frances Lincoln Ltd
New Holland Publishers
Octopus Publishing Group Ltd
Orion Publishing Group Ltd
Pan Macmillan
Quarto Publishing plc
Reader's Digest Association Ltd
Ryland, Peters & Small
Salamander Books Ltd
Souvenir Press Ltd

Health/Medical

Bantam Press
Breslich & Foss
Cambridge University Press
Carroll & Brown Publishers
Kyle Cathie Ltd
Chrysalis Books Group
Constable & Robinson
Dorling Kindersley
Ebury Press
Focus Publishing
W. Foulsham & Co Ltd
Grub Street
Piatkus Books
Quarto Publishing plc
Souvenir Press Ltd
Transworld Publishers

Interior Design

David & Charles Publishing Ltd
Chrysalis Books Group
Dorling Kindersley
Ebury Press
Frances Lincoln Ltd
New Holland Publishers
Octopus Publishing Group Ltd
Orion Publishing Group Ltd
Ryland, Peters & Small
Thames & Hudson

Military

Ian Allan Publishing
Amber Books Ltd
Cassell Military
Chrysalis Books Group
Constable & Robinson
The Crowood Press
Robert Hale Ltd
Osprey Publishing
Salamander Books Ltd
Transworld Publishers
Spellmount Ltd
Sutton Publishing Ltd
Weidenfeld & Nicolson Ltd

Motoring

Ian Allan Publishing
The Crowood Press
Haynes Publishing
Salamander Books Ltd
Sutton Publishing Ltd

Music

Bantam Press
Boxtree
Cambridge University Press
Ebury Press
Faber & Faber Ltd

Guinness Publishing Ltd
Robert Hale Ltd
Headline Book Publishing
Omnibus Press/Book Sales Ltd
Pan Macmillan
Plexus Publishing Ltd
Quartet Books
Sheldrake Press Ltd
Thames & Hudson
Virgin Books Ltd

Natural History

Appletree Press
A & C Black (Publishers) Ltd
Cambridge University Press
The Crowood Press
Robert Hale Ltd
Christopher Helm Publishers Ltd
Kingfisher Publications
New Holland Publishers
Orion Publishing Group Ltd
T & A D Poyser
Reader's Digest Association Ltd
Salamander Books Ltd
Savitri Books Ltd
Souvenir Press Ltd
Usborne Publishing

Photography

Breedon Books Publishing Co
Chrysalis Books Group
David & Charles Publishing Ltd
Guild of Master Craftsman Publications Ltd
Phaidon Press Ltd
RotoVision
Thames & Hudson Ltd

Politics/Current Affairs

Bantam Press
Bloomsbury Publishing Ltd
Jonathan Cape
Century
Chatto & Windus
Constable & Robinson
Faber & Faber Ltd
Fourth Estate Ltd
Hutchinson
Manchester University Press
Pan Macmillan
Yale University Press

Railways

Ian Allan Publishing
Railways – Milepost 92½
Salamander Books Ltd
Sutton Publishing Ltd

Science

Amber Books Ltd
Bantam Press
Cambridge University Press
Fourth Estate Ltd
Headline Book Publishing
Lutterworth Press
Orion Publishing Group Ltd
Transworld Publishers
Weidenfeld & Nicolson Ltd

Sport

A & C Black (Publishers) Ltd
Boxtree
Breedon Books Publishing Co
The Crowood Press
Dorling Kindersley
Ebury Press
Focus Publishing
W. Foulsham & Co Ltd
Guinness Publishing Ltd
Robert Hale Ltd
Headline Book Publishing
Octopus Publishing Group Ltd
Orion Publishing Group Ltd
Transworld Publishers
Virgin Books Ltd

Travel

AA Publishing
Amber Books Ltd
Appletree Press
BBC Books
Bantam Press
A & C Black (Publishers) Ltd
Bloomsbury Publishing Ltd
Cambridge University Press
Chatto & Windus
Chrysalis Books Group
Constable & Robinson
The Crowood Press
Dorling Kindersley
Ebury Press

Book Publishers

AA PUBLISHING
Automobile Association, Fanum House, Basingstoke, Hampshire RG21 2EA.
Tel: 01256 491588. Fax: 01256 492440. E-mail: travelimages@theaa.com
Contact: Debbie Ireland, Head of Picture Library; Liz Allen, Picture Sales Manager.
Subjects: Travel images for guide books, maps and atlases. Commissions only.

ADLARD COLES NAUTICAL – see A & C BLACK

AIRLIFE PUBLISHING – see THE CROWOOD PRESS

ALBION PRESS LTD
Spring Hill, Idbury, Oxfordshire OX7 6RU.
Tel: 01993 831094. Fax: 01993 831982.
Subjects: Children's, cookery, fine arts, social history.

IAN ALLAN PUBLISHING
Riverdene Business Park, Molesey Road, Hersham, Surrey KT12 4RG.
Tel: 01932 266600. Fax: 01932 266601.
Subjects: Aviation, military, motoring, railways, road transport.

AMBER BOOKS LTD
Bradley's Close, 74-77 White Lion Street, London N1 9PF.
Tel: 020 7520 7600. Fax: 020 7520 7606. E-mail: natasha@amberbooks.co.uk
Web: www.amberbooks.co.uk
Contact: Natasha Jones, Picture Manager.
Imprints: Brown Packaging Books Ltd.
Subjects: General; aviation, fitness and survival, military, naval, popular science, transport.

ANNESS PUBLISHING LTD
Hermes House 88-89 Blackfriars Road, London SE1 8HA.
Tel: 020 7401 2077. Fax: 020 7633 9499.
Contact: Gary Murphy, Picture Library Manager.
Imprints: Aquamarine, Hermes House, Lorenz Books, Southwater.
Subjects: Crafts, cookery, gardening, health, reference.

ANTIQUE COLLECTORS CLUB LTD
Sandy Lane, Old Martlesham, Woodbridge, Suffolk IP12 4SD.
Tel: 01394 389950. Fax: 01394 389999.
Contact: Diana Steel, Managing Director (by letter only).
Subjects: Antiques, architecture, art, gardening.

APPLETREE PRESS LTD
14 Howard Street South, Belfast BT7 1AP.
Tel: 028 90 243074. Fax: 028 90 246756.
Web: www.appletree.ie
Contact: Jean Brown, Desk & Marketing Editor.
Subjects: Irish and Scottish interest; arts & crafts, cookery, nature, travel.

AQUAMARINE – see ANNESS PUBLISHING

BBC BOOKS
BBC Worldwide Publishing, Room A3126, Woodlands, 80 Wood Lane, London W12 0TT.
Tel: 020 8433 2000. Fax: 020 8749 8766.
Contact: David Cottingham, Picture Research Manager.
Subjects: General non-fiction, tie-ins to BBC TV and radio programmes; business, cookery, gardening, history, travel.

BANTAM PRESS
Transworld Publishers, 61-63 Uxbridge Road, London W5 5SA.
Tel: 020 8579 2652. Fax: 020 8579 5479.
Subjects: General; biography, food & drink, health, history, music, new age, politics, science, social history, travel.

A & C BLACK (PUBLISHERS) LTD
Alderman House, 37 Soho Square, London W1D 3QZ.
Tel: 020 7758 0200. Fax: 020 7758 0222. E-mail: enquiries@acblack.co.uk
Contact: John Turner.
Imprints: Adlard Coles Nautical, Christopher Helm, Herbert Press, T&AD Poyser.
Subjects: Arts and crafts, children's educational, nautical, ornithology, reference, sport, theatre, travel, ceramics.

BLANDFORD – see OCTOPUS PUBLISHING GROUP

BLOOMSBURY PUBLISHING PLC
38 Soho Square, London W1D 3HB.
Tel: 020 7494 2111. Fax: 020 7434 0151.
Subjects: General; biography, children's, current affairs, reference, travel.

BOXTREE LTD
Macmillan Publishers Ltd, 25 Eccleston Place, London SW1W 9NF.
Tel: 020 7881 8000. Fax: 020 7881 8280.
Contact: Emma Marriott, Commissioning Editor.
Subjects: General illustrated, cookery, gardening, history, popular music, sport.

BRASSEY'S – see CHRYSALIS BOOKS GROUP

BREEDON BOOKS
Breedon House, 3 The Parker Centre, Derby DE21 4SZ.
Tel: 01332 384235. Fax: 01332 292755.
Contact: Steve Caron, Managing Director; Susan Last, Commissioning Editor.
Subjects: Archive photography, British heritage and local history, sport (especially football).

BRESLICH & FOSS LTD
2a Union Court, 20-22 Union Road, London, SW4 6JP
Tel: 020 7819 3990. Fax: 020 7819 3998. E-mail: editorial@breslichfoss.com
Contact: Janet Ravenscroft.
Subjects: Arts, children's, crafts, gardening, health, lifestyle.

BROWN PACKAGING BOOKS – see AMBER BOOKS

CAMBRIDGE UNIVERSITY PRESS
The Edinburgh Building, Shaftesbury Road, Cambridge CB2 2RU.
Tel: 01223 312393. Fax: 01223 315052. E-mail: info@cup.cam.ac.uk
Subjects: Archaeology, architecture, art, astronomy, biology, drama, geography, history, medicine, music, natural history, religion, science, sociology, travel.

JONATHAN CAPE LTD
Random House, 20 Vauxhall Bridge Road, London SW1V 2SA.
Tel: 020 7840 8400. Fax: 020 7233 6117.
Subjects: Archaeology, biography and memoirs, current affairs, history, travel.

CARROLL & BROWN PUBLISHERS LTD
20 Lonsdale Road, London NW6 6RD.
Tel: 020 7372 0900. Fax: 020 7372 0460.
Subjects: Food and drink, gardening, health, general illustrated.

CASSELL ILLUSTRATED – see OCTOPUS PUBLISHING GROUP

CASSELL MILITARY – see WEIDENFIELD & NICHOLSON

CASSELL REFERENCE – see WEIDENFIELD & NICHOLSON

KYLE CATHIE LTD
122 Arlington Road, London NW1 7HP.
Tel: 020 7692 7215. Fax: 020 7692 7260. E-mail: vicki.murrell@kyle-cathie.com
Contact: Caroline Taggart, Editor.
Subjects: Beauty, food and drink, gardening, health, reference.

CENTURY
Random House, 20 Vauxhall Bridge Road, London SW1V 2SA.
Tel: 020 7840 8557. Fax: 020 7233 6127.
Subjects: Biography, current affairs, food and drink.

CHATTO & WINDUS LTD
Random House, 20 Vauxhall Bridge Road, London SW1V 2SA.
Tel: 020 7840 8400. Fax: 020 7233 6117.
Subjects: General; biography and memoirs, current affairs, history, travel.

CHRYSALIS BOOKS GROUP
Chrysalis Buildings, Bramley Road, London W10 6SP.
Tel: 020 7314 1400. Fax: 020 7221 6455.
Web: www.chrysalisbooks.co.uk
Contact: Zoë Holtermann.
Imprints: Batsford, Brassey's, Collins & Brown, Conway Maritime Press, PRC, Pavilion, Putnam Aeronautical, Robson, Salamander.
Subjects: General illustrated; architecture, arts & crafts, biography, cookery, gardening, health, military, photography, transport.

CLARENDON PRESS – see OXFORD UNIVERSITY PRESS

COLLINS – see HARPERCOLLINS PUBLISHERS

COLLINS & BROWN– see CHRYSALIS BOOKS GROUP

CONRAN OCTOPUS – see OCTOPUS PUBLISHING GROUP

CONWAY MARITIME PRESS – see CHRYSALIS BOOKS GROUP

THE CROWOOD PRESS LTD
The Stable Block, Crowood Lane, Ramsbury, Marlborough, Wiltshire SN8 2HR.
Tel: 01672 520320. Fax: 01672 520280. E-mail: enquiries@crowood.com
Subjects: Angling, aviation, climbing, country interests, crafts, DIY, equestrian, gardening, motoring, military, natural history, sport, travel.

DAVID & CHARLES PUBLISHING LTD
Brunel House, Newton Abbot, Devon TQ12 4PU.
Tel: 01626 323200. Fax: 01626 323317.
Contact: Sue Cleave.
Subjects: Arts and crafts, equestrian, interiors, practical art and photography.

DORLING KINDERSLEY
80 Strand, London WC2R 0RL.
Tel: 020 7010 3000. Fax: 020 7010 3294.
Web: www.dkimages.com
Contact: Sue Hadley, Library Services Manager.
Subjects: General illustrated and reference; arts & crafts, children's, decorating & DIY, food & drink, gardening, health, hobbies, parenting, pets, sports, travel. (Also maintains separate picture library, DK Images, for onward selling of material originally commissioned for books).

EBURY PRESS
Random House, 20 Vauxhall Bridge Road, London SW1V 2SA.
Tel: 020 7840 8400. Fax: 020 7840 8406.
Contact: Helen Hutton, Editorial Assistant.
Imprints: Fodor's, Rider,Vermilion.
Subjects: Biography, cookery, crafts, decorating and interiors, health and beauty, history, music, natural therapies, parenting, sport, travel guides. (Digital not accepted).

FABER & FABER LTD
3 Queen Square, London WC1N 3AU.
Tel: 020 7465 0045. Fax: 020 7465 0034.
Subjects: Biography, film, music, politics, theatre, wine.

FOCUS PUBLISHING
11A St Botolph's Road, Sevenoaks, Kent TN13 2EB.
Tel: 01732 742456. Fax: 01732 743381. E-mail: caroline@focus-publishing.co.uk
Web: www.focus-publishing.co.uk
Contact: Caroline Watson, Publishing Manager.
Subjects: General illustrated; crafts, DIY, food and drink, gardening, health, sport, transport.

FODOR'S – see EBURY PRESS

G. T. FOULIS – see HAYNES PUBLISHING

W. FOULSHAM & CO
The Publishing House, Bennetts Close, Cippenham, Slough, Berkshire SL1 5AP.
Tel: 01753 526769. Fax: 01753 535003.
Web: www.foulsham.com
Contact: Emma Hamilton, Editorial Administrator.
Subjects: Crafts, collecting, cookery, DIY, gardening, health, hobbies, sport, travel.

FOURTH ESTATE LTD
77-85 Fulham Palace Road, London W6 8JB.
Tel: 020 8741 4414. Fax: 020 8307 4466. E-mail: general@4thestate.co.uk
Contact: Silvia Crompton, Editorial Assistant.
Digital not accepted.
Subjects: Biography, current affairs, history, popular culture, popular science.

GRUB STREET PUBLISHING
4 Rainham Close, London SW11 6SS.
Tel: 020 7924 3966. Fax: 020 7738 1009. E-mail: post@grubstreet.co.uk
Web: www.grubstreet.co.uk
Subjects: Aviation history, cookery.

GUILD OF MASTER CRAFTSMAN PUBLICATIONS LTD
86 High Street, Lewes, East Sussex BN7 1XN.
Tel: 01273 477374. Fax: 01273 402849.
Contact: Anthony Bailey, Chief Photographer.
Subjects: Crafts; gardening, needlework, photography, woodworking.

GUINNESS WORLD RECORDS LTD
338 Euston Road, London NW1 3BD.
Tel: 020 7891 4567. Fax: 020 7891 4501.
Contact: Design Department.
Subjects: Guinness World Records book, TV and merchandising, sport and popular music.

HACHETTE ILLUSTRATED – see OCTOPUS PUBLISHING GROUP

HALDANE MASON
PO Box 34196, London NW10 3YB.
Tel: 020 8459 2131. Fax: 020 8728 1216. E-mail: info@haldanemason.com
Contact: Ron Samuel, Art Director.
Subjects: General illustrated non-fiction, and children's non-fiction.

ROBERT HALE LTD
Clerkenwell House, 45-47 Clerkenwell Green, London EC1R 0HT. HALE
Tel: 020 7251 2661. Fax: 020 7490 4958.
Contact: Susan Hale.
Subjects: General; architecture, cookery, crafts, equestrian, gemmology, horology, military, music, natural history, sport, travel.

HAMISH HAMILTON – see PENGUIN GROUP

HAMLYN – see OCTOPUS PUBLISHING GROUP

HARPERCOLLINS PUBLISHERS
77-85 Fulham Palace Road, London W6 8JB.
Tel: 020 8741 7070. Fax: 020 8307 4440.
Imprints: Collins, Fourth Estate, Thorsons.
Subjects: General.

HAYNES PUBLISHING
Sparkford, Yeovil, Somerset BA22 7JJ.
Tel: 01963 440635. Fax: 01963 440023.
Web: www.haynes.co.uk
Imprints: G.T.Foulis, Patrick Stephens.
Contact: Christine Smith, Adminstration Manager.
Subjects: Cars, motoring and motor racing, motorcycles, motoring biography, DIY.

HEADLINE BOOK PUBLISHING
338 Euston Road, London NW1 3BH.
Tel: 020 7873 6000. Fax: 020 7873 6122. E-mail: bryone.picton@headline.co.uk
Contact: Bryone Picton, Production Director; Lorraine Jerram, Managing Editor Non-Fiction.
Subjects: Biography, food and wine, history, music, sport.

WILLIAM HEINEMANN
Random House, 20 Vauxhall Bridge Road, London SW1V 2SA.
Tel: 020 7840 8400. Fax: 020 7233 6127.
Contact: Emily Sweet.
Subjects: General non-fiction.

CHRISTOPHER HELM PUBLISHERS
37 Soho Square, London W1D 3QZ.
Tel: 020 7758 0200. Fax: 020 7758 0222.
Contact: Nigel Redman, Commissioning Editor.
Subjects: Ornithology and natural history.

HERBERT PRESS – see A & C BLACK

HERMES HOUSE – see ANNESS PUBLISHING

HODDER EDUCATION
338 Euston Road, London NW1 3BH.
Tel: 020 7873 6000. Fax: 020 7873 6325.
Contact: Helen Townson.
Subjects: Education including geography, health, history, science, travel.

HODDER HEADLINE LTD
338 Euston Road, London NW1 3BH.
Tel: 020 7873 6000. Fax: 020 7873 6024.
Imprints: Headline, Hodder Arnold, Hodder & Stoughton.
Subjects: General; academic, children's.

HODDER & STOUGHTON – see HODDER HEADLINE

HUTCHINSON
Random House, 20 Vauxhall Bridge Road, London SW1V 2SA.
Tel: 020 7840 8400. Fax: 020 7233 6127.
Contact: Sue Freestone.
Subjects: Biography, current affairs, history, travel.

MICHAEL JOSEPH – see PENGUIN GROUP

LAURENCE KING PUBLISHING LTD
71 Great Russell Street, London WC1B 3BP.
Tel: 020 7430 8850. Fax: 020 7430 8880. E-mail: sue@laurenceking.co.ok
Web: www.laurenceking.co.ok
Contact: Susan Bolsom, Picture Manager.
Subjects: Arts and architecture, design.

KINGFISHER PUBLICATIONS
New Penderel House, 283-288 High Holborn, London WC1V 7HZ.
Tel: 020 7903 9836. Fax: 020 7242 4979.
Contact: Cee Weston-Baker.
Subjects: Children's non-fiction, natural history, reference.

FRANCES LINCOLN LTD
4 Torriano Mews, Torriano Avenue, London NW5 2RZ.
Tel: 020 7284 4009. Fax: 020 7267 5249.
Subjects: General; art, gardening, interior design, travel.

LITTLE BROWN & COMPANY (UK)
Brettenham House, Lancaster Place, London WC2E 7EN.
Tel: 020 7911 8000. Fax: 020 7911 8100.
Web: www.littlebrown.co.uk
Subjects: General.

LORENZ BOOKS – see ANNESS PUBLISHING

THE LUTTERWORTH PRESS
P O Box 60, Cambridge CB1 2NT.
Tel: 01223 350865. Fax: 01223 366951. E-mail: publishing@lutterworth.com
Contact: Adrian Brink
Subjects: Antiques, art and architecture, biography, crafts, natural history, reference, religion, science.

MACMILLAN – see PAN MACMILLAN

MANCHESTER UNIVERSITY PRESS
Oxford Road, Manchester M13 9NR.
Tel: 0161 273 5539. Fax: 0161 274 3346. E-mail: mup@man.ac.uk
Contacts: Jonathan Bevan (art history, history); Kate Fox (architecture, culture, design, media, photography, theatre).
Subjects: As above.

MITCHELL BEAZLEY – see OCTOPUS PUBLISHING GROUP

NEW HOLLAND PUBLISHERS (UK) LTD
Garfield House, 86-88 Edgware Road, London W2 2EA.
Tel: 020 7724 7773. Fax: 020 7258 1293. E-mail: postmaster@nhpub.co.uk
Web: www.newhollandpublishers.com
Subjects: Adventure sports, diving, crafts, cookery, gardening, interior design, natural history, travel.

OCTOPUS PUBLISHING GROUP LTD
2-4 Heron Quays, London E14 4JP.
Tel: 020 7531 8400. Fax: 020 7531 8650. E-mail: liz.fowler@hamlyn.co.uk
Contact: Liz Fowler.
Imprints: Blandford, Cassell Illustrated, Conran Octopus, Hachette Illustrated, Hamlyn, Mitchell Beazley, Philip's, Ward Lock.
Subjects: Illustrated general reference and non-fiction.

OMNIBUS PRESS/MUSIC SALES LTD
8/9 Frith Street, London W1V 5TZ.
Tel: 020 7434 0066. Fax: 020 7734 2246.
Contact: Chris Charlesworth, editor; Sarah Bacon, picture researcher.
Subjects: Rock, pop and classical music.

ORION PUBLISHING GROUP LTD
Orion House, 5 Upper St Martin's Lane, London WC2H 9EA.
Tel: 020 7240 3444. Fax: 020 7240 4822.
Subjects: General; biography, cookery, design, gardening, history, interiors, natural history, popular science, sport, travel.

OSPREY PUBLISHING LTD
Elms Court, Chapel Way, Botley, Oxford OX2 9LP.
Tel: 01865 727022. Fax: 01865 727017. E-mail: info@ospreypublishing.com
Web: www.ospreypublishing.com
Subjects: Illustrated military history and aviation.

OXFORD PUBLISHING COMPANY – see IAN ALLAN PUBLISHING

OXFORD UNIVERSITY PRESS
Great Clarendon Street, Oxford OX2 6DP.
Tel: 01865 556767. Fax: 01865 556646.
Imprints: Clarendon Press, Oxford Paperbacks.
Subjects: General; academic, educational, reference.

PRC PUBLISHING – see CHRYSALIS BOOKS GROUP

PAN MACMILLAN
20 New Wharf Road, London N1 9RR.
Tel: 020 7014 6000. Fax: 020 7014 6001.
Web: www.panmacmillan.com
Imprints: Macmillan, Pan, Picador, Sidgwick & Jackson.
Subjects: General; biography, cookery, crafts, current affairs, gardening, music, popular history, practical, travel.

PAVILION BOOKS – see CHRYSALIS BOOKS GROUP

PENGUIN GROUP (UK)
80 Strand, London WC2R 0RL.
Tel: 020 7010 3000. Fax: 020 7010 3294. E-mail: kate.brunt@penguin.co.uk
Imprints: Allen Lane, Hamish Hamilton, Michael Joseph, Penguin, Viking.
Contacts: Kate Brunt, Samantha Johnson (Picture Editors).
Subjects: General.

PHAIDON PRESS LTD
18 Regents Wharf, All Saints Street, London N1 9PA.
Tel: 020 7843 1000. Fax: 020 7843 1010.
Subjects: Architecture, decorative and fine arts, design, photography.

PHILIP'S – see OCTOPUS PUBLISHING GROUP

PIATKUS BOOKS
5 Windmill Street, London W1T 2JA.
Tel: 020 7631 0710. Fax: 020 7436 7137. E-mail: info@piatkus.co.uk
Contact: Alice Davis, Managing Editor.
Subjects: General, biography, cookery, health, leisure, mind body & spirit, women's interests.

PICADOR – see PAN MACMILLAN

PLAYNE BOOKS LTD
Chapel House, Trefin, Haverfordwest, Pembrokeshire SA62 5AU.
Tel: 01348 837073. Fax: 01348 837063. E-mail: playne.books@virgin.net
Contact: Gill Davies, Editorial Director.
Subjects: General illustrated books for adults and children.

PLEXUS PUBLISHING LTD
55a Clapham Common Southside, London SW4 9BX.
Tel: 020 7622 2440. Fax: 020 7622 2441.
Contact: Sandra Wake.
Subjects: Biography, fashion, film, music, popular culture.

PUTNAM AERONAUTICAL – see CHRYSALIS BOOKS GROUP

T&AD POYSER – see CHRISTOPHER HELM

QUARTET BOOKS
27 Goodge Street, London W1T 2LD.
Tel: 020 7636 3992. Fax: 020 7637 1866. E-mail: quartetbooks@easynet.co.uk
Subjects: Biography, history, music and popular culture.

QUARTO PUBLISHING PLC
The Old Brewery, 6 Blundell Street, London N7 9BH.
Tel: 020 7700 6700. Fax: 020 7700 4191.
Contact: Penny Cobb, Assistant Art Director.
Subjects: General; arts and crafts, cookery, gardening, health, home interest, new age, travel.

RAILWAYS – MILEPOST 92½
Newton Harcourt, Leicestershire LE8 9FH.
Tel: 0116 259 2068. Fax: 0116 259 3001. E-mail: contacts@milepost92-half.co.uk
Contacts: Colin Garratt, Director; Colin Nash, Picture Library Manager.
Subjects: Railways worldwide – past and present.

RANDOM HOUSE UK LTD
Random House, 20 Vauxhall Bridge Road, London SW1V 2SA.
Tel: 020 7840 8400. Fax: 020 7233 8791.
Web: www.randomhouse.co.uk
Contact: Design Department.
Relevant Imprints: Jonathan Cape, Century, Chatto & Windus, Ebury Press, William Heinemann, Hutchinson, Secker & Warburg.
Subjects: Various; see individual imprints.

READER'S DIGEST ASSOCIATION
11 Westferry Circus, Canary Wharf, London E14 4HE.
Tel: 020 7715 8000. Fax: 020 7715 8181.
Subjects: General illustrated; cookery, crafts, DIY, encyclopaedias, folklore, gardening, guide books, history, natural history.

ROBSON – see CHRYSALIS BOOKS GROUP

ROTOVISION
Sheridan House, 112/116A Western Road, Hove BN3 1DD.
Tel: 01273 727268. Fax: 01273 727269. E-mail: mail@rotovision.com
Subjects: Design, photography.

ROUTLEDGE
11 New Fetter Lane, London EC4P 4EE.
Tel: 020 7842 2071. Fax: 020 7842 2298.
Contact: Design Department.
Subjects: Academic, professional and reference.

RYLAND PETERS & SMALL LTD
Kirkman House, 12-14 Whitfield Street, London W1T 2RP.
Tel: 020 7436 9090. Fax: 020 7436 9790. E-mail: info@rps.co.uk
Contact: Gabriella Le Grazie, Art Director.
Subjects: Food and drink, gardening, interior design.

SALAMANDER BOOKS LTD
The Chrysalis Building, Bramley Road, London W10 6SP.
Tel: 020 7314 1437. Fax: 020 7314 1596. E-mail: lwilson@chrysalisbooks.co.uk
Web: www.chrysalisbooks.co.uk
Contact: Leslie Wilson, Senior Commissioning Editor.
Subjects: Cookery, gardening, history, military, natural history, transport.

SAVITRI BOOKS LTD
25 Lisle Lane, Ely, Cambridgeshire CB7 4AS.
Tel/fax: 01353 654327. E-mail: munni@savitribooks.demon.co.uk
Contact: Mrinalini Srivastava, Director.
Subjects: General; crafts, ecology, natural history.

SECKER & WARBURG
Random House, 20 Vauxhall Bridge Road, London SW1V 2SA.
Tel: 020 7840 8570. Fax: 020 7233 6117.
Subjects: General non-fiction.

SHELDRAKE PRESS LTD
188 Cavendish Road, London SW12 0DA.
Tel: 020 8675 1767. Fax: 020 8675 7736. E-mail: mail@sheldrakepress.demon.co.uk
Web: www.sheldrakepress.demon.co.uk
Contact: Simon Rigge.
Subjects: General; architecture, cookery, design, history, music, travel.

SIDGWICK & JACKSON – see PAN MACMILLAN

SIMON & SCHUSTER
Africa House, 64-78 Kingsway, London WC2B 6AH.
Tel: 020 7316 1900. Fax: 020 7316 0332.
Imprints: Martin Books.
Subjects: Biography, cookery, history.

SOUTHWATER – see ANNESS PUBLISHING

SOUVENIR PRESS LTD
43 Great Russell Street, London WC1B 3PD.
Tel: 020 7580 9307. Fax: 020 7580 5064.E-mail: souvenirpress@ukonline.co.uk
Subjects: General; archaelogy, art, animals, childcare, cookery, gardening, health, hobbies, plants, practical, sociology. (Digital not accepted).

SPELLMOUNT LTD
The Village Centre, Staplehurst, Kent TN12 0AZ.
Tel: 01580 893730. Fax: 01580 893731.
Web: www.spellmount.com
Contact: Jamie Wilson, Managing Director.
Subjects: History and military history.

PATRICK STEPHENS – see HAYNES PUBLISHING

SUTTON PUBLISHING LTD
Phoenix Mill, Thrupp, Stroud, Gloucestershire GL5 2BU.
Tel: 01453 731114. Fax: 01453 884150.
Subjects: Archaeology, architectural history, aviation, biography, canals, military and naval history, railway history, sport history.

THAMES & HUDSON LTD
181a High Holborn, London WC1V 7QX.
Tel: 020 7845 5000. Fax: 020 7845 5050. E-mail: s.ruston@thameshudson.co.uk
Web: www.thamesandhudson.com
Contact: Sam Ruston, Head of Picture Research.
Subjects: Art, architecture, archaeology, anthropology, cinema, fashion, interior design, music, photography, practical guides, religion and mythology, theatre, travel.

THORSONS – see HARPERCOLLINS PUBLISHERS

TOUCAN BOOKS LTD
3rd Floor, 89 Charterhouse Street, London EC1M 6PE.
Tel: 020 7250 3388. Fax: 020 7250 3123. E-mail: info@toucanbooks.co.uk
Subjects: General illustrated.

TRANSWORLD PUBLISHERS
61-63 Uxbridge Road, London W5 5SA.
Tel: 020 8579 2652. Fax: 020 8579 5479.
Imprints: Bantam, Corgi, Doubleday.
Subjects: General non-fiction; autobiography, cookery, health, military, popular science, sport.

USBORNE PUBLISHING
83-85 Saffron Hill, London EC1N 8RT.
Tel: 020 7430 2800. Fax: 020 7242 0974.
Contacts: Steve Wright; Mary Cartwright.
Subjects: General children's; crafts, natural history, practical, reference.

VERMILION – see EBURY PRESS

VIKING – see PENGUIN GROUP

VIRGIN BOOKS LTD
Thames Wharf Studios, Rainville Road, London W6 9HA.
Tel: 020 7386 3300. Fax: 020 7386 3360. E-mail: amartin@virgin-books.co.uk
Contacts: Anna Martin (In-house Design),Vanessa Daubney (general, sport), Carolyn Thorne (music, arts, lifestyle).
Subjects: General; arts, lifestyle, music, sport.

WARD LOCK – see OCTOPUS PUBLISHING GROUP

WATERLINE – see AIRLIFE PUBLISHING

WEIDENFELD & NICOLSON LTD
Orion House, 5 Upper St Martin's Lane, London WC2H 9EA.
Tel: 020 7240 3444. Fax: 020 7240 4822.
Imprints: Cassell Military, Cassell Reference, Weidenfeld.
Subjects: Biography, history, military, science.

YALE UNIVERSITY PRESS
47 Bedford Square, London WC1B 3DP.
Tel: 020 7079 4900. Fax: 020 7079 4901. E-mail: emily.lees@yaleup.co.uk
Contact: Emily Lees, Picture Manager.
Subjects: Architecture, art, history, politics, sociology.

CARDS & CALENDARS

This section lists publishers of postcards, greetings cards and calendars, along with their requirements. Additionally, companies producing allied material, such as posters and prints, are also included, though there is considerable overlap with many of the companies listed here producing a range of products.

With the exception of traditional viewcard producers, who have always offered rather meagre rates for freelance material, fees in this area are generally good. However, only those who can produce precisely what is required as far as subject matter, quality and format are concerned, are likely to succeed.

Market requirements

Traditionally, these publishers have required larger format transparencies of the highest quality. While they still demand optimum quality, the requirement for the really large format has eased up in recent years and most of the companies listed here will consider top quality 35mm. Nevertheless, if you want to make a real impact in this field, you should seriously consider working in the larger "landscape" formats, such as 6x7cm or 6x9cm. Digital is beginning to be accepted in some of these markets, but generally this field still prefers transparencies.

The need for material of the highest quality cannot be too strongly emphasised. The market is highly specialised with very specific requirements. If you aim to break into this field, you must be very sure of your photographic technique. You must be able to produce professional quality material that is pin sharp and perfectly exposed with excellent colour saturation.

You must also know and be able to supply *exactly* what the market requires. The listings will help you, but you should also carry out your own field study by examining the photographic products on general sale.

After a period in the doldrums the photographic greetings card has been making something of a comeback in recent years. Neverthless, the big mass-market card publishers still employ mostly art or graphics. Those that do use photography tend to be smaller, specialised companies, many of them publishing a full range of photographic products. These companies also use a lot of work from top photographers or picture libraries, which means that there is greater competition than ever to supply material for these products.

The calendar market is equally demanding, though fortunately there are still large numbers of calendars using photographs being produced every year. Many calendar producers obtain the material they need from picture agencies, but this is not to say that individual photographers cannot successfully break into this field. Once again, though, you must be sure of your photographic technique and be able to produce really top quality work.

Make a point of studying the cards, calendars or posters that you see on general sale or hanging up in places you visit. Don't rely solely on what *you* think would make a good card or calendar picture; familiarise yourself with the type of pictures actually being used by these publishers.

Finally, it is worth noting that whilst many firms will consider submissions at any time, some in the calendar or greetings card market only select material at certain times of the year or when they are renewing their range. So when contemplating an approach to one of these firms, always check first to see if they are accepting submissions at the time.

Rights and fees

Where provided by the company concerned, fee guidelines are quoted. Some companies prefer to negotiate fees individually, depending upon the type of material you offer. If you are new to this field, the best plan is to make your submission (preferably after making an initial enquiry, outlining the material you have available) and let the company concerned make you an offer. Generally speaking, you should not accept less than about £75 for Greetings Card or Calendar Rights.

Remember, you are not selling your copyright for this fee; you are free to submit the same photograph to any *non-competitive* market (for example, a magazine) at a later date. But you should not attempt to sell the picture to another greetings card publisher once you have sold Greetings Card Rights to a competing firm.

ABACUS CARDS LTD
Gazeley Road, Kentford, Newmarket, Suffolk CB8 7RH.
Tel: 01638 552399. Fax: 01638 554082. E-mail: liz.ellis@abacuscards.co.uk
Contact: Liz Ellis (Art Editor).
Products: Greetings cards.
Will consider top-quality carefully-composed garden scenes, landscapes, winter scenes (British), pets, action or extreme sports. Limited scope as much is produced in-house or obtained from libraries.
Formats: Transparencies all formats, or digital files.
Fees: Around £200 for three-year world rights.

CHRIS ANDREWS PUBLICATIONS
15 Curtis Yard, North Hinksey Lane, Oxford OX2 0LX.
Tel: 01865 723404. Fax: 01865 725294. E-mail: chris.andrews1@btclick.com
Web: www.cap-ox.com
Contact: Chris Andrews (Partner).
Products: Calendars, postcards, guidebooks, diaries, address books.
Require atmospheric colour images of recognisable places (towns, villages) throughout central England, specifically the Cotswolds, Oxfordshire, Cherwell Valley, Thames and Chilterns. Winterscapes especially welcome. Photographs not required for immediate use may be accepted into the Oxford Picture Library which is run in parallel.
Formats: Any considered.
Fees: By negotiation.

THOMAS BENNACI
Unit 9, Bessemer Park, 250 Milkwood Road, London SE24 0HG.
Tel: 020 7924 0635. Fax: 020 7924 0636. E-mail: nelrom@aol.com
Contact: Romano Di Giulio (Manager).
Products: Postcards.
Always interested in new views of London for sale to the tourist market – landmarks, scenes and buildings that are easily recognisable or interesting to tourists. Images should be bright and lively.
Formats: All considered.
Fees: £50 for postcard rights.

BRUNEL PROMOTIONS
Hope Road, Bedminster, Bristol BS3 3NZ.
Tel: 0117 963 6161. Fax: 0117 966 4235. E-mail: richardc@brunel-promotions.co.uk
Contact: Richard Childs, Picture Researcher.
Products: Calendars.
Will consider a range of subjects suitable for company advertising calendars, especially UK scenics, British and world wildlife. Limited amount of glamour considered. Submissions usually required February/March for the following year's products.
Formats: 5x4in transparencies preferred; medium format accepted.
Fees: By negotiation.

CARD CONNECTION
Park House, Hickleys Court, South Street, Farnham, Surrey GU9 7QQ.
Tel: 01252 892300. Fax: 01252 892339.
Web: www.card-connection.co.uk
Contact: Alison Mahoney, Senior Product & Marketing Manager.
Products: Greetings cards, giftwrap.

Will consider humorous or cute animal images (domestic or wild), florals, still life, landscapes and sporting images. Also humorous B&W (or colour for use as B&W) "scenes from daily life".
Formats: Medium format transparencies required for colour products, though very high quality prints may be considered. Digital also accepted.
Fees: By negotiation, for 2–5 year world greetings card rights.

GB POSTERS LTD
1 Russell Street, Sheffield S3 8RW.
Tel: 0114 276 7454. Fax: 0114 272 9599. E-mail: max@gbposters.com
Web: www.gbposters.com
Contact: Max Arguile (Licensing Manager).
Products: Posters and postcards.
Interested in pin-up type images of youth-culture celebrities – contemporary pop stars, young film and TV actors/actresses, popular young sports stars. Colour or B&W, but must have immediate appeal to the youth market. Also open to new ideas for possible generic titles – landscapes, animals, humour, etc.
Formats: 35mm considered but medium format preferred. Digital accepted, 32x45cm at 300dpi.
Fees: Negotiable.

HALLMARK CARDS PLC
Bingley Road, Bradford BD9 5SD.
Tel: 01274 252000. Fax: 01274 252675.
Contact: Mary Crowther (Studio Manager).
Products: Greetings cards, postcards, giftwrap.
Will consider any B&W and colour images suitable for these products.
Formats: All considered.
Fees: Dependent on work and use.

IMAGES & EDITIONS LTD
Bourne Road, Essendine, Nr Stamford, Lincs PE9 4UW.
Tel: 01780 757118. Fax: 01780 754629.
Contact: Design Studio.
Products: Greetings cards and stationery.
Will consider British landscapes and wildlife, domestic pets (especially cats, dogs, horses), florals.
Formats: Top quality 35mm acceptable but larger formats preferred.
Fees: By negotiation or on 5 per cent royalty basis, for world rights for greetings cards for three years.

INDEPENDENT POSTERS
PO Box 7259, Brentwood, Essex CM14 5ZA.
Tel: 01277 372000. Fax: 01277 375333. E-mail: kim@independentposters.co.uk
Web: www.independentposters.co.uk
Contact: Kim Miller (Publishing Manager).
Products: Posters, miniposters.
Will consider top quality images of: rock and pop personalities – studio or in performance; motorbikes and dream cars – static or action; glamour – high quality, celebrity models only.
Formats: All formats considered. Large format transparencies preferred.
Fees: Variable, for worldwide rights.

INDIGO ART LTD
Indigo House, Brunswick Place, Liverpool L20 8DT.
Tel: 0151 933 9779. Fax: 0151 922 1524. E-mail: kaye@indigoart.co.uk
Web: www.indigoart.co.uk
Contact: Kaye Kent (Art Consultant).

Products: Large-scale display prints for use in the hotel/leisure industry.
Striking colour or B&W images with a modern/contemporary look. Wide variety of styles considered: abstracts, close-ups, experimentation with light, angles or digital manipulation. Also monochrome landscape or lifestyle images. See website for current range of subjects/styles.
Formats: Transparencies, prints or high-res scans.
Fees: On a royalties basis, usually 10%.

INFOCADO
PO Box 172, Stamford, Lincs PE9 4QB.
Tel: 01780 767711. Fax: 01780 489218. E-mail: info@infocado.co.uk
Web: www.infocado.co.uk
Contact: David Pike (Director).
Products: Calendars.
Will consider anything depicting "the true character of Britain". British countryside; architecture and heritage; flowers and gardens; animals both domestic and wild, natural and humorous; transport.
Formats: Any transparency size as long as good quality – but preferably square. Digital also accepted.
Fees: Royalties, subject to negotiation.

JUDGES POSTCARDS LTD
176 Bexhill Road, St Leonard's on Sea, East Sussex TN38 8BN.
Tel: 01424 420919. Fax: 01424 438538. E-mail: richard.isaac@judges.co.uk
Web: www.judges.co.uk
Contact: Richard Isaac (Product Developer).
Products: Postcards, calendars, greetings cards.
Will consider images of England and Wales, local and regional, appealing to the tourist industry. Must be bright, sunny and vibrant. Landscapes, flowers, animals and any other imagery may be considered.
Formats: Any considered, including digital.
Fees: Dependent on quality and quantity.

KARDORAMA LTD
PO Box 85, Potters Bar, Herts EN6 5AD.
Tel: 01707 652781.
Contact: Brian Elwood (Managing Director).
Products: Postcards.
Always seeking new views of London – major tourist sights or subjects that tourists would consider typical such as red buses, phone boxes, policemen, taxis, etc. Should be good record shots but with "a hint of romance" and plenty of detail in the main subject. Also, humorous images, any subject or location providing the image needs no explanation, but must be sharp and well exposed under good lighting conditions.
Formats: 35mm transparencies are acceptable, but medium format is preferred. Digital and prints also considered.
Fees: Variable, depending on quality of work, subject matter and quantities

KEVIN MAYHEW PUBLISHERS
Buxhall, Stowmarket, Suffolk IP14 3BW.
Tel: 01449 737978. Fax: 01449 737834. E-mail: chriscoe@kevinmayhewltd.com
Contact: Miss Chris Coe (Greetings Card Manager).
Products: Greetings cards.
Images suitable for both religious and secular greetings cards of all kinds. Landscapes, seascapes,

rural scenes, mountains, water images, florals, garden images. Must be strong, bright images with good atmosphere.
Formats: Original transparencies or high-res digital.
Fees: Negotiable, usually around £50–£75 for greetings card rights.

PINEAPPLE PARK LTD
58 Wilbury Way, Hitchin, Herts SG4 0TP.
Tel: 01462 442021. Fax: 01462 440418. E-mail: info@pineapplepark.co.uk
Contact: Sarah M Parker (Director).
Products: Greetings cards.
Seek high quality colour images of: 1) Florals – contemporary and traditional needed for female-orientated range of greetings cards. Country kitchen type arrangements including china, country dressers etc also needed. 2) Male subjects, eg collection of wine bottles, sporting items, cars etc for male-orientated greetings cards. 3) Gardens and gardening.
Formats: 35mm quite acceptable.
Fees: By negotiation, for worldwide greetings card rights.

PORTFOLIO COLLECTION LTD
105 Golborne Road, London W10 5NL.
Tel: 020 8960 1826. Fax: 020 8960 6570.
Contact: Jayne Diggory (Director).
Products: Greetings cards and posters.
Specialists in creative black and white photography. Strong, contemporary, expressive images – landscapes, cityscapes, people, etc. Also nostalgic images from the '60s and '70s – pop stars, swinging London, flower power, etc.
Formats: Prints from 10x8in up.
Fees: Usually on royalty basis at 12 per cent of distribution price. Flat fees may be negotiated.

NIGEL QUINEY PUBLICATIONS
Cloudesley House, Shire Hill, Saffron Walden, Essex CB11 3FB.
Tel: 01799 520200. Fax: 01799 520100. E-mail: jarkinstall@nigelquiney.com
Contact: Jo Arkinstall (Product Manager).
Products: Greetings cards.
Top quality colour images of animals (domestic and wild) in humorous or interesting situations, and florals – bright, modern, contemporary. Will also consider images suitable for anniversary, new baby, etc.
Formats: 5x4in transparencies.
Fees: Dependent on product/design, for world rights for five years.

RIVERSIDE CARDS
Jubilee Way, Grange Moor, Wakefield WF4 4TD.
Tel: 01924 840500. Fax: 01924 840600. E-mail: sue@riversidecards.com
Web: www.riversidecards.com
Contact: Sue Pickles (Design Manager).
Products: Greetings cards.
Interested in cute colour photographs of domestic pets (kittens and puppies) and still-life floral compositions.
Formats: Any considered.
Fees: By negotiation.

ROSE OF COLCHESTER LTD
Clough Road, Severalls Industrial Park, Colchester CO4 4QT.
Tel: 01206 844500. Fax: 01206 845872. E-mail: simon@rosecalendars.co.uk
Contact: Simon Williams (Publishing Manager).

Products: Calendars for business promotion.
Will consider British and worldwide landscapes and wildlife. Also glamour, classic and supercars, domestic and farm animals, adventure sport. Submit January for annual selection process.
Formats: 10x8in, 5x4in and medium formats. Minimum acceptable size 6x6cm. XPan considered for landscapes. 35mm acceptable for wildlife. High-end professional scans and digital capture (minimum 6MP professional cameras) also accepted.
Fees: Negotiable depending on subject matter.

SANTORO GRAPHICS
Rotunda Point, 11 Hartfield Crescent, Wimbledon, London SW19 3RL.
Tel: 020 8781 1100. Fax: 020 8781 1101. E-mail: submissions@santorographics.com
We: santorographics.com
Contact: Meera Santoro (Projects Director).
Products: Posters, postcards and greetings cards.
Requires striking and attractive images appealing to the typical young poster/postcard buyer: nostalgic, contemporary, romantic, humorous. B&W a speciality, but colour images in contemporary styles are also sought.
Formats: Any considered, digital accepted.
Fees: By negotiation for worldwide rights.

STATICS
Unit 7, Victoria Industrial Estate, London W3 6UU.
Tel: 020 8992 8990. Fax: 020 8992 8996.
Contact: Christopher Douglas-Morris (Art Director).
Products: Postcards, greetings cards, yearbooks and calendars.
Will consider cute or humorous shots of children or of "popular" animals (eg pigs, cats, dogs, orang-utans). Must be shot on location or in contextual settings, not in the studio. Colour and B&W considered.
Formats: Any considered.
Fees: Postcards, £120; greetings cards, £160; page in yearbook, £75; page in mini-calendar, £75.

VILLAGE MILL
16 Plantagenet Road, Barnet, Herts EN5 5JG.
Tel: 020 8441 2571.
Contact: Peter Morrish (Picture Editor).
Products: Desk calendars.
Landscape views required for the "British Highlights" and "Nature's Art", and "Worldwide Panoramas" desk calendars. Pictures of principal British and world countryside, and exotic or spectacular places around the world, always of interest if well-composed and colourful. Preference for scenes without people. Compositions must be suited to fit an elongated landscape shape. Selection during November/December.
Formats: Medium format transparencies.
Fees: £60 for non-exclusive UK rights.

AGENCIES

Picture libraries and agencies are in the business of selling pictures. They are not in the business of teaching photography or advising photographers how to produce saleable work – although they can sometimes prove remarkably helpful in the latter respect to those who show promise. Their purpose is strictly a business one: to meet the demand for stock pictures from such markets as magazine and book publishers, advertising agencies, travel operators, greetings card and calendar publishers, and many more.

Many photographers look upon an agency as a last resort; they have been unable to sell their photographs themselves, so they think they might as well try unloading them on an agency. This is the wrong attitude. No agency will succeed in placing pictures which are quite simply unmarketable. In any event, the photographer who has had at least some success in selling pictures is in a far better position to approach an agency.

Agency requirements

If you hope to interest an agency in your work, you must be able to produce pictures which the agency feels are likely to sell to one of their markets. Although the acceptance of your work by an agency is no guarantee that it will sell, an efficient agency certainly will not clutter up its files with pictures which do not stand a reasonably good chance of finding a market.

Agents handle pictures of every subject under the sun. Some specialise in particular subjects – sport, natural history, etc – while others act as general agencies, covering the whole spectrum of subject matter. Any photograph that could be published in one form or another is a suitable picture for an agency.

Even if you eventually decide that you want to place all your potentially saleable material with an agency, you cannot expect to leave every aspect of the business to them. You must continue to study the market, watching for trends; you must continue to study published pictures.

For example, if your speciality is travel material, you should use every opportunity to study the type of pictures published in current travel brochures and other markets using such material. Only by doing this – by being aware of the market – can you hope to continue to provide your agency with marketable pictures.

Nowadays most agencies do a great deal of their business on-line and maintain extensive websites displaying the images they hold. Indeed, many newer agencies are "on-line only" and deal only in digitally-captured or scanned images.

Although agency websites are primarily aimed at potential picture buyers, they are well worth looking at for the photographer considering an approach, since they will give a good indication of the type of subject and style of work the agency handles.

Commission and licensing

Agencies generally work on a commission basis, 50 per cent being the most usual rate – if they receive £100 for reproduction rights in a picture, the photographer gets £50 of this. The more heavily digitised or Web-based agencies have more variable rates, depending on whether photographer or agency is expected to bear the cost of producing high-resolution scans.

The percentage taken may seem high, but it should be remembered that a picture agency, like any other business, has substantial overheads to account for.

There can also be high costs involved in making prospective buyers aware of the pictures that are available. The larger agencies produce lavish colour catalogues featuring selections of their best pictures, while smaller agencies regularly send out flyers. All are involved in constantly maintaining and updating their websites.

Agents do not normally sell pictures outright. As would the individual photographer, they merely sell reproduction rights, the image being licensed to the buyer for a specific purpose. Images may be licensed by size of reproduction, by territory in which they are published, by the medium in which they are reproduced, by time and/or quantity of reproductions, and can be exclusive or non-exclusive. Selling in this way is known as "rights-managed" licensing.

The other form of selling undertaken by some agencies is "royalty-free". Under this method images are sold as part of a collection purchased for a flat fee and pre-licensed for a specified range of uses.

A long-term investment

When dealing with a photographer for the first time, most agencies require a minimum initial submission – which can consist of anything from a few to 500 or more pictures. Most also stipulate that you must keep your material with them for a minimum period of anything from one to five years.

When an agency takes on the work of a new photographer, they are involved in a lot of work – scanning, categorising, filing, key-wording, cross-indexing and more.

The next step will be to make it known to picture buyers that these new pictures are available, perhaps including reproductions of them in any new catalogues or publicity material and getting an initial selection onto the website.

Having been involved in all this work and expense, it is not unreasonable for them to want to be given a fair chance to market the pictures. If the photographer were able to demand the withdrawal of the images after only a few months, the agency will have been involved in a lot of work and expense for nothing.

Dealing with an agency must therefore be considered a long-term investment. Having initially placed, say, a few hundred pictures with an agency, it could be at least several months before any are selected by a picture buyer, and even longer before any monies are seen by the photographer.

Normally, the photographer will also be expected to regularly submit new material to the library. Indeed, only when you have several hundred pictures lodged with the library can you hope for regular sales – and a reasonable return on your investment.

Making an approach

When considering placing work with an agency, the best plan is to make an initial short-list of those that seem most appropriate to your work.

Then contact the agency or agencies of your choice outlining the material you have available. It may also be worth mentioning details of any sales you have made yourself. If an agency is interested they will probably ask that you first post or e-mail some samples to them. Later they may suggest an appointment when you can bring a wider selection material to show them in person.

But remember that there is little point in approaching an agency until you have a sizeable collection of potentially saleable material. Most will not feel it worth their while dealing with a photographer who has only a dozen or so marketable pictures to offer – it just wouldn't be worth all the work and expense involved. And the chance of the photographer seeing a worthwhile return on just a dozen pictures placed with an agency are remote indeed; you'd be lucky to see more than one cheque in ten years!

In the listings that follow you'll find information on more than 100 agencies: the subjects they handle, the markets they supply, the formats they stock, their terms of business (including any minimum submission quantity and minimum retention period), and their standard commission charged on sales.

Prefacing the listings you'll find an Agency Subject Index. This is a guide to agencies which have a special interest in those subjects, though many other agencies may also cover the same subjects within their general stock.

Remember: simply placing material with an agency doesn't guarantee sales. And no agency can sell material for which there is no market. On the other hand, if you are able to produce good quality, marketable work, and can team up with the right agency, you could see a very worthwhile return from this association.

**An asterisk against an agency name in the main listings indicates membership of the British Association of Picture Libraries & Agencies (BAPLA).*

Subject Index

Geography/Environment

Bruce Coleman Collection
Sylvia Cordaiy Photo Library
Ecoscene
Eye Ubiquitous
FLPA – Images of Nature
Holt Studios International
Hutchison Picture Library
Impact Photos
Link Picture Library
NHPA Ltd
Natural Image
Natural Science Photos
OSF Ltd
Panos Pictures
Papilio Natural History Library
Picturebank Photo Library Ltd
Royal Geographical Society Picture Library
SCR Photo Library
Swift Imagery
Tropix Photo Library

Glamour/Nude

Camera Press Ltd
Picturebank Photo Library Ltd

Historical

Ancient Art & Architecture Collection
Bridgeman Art Library
Sylvia Pitcher Photo Library
Popperfoto.com
Royal Geographical Society Picture Library

Landscapes

Arcblue.com
Cornish Picture Library
ImageState Ltd
NHPA Ltd
OSF Ltd
Pure Images
Still Moving Picture Company
StockScotland.com

Music

All Action Digital Ltd
Arena PAL
Camera Press Ltd
Capital Pictures
Famous
Jazz Index Photo Library
Lebrecht Music & Arts Photo Library
Sylvia Pitcher Photo Library
Redferns Music Picture Library
Retna Pictures Ltd
S.I.N.

Natural History

Acestock.com
Bruce Coleman Collection
FLPA – Images of Nature
Holt Studios International
NHPA Ltd
Natural Image
Natural Science Photos
OSF Ltd
Papilio Natural History Library
Photega
StockScotland.com
Windrush Photos

News/Current Affairs

Camera Press Ltd
Express Syndication
Getty Images News & Sport
Rex Features Ltd
World Picture News

People/Lifestyle

Acestock.com
Alamy Images
Greystock
PYMCA
Photega
Picturebank Photo Library Ltd
Photofusion Picture Library
Pure Images
Retna Pictures Ltd
Rex Interstock
S.I.N.
StockScotland.com
Swift Imagery
TheImagefile.com

Personalities/Celebrities

Alamy Images
All Action Digital Ltd
Camera Press Ltd

Capital Pictures
Express Syndication
Famous
Getty Images News & Sport
Monitor Picture Library
Newscast
Nunn Syndication
Retna Pictures Ltd
Rex Features Ltd
S.I.N.

Science/Technology

Acestock.com
Camera Press Ltd
Bruce Coleman Collection
Leslie Garland Picture Library
ImagingBody
Photega
Powerstock/Superstock
OSF Ltd
Picturebank Photo Library Ltd
SCR Photo Library
Science Photo Library

Social Documentary

Bubbles Photo Library
Collections
Educational Images
Eye Ubiquitous
Impact Photos
Link Picture Library
PYMCA
Panos Pictures
Photega
Photofusion Picture Library
Swift Imagery
World Religions Photo Library

Sport

Action Images Ltd
Airsport Photo Library
All Action Digital Ltd
Alvey & Towers
Cut and Deal Ltd
Empics Sports Photo Agency
Getty Images News & Sport
Kos Picture Source Ltd
Powerstock/Superstock
Retna Pictures Ltd
Pure Images
Skishoot – Offshoot
Skyscan Photolibrary
Sporting Pictures (UK) Ltd
Still Moving Picture Company
Stock Shot

Transport

Acestock.com
Alvey & Towers
Edinburgh Photographic Library
Flight Collection
Impact Photos
Milepost 92½
Photega
Powerstock/Superstock
Skyscan Photolibrary
TRH Pictures
Travel Ink

Travel/Tourist

Acestock.com
Alamy Images
Alvey & Towers
Andes Press Agency
Anthony Blake Photo Library
Bruce Coleman Collection
Sylvia Cordaiy Photo Library
Eye Ubiquitous/JDTP
E-Picture Library Ltd
Hutchison Picture Library
Images of France
ImageState Ltd
Kos Picture Source Ltd
1dpi
Photega
Picturebank Photo Library Ltd
Pictures Colour Library
Rex Interstock
Royal Geographical Society Picture Library
Skishoot – Offshoot
Spectrum Colour Library
Still Moving Picture Company
Stock Shot
Swift Imagery
TheImagefile.com
Topham Picturepoint
Travel Ink
The Travel Library
World Pictures

Underwater

Bruce Coleman Collection
FLPA – Images of Nature
Sylvia Cordaiy Photo Library
Kos Picture Source Ltd
OSF Ltd
Papilio Natural History Library

ACESTOCK.COM*
Satellite House, 2 Salisbury Road, Wimbledon, London SW19 4EZ.
Tel: 020 8944 9944. Fax: 020 8944 9940. E-mail: john@acestock.com
Web: www.acestock.com
Contact: John Panton (Director).
Specialist subjects/requirements: General: Architecture, business, concepts, industry, nature/environment, people/lifestyles, science/medical, sports/leisure, still-life, technology, transport, wildlife, world travel.
Markets supplied: Advertising; design; publishing.
Stock: Mainly colour. All formats; digital preferred. Top quality portfolio work only.
Usual terms of business: Minimum initial submission: 200 accepted images. Minimum retention period: 3 years.
Commission: 50 per cent.
Additional information: Submit 100 low-res images for initial assessment.

ACTION IMAGES PLC*
Image House, Station Road, Tottenham, London N17 9LR.
Tel: 020 8885 3000. Fax: 020 8267 2035. E-mail: info@actionimages.com
Web: www.actionimages.com
Contact: James Pinniger (Picture Editor).
Specialist subjects/requirements: High quality sports pictures, especially of any unusual or spectacular incident.
Markets supplied: Newspapers, magazines, books, etc.
Stock: Colour. Digital only; minimum 18MB files.
Usual terms of business: No minimum initial submission, but phone first to discuss possible submissions.
Commission: Negotiable.

ADAMS PICTURE LIBRARY*
Unit 50b, Canalot Production Studios, 222 Kensal Road, London W10 5BN.
Tel: 020 8964 8007. Fax: 020 8960 8609. E-mail: info@adamspicturelibrary.com
Web: www.adamspicturelibrary.com
Contact: Dave Jarvis, Tamsyn Whitmarsh (Partners).
Specialist subjects/requirements: All subjects except hot news.
Markets supplied: All markets including advertising, publishing, calendars and posters.
Stock: Colour. All formats, but digital submissions preferred (A4 at 300dpi).
Usual terms of business: Minimum initial submission: 100 images. Minimum retention period: 5 years; 1 year's notice required for withdrawal.
Commission: 50 per cent (for exclusive images).

AIRSPORT PHOTO LIBRARY*
East Farm Studio, Nordelph, Downham Market, Norfolk PE38 0BG.
Tel: 01366 324346; 0403 542804 (mobile). E-mail: library@airsport-photo.co.uk
Web: www.airsport-photo.co.uk
Contact: David Wootton (Proprietor).
Specialist subjects/requirements: All forms of airsports: ballooning, hang gliding, paragliding, skydiving, kiting, bungee jumping, microlighting, light aircraft, etc.
Markets supplied: Editorial, advertising, books, internet.
Stock: Colour transparencies/digital.
Usual terms of business: No minimum initial submission but like to see at least 20 to begin with.
Commission: 50 per cent.
Additional information: Pictures should be bright, colourful and dramatic to show the sports at their best. Phone or e-mail before submitting. The library also specialises in commercial aerial photography.

ALAMY IMAGES*
6F Milton Park, Abingdon, Oxon OX14 4RR.
Tel: 01235 844608. Fax: 01235 844650. E-mail: memberservices@alamy.com
Web: www.alamy.com
Contact: Alan Capel (Head of Content); Alexandra Bortkiewicz (Director of Photography).
Specialist subjects/requirements: Quality images of all subjects – business, lifestyle, travel, vacations, sports, food, abstracts, concepts, still life, science, wildlife, celebrities, special interest, historical, reportage.
Markets supplied: Advertising, business clients and publishing worldwide.
Stock: Digital scans only, usually 48–70MB RGB TIFF files. See website for full technical requirements.
Usual terms of business: Submit initial test CD of 10–15 images; if accepted no minimum submission applies.
Commission: 65 per cent to photographer.
Additional information: Photographers must supply their own scans and keywording. Alamy do not edit photographers' submissions but scans are checked for technical accuracy before being allowed online. For initial approach first register at the website.

ALL ACTION DIGITAL LTD*
32 Great Sutton Street, London EC1V 0NB.
Tel: 020 7250 0350. Fax: 020 7250 3376. E-mail: info@allaction.co.uk
Web: www.allaction.co.uk
Contact: Tristan Rogers (Managing Director).
Specialist subjects/requirements: Celebrities and personalities in the worlds of contemporary music, fashion, sport, showbiz and politics.
Markets supplied: Magazines, newspapers, TV production, publishers, websites.
Stock: Digital only.
Usual terms of business: No minimum terms.
Commission: 50 per cent.
Additional information: Picture desk can receive via FTP, modem and ISDN; call for details.

ALVEY & TOWERS*
The Springboard Centre, Mantle Lane, Coalville, Leicestershire LE67 3DW.
Tel/fax: 01530 450011. E-mail: alveytower@aol.com
Web: www.alveyandtowers.com
Contact: Emma Rowen (Library Manager).
Specialist subjects/requirements: Agriculture, business, industry, leisure, people, transport and travel. Specialist modern railway library incorporating all aspects of this particular industry.
Markets supplied: Advertising, books, magazines, corporate brochures, calendars, audio visual.
Stock: Colour. All formats, including digital.
Usual terms of business: On application.
Commission: 50 per cent.
Additional information: It is essential that potential contributors make contact prior to making any submission in order to discuss precise requirements. All images must be mounted, and numbered with captions on accompanying sheet of paper, not on transparency mounts.

ANCIENT ART & ARCHITECTURE COLLECTION LTD
Suite 1, 410-420 Rayners Lane, Pinner, Middlesex HA5 5DY.
Tel: 020 8429 3131. Fax: 020 8429 4646. E-mail: librarian@aaacollection.co.uk
Web: www.aaacollection.com
Contact: Michelle Williams (Librarian).
Specialist subjects/requirements: Historical art and artifacts mainly from pre-history up to the Middle Ages; everything which illustrates the civilisations of the ancient world, its cultures and technologies, religion, ideas, beliefs and development. Also warfare, weapons, fortifications and

military historical movements. Statues, portraits and contemporary illustrations of historically important people – kings and other rulers.
Markets supplied: Mainly book publishers, but including magazines and TV.
Stock: B&W and colour. 6x6cm or larger formats preferred (though some 35mm accepted from remote overseas locations.)
Usual terms of business: Minimum retention period: 3 years. 24 months notice of return.
Commission: 50 per cent.
Additional information: All submissions must be accompanied by return sae. Only material of the highest quality can be considered.

ANDES PRESS AGENCY*
26 Padbury Court, London E2 7EH.
Tel: 020 7613 5417. Fax: 020 7739 3159. E-mail: photos@andespressagency.com
Web: www.andespressagency.com
Contact: Valeria Baker.
Specialist subjects/requirements: Latin America, including the Caribbean; world religions.
Markets supplied: Books, newspapers, magazines.
Stock: Colour only. 35mm and medium format.
Usual terms of business: Minimum initial submission: 100 transparencies. Minimum retention period: 3 years.
Commission: By negotiation.

ARCBLUE.COM*
93 Gainsborough Road, Richmond, Surrey TW9 2ET.
Tel: 020 8940 2227. Fax: 020 8940 6570. E-mail: info@arcblue.com
Web: www.arcblue.com
Contact: Peter Durant (Library Manager).
Specialist subjects/requirements: Modern contemporary architecture and built environment. Also interiors and landscape.
Markets supplied: General publishing, advertising and design.
Stock: B&W and colour transparencies, digital (50MB, RGB, 300dpi).
Usual terms of business: Minimum initial submission: 30 images. Minimum retention period: 2 years.
Commission: 50 per cent.
Additional information: Prefer to see coherent sets of images that work together as well as individually. Send sample set of images in the first instance, by mail or e-mail, preferably 6–20 images in digital format or tearsheets/photocopies.

ARENA PAL*
1st Floor, 55 Southwark Street, London SE1 1RU.
Tel: 020 7403 8542. Fax: 020 7403 8561. ISDN: 020 7407 3764. E-mail: searches@arenapal.com
Web: www.arenapal.com
Contact: Biddy Hayward (Managing Director).
Specialist subjects/requirements: Performing arts and the entertainment industry – theatre, dance, film, TV, music, opera, circus, festivals and venues.
Markets supplied: All media including publishing, arts bodies, advertising, design companies.
Stock: B&W and colour, all formats. Digital submissions accepted on CD.
Usual terms of business: No minimum initial submission, but expects around 100 images. Minimum retention period: 3 years.
Commission: 60/40 split in first year; 50 per cent thereafter or if digital files provided.
Additional information: Incorporates the former Performing Arts Library. Looks for photographers with a well-presented portfolio and a solid base in the performing arts. Also acts as a photographer's agent with commissions often available to established contributors.

ART DIRECTORS/TRIP PHOTO LIBRARY*
57 Burdon Lane, Cheam, Surrey SM2 7BY.
Tel: 020 8642 3593. Fax: 020 8395 7230. E-mail: images@artdirectors.co.uk
Web: www.artdirectors.co.uk
Contact: Bob Turner (Partner).
Specialist subjects/requirements: All subjects and all locations. Art Directors supplies images mainly for advertising; TRIP handles general travel material and in-depth, extensive coverage of all religions.
Markets supplied: Advertising and editorial.
Stock: Colour. All formats; digital preferred.
Usual terms of business: Minimum initial submission: 100 images. Minimum retention period: 3 years.
Commission: 50 per cent.
Additional information: Ask for Photographers' Guidelines or view them on website.

THE ANTHONY BLAKE PHOTO LIBRARY LTD*
20 Blades Court, Deodar Road, Putney, London SW15 2NU.
Tel: 020 8877 1123. Fax: 020 8877 9787. E-mail: info@abpl.co.uk
Web: www.abpl.co.uk
Contact: Anna Weller (Library Manager).
Specialist subjects/requirements: Food and wine related images. High quality, original material on all aspects from farming, fishing, country trades, markets and vineyards to raw ingredients, finished dishes, chefs, restaurants and kitchens. Also worldwide travel.
Markets supplied: Publishing, advertising, etc.
Stock: Colour. All formats, including digital.
Usual terms of business: Minimum initial submission: usually 100+ images but depends on quality/subjects covered. Minimum retention period: 3 years.
Commission: 40 per cent to photographer in the first year, 50 per cent thereafter.
Additional information: Always call before submitting. A regular wants list is sent to contributors.

BRIDGEMAN ART LIBRARY*
17-19 Garway Road, London W2 4PH.
Tel: 020 7727 4065. Fax: 020 7792 8509. E-mail: info@bridgeman.co.uk
Web: www.bridgeman.co.uk
Contact: Adrian Gibbs (Collections Manager).
Specialist subjects/requirements: American, European and Oriental paintings and prints, antiques, antiquities, arms and armour, botanical subjects, ethnography, general historical subjects and personalities, maps and manuscripts, natural history, topography, transport, etc.
Markets supplied: Publishing, advertising, television, greetings cards, calendars, etc.
Stock: Mainly colour but some B&W. Minimum 5x4in transparencies.
Usual terms of business: No minimum initial submission. Retention period negotiable.
Commission: 50 per cent.
Additional information: Website catalogue: www.bridgeman.co.uk

BUBBLES PHOTO LIBRARY*
3 Rose Lane, Ipswich IP1 1XE.
Tel: 01473 288605. E-mail: info@bubblesphotolibrary.co.uk
Web: www.bubblesphotolibrary.co.uk
Contact: Sarah Robinson, Loisjoy Thurstun (Partners).
Specialist subjects/requirements: Babies, children, pregnancy, mothercare, child development, education, teenagers, old age, family life, women's health and medical, still lives of food, vegetables, herbs, etc.
Markets supplied: Books, magazines, newspapers and advertising.

Stock: Colour and B&W. All formats; scans accepted (A4 at 300dpi)
Usual terms of business: Minimum submission: 100 images. Regular contributions expected. Minimum retention period: 3 years.
Commission: 50 per cent.
Additional information: Attractive women and children sell best. Always looking for multicultural and multiracial children/adults. Photographers must pay close attention to selecting models that are healthy-looking and ensure that backgrounds are uncluttered. Best clothes to wear are light coloured and neutral fashion.

CAMERA PRESS LTD*
21 Queen Elizabeth Street, London SE1 2PD.
Tel: 020 7378 1300. Fax: 020 7407 2635. E-mail: j.wald@camerapress.com
Web: www.camerapress.com
Contact: Jacqui Ann Wald (Managing Editor).
Specialist subjects/requirements: Mainly celebrity, pop, photo reportage, personality portraits. Also material suitable for women's magazines and general interest features, humour, travel, and some general stock.
Stock: B&W and colour. Digital preferred but scanning still undertaken.
Usual terms of business: By mutual agreement.
Commission: 50 per cent.

CAPITAL PICTURES*
85 Randolph Avenue, London W9 1DL.
Tel: 020 7286 2212. Fax: 020 7286 1218. E-mail: sales@capitalpictures.com
Web: www.capitalpictures.com
Contact: Phil Loftus (Manager).
Specialist subjects/requirements: Celebrities and personalities from the worlds of showbusiness, film and TV, rock and pop, politics and royalty.
Markets supplied: Consumer magazines, newspapers, etc.
Stock: Colour, digital only.
Usual terms of business: Minimum initial submission: 100 images. Minimum retention period: 1 month.
Commission: 50 per cent.

BRUCE COLEMAN COLLECTION
Chalfont House, Hampden Road, Chalfont St Peter, Bucks SL9 9RY.
Tel: 0870 420 4186. Fax: 0870 420 4187. E-mail: pix@brucecoleman.co.uk
Contact: Picture Editor.
Specialist subjects/requirements: Natural history, geographical, landscapes, agriculture, horticulture, marine, space.
Markets supplied: Book publishers, magazines, advertising agencies, calendar publishers.
Stock: Colour. All formats.
Usual terms of business: Minimum submission: 250 transparencies. Minimum retention period: 5 years.
Commission: 50 per cent.
Additional information: Contributors are asked to write for library literature first.

COLLECTIONS*
13 Woodberry Crescent, London N10 1PJ.
Tel: 020 8883 0083. Fax: 020 8883 9215. E-mail: salshuel@btinternet.com
Web: www.collectionspicturelibrary.com/www.collectionspicturelibrary.co.uk
Contact: Brian & Sal Shuel (Directors).
Specialist subjects: The British Isles and Ireland.
Markets supplied: All, particularly on the editorial side.

Stock: Colour in all formats and B&W prints.
Usual terms of business: By arrangement; "easy going and on the side of the contributor."
Commission: 50 per cent.
Additional information: The library aims to stock pictures of as many places, things, happenings on these islands as possible.

CORBIS*
111 Salusbury Road, London NW6 6RG.
Tel: 020 7731 9995. Fax: 020 7644 7645. E-mail: info@corbis.com
Web: www.corbis.com
Contact: Vanessa Kramer (Director of Artistic Relations).
Specialist subjects/requirements: General library handling most subjects, on both a licensed and royalty-free basis.
Markets supplied: Advertising, publishing, design, etc.
Stock: Colour, and historic B&W. Now accepting only digital files, minimum 17MB (digital capture) or 33MB (scans) for editorial images. Larger file sizes required for advertising, fashion and royalty-free images.
Usual terms of business: Minimum initial submission variable. Minimum retention period: 3 years.
Commission: 20–50 per cent, depending on client and use.
Additional information: For contributor submission information see http://studioplus.corbis.com

SYLVIA CORDAIY PHOTO LIBRARY*
45 Rotherstone, Devizes, Wiltshire SN10 2DD.
Tel: 01380 728327. Fax: 01380 728328. E-mail: info@sylvia-cordaiy.com
Web: www.sylvia-cordaiy.com
Contact: Sylvia Cordaiy (Proprietor).
Specialist subjects/requirements: Worldwide travel, architecture, exploration, wildlife, places, domestic animals and livestock, marine biology, environmental issues.
Markets supplied: General publishing, cards and calendars, brochures, exhibitions, advertising.
Stock: Colour. All formats including digital (minimum 50MB TIFF).
Usual terms of business: Minimum initial submission: 100 images. Minimum retention period: 3 years.
Commission: 50 per cent.
Additional information: Prefers Fuji film stock for transparencies. Only top quality images considered and all must be accurately captioned.

CORNISH PICTURE LIBRARY*
40b Fore Street, St Columb Major, Cornwall TR9 6RH.
Tel: 01637 880103/01503 250673. E-mail: paul@imageclick.co.uk
Web: www.imageclick.co.uk
Contact: Paul Watts (Proprietor).
Specialist subjects/requirements: Cornwall and the West Country (Devon, Dorset, Somerset, Wiltshire, Isles of Scilly, Channel Isles) – landscapes, historic sites, gardens, people, activities, attractions, wildlife.
Markets supplied: Magazines, books, tourism, etc.
Stock: Colour, medium format or larger transparencies preferred but top quality 35mm considered. B&W archive (pre-1960) images of Cornwall. Digital files from 6MP cameras upwards, minimum 16MB TIFF; must be colour correct preferably with Adobe 1998 profile.
Usual terms of business: No minimum submission. Minimum retention period: 2 years.
Commission: 50 per cent.

Additional information: Contact by e-mail or letter with details of subjects covered before sending submission. Browse website for more info and to view images already held; very similar images not required, only better shots or different views. Contributors' guidelines available on request.

CUT AND DEAL LTD
Suite 299, 2 Landsdowne Row, London SW18 3SX.
Tel: 07951 537370. E-mail: submissions@cutanddeal.com
Web: www.cutanddeal.com
Contact: Glen Conybeare (Director).
Specialist subjects/requirements: Images relating to gambling of all kinds. Gambling locations, gaming subjects and sports betting, including images of sports that people bet on such as horse racing, dog racing, football, basketball, cricket, golf, rugby, etc.
Markets supplied: Design industry, advertising, general publishing.
Stock: Digital. Uncompressed files at least 10MB.
Usual terms of business: Minimum initial submission: 25 images.
Commission: 50 per cent.
Additional information: Potential contributors should submit 5 sample images (or a link to a website) with details of what other subjects can be provided.

THE DEFENCE PICTURE LIBRARY LTD*
1 Creykes Court, The Millfields, Plymouth PL1 3JB.
Tel: 01752 312061. Fax: 01752 312063. E-mail:dpl@defencepictures.com
Web: www.defencepictures.com
Contact: David Reynolds (Director), Andrew Chittock (Picture Editor).
Specialist subjects/requirements: Military images covering all aspects of the armed forces worldwide, in training and on operations. Pictures of UK and international forces across the globe are always of interest.
Markets supplied: Publishers, advertising agencies, national media.
Stock: Colour. 35mm and medium format; high-resolutions TIFFS.
Usual terms of business: Minimum initial submission: 50 quality images. Minimum retention period: 5 years.
Commission: 50 per cent.
Additional information: The library is the UK's leading specialist source of military and defence images.

E & E PICTURE LIBRARY*
Beggars Roost, Woolpack Hill, Brabourne Lees, Nr Ashford, Kent TN25 6RR.
Tel: 01303 812608. Fax: 01303 812608. E-mail: isobel@picture-library.freeserve.co.uk
Web: www.picture-library.freeserve.co.uk
Contact: Isobel Sinden (Proprietor).
Specialist subjects/requirements: Worldwide religions – art, architecture, objects, clergy, vestments, rituals, festivals, ceremonies, funerals and burials, saints, pilgrims, holy places, manuscripts, illustrations, etc. Eccentricities and oddities – architectural, historical and contemporary.
Markets supplied: General publishing, newspapers, TV.
Stock: Colour, transparencies preferred; high-res digital accepted.
Usual terms of business: Minimum initial submission: 50 images; less if specialist subject matter. Minimum retention period: 4 years.
Commission: 50 per cent.

E-PICTURE LIBRARY LTD
Horizon House, Route de Picaterre, Alderney, Guernsey GY9 3UP.
Tel: 01481 824200. Fax: 01481 823880. E-mail: info@e-picturelibrary.net
Web: www.e-picturelibrary.net

Contact: Mark Burns (Managing Director).
Specialist subjects/requirements: General – landscapes, architecture, business, cities, lifestyle, wildlife, weather, sport, travel, etc.
Markets supplied: General publishing, advertising, etc.
Stock: Digital images scanned from original transparencies.
Usual terms of business: Minimum initial submission: 100 images. Minimum term of agreement: 1 year.
Commission: Variable according to stock quantities – see website.
Additional information: This a marketing service rather than a conventional stock library, selling both rights-managed and royalty-free. See website for more information.

ECOSCENE*
The Oasts, Headley Lane, Passfield, Liphook, Hampshire GU30 7RX.
Tel: 01428 751056. E-mail: sally@ecoscene.com
Web: www.ecoscene.com
Contact: Sally Morgan (Proprietor).
Specialist subjects/requirements: Environmental issues worldwide including agriculture, conservation, energy, pollution, transport, organic vs GM issues.
Markets supplied: Books, magazines, organisations, etc.
Stock: Colour. All transparency formats and digital files at 50MB.
Usual terms of business: Minimum initial submission: 100 quality images. Minimum retention period: 4 years.
Commission: 55 per cent to photographer.
Additional information: Contributors' guidelines available on request – can also be found on the library's website along with details of specific current requirements.

EDUCATIONAL IMAGES
24 Victoria Street, Torpoint, Cornwall PL11 2HE.
Tel/fax: 01752 814151. E-mail: enquiries@educationalimages.co.uk
Contact: Jim Merrett (Manager).
Web: www.educationalimages.co.uk
Specialist subjects/requirements: Education – photographs taken in schools, colleges, university, of children/young people undertaking educational activities. All ages and subjects.
Markets supplied: Educational book and magazine publishers.
Stock: B&W and colour, all formats including digital.
Usual terms of business: Minimum initial submission: 50 images. Minimum retention period: 3 years.
Commission: 50 per cent.
Additional information: Photographs should be bright, clear, colourful and informative.

EMPICS*
Pavilion House, 16 Castle Boulevard, Nottingham NG7 1FL.
Tel: 0115 844 7447. Fax: 0115 844 7448. E-mail: photographers@empics.com
Web: www.empics.com
Contact: Neal Simpson (Photographic Director).
Specialist subjects/requirements: Sport; most interested in the unusual, not run-of-the-mill coverage. The agency has an electronic picture desk and wire service for extensive syndication.
Markets supplied: Newspapers, magazines, advertising agencies, governing bodies, etc.
Stock: Colour. 35mm colour neg and transparency. Delivered in digital formats.
Usual terms of business: No minimum terms.
Commission: 50 per cent.
Additional information: Always happy to consider any unusual, exclusive and historical sports material.

EPICSCOTLAND*
Unit 5 Hathaway Business Centre, 21-29 Hathaway Street, Glasgow G20 8TD.
Tel: 0141 945 0000. Fax: 0141 945 0083. Email: info@epicscotland.com
Web: www.epicscotland.com
Contact: Sarah Chandler (Picture Library Manager).
Specialist subjects/requirements: All aspects of Scotland and Scottish life.
Markets supplied: Newspapers, magazines, publishers, design agencies.
Stock: Mainly colour, all formats. Digital if above 10MB and of high quality.
Usual terms of business: No minimum terms.
Commission: 50 per cent.
Additional information: No submitting without prior contact. Digital files must be checked by e-mail before submission.

EXPRESS SYNDICATION
Ludgate House, 245 Blackfriars Road, London SE1 9UX.
Tel: 020 7922 7884. Fax: 020 7922 7871. E-mail: adam.williams@express.co.uk
Web: www.expresspictures.com
Contact: Adam Williams (Syndication Manager).
Specialist subjects/requirements: Current news, features and personalities.
Markets supplied: Magazines and newspapers, UK and overseas.
Stock: B&W and colour. All formats.
Usual terms of business: Minimum retention period: 90 days.
Commission: 50 per cent.

EYE UBIQUITOUS*
65 Brighton Road, Shoreham, West Sussex BN43 6RE.
Tel: 01273 440113. Fax: 01273 440116. E-mail: library@eyeubiquitous.com
Web: www.eyeubiquitous.com
Contact: Paul Seheult (Proprietor).
Specialist subjects/requirements: General stock and social documentary material – people, lifestyles, work, environment, etc. Also incorporates the James Davis Travel Photography collection for worldwide travel material suitable for the tourist industry – scenics, resorts, beaches, major sights, etc.
Markets supplied: Publishing markets, travel industry, UK and European advertising agencies.
Stock: Colour. 35mm acceptable for documentary and people images; medium format required for travel stock. Generally prefer Fuji material.
Usual terms of business: Suggested minimum submission 200 transparencies, but terms open to discussion.
Commission: 50 per cent.
Additional information: The two collections are run as separate entities, though contributing photographers may have work with both.

FLPA – IMAGES OF NATURE
Pages Green House, Wetheringsett, Stowmarket, Suffolk IP14 5QA.
Tel: 01728 860789. Fax: 01728 860222. E-mail: pictures@flpa-images.co.uk
Web: www.flpa-images.co.uk
Contact: Jean Hosking, David Hosking (Directors).
Specialist subjects/requirements: Natural history and weather phenomena: birds, clouds, fish, fungi, insects, mammals, pollution, rainbows, reptiles, sea, snow, seasons, trees, underwater, hurricanes, earthquakes, lightning, volcanoes, dew, rain, fog, etc. Ecology and the environment. Horse, dog and cat breeds.
Markets supplied: Book publishers, advertising agencies, magazines.
Stock: Colour. 35mm (Fujichrome preferred) and medium format transparencies, digital files at 50MB (contact agency for digital guidelines).

Usual terms of business: Minimum initial submission: 250 images. Minimum retention period: 3 years.
Commission: 50 per cent.
Additional information: Competition in the natural history field is fierce, so only really sharp, well-composed pictures are needed. Sales are slow to start with, and a really keen photographer must be prepared to invest money in building up stock to the 1,000 mark.

FAMOUS*
13 Harwood Road, London SW6 4QP.
Tel: 020 7731 9333. Fax: 020 7731 9330. ISDN: 020 7731 9331. E-mail: info@famous.uk.com
Web: www.famous.uk.com
Contact: Rob Howard (Managing Director).
Specialist subjects/requirements: Celebrity photographs, especially personalities in the TV, movie, music, fashion and Royal fields. Taken in any situation: performance, studio, party, at home and paparazzi-style.
Markets supplied: General press and publishing.
Stock: Colour. Digital only.
Usual terms of business: No minimum submission or retention period.
Commission: 50 per cent.
Additional information: Always looking for photographers who can supply relevant pictures fast.

THE FLIGHT COLLECTION*
Quadrant House, The Quadrant, Sutton, Surrey SM2 5AS.
Tel: 020 8652 8888/3427. Fax: 020 8652 8933. E-mail: qpl@rbi.co.uk
Web: www.theflightcollection.com
Contact: Kim Hearn (Head of Picture Library).
Specialist subjects/requirements: All aspects of aviation – civil, military, helicopters, airports, crew, aircraft interiors, maintenance, etc.
Markets supplied: Books, magazines, advertising, exhibitions, etc.
Stock: Mainly colour; B&W historical. All formats, original /dupe transparencies or digital (300dpi, 20MB, cleaned and colour balanced, caption added to file info box).
Usual terms of business: Minimum initial submission: 50 transparencies or CD for inspection. Minimum retention period: 2 years.
Commission: 50 per cent.
Additional information: Call first for "wants" list.

FOOD FEATURES*
5 Upper Church Lane, Farnham, Surrey GU9 7PW.
Tel: 01252 735240. Fax: 01252 735242. E-mail: frontdesk@foodpix.com
Web: www.foodpix.com
Contact: Steve Moss, Alex Barker (Partners).
Specialist subjects/requirements: Food and drink, especially images involving people – dining, cooking, dinner parties, al fresco, chefs, etc.
Markets supplied: Publishing, advertising, etc.
Stock: Colour only. 35mm acceptable for location shots but larger formats preferred. Digital submissions minimum 30MB TIFF; 50MB preferred.
Usual terms of business: No minimum initial submission. Minimum retention period: 3 years.
Commission: By agreement.

GARDEN PICTURE LIBRARY*
Unit 12, Ransome's Dock, 35 Parkgate Road, London SW11 4NP.
Tel: 020 7228 4332. Fax: 020 7924 3267. E-mail: lorraine@gardenpicture.com
Web: www.gardenpicture.com
Contact: Lorraine Shill (Picture Research Manager).

Specialist subjects/requirements: Gardens, plants (mainly cultivated), people and animals in the garden, practical gardening, food al fresco, outdoor living, flower shows, floral still life, and garden features.
Markets supplied: General publishing, greetings cards and calendars, advertising and design.
Stock: Colour only. All formats. Digital media accepted – contact for specifications.
Usual terms of business: Minimum initial submission: 100 images.
Commission: 50 per cent.
Additional information: Submission guidelines available on request or via website.

GARDEN WORLD IMAGES*
(Incorporating The Harry Smith Collection)
Grange Studio, Woodham Road, Battlesbridge, Wickford, Essex SS11 7QU.
Tel: 01245 325725. Fax: 01245 429198. E-mail: info@gardenworldimages.com
Web: www.gardenworldimages.com
Contact: Françoise Davis, Lisa Smith (Partners).
Specialist subjects/requirements: All aspects of horticulture, plants, vegetables, fruit, herbs, trees, gardens, pools, patios, etc. Also gardening action shots, people doing things, step-by-step, making patios, etc. Creative abstract images. Also fauna.
Markets supplied: Publishing, calendars, seed catalogues, etc.
Stock: Colour. 35mm and medium format transparencies, and digital images.
Usual terms of business: Minimum initial submission: 50 images. No minimum retention period.
Commission: 50 per cent for transparencies, 40 per cent for digital.
Additional information: Plant portraits must be identified with Latin name.

LESLIE GARLAND PICTURE LIBRARY
"High Pasture", Yarrow, Falstone, Hexham, Northumberland NE48 1BG.
Tel/fax: 01434 240324. E-mail: pictures@lesliegarland.co.uk
Web: www.lesliegarland.co.uk
Contact: Leslie Garland, ARPS, ABIPP (Proprietor).
Specialist subjects/requirements: General coverage of Northern England (Derbyshire to the Border), Wales, Ireland, Scotland and Scandinavia; all subjects, though especially industry, engineering, science and technology.
Markets supplied: Advertising, books, brochures, exhibitions, magazines, etc.
Stock: Colour. Medium format or larger transparencies preferred, exceptional 35mm considered depending on subject matter.
Usual terms of business: Minimum initial submission 25 accepted images. Minimum retention period: 3 years.
Commission: 50 per cent.
Additional information: All pictures must be of top quality professional standard with precise captions. View contributor guidelines etc on net before submitting.

GEO AERIAL PHOTOGRAPHY*
4 Christian Fields, London SW16 3JZ.
Tel/fax: 020 8764 6292 or 0115 981 9418. E-mail: geo.aerial@geo-group.co.uk
Web: www.geo-group.co.uk
Contact: John Douglas (Director), Kelly White (Consultant).
Specialist subjects/requirements: Worldwide oblique aerial photographs.
Markets supplied: Books, magazines, advertising, etc.
Stock: Colour. 35mm or larger format.
Usual terms of business: Negotiable.
Commission: 50 per cent.
Additional information: Locations must be identified in detail. Do not send samples of work but contact by letter first.

GETTY IMAGES*
101 Bayham Street, London NW1 0AG.
Tel: 020 7267 8988. Fax: 020 7267 6540. E-mail: editor@gettyartists.com
Web: http://creative.gettyimages.com
Contact: Picture Editor.
Specialist subjects/requirements: Conceptual and general stock photography on all subjects.
Markets supplied: Advertising, publishing, design agencies, etc.
Stock: B&W and colour. All formats.
Usual terms of business: On application, for rights-managed and royalty-free sales.
Commission: Variable.
Additional information: The Getty Images Creative division incorporates several major collections including The Image Bank, Stone and Photodisc. For contributor information see www.gettyartists.com

GETTY IMAGES NEWS & SPORT*
116 Bayham Street, London NW1 0AG.
Tel: 0800 376 7981. E-mail: hugh.pinney@gettyimages.com/steve.rose@gettyimages.com/georges.dekeerle@gettyimages.com
Web: http://editorial.gettyimages.com
Contact: Editors – Hugh Pinney (news), Steve Rose (sport), Georges de Keerle (entertainment).
Specialist subjects/requirements: Contemporary news, sport and entertainment images.
Markets supplied: Newspapers, magazines, television, etc.
Stock: Mainly colour. 35mm and digital (for news).
Usual terms of business: Minimum retention period: 3 years.
Commission: 50 per cent.

GREYSTOCK*
Millennium Plc, Windhill Manor, Leeds Road, Shipley, West Yorkshire BD18 1BP.
Tel: 01274 538888. Fax: 01274 538899. E-mail: tracey.mcnulty@millenniumdirect.com
Web: www.greystockimages.co.uk
Contact: Tracey McNulty (Library Manager).
Specialist subjects/requirements: Images of older people, 50–80, in everyday situations: at home, on holiday, at work, with family, going out, dining out, playing sports, etc. Also B&W archive subjects of interest to older people.
Markets supplied: Primarily advertising and marketing.
Stock: Colour and B&W. All formats. Submissions on CD accepted.
Usual terms of business: No minimum initial submission or retention period.
Commission: 50 per cent.
Additional information: Prefer real people in real environments to posed professional models, but all images must be positive and evoke "living life to the full".

ROBERT HARDING WORLD IMAGERY*
58-59 Great Marlborough Street, London W1V 1DD.
Tel: 020 7478 4146. Fax: 020 7478 4161. E-mail: submissions@robertharding.com
www.robertharding.com
Contact: Fraser Hall (Library Manager).
Specialist subjects/requirements: People, lifestyle, industry, travel.
Markets supplied: Publishers, advertising agencies, design groups, calendar publishers, etc.
Stock: Colour. All formats; digital preferred (48MB non-interpolated for scans, 30MB non-interpolated for digital capture).
Usual terms of business: Minimum initial submission: 100 images. Minimum retention period: 7 years; 12 months notice of withdrawal.
Commission: As per contract; usually 40% to photographer.

HOLT STUDIOS INTERNATIONAL*
Coxes Farm, Bulstone Lane, Branscombe, East Devon EX12 3BJ.
Tel: 01297 680569. Fax: 01297 680478. E-mail: library@holt-studios.co.uk
Web: www.holt-studios.co.uk
Contact: Graham Everitt (Library Manager).
Specialist subjects/requirements: Pictorial and technical photographs of worldwide agriculture and horticulture, crop production and protection, livestock, pests, conservation, the environment and wildlife.
Markets supplied: Agricultural organisations, educational and technical publishers, advertising agencies, etc.
Stock: Colour. 35mm and medium format, digital.
Usual terms of business: To be negotiated.
Commission: Usually 50 per cent.
Additional information: Contributing photographers must combine specialist technical, scientific or agricultural knowledge with their photographic skills to produce outstanding photographs.

HUTCHISON PICTURE LIBRARY*
65 Brighton Road, Shoreham, West Sussex BN43 6RE.
Tel: 01273 440113. Fax: 01273 440116. E-mail: library@eyeubiquitous.com
Web: www.hutchisonpictures.co.uk
Contact: Stephen Rafferty (Library Manager).
Specialist subjects/requirements: Worldwide coverage of agriculture, industry, landscapes, festivals and ceremonies, decoration, religion, urban and village life, tourism, flora and fauna, medicine and education, architecture, art, craft, etc.
Markets supplied: Publishing, company reports, calendars, advertising, audio visual.
Stock: Colour. 35mm and medium format.
Usual terms of business: Minimum initial submission: 1,000 transparencies. Minimum retention period: 3 years.
Commission: 50 per cent.
Additional information: Now allied with the Eye Ubiquitous library. Only occasionally take on new photographers with large collections of in-depth documentary work (medical, environment, agriculture, etc) or as varied as possible in geographical and subject coverage.

IMAGES OF FRANCE
Tel: 07785 353290. E-mail: info@imagesfrance.com
Web: www.imagesfrance.com
Contact: David Martyn Hughes (Proprietor).
Specialist subjects/requirements: All aspects of France and French life.
Markets supplied: Travel industry, advertising, general publishing.
Stock: Digital capture files only; no scans. Images taken on 5MP cameras and above.
Usual terms of business: No minimum initial submission. Minimum retention period: 1 year. Exclusivity not required.
Commission: 50 per cent.
Additional information: Check the website first to see what kind of images the library sells. Initial contact should be made by e-mail stating what stock a photographer has to offer.

IMAGESTATE LTD*
Ramillies House, 1-2 Ramillies Street, London W1F 7LN.
Tel: 020 7734 7344. Fax: 020 7287 3933. E-mail: submissions@imagestate.co.uk
Web: www.imagestate.co.uk
Contact: Diana Leppard (Picture Editor).
Specialist subjects/requirements: General contemporary stock – lifestyle, business, industry, landscapes, travel, leisure, etc
Markets supplied: Advertising and publishing.

Stock: Mainly colour; some B&W.
Usual terms of business: Minimum initial submission dependent on quality. Minimum retention period: 5 years.
Commission: Subject to contract.
Additional information: The agency sells both rights-managed and royalty-free stock.

IMAGING BODY*
55 Craiglockhart Terrace, Edinburgh EH14 1XH.
Tel: 0131 443 9825. E-mail: info@imagingbody.com
Web: www.imagingbody.com
Contact: Sarah Keer-Keer (Manager).
Specialist subjects/requirements: Medical science, healthcare (hospital scenes, medical situations, health issues) and the human body (clinical, creative or detail images – must be model released).
Markets supplied: Publishing, advertising, etc.
Stock: Digital.
Usual terms of business: No minimum submission. Minimum retention period: 3 years.
Commission: From 40 per cent if agency required to scan, to 50 per cent if high-res scans supplied by photographer.
Additional information: Submit an initial selection of around 20 low-res images by e-mail.

IMPACT PHOTOS*
18-20 St John Street, London EC1M 4NX.
Tel: 020 7251 5091. Fax: 020 7608 0114. E-mail: library@ impactphotos.demon.co.uk
Web: www.impactphotos.com
Contact: Zute Lightfoot (Picture Editor).
Specialist subjects/requirements: Worldwide coverage of people in their environment – agriculture, industry, health, religion, transport, modernisation, education, social issues and travel.
Markets supplied: Newspapers, magazines, book, charities, etc.
Stock: Colour. 35mm transparencies; digital on CD preferred (50MB RGB TIFF uncompressed at 300dpi).
Usual terms of business: No minimum initial submission. Minimum retention period: 3 years.
Commission: 50 per cent.
Additional information: Digital contributors should also supply low-res images for quick edit.

J.S. LIBRARY INTERNATIONAL
101a Brondesbury Park, London NW2 5JL.
Tel: 020 8451 2668. Fax: 020 8459 0223. E-mail: sales@jslibrary.com
Web: www.jslibrary.com
Contact: John Shelley (Proprietor).
Specialist subjects/requirements: All subjects.
Markets supplied: Newspapers, magazines, book publishers, etc.
Stock: Colour. All transparency formats, and digital files.
Usual terms of business: No minimum initial submission, but regular submissions of large quantities recommended to maximise sales. Minimum retention period: None stated.
Commission: 50 per cent.
Additional information: The agency website also has an extensive gallery section where photographers can display single images or portfolios of work.

JAZZ INDEX PHOTO LIBRARY*
26 Fosse Way, London W13 0BZ.
Tel: 020 8998 1232. Fax: 020 8998 2880. E-mail: christianhim@jazzindex.co.uk
Web: www.jazzindex.co.uk
Contact: Christian Him (Principal).

Specialist subjects/requirements: Jazz, blues and contemporary music. Good atmospheric shots of musicians. Both contemporary and archive material of interest.
Markets supplied: Newspapers, book publishers, videos, television.
Stock: Colour, all formats; B&W, prints or negs.
Commission: 50 per cent.
Usual terms of business: No minimum submission.
Additional information: Always interested on jazz photos from the '60s or '70s. Contributors must phone first to enquire if material is suitable.

KOS PICTURE SOURCE LTD*
7 Spice Court, Ivory Square, Plantation Wharf, London SW11 3UE.
Tel: 020 7801 0044. Fax: 020 7801 0055. E-mail: images@kospictures.com
Web: kospictures.com
Contact: Caroline Hillier (Manager).
Specialist subjects/requirements: Water-related images from around the world. International yacht racing, all watersports, seascapes, underwater photography, and general travel.
Markets supplied: Advertising, design, publishing.
Stock: Colour only. 35mm and digital files.
Usual terms of business: No minimum initial submission. Minimum retention period: 2 years.
Commission: 50 per cent.

LEBRECHT MUSIC & ARTS PHOTO LIBRARY*
58b Carlton Hill, London NW8 0ES.
Tel: 020 7625 5341. Fax: 020 7625 5341. E-mail: pictures@lebrecht.co.uk
Web: www.lebrecht.co.uk
Contact: Elbie Lebrecht (Proprietor).
Specialist subjects/requirements: All aspects of music – classical, opera, jazz, rock – and the arts. Instruments, composers, musicians, singers, writers, artists, playwrights, philosophers. Interiors and exteriors of concert halls and opera houses, statues and tombs of famous composers in the UK and abroad.
Markets supplied: Specialist magazines, national press, record companies, book publishers.
Stock: B&W and colour. Digital submissions preferred (300dpi 25MB TIFF).
Usual terms of business: No minimum initial submission or retention period.
Commission: 50 per cent.

LINK PICTURE LIBRARY*
33 Greyhound Road, London W6 8NH.
Tel: 020 7381 2433. E-mail: lib@linkpicturelibrary.com
Web: www.linkpicturelibrary.com
Contact: Orde Eliason (Proprietor).
Specialist subjects/requirements: General documentary coverage of countries worldwide, but particularly Africa – communications, culture, education, environment, health, industry, people and politics. Special interest in South Africa, South East Asia, India and Israel.
Markets supplied: Newspapers, general publishing.
Stock: Colour. 35mm transparencies and digital images at 300dpi for 5x7in output.
Usual terms of business: Minimum initial submission: 50 images. Minimum retention period: 3 years.
Commission: 50 per cent.

MILEPOST 92½*
Newton Harcourt, Leicestershire LE8 9FH.
Tel: 0116 259 2068. Fax: 0116 259 3001. E-mail: contacts@milepost92-half.co.uk
Web: www.milepost92-half.co.uk
Contact: Colin Nash (Library Manager).

Specialist subjects/requirements: Railways – all aspects, national and international, contemporary and archive.
Markets supplied: Advertising, publishing, design, corporate railways.
Stock: Colour, 35mm or medium format. Archive B&W.
Usual terms of business: Minimum initial submission 25 pictures. No minimum retention period.
Commission: 50 per cent.
Additional information: All material must be of the highest quality. Transparencies must be mounted and captioned with brief, accurate details.

MILITARY PICTURE LIBRARY INTERNATIONAL LTD*
PO Box 3350, Shepton Mallet, Somerset BA4 4WX.
Tel: 01749 850560. Fax: 01749 850689. E-mail: info@mpli.co.uk
Web: www.militarypicturelibrary.com
Contact: Julie Collins (Contributor Accounts Handler).
Specialist subjects/requirements: UK and international military forces (land, sea and air), including current and historic military operations.
Markets supplied: World press, magazines, book publishers, etc.
Stock: Colour and B&W.
Usual terms of business: No minimum initial submission. Minimum retention period: 12 months.
Commission: 50 per cent.
Additional information: Not interested in images from air shows and similar events open to the public unless especially striking or unusual.

MONITOR PICTURE LIBRARY*
The Forge, Harlow Road, Roydon, Nr Harlow, Essex CM19 5HH.
Tel: 01279 792700. Fax: 01279 792600. E-mail: elly@monitorpicturelibrary.com
Web: www.monitorpicturelibrary.com
Contact: Elly White (Picture Editor).
Specialist subjects/requirements: Photographs of personalities from politics, business, sport, entertainment, royalty. Both current and archive material of interest.
Markets supplied: National and international press, television, advertising, publishers, etc.
Stock: B&W and colour. 35mm, medium format and digital (high-res TIFF).
Usual terms of business: No minimum submission.
Commission: 50 per cent, but may make outright purchase offer for suitable material.

NHPA LIMITED*
Little Tye, 57 High Street, Ardingly, Sussex RH17 6TB.
Tel: 01444 892514. Fax: 01444 892168. E-mail: nhpa@nhpa.co.uk
Web: www.nhpa.co.uk
Contact: Tim Harris (Manager).
Specialist subjects/requirements: Worldwide wildlife, domestic animals and pets, plants and gardens, landscapes, agriculture and environmental subjects. Endangered and appealing wildlife of particular interest.
Markets supplied: Books, magazines, advertising and design, cards and calendars, electronic publishing, exhibitions, etc (UK and overseas).
Stock: Colour. 35mm, medium format and larger original transparencies. High quality large format dupes. Digital subject to agency guidelines.
Usual terms of business: Minimum initial submission: 200 transparencies.
Commission: 50 per cent.
Additional information: Pictures should be strong, active and well-composed. Write before submitting material. First submissions should be of transparencies. Full submissions guidelines available on website.

NATURAL IMAGE
24 Newborough Road, Wimborne, Dorset BH21 1RD.
Tel: 01202 849142. Fax: 01202 848419. E-mail: bob.gibbons@which.net
Contact: Bob Gibbons (Proprietor).
Specialist subjects/requirements: Natural history, the countryside, gardens and gardening, worldwide travel with a wildlife or conservation bias.
Markets supplied: Books, magazines, etc.
Stock: Colour. 35mm upwards.
Usual terms of business: Minimum initial submission: 50 slides. Minimum retention period: 1 year.
Commission: 50 per cent.
Additional information: Material must be accurately and informatively captioned.

NATURAL SCIENCE PHOTOS*
33 Woodland Drive, Watford, Hertfordshire WD17 3BY.
Tel: 01923 245265. Fax: 01923 246067. E-mail: ph_ward@talk21.com
Contact: Peter Ward (Partner).
Specialist subjects/requirements: All types of living organisms including wildlife of every description, domestic animals and fowl, botany, ecology, geology, geography, climate and effects, astronomy, pollution and effects, primitive people and their ways of life, countryside topics and scenics, latter mostly without artifacts. Also angling, both sea and freshwater.
Markets supplied: Books, magazines, newspapers, calendars, audio-visual, television and advertising, UK and overseas. Some inter-agency deals.
Stock: Colour. Mainly 35mm, but larger formats accepted.
Usual terms of business: No minimum submission. Standard contract allows for 3 years retention and is non-exclusive.
Commission: 33 per cent.
Additional information: All material to be clearly captioned and well documented – English and scientific names, locality and photographer; also any useful additional information.

NEWSCAST LTD*
PO Box 10, London EC1V 0PQ.
Tel: 020 7608 1000. E-mail: photo@newscast.co.uk
Web: www.newscast.co.uk
Contact: Bob Collins (Picture Editor).
Specialist subjects/requirements: Images relevant to business and corporate activities worldwide. Portraits of business people, politicians, company buildings and company activities.
Markets supplied: Magazines, newspapers and broadcasting media worldwide.
Stock: Colour. All formats.
Usual terms of business: No minimum initial submission. Minimum retention period: 2 years.
Commission: 50 per cent.
Additional information: This is an entirely Web-based syndication service. For image security the website is password-protected and all images watermarked.

NUNN SYNDICATION*
13a Shad Thames, Butlers Wharf, London SE1 2PU.
Tel: 020 7407 4666. Fax: 020 7407 5666. E-mail: production@nunn-syndication.com
Web: www.nunn-syndication.com
Contact: Robin Nunn (Managing Director).
Specialist subjects/requirements: All aspects of the British royal family, including state occasions, foreign tours, informal shots, etc. Also foreign royalty and general celebrities.

Markets supplied: General publishing.
Stock: Colour. 35mm transparencies.
Usual terms of business: No minimum terms specified.
Commission: 40 per cent.

OSF LTD*
Network House, Station Yard, Thame, Oxfordshire OX9 3UH.
Tel: 01844 262370. Fax: 01844 262380. E-mail: photo.library@osf.uk.com
Web: www.osf.uk.com
Contact: Gilbert Woolley (Creative Director).
Specialist subjects/requirements: High quality wildlife photography, plus the environment, botanical, science, travel, pollution and conservation, landscapes, agriculture, high-speed photography, special effects, underwater, creative plant shots, indigenous people, pets.
Markets supplied: Magazines, book publishers, advertising/design companies, merchandising etc.
Stock: Colour. All formats up to and including 5x4in and panoramics.
Usual terms of business: Minimum initial submission 100 transparencies. Minimum retention period: 5 years.
Commission: Negotiable.
Additional information: All material must be of a very high technical standard – perfectly sharp and exposed, well composed, creative and visually stunning. Contact the library for a photographer's pack.

1dpi*
Suite 43, The Media Centre, 7 Northumberland Street, Huddersfield HD1 1RL.
Tel: 0870 990 5197. E-mail: linda.whitwam@1dpi.com
Web: www.1dpi.com
Contact: Linda Whitwam (Visual Director).
Specialist subjects/requirements: High-quality travel, particularly Western Europe and Britain. Subject areas include landscapes, cityscapes, architecture, culture, nature, mood images and concepts.
Markets supplied: Magazines, travel brochures, books, calendars, design etc.
Stock: High-resolution digital.
Usual terms of business: Minimum initial submission: 200 images. Minimum retention period: 3 years.
Commission: 40 per cent to photographer.
Additional information: Only top-quality work will be considered, preferably offering a new take on familiar subjects. Images can be submitted as high-res digital (must have been cleaned in Photoshop to agency standard) or transparencies for scanning by the agency (no charge). Images from digital cameras must be from Canon/Nikon 6-megapixel cameras or higher. Initial contact by e-mail preferred.

PANOS PICTURES*
Studio 3B, 38 Southwark Street, London SE1 1UN.
Tel: 020 7234 0010. Fax: 020 7357 0094. E-mail: pics@panos.co.uk
Web: www.panos.co.uk
Contact: Adrian Evans (Director).
Specialist subjects/requirements: Documentary coverage of the Third World and Eastern Europe, focusing on social, economic and political issues and with special emphasis on environment

and development. Also agriculture, education, energy, health, industry, landscape, people, religions.
Markets supplied: Newspapers and magazines, book publishers, development agencies.
Stock: B&W and colour. 35mm. Digital media accepted.
Usual terms of business: No minimum initial submission or retention period.
Commission: 50 per cent.
Additional information: 50 per cent of all profits from the library are covenanted to the Panos Institute, an international development studies group.

PAPILIO NATURAL HISTORY LIBRARY
155 Station Road, Herne Bay, Kent CT6 5QA.
Tel: 01227 360996. E-mail: library@papiliophotos.com
Contact: Justine Pickett (Director).
Specialist subjects/requirements: All aspects of natural history worldwide: plants, insects, birds, mammals and marine life.
Markets supplied: Books, magazines, advertising, etc.
Stock: Colour. 35mm, medium format and digital.
Usual terms of business: Minimum initial submission: 200 images. Minimum retention period: 3 years.
Commission: 50 per cent.
Additional information: Contact first before sending digital submissions, to obtain full detailed requirements.

PHOTEGA*
Telford Way, Waterwells Business Park, Quedgeley, Gloucester GL2 2AB.
Tel: 01452 541221. Fax: 01452 541230. E-mail: contributor@photega.com
Web: www.photega.com
Contact: Helen Leigh-Rush (Library Manager).
Specialist subjects/requirements: All subjects including people (European lifestyle rather than American lifestyle), objects, concepts, seasons, nature, health, business, travel, education, social, cultural and historic.
Markets supplied: Publishing, advertising, design, PR, etc.
Stock: Digital only. For submission specifications see website.
Usual terms of business: Minimum initial submission: 5–10 images on CD showing a good cross-section of work. Minimum retention period: 12 months, thereafter 3 month termination notice applies.
Commission: 50 per cent.
Additional information: The agency offers a unique searching facility said to be of greater accuracy than other models. A small administration fee is charged for accepted images to cover the maintenance of search system integrity. Full contributors' information can be found on the website.

PHOTOFUSION PICTURE LIBRARY*
17a Electric Lane, Brixton, London SW9 8LA.
Tel: 020 7733 3500. Fax: 020 7738 5509. E-mail: library@photofusion.org
Web: www.photofusion.org
Contact: Liz Somerville (Library Manager).
Specialist subjects/requirements: All aspects of contemporary life with an emphasis on environmental and social issues. Specialist areas include children, disability, education, environment, the elderly, families, health, housing & homelessness, plus people generally.

Markets supplied: UK book and magazine publishing, newspapers, charities, annual reports, etc.
Stock: Colour transparencies and prints; B&W prints, digital files (minimum 24MB).
Usual terms of business: Minimum initial submissions: 100 photos. Minimum retention period: 3 years.
Commission: 50 per cent.

PHOTONICA*
10 Regents Wharf, All Saints Street, London N1 9RL.
Tel: 020 7278 4117. Fax: 020 7278 4118. E-mail: info@photonica.co.uk
Web: www.photonica.com
Contact: Mark Turner (Creative Director).
Specialist subjects/requirements: Strong metaphorical and conceptual images – abstract, creative, expressive.
Markets supplied: Advertising, design, editorial.
Stock: B&W and colour. All formats.
Usual terms of business: Minimum initial submission: by negotiation. Minimum retention period: 3 years.
Commission: Variable.

PICTUREBANK PHOTO LIBRARY LTD*
Parman House, 30–36 Fife Road, Kingston-upon-Thames, Surrey KT1 1SY.
Tel: 020 8547 2344. Fax: 020 8974 5652.E-mail info@picturebank.co.uk
Web: www.picturebank.co.uk
Contact: Martin Bagge (Managing Director).
Specialist subjects/requirements: Worldwide travel and tourism, UK cities and countryside, people (glamour, families, children, ethnic peoples), environment, animals (domestic and wild), business, industry and technology.
Markets supplied: Magazines, calendars, travel industry, advertising, etc.
Stock: Colour. 35mm acceptable if subject matter is exceptional; larger formats preferred. Digital files at 35MB+.
Usual terms of business: Minimum initial submission: 100 images. Minimum retention period: 5 years.
Commission: Variable – maximum 50 per cent.

PICTURES COLOUR LIBRARY*
10 James Whatman Court, Turkey Mill, Ashford, Kent ME14 5SS.
Tel: 01622 609809. Fax: 01622 609806. E-mail: karen@picturescolourlibrary.co.uk
Web: www.picturescolourlibrary.co.uk
Contact: Karen McCunnail (Submissions Manager).
Specialist subjects/requirements: General, but with strong emphasis on travel and travel-related images.
Markets supplied: Magazines, newspapers, travel companies, advertising and design.
Stock: Colour only. All formats including digital (minimum file size 48MB).
Usual terms of business: Minimum initial submission: 500 images. Minimum retention period: 3 years.
Commission: 50 per cent.

POPPERFOTO.COM*
Paul Popper Ltd, The Old Mill, Overstone Farm, Overstone, Northampton NN6 0AB.
Tel: 01604 670670. Fax: 01604 670635. E-mail:inquiries@ popperfoto.com
Web: www.popperfoto.com
Contact: Ian Blackwell (Sales Director).
Specialist subjects/requirements: General library of 14+ million images – historical/modern

archive material and stock. No longer accepting contributing photographers but interested in buying photographs outright, particularly vintage social history, family archives, or general historical collections.
Markets supplied: All media worldwide including books, newspapers, magazines, TV and advertising.
Stock: All formats, B&W and colour.
Usual terms of business: Outright purchase only.
Commission: N/A.

POWERSTOCK/SUPERSTOCK*
Unit G10, 59 Chilton Street, London E2 6EA.
Tel: 020 7729 7473. Fax: 020 7729 7476. E-mail: info@powerstock.com
Web: www.powerstock.com
Contact: Ian Lishman (Creative Director).
Specialist subjects/requirements: Business, lifestyle, travel, nature, food, sport, people, technology, industry, transport, manufacturing, conceptual ideas, vintage, fine art.
Markets supplied: Advertising, publishing, editorial, audio visual, public relations, travel.
Stock: Colour and B&W. All formats.
Usual terms of business: Minimum initial submission: 50 transparencies. Also supplies royalty-free.
Commission: 50 per cent.

PYMCA*
Unit C, Zetland House, 5-25 Scrutton Street, London EC2A 4HJ.
Tel: 020 7613 3725. Fax: 020 7613 3437. E-mail: info@pymca.com
Web: www.pymca.com
Contact: Jake Cunningham (Image Manager).
Specialist subjects/requirements: All images related to youth and subcultures, from the past (1940s/50s) to the present day, UK and abroad. Areas of particular interest: street fashions; lifestyle; social documentary; music/clubbing; recreational sport; related incidental imagery.
Markets supplied: General publishing, advertising, etc.
Stock: B&W and colour. All formats.
Usual terms of business: Minimum initial submission: 20 pictures. Minimum retention period: 1 year.
Commission: 50 per cent.
Additional information: Particularly interested in older material, which is hard to source. Also the very new – latest fashions, fads and trends.

RED COVER LIMITED*
Unit 7, Aura House, 53 Oldridge Road, London SW12 8PP.
Tel: 020 8772 1110. Fax: 020 8772 3113. E-mail: info@redcover.com
Web: www.redcover.com
Contact: Sally Griffiths (Senior Picture Editor).
Specialist subjects/requirements: Architecture, interiors, gardens and food.
Markets supplied: International publishing, advertising, design.
Stock: Colour transparencies, all formats, and digital images.
Usual terms of business: Minimum initial submission: 20–50 images. Minimum retention period: 4 years.
Commission: 50 per cent.
Additional information: The agency markets complete features as well as single images. For initial viewing only, scanned images may be submitted on CD or via e-mail.

REDFERNS MUSIC PICTURE LIBRARY*
7 Bramley Road, London W10 6SZ.
Tel: 020 7792 9914. Fax: 020 7792 0921. E-mail: info@redferns.com
Web: www.redferns.com
Contact: Dede Millar (Partner).
Specialist subjects/requirements: All forms of popular music from the 1920s onwards, but with special concentration on the past 40 years. Also related subjects such as musical instruments, dance, stage shows.
Markets supplied: Newspapers, magazines, books, record companies, advertising and design companies.
Stock: B&W and colour. 35mm and medium format. Digital submissions also accepted.
Usual terms of business: Negotiable.
Commission: 45 per cent.

RETNA PICTURES LTD*
Stills Road, Pinewood Studios, Pinewood Road, Iver Heath, Buckinghamshire SL0 0NH.
Tel: 01753 785450. Fax: 01753 785451. E-mail: ukinfo@retna.com
Web: www.retna.com
Contact: Verity Briggs (lifestyle), Camilla Dowse (music/events).
Specialist subjects/requirements: Lifestyle images: women, couples, family life, health and beauty, leisure, babies, children, teenagers, men, business and food. Celebrity/music images: portraiture, studio and events photography.
Markets supplied: Newspapers, magazines, books, record companies, advertising.
Stock: B&W and colour, any format. Digital media accepted.
Usual terms of business: Minimum initial submission: 40–50 images. Minimum retention period: 3 years.
Commission: Negotiable, depending on material.
Additional information: Lifestyle images must be fully model-released

REX FEATURES*
18 Vine Hill, London EC1R 5DZ.
Tel: 020 7278 7294. Fax: 020 7696 0974. E-mail: rex@rexfeatures.com
Web: www.rexfeatures.com
Contact: Glen Marks (Library Manager).
Specialist subjects/requirements: Human interest and general features, current affairs, personalities, animals (singles and series), humour, travel.
Markets supplied: UK national newspapers and magazines, book publishers, audio visual, television and international press. Daily worldwide syndication.
Stock: B&W and colour. All formats including digital.
Usual terms of business: No minimum submission. Preferred minimum retention period: 2 years.
Commission: 50 per cent.

REX INTERSTOCK*
18 Vine Hill, London EC1R 5DZ.
Tel: 020 7278 6989. Fax: 020 7696 0973. E-mail: interstock@rexfeatures.com
Web: www.rexinterstock.com
Contact: Paul Brown (Library Manager).
Specialist subjects/requirements: General stock material, especially lifestyle and illustrative photography.
Markets supplied: General media. publishing, advertising and design.
Stock: B&W and colour. All formats and digital.

Usual terms of business: Minimum submission negotiable. Minimum retention period: 2 years.
Commission: 50 per cent.
Additonal information: Submit brief description of the type of work and quantities available. Material is accepted for online, stock and catalogue distribution worldwide.

ROYAL GEOGRAPHICAL SOCIETY PICTURE LIBRARY*
1 Kensington Gore, London SW7 2AR.
Tel: 020 7591 3060. Fax: 020 7591 3061. E-mail: pictures@rgs.org
Web: www.rgs.org/picturelibrary
Contact: Justin Hobson (Library Sales Manager).
Specialist subjects/requirements: Exploration and geographical coverage, both historic and current. Travel photography from remote destinations: indigenous peoples and daily life, landscapes, environmental and geographical phenomena, agriculture, crafts, human impact on the environment.
Markets supplied: Commercial publishing and academic research.
Stock: Colour, all formats. Historic B&W.
Usual terms of business: Minimum initial submission: 250 pictures. Minimum retention period: none specified, but like to hold material for at least 2 years.
Commission: 50 per cent.

SCR PHOTO LIBRARY
Society for Co-operation in Russian and Soviet Studies, 320 Brixton Road, London SW9 6AB.
Tel: 020 7274 2282. Fax: 020 7274 3230. E-mail: ruslibrary@scrss.org.uk
Web: www.scrss.org.uk
Contact: J Cunningham (Librarian).
Specialist subjects/requirements: Pictures from Russia and all Republics of the former Soviet Union. General/everyday scenes, landscapes, architecture, towns and cities, politics, arts, industry, agriculture, science, etc.
Markets supplied: General.
Stock: All formats.
Usual terms of business: No minimum submission. Minimum retention period: 2 years.
Commission: 50 per cent.

S.I.N. (SYNDICATED INTERNATIONAL NETWORK)*
89a North View Road, Crouch End, London N8 7LR.
Tel: 020 8348 8061. Fax: 020 8340 8517. E-mail: sales@sin-photo.co.uk
Web: www.sin-photo.co.uk
Contact: Marianne Lasson (Proprietor).
Specialist subjects/requirements: Rock and pop music and performers. Also youth culture from all eras, including clubbing, festivals, raves, street fashion, skateboarding, etc.
Markets supplied: Music industry and general publishing.
Stock: Colour and B&W.
Usual terms of business: No minimum initial submission. Minimum retention period: 3 years.
Commission: 55 per cent to photographer.
Additional information: Material must be of a very high standard; prefers initial submissions on CD-ROM.

SOA PHOTO AGENCY*
Lovells Farm, Dark Lane, Stoke St Gregory, Taunton TA3 6EU.
Tel: 0870 333 6062. Fax: 0870 333 6082. E-mail: info@soaphotoagency.com
Web: www.soaphotoagency.com
Contact: Sabine Oppenlander (Director).
Specialist subjects/requirements: Very high-quality, modern, creative, avant-garde images of varied subject matter.
Markets supplied: Mainly advertising and design via online distribution and worldwide network of

other small agencies.
Stock: B&W and colour. All formats. Digital preferred.
Usual terms of business: See website for details.
Commission: 60-50 per cent.
Additional information: Promises photographers a personalised service with regular sales reports and prompt payment. Don't send on spec; e-mail in the first instance with details of material available.

SCIENCE PHOTO LIBRARY*
327-329 Harrow Road, London W9 3RB.
Tel: 020 7432 1100. Fax: 020 7286 8668. E-mail: rose@sciencephoto.co.uk
Web: www.sciencephoto.com
Contact: Rosemary Taylor (Director).
Specialist subjects/requirements: All types of scientific, industrial and medical imagery, from micrography to astronomical photography. Also includes photographs of equipment, laboratories, factories and relevant personalities.
Markets supplied: Books, magazines, advertising, design, corporate, audio visual.
Stock: Mainly colour. Analogue and digital accepted (contact for details).
Usual terms of business: No minimum submission. Minimum retention period: 5 years.
Commission: 50 per cent.
Additional information: All photographs must be accompanied by full caption information, but preferably in non-technical language.

SKISHOOT– OFFSHOOT*
Hall Place, Upper Woodcott, Whitchurch, Hants RG28 7PY.
Tel: 01635 255527. Fax: 01635 255528. E-mail: skishootsnow@aol.com
Web: www.skishoot.co.uk
Contact: Kate Parker, Jo Crossley.
Specialist subjects/requirements: Skishoot: skiing and snowboarding, ski resorts in Europe and North America. Offshoot: major cities and tourist areas in France. Special interest in beaches and local colour.
Markets supplied: Travel industry, general publishing, and advertising.
Stock: Colour. 35mm and medium format transparencies; digital on CD preferred.
Usual terms of business: Minimum initial submission: 50 images. No minimum retention period.
Commission: 50 per cent.

SKYSCAN PHOTOLIBRARY*
Oak House, Toddington, Cheltenham GL54 5BY.
Tel: 01242 621357. Fax: 01242 621343. E-mail: info@skyscan.co.uk
Web: www.skyscan.co.uk
Contact: Brenda Marks (Library Manager).
Specialist subjects/requirements: Anything aerial – air to ground; aircraft; general aviation; aerial sports (skydiving, ballooning, etc).
Markets supplied: Editorial, advertising, design, calendars.
Stock: B&W and colour. All formats. Digital files of 10+MB (preferably 50+MB).
Usual terms of business: Minimum initial submission: 20+ images. Minimum retention period: 2 years.
Commission: 50 per cent.
Additional information: Also operates a brokerage service which is sometimes more appropriate than agency terms. Photographs are retained by the photographer; picture requests are initiated and negotiated by Skyscan and fees split 50/50.

SPECTRUM COLOUR LIBRARY
227 Stratford Workshops, Burford Road, London E15 2SP.
Tel: 020 8522 0888. Fax: 020 8522 0666. E-mail: spectrumphotos@btinternet.com
Leeds Office: 13, Holly Park Mills, Calverley, Pudsey, West Yorkshire LS28 5QS.
Tel: 0113 239 4020. Fax: 0113 236 1506.
Web: www.spectrumphotos.com
Contact: Keith Jones, Ann Jones (Directors). Leeds Office: Peter Dransfield (Manager).
Specialist subjects/requirements: Travel, natural history, people, general.
Markets supplied: Advertising, publishing, travel brochures, etc.
Stock: Colour. All formats.
Usual terms of business: Minimum initial submission: 500 slides; no minimum submission for digital. Minimum retention period: 5 years.
Commission: 50 per cent.
Additional information: Contributing photographers are expected to make regular submissions of work, at least quarterly and preferably monthly. Digital images may be uploaded at the website – see site for details.

SPORTING PICTURES (UK) LTD*
7a Lambs Conduit Passage, London WC1R 4RG.
Tel: 020 7405 4500. Fax: 020 7831 7991. E-mail: photos@sportingpictures.com
Web: www.sportingpictures.com
Contact: Steven Bloor (Picture Editor).
Specialist subjects/requirements: Leisure and adventure activities and extreme or unusual sport. People involved in minority interests – any age (primarily for advertising), model-released if possible. General view and aerial shots of all sports.
Markets supplied: Magazines, books, advertising etc.
Stock: Colour 35mm and digital.
Usual terms of business: No minimum initial submission.
Commission: 50 per cent.
Additional information: Digital submissions preferred. Main scope for contributors is for minority and leisure sports as above; most mainstream sporting coverage is handled by the agency's own staff, but please enquire.

STILL MOVING PICTURE COMPANY
1 Castlehill, Doune, Perthshire FK16 6BU.
Tel: 01786 842200. E-mail: info@stillmovingpictures.com
Web: www.stillmovingpictures.com/www.stilldigital.co.uk
Contact: John Hutchinson, Sue Hall (Directors).
Specialist subjects/requirements: All Scottish subjects; scenics, travel, commerce, industry, wildlife, sport and culture.
Markets supplied: Publishing, advertising, tourism, etc.
Stock: Colour. All formats.
Usual terms of business: No minimum initial submission or retention period.
Commission: 50 per cent.
Additional information: Now operating entirely digital service through www.stilldigital.co.uk. A full "wants" list can be supplied on request.

STOCK-CUBE
Unit 8, Level 5 South, New England House, New England Street, Brighton BN1 4GH.
Tel: 01273 620222. E-mail: submissions@stock-cube.com
Web: www.stock-cube.com
Contact: Sam Williams (Library Manager).
Specialist subjects/requirements: Creative and individual work on a broad range of subjects, to

be sold as royalty-free CD collections. Themed or stylistically consistent selections rather than mixed subjects.
Markets supplied: Advertising, design agencies, websites, etc.
Stock: Colour and B&W. Digital preferred, 50MB RAW files. All stock is digital but transparencies or high-quality prints accepted for scanning.
Usual terms of business: Minimum initial submission: Negotiable, but ideally 80–100 images. Minimum retention period: 5 years.
Commission: 50 per cent.
Additional information: Submit 5 small JPEG samples or link to a website in the first instance. The library is run "by artists for artists" hence the higher than normal commission rate for royalty-free.

STOCK SHOT*
2b St Vincent Street, Edinburgh EH3 6SH.
Tel: 07071 201 440. Fax: 0131 556 8282. E-mail: info@stockshot.co.uk
Web: www.stockshot.co.uk
Contact: Bridget Clyde (Library Manager).
Specialist subjects/requirements: Skiing and other winter sports; adventure sports; adventure travel.
Markets supplied: Publishers, newspapers, advertising, tour operators and travel companies.
Stock: Colour only. 35mm.
Usual terms of business: No minimum terms.
Commission: 50 per cent.
Additional information: Seek quality rather than quantity, with dynamic, unusual angles etc. Only limited scope for new contributors.

STOCKSCOTLAND.COM*
Croft Studio, Croft Roy, Crammond Brae, Tain IV19 1JG.
Tel/fax: 01862 892298. E-mail: info@stockscotland.com
www.stockscotland.com
Contact: Hugh Webster (Library Manager).
Specialist subjects/requirements: All aspects of Scotland and Scottish life – landscapes, castles, Highland games, natural history, industry, whisky, people, lifestyles, etc.
Markets supplied: General publishing, advertising, travel industry.
Stock: B&W and colour, all formats. High-res scans (30Mb+).
Usual terms of business: No minimum initial submission. Minimum retention period: 3 years.
Commission: 50 per cent.
Additional information: Images should be edited rigorously before submission. Do not send lots of very similar images. For more submission details see website.

TRH PICTURES*
Bradley's Close, 74–77 White Lion Street, London N1 9PF.
Tel: 020 7520 7647. Fax: 020 7520 7606. E-mail: trh@trhpictures.co.uk
Web: www.trhpictures.co.uk/www.codyimages.com
Contact: Ted Nevill (Director).
Specialist subjects/requirements: All aspects of aviation, defence, transport (shipping, railways, road) and space exploration – worldwide, historical and modern.
Markets supplied: Books, magazines, newspapers, multi-media, etc.
Stock: B&W and colour, all formats.
Usual terms of business: Minimum initial submission: 200 images. Minimum retention period: 3 years.
Commission: 50 per cent.
Additional information: Ring first to discuss submission and agency requirements.

THEIMAGEFILE.COM
PO Box 241, Chertsey, Surrey KT16 0YZ.
Tel: 0870 224 2454. Fax: 0870 224 2455. E-mail: membership@theimagefile.com
Web: www.theimagefile.com
Contact: James Duncan (Director).
Specialist subjects/requirements: All major commercial subjects.
Markets supplied: Advertising, design agencies, general publishing.
Stock: Digital only.
Usual terms of business: No minimum initial submission or retention period.
Commission: 75 per cent, but because of the personalised facilities offered there is a monthly subscription charge of £25.
Additional information: Contributing photographers have their own account through which they set their own prices for images sold. They are able to deal direct with purchasers if they wish and also obtain commissions. Other facilities include direct uploading of images and real time payment tracking.

TOPHAM PICTUREPOINT*
PO Box 33, Edenbridge, Kent TN8 5PB.
Tel: 01732 863939. Fax: 01732 860215. E-mail: admin@topfoto.co.uk
Web: www.topfoto.co.uk
Contact: John Balean (Stock Manager).
Specialist subjects/requirements: World coverage of general subjects; sports, pastimes, industry, travel, personalities, etc.
Markets supplied: Books, travel industry, advertising, etc.
Stock: Digital only, 300dpi at A4.
Usual terms of business: Minimum initial submission: 100 images. Minimum contract period: 3 years (12 months notice).
Commission: 50 per cent.

TRAVEL INK*
The Old Coach House, 14 High Street, Goring-on-Thames, Berkshire RG8 9AR.
Tel: 01491 873011. Fax: 01491 875558. E-mail: info@travel-ink.co.uk
Web: www.travel-ink.co.uk
Contact: Amanda Greenwood (Library Manager).
Specialist subjects/requirements: All aspects of travel and tourism, from destinations to forms of transport, food, things to buy, famous sights, hotel shots to native lifestyles. All countries including the UK. Particularly interested in travel lifestyle images.
Markets supplied: Travel industry, magazines, books, newspapers, advertising etc.
Stock: Colour, all formats including digital (minimum 18MB).
Usual terms of business: Minimum submission: 200. Minimum retention period 3 years.
Commission: 40 per cent to photographer.
Additional information: If submitting digital send initial sample of 10 images on CD.

THE TRAVEL LIBRARY*
Unit 7, The Kiln Workshops, Pilcot Road, Crookham Village, Fleet, Hants GU51 5RY.
Tel: 01252 627233. Fax: 01252 812399. E-mail: info@travel-library.co.uk
Web: www.travel-library.co.uk
Contact: Philip Enticknap (Director), Sally Sherwood (Marketing Manager).

Specialist subjects/requirements: Top quality tourist travel material covering destinations worldwide.
Markets supplied: UK tour operators and travel industry, advertising, design and corporate.
Stock: Colour. Medium or larger format transparencies preferred, 35mm only if top quality. Digital files, minimum 18MB RAW TIFF.
Usual terms of business: Minimum initial submission: 100 images. Minimum retention period 3 years.
Commission: 50 per cent.

TROPIX PHOTO LIBRARY*
44 Woodbines Avenue, Kingston upon Thames, KT1 2AY.
Tel: 020 8546 0823. Fax: 0870 706 1317. E-mail: images@tropix.co.uk
Web: www.tropix.co.uk
Contact: Veronica Birley (Librarian).
Specialist subjects/requirements: Progressive and up-beat images of the developing world, exotic travel and wildlife.
Markets supplied: Advertising and general publishing, international clients, etc.
Stock: Colour. All formats from 35mm up.
Usual terms of business: Subject to negotiation.
Commission: 50 per cent.
Additional information: Model releases essential for people shots. Send no images initially; photographers with suitable material should check website first then e-mail with details of their photography.

ELIZABETH WHITING & ASSOCIATES*
70 Mornington Street, London NW1 7QE.
Tel: 020 7388 2828. Fax: 020 7874 1108. E-mail: liz@elizabethwhiting.com
Web: www.elizabethwhiting.com
Contact: Liz Whiting (Director).
Specialist subjects/requirements: Home interest topics – architecture, interiors, design, DIY, crafts, gardens, food. Some travel and scenic material.
Markets supplied: Book and magazine publishers, advertising, design companies.
Stock: Colour transparencies and digital (60 MB files).
Usual terms of business: No minimum initial submission, but a contract is only entered into if both parties envisage a long-term commitment. Minimum retention period: 1 year.
Commission: 50 per cent.

WINDRUSH PHOTOS*
99 Noahs Ark, Kemsing, Sevenoaks, Kent TN15 6PD.
Tel: 01732 763486. Fax: 01732 763285. E-mail: dt@windrushphotos.demon.co.uk
Web: www.windrushphotos.com
Contact: David Tipling (Director).
Specialist subjects/requirements: High quality bird photography.
Markets supplied: Magazines, book publishers, etc.
Stock: Colour. Now only accepting digital submissions.
Usual terms of business: No minimum initial submission. Minimum retention period 3 years.
Commission: 50 per cent.
Additional information: Specialists in birds and bird watching, the library also acts as ornithological consultants. Do not submit on spec – always telephone first to discuss requirements.

WORLD PICTURE NEWS
Tel: +1 212 871 1207. Fax: +1 212 925 4569. E-mail: info@worldpicturenews.com
Web: www.worldpicturenews.com
Contact: Seamus Conlan (Director).

Specialist subjects/requirements: International news and photojournalism for on-line supply.
Markets supplied: National and international magazines, newspapers, broadcasting organisations.
Stock: Digital.
Usual terms of business: No minimum terms.
Commission: 50 per cent.
Additional information: Although established in London, HQ is now in New York. Business is conducted entirely on-line and photographers must first register on the website. Contributors must be familiar with scanning procedures, able to process images quickly and have the facility to up-load on-line. For further information see website.

WORLD PICTURES*
43-44 Berners Street, London W1T 3ND.
Tel: 020 7580 1845. Fax: 020 7580 4146. E-mail: mail@worldpictures.co.uk
Web: www.worldpictures.co.uk
Contact: David Brenes (Director).
Specialist subjects/requirements: Travel material: cities, resorts, hotels worldwide plus girls, couples and families on holiday suitable for travel brochure, magazine and newspaper use.
Markets supplied: Tour operators, airlines, design houses, advertising agencies.
Stock: Colour. 6x7cm, 6x9cm and 5x4in. No 35mm.
Usual terms of business: No minimum submission but usually likes the chance of placing material for minimum period of 2 years.
Commission: 50 per cent.

WORLD RELIGIONS PHOTO LIBRARY*
53a Crimsworth Road, London SW8 4RJ.
Tel/fax: 020 7720 6951. E-mail: copix@clara.co.uk
Web: www.worldreligions.co.uk/www.copix.co.uk
Contact: Christine Osborne (Proprietor).
Specialist subjects/requirements: World religions, images relating to rites of passage, places of worship and pilgrimage, festivals, sacred shrines. Travel and lifestyle images from specialist regions: Middle East and Arab world, Africa, South and S.E. Asia.
Markets supplied: General publishing, travel industry, internet.
Stock: Colour. 35mm transparencies accepted but digital files preferred.
Usual terms of business: Minimum initial submission: 40 images (preferrably on CD) to assess quality, followed by ability to deposit at least 100. Minimum retention period: 3 years.
Commission: 50 per cent.
Additional information: Images with inadequate caption information will not be considered.

SERVICES

This section lists companies providing products and services of use to the photographer. A number of those listed offer discounts to BFP members. To obtain the discounts indicated, members should simply produce their current membership card. In the case of mail order transactions, enclose your membership card with your order, requesting that this be returned with the completed order or as soon as membership has been verified. But in all cases, ensure that your membership card is valid: the discount will not be available to those who present an expired card.

Computer Software

SIGNUM TECHNOLOGIES LTD
Dunraven House, 5 Meadow Court, High Street, Witney, Oxfordshire, OX28 6ER.
Tel: 01933 776929. Fax: 01933 776939. E-mail: signum@signumtech.com
Web: www.signumtech.com
SureSign digital watermarking plug-ins for Photoshop, for copyright protection and communication.

SPANSOFT
8 Juniper Hill, Glenrothes, Fife KY7 5TH.
Tel/fax: 01592 743110. E-mail: support@spansoft.org
Web: www.spansoft.org
Slide Librarian shareware package for cataloguing transparency collections on PC.

Equipment Hire

ANGLIA CAMERAS
15-15a St Matthew's Street, Ipswich IP1 3EL.
Tel/fax: 01473 258185. E-mail: info@angliacameras.fsnet.co.uk
Web: www.anglia-cameras.co.uk
Hire of AV equipment, overhead projectors, screens, etc.

CALUMET
Promandis House, Bradbourne Drive, Tilbrook, Milton Keynes MK7 8AJ.
Tel: 01908 366344. Fax: 01908 366322.
Branches: London, Aberdeen, Belfast, Birmingham, Bristol, Edinburgh, Glasgow, Liverpool, Manchester and Nottingham.
Comprehensive equipment hire service featuring cameras, lenses, lighting, tripods, backgrounds, digital & AV equipment & accessories.
Discount to BFP members: 15%

EDRIC AUDIO VISUAL LTD
Oak End Way, Gerrards Cross, Bucks SL9 8BR.
Tel: 01753 481400. Fax: 01753 887163.
Web: www.edric-av.co.uk
Also at Manchester: 0161 773 7711; Bristol: 01454 201313; Birmingham: 0121 359 4666.
Hire and sale of AV equipment, film production and video production equipment.

THE FLASH CENTRE
54 Brunswick Centre, Bernard Street, London WC1N 1AE.
Tel: 020 7837 6163. Fax: 020 7833 4737. E-mail: hire@theflashcentre.co.uk
2nd Floor, Mill 1, Mabgate Mills, Mabgate, Leeds LS9 7DZ.
Tel: 0113 247 0937. Fax: 0113 247 0038.
Web: www.theflashcentre.com
Hire of lighting and digital photographic equipment.

PROFESSIONAL PHOTOGRAPHIC RETAIL
Unit 5, Westway Centre, St Marks Road, London W10 6JG.
Tel/fax: 020 8969 0234. E-mail: arun@film-plus.com
Specialist photographic retail and hire including film, paper and chemicals.
Discount to BFP members: 10%

Equipment Repair

BOURNEMOUTH PHOTOGRAPHIC (REPAIR) SERVICES LTD
251 Holdenhurst Road, Bournemouth, Dorset BH8 8DA.
Tel: 01202 301273. Fax: 01202 301273
Professional repairs to all makes of equipment. Full test facilities including modern electronic diagnostic test equipment.
Discount to BFP members: 5% off labour charges (cash sales).

CALUMET
Promandis House, Bradbourne Drive, Tilbrook, Milton Keynes MK7 8AJ.
Tel: 01908 366344. Fax: 01908 366322.
Branches: London, Aberdeen, Belfast, Birmingham, Bristol, Edinburgh, Glasgow, Liverpool, Manchester and Nottingham.
Full range of equipment repair.
Discount to BFP members: Free loan or discounted rental equipment with selected repairs.

CAM SERV
37 Hope Street, Hanley, Stoke-on-Trent ST1 5BS.
Tel: 01782 280789. Fax: 01782 281548. E-mail: camserv@msn.com
Repairs to all makes of cameras, camcorders, flash units, etc.
Discount to BFP members: 20%.

THE CAMERA REPAIR CENTRE
47 London Road, Southborough,Tunbridge Wells, Kent TN4 0PB.
Tel: 01892 619136. Fax: 01892 540362.
Web: www.camerarepaircentre.co.uk
Repairs to all makes of photographic equipment, including camcorders and digital.

CENTRAL CAMERAS
29 Salters Road, Walsall Wood, West Midlands WS9 9JD.
Tel: 01543 370263. Fax: 01543 454144.
General photographic repairs (not AV). Specialist in 35mm cameras, lenses and medium format equipment.
Discount to BFP members: 10% of labour costs.

COUSINS & WRIGHT
5 The Halve, Trowbridge, Wiltshire BA14 8SB.
Tel: 01225 754242.
Camera, camcorder and photographic equipment servicing and repair.

THE FLASH CENTRE
54 Brunswick Centre, Bernard Street, London WC1N 1AE.
Tel: 020 7837 6163. Fax: 020 7833 4737. E-mail: service@theflashcentre.co.uk
2nd Floor, Mill 1, Mabgate Mills, Mabgate, Leeds LS9 7DZ.
Tel: 0113 247 0937. Fax: 0113 247 0038.
Web: www.theflashcentre.com
Specialists in studio flash repair.

A J JOHNSTONE & CO LTD
395 Central Chambers, 93 Hope Street, Glasgow G2 6LD.
Tel: 0141 221 2106. Fax: 0141 221 9166.
Web: www.ajjohnstone.co.uk
All equipment repairs, including AV equipment. Authorised service centre for Canon, Olympus, Nikon, Bronica and Jobo processing equipment. Canon and Nikon warranty repairs.
Discount to BFP members: 10%.

T J KENYON LTD
Head office and general repairs: Bessemer Drive, Stevenage, Herts SG1 2DL.
Professional Division: 891 Ashton New Road, Clayton, Manchester M11 4PB.
Tel: 01438 720888. Fax: 01438 7438 743551. E-mail: tjkrepairs@aol.com
Web: www.camerarepairs.co.ukh
Comprehensive, nationwide photographic repairs and servicing, including large, medium and 35mm cameras, lenses, digital cameras, scanners, camcorders and computer equipment.

SENDEAN LTD
9-12 St Anne's Court, London W1F 0BB.
Tel: 020 7439 8418. Fax: 020 7734 4046. E-mail: mail@sendeancameras.com
General repair service. Estimates free.
Discount to BFP members: 10%.

Insurance

AUA INSURANCE
De Vere House, 90 St Faiths Lane, Norwich NR1 1NL.
Tel: 01603 628034. Fax: 01603 761384. E-mail: info@aua-insurance.com
14 Fenchurch Avenue, London, EC3M 5AT.
Tel: 020 7265 1166. Fax: 020 7265 1857.
Web: www.aua-insurance.com
Insurance for professional, semi-rpofessional and freelance photographers.
Discount to BFP members: 10%.

CAMERASURE ALLIANCE
Funtley Court, Funtley Hill, Fareham, Hampshire PO16 7UY.
Tel: 0870 4115511. Fax: 0870 4115515.
Web: www.towergate.co.uk
A complete insurance service for the professional photographic and multimedia industries, including a comprehensive policy covering equipment, studios, work in progress and legal liabilities (Public, Products and Employers).
Discount to BFP members: on application.

ENTERTAINMENT & LEISURE INSURANCE SERVICES LTD
PO Box 100, Ouseburn, York YO26 9SZ. E-mail: info@eandl.co.uk
Tel: 08707 423710. Fax: 08707 423810.
Web: www.eandl.co.uk
Specialist photographic insurance scheme covering private, domestic or commercial photo equipment.

GLOVER & HOWE LTD
1 Culver Walk, Colchester, Essex CO1 1XJ.
Tel: 01206 814502. Fax: 01206 814501. E-mail: info@gloverhowe.co.uk
Web: www.gloverhowe.co.uk
Insurance for photographic equipment and associated risks, for the amateur, semi-pro or professional.
Discount to BFP members: 10%.

GOLDEN VALLEY INSURANCE
The Olde Shoppe, Ewyas Harold, Herefordshire HR2 0ES.
Tel: 01981 240536. Fax: 01981 240451. E-mail: gvinsurance@aol.com
Comprehensive insurance cover for all photographic, video and sound recording equipment, binoculars and telescopes, computers, home office/studio, all accessories etc.
Discount to BFP members: 10%.

MARTIN HALE INSURANCE
Aztec Centre, Aztec West, Almondsbury, Bristol BS32 4TD.
Tel: 01454 203610. Fax: 01454 203611. E-mail: bristol@martinhale.co.uk
Web: www.martinhale.co.uk/photographers
Comprehensive insurance cover for professional photographers in one flexible package.
Discount to BFP members: 5%.

MORGAN RICHARDSON LTD
Freepost CL4071, Westgate Court, Western Road, Billericay, Essex CM12 9ZZ.
Tel: 01277 630666. Fax: 01277 632255. Free Call: 0800 731 2940.
Specialist "Policy Portfolio" and "Photographers' Economy" insurance for photographers. Tailored package. Professional indemnity automatically insured up to £50,000.

WEALD INSURANCE BROKERS LTD
Falcon House, Black Eagle Square, Westerham, Kent TN16 1SE.
Tel: 01959 565678; freephone 0800 074 7016. Fax: 01959 569988.
Web: www.weald-insurance.co.uk
Comprehensive specialist insurance policies for professional and semi-pro photographers.
Discount to BFP members: 5%.

Postcard Printers

ABACUS (COLOUR PRINTERS) LTD
Lowick, Near Ulverston, Cumbria LA12 8DX.
Tel: 01229 885361/885381. Fax: 01229 885348. E-mail: sales@abacusprinters.co.uk
Web: www.abacusprinters.co.uk
Quality printers specialising in colour postcards & greetings cards. Minimum quantity 500.

BUTTERFLY CARDS
25 Princes Road, Teddington, Middlesex TW11 0RL.
Tel: 020 8943 1496.
Web: www.butterflycards.co.uk
Design, artwork and printing of publicity cards, postcards, greetings cards.
Discount to BFP members: 5%.

JUDGES POSTCARDS LTD
176 Bexhill Road, St Leonards on Sea, East Sussex TN38 8BN.
Tel: 01424 420919. Fax: 01424 438538.
Web: www.judges.co.uk
Printers of postcards, greetings cards and calendars. Minimum quantity: 500.
Discount to BFP members: 10%.

THE POSTCARD COMPANY
51 Gortin Road, Omagh BT79 7HZ.
Tel: 028 8224 9222. Fax: 028 8224 9886. E-mail: sales@thepostcardcompany.com
Web: www.thepostcardcompany.com
Printers of postcards, greetings cards and product cards. No minimum quantity.

THE SHERWOOD PRESS (NOTTINGHAM) LTD
Hadden Court, Glaisdale Parkway, Glaisdale Drive West, Nottingham NG8 4GP.
Tel: 0115 928 7766. Fax: 0115 928 0271.
Quality printers specialising in the production of greetings cards, fine art prints, postcards and calendars.

THOUGHT FACTORY
Group House, 40 Waterside Road, Hamilton Industrial Park, Leicester LE5 1TL.
Tel: 0116 276 5302. Fax: 0116 246 0506. E-mail: sales@thoughtfactory.co.uk
Web: www.thoughtfactory.co.uk
Minimum quantity: 250. Price: £54 + VAT.
Discount to BFP members: On application.

Processing & Finishing

ACTPIX LTD
4 East Street Industrial Estate, Rhayader, Powys LD6 5ER.
Tel: 01597 810003. Fax: 01597 811265. E-mail: info@actpix.com
Web: www.actpix.com
Full digital services include drum scanning, retouching, FTP, file storage and inkjet printing.
Discount to BFP members: 5% on orders over £150.

ANGEL PRINTS
29 Upper Street, Islington, London N1 0PN.
Tel: 020 7359 9210. E-mail: sales@angelprints.co.uk
Web: www.angelprints.co.uk
Digital imaging specialists. Processing and printing of E6, C41 and B&W, plus full-range printing from memory cards, CD, Zip or floppy. Also image editing and transfers to cards, T-shirts, mugs, etc (see: www.imagealia.com)

AVONCOLOUR IMAGING
131 Duckmoor Road, Ashton Gate, Bristol BS3 2BJ.
Tel: 01179 633456. Fax: 01179 635186. E-mail: info@avoncolour.co.uk
Web: avoncolour.co.uk
Full service imaging centre. E6, C41, duping, copying, mounting, laminating, machine and hand printing in colour and B&W, digital printing.
Discount to BFP members: Up to 20%. Tel: Ron Munn.

CC IMAGING
7 Scala Court, Leathley Road, Leeds LS10 1JD.
Tel: 0113 244 8329. Fax: 0113 244 0115. E-mail: info@ccimaging.co.uk
Web: www.ccimaging.co.uk
Comprehensive colour and B&W processing services. Specialist reversal print service. Full mounting and finishing services. Colour laser copying. Digital imaging, retouching and printing.
Discount to BFP members: 15%.

CHANDOS PHOTOGRAPHIC SERVICES LTD
Europa House, 13/17 Ironmonger Row, London EC1V 3QG.
Tel: 020 7253 9993/4. Fax: 020 7253 9995.
Web: www.chandosphotographic.com
Comprehensive colour and B&W processing services. Full range of duplicate transparencies. Digital outputting.

COLAB GROUP LTD
Herald Way, Binley, Coventry CV3 1BB.
Tel: 024 76 440404. Fax: 024 76 444219. E-mail: info@colab.com
Web: www.colab.com
Branches: Birmingham, Cardiff, Cheltenham.
Comprehensive colour processing and digital imaging services.

COLCHESTER COLOUR IMAGING
7 Brunel Court, Severalls Park, Colchester, Essex CO4 9XW.
Tel: 01206 751241. Fax: 01206 855134.
Web: www.colchester-colour.co.uk
Colour and B&W processing, electronic imaging.
Discount to BFP members: 5%.

COLOUR PROCESSING LABORATORIES LTD
Head Office: Heath House, Crockham Hill, Edenbridge, Kent TN8 6ST.
Tel: 01732 860393. Fax: 01732 866560.
Web: www.cplnet.co.uk
Branches: London, Southampton, Reading.
E6 and C41 processing. All forms of photographic printing including Cibachrome and Duratrans. Film scanning, retouching, film writing. Kodak Pro Photo CD. Archiving to CD-ROM. Large format digital printing. Photographic images onto fabric. ISDN service.

DUNNS IMAGING GROUP PLC
Chester Road, Cradley Heath, West Midlands B64 6AA.
Tel: 01384 564770. E-mail: enquiries@dunns.co.uk
Web: www.dunns.co.uk
Comprehensive colour and B&W processing, digital photographic printing, scanning and image management services. Also schools and package printing.

GENESIS DIGITAL IMAGING
The Depot, 2 Michael Road, Fulham, London SW6 2AD.
Tel: 020 7731 2227. Fax: 020 7731 8778. E-mail: info@genesis-digital.net
Web: www.genesis-digital.net
E6, C41, B&W processing, colour and B&W hand prints and print runs, dupes, pro digital mini-lab and X-pan services, digital image retouching, digital film writing, large format (Lambda) printing, on-line ePrints and prints from digital media cards, drum and flatbed scanning, mounting and laminating.

HMD GROUP PLC
Olympia House, 4 Garnett Close, Watford, WD24 7JY.
Tel: 01923 237012 . Fax: 01923 817421.
Web: www.hmdgroup.com
Comprehensive colour and B&W processing services.
Discount to BFP members: 15%.

HOME COUNTIES COLOUR SERVICES LTD
17-21 Hastings Street, Luton, Bedfordshire LU1 5DF.
Tel: 01582 731899. Fax: 01582 402410. E-mail: sales@hccs.co.uk
Web: www.hccs.co.uk
Photographic processing services for photographers, including digital.
Discount to BFP members: On volume work only; open to negotiation.

KAY MOUNTING SERVICE LTD
4c Athelstane Mews, London N4 3EH.
Tel: 020 7272 7799. Fax: 020 7272 9888.
Mounting, canvas-bonding and heat-sealing. Specialists in Diasec bonding behind acrylic, mounting to aluminium, canvas, Foamex, etc.
Discount to BFP members: 10%

THE LAB
51 Cleveland Street, London W1T 4JH.
Tel: 020 7631 1111. Fax: 020 7631 0011. Sales@thelab.co.uk
Web: www.thelab.co.uk
E6 processing, C41, contacts, colour, B&W and digital printing, scanning, data transfer.
Discount to BFP members: 10%.

PEAK IMAGING PROFESSIONAL
Rockingham House, Broad Lane, Sheffield S1 3PP.
Tel: 0114 224 3200. Fax: 0114 224 3205. E-mail: sales@peak-professional.com
Web: www.peak-professional.com
Comprehensive professional colour and B&W imaging services.
Discount to BFP members: 10% on pro lab services.

PINEWOOD PHOTOGRAPHIC CENTRE
Stills Road, Pinewood Studios, Pinewood Road, Iver Heath, Buckinghamshire SL0 0NH.
Tel: 01753 657198. E-mail: sales@pinewoodphoto.com
Web: www.pinewoodphoto.com
Professional photo lab with full range of conventional and digital services. B&W, colour, printing, scanning and processing. Services include physical and on-line storage and free daily collection to and from London.

PRIMARY COLOUR
80 Kingsland Road, London E2 8DP.
Tel: 020 7729 7140. Fax: 020 7729 2080. E-mail: citylab@primary-uk.com
Web: www.primary-uk.com
E6, C41, B&W processing, colour and B&W hand prints and print runs, dupes, pro digital mini-lab and X-pan services, exclusive UK processing of Agfa Scala B&W transparency film, digital film writing, large format (Lambda) printing, fine art archival inkjet printing, prints from digital media cards, drum and flatbed scanning, mounting and laminating, film sales of all leading brands.

PROFOLAB IMAGING LTD
Unit 4, Surrey Close, Granby Industrial Estate, Weymouth, Dorset DT4 9TY.
Tel: 01305 774098. Fax: 01305 778746. E-mail: info@profolab.co.uk
Web: www.profolab.co.uk
E6, C41 processing and printing up to 30x40in; specialist reproduction-quality slide duplicating service; digital service.

QUICK IMAGING PHOTOSTICKERS
12 Alston Road, Solihull B91 2RQ.
Tel/fax: 0121 703 3123.
Web: www.quickimagingphotostickers.50megs.com
Full range of professional laboratory services, plus photoleaflets and photostickers.
Discount to BFP members: 10% against cwo.

RUSSELL PHOTO IMAGING
17 Elm Grove, Wimbledon, London SE19 4HE. E-mail: info@russellphotomarketing.co.uk
Web: www.russellphotomarketing.co.uk
Tel: 020 8947 6172. Fax: 020 8944 2064.
Comprehensive colour processing services; 2-hour E6 processing, C41, dupes, copy trans, copy negs, machine and hand line printing, exhibition printing and mounting service. Digital services. Also complete B&W service.
Discount to BFP members: 5%.

SCL
16 Bull Lane, Edmonton, London N18 1SX.
Tel: 020 8807 0725. Fax: 020 8807 2539. E-mail: davids@sclimage.net
Web: www.sclimage.net
Comprehensive colour and B&W processing plus full range of digital output services.

TRANSCOLOUR LTD
7, Tyers Gate, London Bridge, London SE1 3HX.
Tel: 020 7403 0048. Fax: 020 7403 1944.
Image manipulations, 11/2 hour E6 processing (8.30am–6pm; 24-hours by arrangement), dupes, retouching, montaging, scanning, C-Types – digital prints.

Specialised Equipment & Materials

CALUMET
Promandis House, Bradbourne Drive, Tilbrook, Milton Keynes MK7 8AJ.
Tel: 01908 366344. Fax: 01908 366322.
Web: www.calumetphoto.co.uk
Branches: London, Aberdeen, Belfast, Birmingham, Bristol, Edinburgh, Glasgow, Liverpool, Manchester and Nottingham.
Distributors of Bowens, Cambo, Fidelity, Manfrotto tripods, Norman, Savage, Tenba, Wein, Zone VI, etc. Complete range of standard and specialist films, papers and chemicals.

CALUMET SOCIAL PHOTOGRAPHIC
Unit 1A, Pixmore Centre, Pixmore Avenue, Letchworth, Hertfordshire SG6 1JG.
Tel: 01462 679388. Fax: 01462 675860. E-mail: sales@midcounties-photographic.co.uk
Comprehensive wholesale supplies of film, paper, chemicals, albums, mounts, etc.

CAMERA BELLOWS LTD
Units 3-5, St Pauls Road, Balsall Heath, Birmingham B12 8NG.
Tel: 0121 440 1695. Fax: 0121 440 0972.
Web: www.camerabellows.com
Bellows for all photographic purposes in leather and other materials. Replacements for modern and antique cameras.
Discount to BFP members: 2%.

COLORAMA PHOTODISPLAY LTD
Ace Business Park, Mackadown Lane, Kitts Green, Birmingham B33 0LD.
Tel: 0121 783 9931. Fax: 0121 783 1674. E-mail: info@coloramaphotodisplay.co.uk
Web: www.coloramaphotodisplay.co.uk
Suppliers of photographic background and background support products including Colorama Background Paper, Colorcrepe, Colorswirl, Rainbow, Colormatt, Colorgloss, Cove-lock coving systems.

THE FLASH CENTRE
66 Brunswick Centre, Bernard Street, London WC1N 1AE.
Tel: 020 7837 6163. Fax: 020 7833 4737. E-mail: sales@theflashcentre.co.uk
2nd Floor, Mill 1, Mabgate Mills, Mabgate, Leeds LS9 7DZ.
Tel: 0113 247 0937. Fax: 0113 247 0038.
Web: www.theflashcentre.com
Specialist suppliers of studio flash systems, photographic lighting and digital imaging equipment.

FOTOLYNX LTD
6b Park Lane Industrial Estate, Park Lane, Corsham, Wiltshire SN13 9LG.
Tel: 01249 715333. Fax: 01249 714999. E-mail: info@ccscentre.co.uk
Web: www.ccscentre.co.uk
Distributors of CCS camera bags and accessories, Kaiser Fototechnik darkroom and processing equipment, Herma products, Walther Albums, Ansmann batteries and chargers.

JESSOPS
Head Office: Jessop House, 98 Scudamore Road, Leicester LE3 1TZ.
Tel: 0116 232 0033. Fax: 0116 232 0060.
Web: www.jessops.com
Specialist suppliers of all photographic and digital imaging equipment including Portaflash portable studio flash, a full range of darkroom equipment and accessories.

KENTMERE PHOTOGRAPHIC LTD
Staveley, Kendal, Cumbria LA8 9PB.
Tel: 01539 821365. Fax: 01539 821399. E-mail: sales@kentmere.co.uk
Web: www.kentmere.co.uk
Manufacturers of the Kentmere range of B&W photographic papers. Comprehensive range of large and small format photobase ink jet media. Specialist films for roll-up, pop-up and backlit display applications.
Discount to BFP members: 15%

OCEAN OPTICS
13 Northumberland Avenue, London WC2N 5AQ.
Tel: 020 7930 8408. Fax: 020 7839 6148. E-mail: optics@oceanoptics.co.uk
Web: www.oceanoptics.co.uk
Specialist suppliers of underwater photography equipment.

PATERSON PHOTOGRAPHIC LTD
4 Malthouse Road, Tipton, West Midlands DY4 9AE.
Tel: 0121 520 4830. Fax: 0121 520 4831.
Web: www.patersonphotographic.com
Paterson darkroom equipment and accessories, Benbo, Bilora and Giotto tripods, Interfit lighting, Olmec inkjet paper.
Discount to BFP members: Special rates on lighting and tripods; phone for details.

SILVERPRINT LTD
12 Valentine Place, London SE1 8QH.
Tel: 020 7620 0844. Fax: 020 7620 0129.
Web: www.silverprint.co.uk
Specialist suppliers of B&W materials. Importers of Oriental Seagull, Maco and Forte fibre-based papers and a wide range of other papers, toners, liquid emulsions, tinting and retouching materials. Products for archival mounting, and archival storage boxes and folio cases. Mail order service.

JAMIE WOOD LTD
1 Green Street, Old Town, Eastbourne, E.Sussex BN21 1QN.
Tel/fax: 01323 727291. E-mail: jamiewood@birdtables.com
Web: www.birdtables.com
Makers of photographic hides and suppliers of photo electronic equipment. Exclusive UK distributor for Jama Electronique, Europe's leading manufacturer of advanced remote control, laser and infra-red photographic technology
Discount to BFP members: 5%.

Storage & Presentation

ABLE DIRECT CENTRE LTD
5 Mallard Close, Earls Barton, Northampton NN6 0LS
Tel: 0870 444 2733. Fax: 0870 444 2766
Web: www.able-labels.co.uk
ABLE-LABELS – printed self-adhesive labels.

ARROWFILE
PO Box 88, Southampton SO14 0ZA.
Tel: 0870 607 2048. Fax: 0870 241 2198. E-mail: customerservices@arrowfile.com
Web: www.arrowfile.com
Photographic storage and presentation specialists. The Arrowfile system organises, stores and protects varying photo sizes, negs, slides, and CDs in one binder album.

AUDIO VISUAL MATERIAL LTD
AVM House, Hawley Lane, Farnborough, Hants GU14 8EH.
Tel: 01252 510363. Fax: 01252 549214.
Optia storage systems; lightboxes, Draper projection screens.
Discount to BFP members: 10%.

BRAYTHORN LTD
Phillips Street, Aston, Birmingham B6 4PT.
Tel: 0121 359 8800. Fax: 0121 359 8412. E-mail: sales@braythorn.co.uk
Web: www.braythorn.co.uk
Suppliers of cardboard mailing tubes and polythene envelopes. Minimum quantities: 1000 envelopes, 100 tubes.
Discount to BFP members: 10%.

CALUMET
Promandis House, Bradbourne Drive, Tilbrook, Milton Keynes MK7 8AJ.
Tel: 01908 366344. Fax: 01908 366322.
Web: www.calumetphoto.com
Branches: London, Aberdeen, Belfast, Birmingham, Bristol, Edinburgh, Glasgow, Liverpool, Manchester and Nottingham.
Full range of storage and presentation equipment and materials, including lightboxes, mounts, frames, storage bags and albums.

CALUMET SOCIAL PHOTOGRAPHIC
Unit 1A, Pixmore Centre, Pixmore Avenue, Letchworth, Hertfordshire SG6 1JG.
Tel: 01462 679388. Fax: 01462 675860.
Wholesalers of albums, mounts, film, frames, papers, chemicals, and equipment.

CHALLONER MARKETING LTD
Raans Road, Amersham, Buckinghamshire HP6 6LL.
Tel: 01494 721270. Fax: 01494 725732.
Web: www.challoner-marketing.com
Suppliers of Fly-Weight envelope stiffener. Minimum quantity: 100.
Discount to BFP members: 5% on orders over 5,000.

DW GROUP LTD
Unit 7, Peverel Drive, Granby, Milton Keynes MK1 1NL.
Tel: 01908 642323. Fax: 01908 640164. E-mail: sales@dw-view.com
Web: www.photopages.com
Filing and presentation systems, masks for all formats, mounts, wallets, storage cabinets, lightboxes, display boxes, viewing booths, viewtowers, ultra-slim light panels. Also CD-ROM production and replication, CD printers and replication systems, floppy disk duping, poster prints.
Discount to BFP members: 10%.

NICHOLAS HUNTER LTD
Unit 8, Oxford Business Centre, Osney Lane, Oxford OX1 1TB.
Tel: 01865 727292. Fax: 01865 200051.
Web: www.photofiling.com
Plastic wallets for presentation of prints, slides and negatives.
Discount to BFP members: 5% if cwo; 10% on orders over £100.

KENRO LTD
Greenbridge Road, Swindon, Wilts SN3 3LH.
Tel: 01793 615836. Fax: 01793 513561. E-mail: sales@kenro.co.uk
Web: www.kenro.co.uk
Black card transparency mounts,strut mounts, photo albums and frames, slide storage systems, clean air dusters, and other presentation and storage accessories.

S.W. KENYON
PO Box 71, Cranbrook, Kent TN18 5ZR.
Tel: 01580 850770. Fax: 01580 850225. E-mail: swkenyon@btinternet.com
Web: www.swkenyon.com
Slide storage systems, K-Line dulling sprays.

LONDON LABELS LTD
20 Oval Road, London NW1 7DJ.
Tel: 020 7267 7105. Fax: 020 7267 1165.
Self-adhesive labels for 35mm slides, printed with name, address or logo. Also plain labels.

RICHFORDS
E M Richford Ltd, Curzon Road, Chilton Industrial Estate, Sudbury, Suffolk CO10 2XW.
Tel: 01787 375241. Fax: 01787 310179. E-mail: sales@richstamp.co.uk
Web: www.richstamp.co.uk
Rubber stamps and inks, including stamps made to order and specialist quick-drying inks.

RUSSELL PHOTO MARKETING
17 Elm Grove, Wimbledon, London SE19 4HE. E-mail: info@russellphotomarketing.co.uk
Web: www.russellphotomarketing.co.uk
Tel: 020 8947 6171. Fax: 020 8944 2064.
D&F Maxima etc. Albums and accessories. Frames to size wood/metal, many colours.
Discount to BFP members: 5% on orders over £150.

SECOL LTD
Howlett Way, Thetford, Norfolk IP24 1HZ.
Tel: 01842 752341. Fax: 01842 762159. E-mail: sales@secol.co.uk
Web: www.secol.co.uk
Wide range of photographic storage and display products including sleeves, filing sheets, storage boxes, black card masks, mounting systems, portfolio cases and portfolio boxes.
Discount to BFP members: 10% on prepaid orders of £100 or more.

SLIDEPACKS
1 The Moorings, Aldenham Road, Bushey, Herts WD23 2NR.
Tel: 01923 254790. Fax: 01923 254789. E-mail: sales@slidepacks.com
Web: www.slidepacks.com
Binders, folders, mounts and wallets for transparency presentation, storage and filing. Custom-made service also available. Also supply labels, lightboxes, lupes and other accessories.

Studio Hire & Services

ALPHA STUDIOS
43a Lodge Lane, London N12 8JG.
Tel: 020 8445 5040. Fax: 0870 137 4641. E-mail: office@alphastudios.co.uk
Web: www.alphastudios.co.uk
Two fully-equipped studios with good daylight, Bowens flash equipment, additional facilities and free parking. Available evenings and weekends by arrangment.
Discount to BFP members: 10% off standard hire rates.

BEEHIVE CENTRE OF PHOTOGRAPHY
37 Camden High Street, London NW1 7JE.
Tel: 020 7388 6261.
Web: www.beehivestudios.org.uk
Three large studios with electronic flash, plus darkroom.
Discount to BFP members: By negotiation.

CHALK FARM STUDIOS
10A Belmont Street, London NW1 8HH.
Tel: 020 7482 1001. Fax: 020 7267 3179. E-mail: chalkfarmstudios@btconnect.com
Web: www.chalkfarmstudios.co.uk
Three studios for hire with daylight and blackout facilities, Elinchrom flash and tungsten.
Discount to BFP members: 17%

CHARNWOOD STUDIO
A37 The Springboard Centre, Mantle Lane, Coalville, Leicestershire LE67 3DW.
Tel: 01530 450012. E-mail: charnwoodstudio@aol.com
Web: www.charnwoodstudio.co.uk
800 square feet of fully equipped studio for hire, inclduing lights, backgrounds and digital camera if required.
Discount to BFP members: 10%.

HOLBORN STUDIOS
49/50 Eagle Wharf Road, London N1 7ED.
Tel: 020 7490 4099. Fax: 020 7253 8120.
Web: www.holbornstudios.com
15 studios to hire, plus very comprehensive equipment hire.
Discount to BFP members: 10% on full week bookings.

LEWIS & KAYE (HIRE) LTD
3b Brassie Avenue, London W3 7DE.
Tel: 020 8749 2121. Fax: 020 8749 9455.
Web: www.lewisandkaye.co.uk
Large collection of silver, glass, china and objets d'art for hire as studio props.
Discount to BFP members: 10% where hire charge is £500 or over.

Are you working from the latest edition of The Freelance Photographer's Market Handbook? It's published on 1 October each year. Markets are constantly changing, so it pays to have the latest edition

MANCHESTER MODEL AGENCY
14 Albert Square, Manchester M2 5PF.
Tel: 01565 722864/07817 650896. E-mail: mavisroper@btinternet.com
Web: www.manchestermodelagency.com/www.mmaphotorep.com
Photographic models – female, male and children for fashion and advertising. Also photographers' representation.

MIDTOWN STUDIOS
50 Acton Mews, London E4 4EA.
Tel: 0845 166 9032. Fax: 020 7241 5663. E-mail: bookings@midtownstudios.co.uk
Web: www.midtownstudios.co.uk
Compact hire studio suitable for fashion, glamour, portraiture or still life. Elinchrom lighting available if required. Close to local lab facilities.
Discount to BFP members: 10%.

MODELS PLUS AGENCY
307 Holdenhurst Road, Bournemouth BH8 8BX.
Tel: 01202 393193. Fax: 01202 301156. E-mail: info@mpagency.co.uk
Web: www.mpagency.co.uk
Commercial, fashion and glamour models. Full commercial studio hire facilities.
Discount to BFP members: 10%.

PINEWOOD PHOTOGRAPHIC STUDIO
Stills Road, Pinewood Studios, Pinewood Road, Iver Heath, Buckinghamshire SL0 0NH.
Tel: 01753 656299. E-mail: tony@pinewoodphoto.com
2,500 sq ft photographic studio based in Pinewood Studios. 39x29x16ft white infinity coving, hair/make-up rooms, kitchen, client space and large front loading doors. Excellent range of equipment availble for hire. Catering, free parking and professional photo lab on site.

SHOOT PHOTOGRAPHIC
Larchwood, Chiddingfold Road, Dunsfold, Surrey GU8 4PB.
Tel: 01483 200079.
Large studio, two acre garden and house for hire.

Web Services

AMAZING INTERNET LTD
Tel: 020 8607 9535. E-mail: contact@amazinginternet.com
Web: www.amazinginternet.com
Website solutions for photographers. Range from fully updateable portfolio websites to large photo library systems, plus full e-commerce facilities and online sales modules for wedding and social photographers.
Discount to BFP members: 10%.

As a member of the Bureau of Freelance Photographers, you'll be kept up-to-date with markets through the BFP Market Newsletter, published monthly. For details of membership, turn to page 9

CONTACT
Surrey House, 31 Church Street, Leatherhead, Surrey KT22 8EF.
Tel: 01372 220330. Fax: 01372 220340. E-mail: mail@contact-uk.com
Web: www.contact-uk.com
Portfolio display service for professionals. Provides creative contacts on the Web, on CD and in the Contact book.

HOLLY BLUE
1 Malvern Terrace, Taunton TA2 7PN.
Tel: 01823 350777. E-mail: info@hollyblue.co.uk
Web: www.hollyblue.co.uk
Web design, hosting and other Internet services for photographers. On-line gallery.
Discount to BFP members: 10%

INTERNATIONAL PHOTONET LTD
The Mallings, 112 Malling Street, Lewes, East Sussex BN7 2RJ.
Tel: 01273 488094. Fax: 01273 488095. E-mail: info@international-photonet.com
Web: www.international-photonet.com
On-line searchable resources centre for professional photographers and labs worldwide. Comprehensive services, from sourcing commissions to gallery and portfolio display facilities. Also digitisation and image shipping/dispatch services.

PHOTONETWORK
44 Beaumont Road, Flitwick, Beds MK45 1WD.
Tel/fax: 01525 635633. E-mail: info@photonetwork.co.uk
Web: www.photonetwork.co.uk
Low-cost service for photographers to upload and display their portfolios on the internet. Includes on-line profile with contact details, personal website and e-mail links. Scanning service available for film users.

PHOTOSHOT
29-31 Saffron Hill, London EC1N 8SW.
Tel: 020 7421 6000. Fax: 020 7421 6006. E-mail: admin@photoshot.com
Web: www.photoshot.com
On-line gallery display and sales service for the serious amateur or semi-pro.

REDSTART
23 Craven Terrace, London W2 3QH.
Tel: 020 7402 6473. Fax: 020 7261 8732. E-mail: support@redstart.co.uk
Web: www.redstart.net
Portfolio display service for professionals. Basic subscription free to those who can upload on-line; full scanning and upload service available for admin fee of £25 plus VAT.

SPEAR SOLUTIONS LTD
Regus House, Cardiff Bay, Cardiff CF10 4RU.
Tel: 02920 504057. E-mail: rupert.bacon@spearsolutions.com
Web: www.spearsolutions.com
Template-based Online Album package for photo display and sales. Functions include rapid uploading, simple album management, and on-line ordering facilities. Site building and hosting also available.
Discount to BFP members: 10%–20% depending on product/service.

USEFUL ADDRESSES

ASSOCIATION OF MODEL AGENTS
122 Brompton Road, London SW3 1JE.
Tel: 020 7584 6466. Fax: 020 7581 2113.

ASSOCIATION OF PHOTOGRAPHERS (AOP)
81 Leonard Street, London EC2A 4QS.
Tel: 020 7739 6669. Fax: 020 7739 8707. E-mail: general@aophoto.co.uk
Web: www.the-aop.org

BRITISH ASSOCIATION OF PICTURE LIBRARIES AND AGENCIES (BAPLA)
18 Vine Hill, London EC1R 5DZ.
Tel: 020 7713 1780. Fax: 020 7713 1211. E-mail: enquiries@bapla.org.uk
Web: www.bapla.org

BRITISH INSTITUTE OF PROFESSIONAL PHOTOGRAPHY (BIPP)
Fox Talbot House, Amwell End, Ware, Hertfordshire SG12 9HN.
Tel: 01920 464011. Fax: 01920 487056. E-mail: info@bipp.com
Web: www.bipp.com

BUREAU OF FREELANCE PHOTOGRAPHERS (BFP)
Focus House, 497 Green Lanes, London N13 4BP.
Tel: 020 8882 3315. Fax: 020 8886 5174. E-mail: info@thebfp.com
Web: www.thebfp.com

CHARTERED INSTITUTE OF JOURNALISTS (CIOJ)
2, Dock Offices, Surrey Quays Road, London SE16 2XU.
Tel: 020 7252 1187. Fax: 020 7232 2302. E-mail: memberservices@ioj.co.uk
Web: www.ioj.co.uk

DESIGN & ARTISTS COPYRIGHT SOCIETY (DACS)
Parchment House, 13 Northburgh Street, London EC1V 0JP.
Tel: 020 7336 8811. Fax: 020 7336 8822. E-mail: info@dacs.co.uk
Web: www.dacs.co.uk

MASTER PHOTOGRAPHERS ASSOCIATION (MPA)
Jubilee House, 1 Chancery Lane, Darlington, Co Durham DL1 5QP.
Tel: 01325 356555. Fax: 01325 357813. E-mail: enq@mpauk.com
Web: www.mpauk.com

NATIONAL ASSOCIATION OF PRESS AGENCIES (NAPA)
41 Lansdowne Crescent, Leamington Spa, Warwickshire CV32 4PR.
Tel: 01926 424181. Fax: 01926 424760. Web: www.napa.org.uk

NATIONAL UNION OF JOURNALISTS (NUJ)
Headland House, 308-312 Gray's Inn Road, London WC1X 8DP.
Tel: 020 7278 7916. Fax: 020 7837 8143. E-mail: acorn.house@nuj.org.uk
Web: www.nuj.org.uk

PHOTO IMAGING COUNCIL (PIC)
Orbital House, 85 Croydon Road, Caterham, Surrey CR3 6PD.
Tel: 01883 334497. Fax: 01883 334490. E-mail: pic@admin.co.uk
Web: www.pic.uk.net

PHOTO MARKETING ASSOCIATION UK (PMA)
Wisteria House, 28 Fulling Mill Lane, Welwyn, Herts AL6 9NS.
Tel: 0870 240 4542. Fax: 01438 716572. E-mail: tchapman@pmai.org
Web: www.pmai.org

PICTURE RESEARCH ASSOCIATION (PRA)
2 Culver Drive, Oxted, Surrey RH8 9HP.
Tel: 01883 730123. Fax: 01883 730144. E-mail: pra@lippmann.co.uk
Web: www.picture-research.org.uk

PRESS ASSOCIATION
292 Vauxhall Bridge Road, London SW1V 1AE.
Tel: 020 7963 7000; Picture Desk: 020 7963 7155. Fax: 020 7963 7191.
Web: www.pressassociation.press.net

REUTERS
85 Fleet Street, London EC4P 4AJ.
Tel: 020 7542 7949 (UK news); 020 7542 8088 (international). E-mail: lon.pictures@reuters.com
Web: http://pictures.reuters.com

ROYAL PHOTOGRAPHIC SOCIETY (RPS)
The Octagon, Milsom Street, Bath BA1 1DN.
Tel: 01225 462841. Fax: 01225 448688. E-mail: rps@rps.org
Web: www.rps.org

SOCIETY OF WEDDING AND PORTRAIT PHOTOGRAPHERS (SWPP/BPPA)
Colomendy House, 6 Bath Street, Rhyl LL16 3EB.
Tel: 01745 356935. Fax: 01745 356953. E-mail: phil@swpp.co.uk
Web: www.swpp.co.uk

INDEX

A

B

C

D

E

F

G

H

I

J

K

L

M

N

O

P

Q

R

S

T

U

V

W

Y

Z